# Beyond the Margin

# Beyond the Margin
## Readings in Italian Americana

Edited by
## Paolo A. Giordano
## and Anthony Julian Tamburri

Madison ● Teaneck
Fairleigh Dickinson University Press
London: Associated University Presses

Associated University Presses
440 Forsgate Drive
Cranbury, NJ 08512

Associated University Presses
16 Barter Street
London WC1A 2AH, England

Associated University Presses
P.O. Box 338, Port Credit
Mississauga, Ontario
Canada L5G 4L8

The paper used in this publication meets the requirements
of the American National Standard for Permanence of Paper
for Printed Library Materials Z39.48–1984.

**Library of Congress Cataloging-in-Publication Data**

Beyond the margin : readings in Italian Americana / edited by Paolo A. Giordano and Anthony Julian Tamburri.
   p.   cm.
Includes bibliographical references and index.
ISBN 0-8386-3732-9 (alk. paper)
   1. American literature—Italian American authors—History and criticism.   2. American literature—20th century—History and criticism.   3. Italian Americans—Intellectual life.   4. Italian Americans—Social life and customs.   5. Italian Americans in literature.   6. Italian Americans in motion pictures.   I. Giordano, Paolo.   II. Tamburri, Anthony Julian.
PS153.I8B4985   1998
810.9'851—dc21                                                        97-21256
                                                                          CIP

PRINTED IN THE UNITED STATES OF AMERICA

# Contents

# Acknowledgments

In editing a book such as *Beyond the Margin: Readings in Italian Americana,* we incurred numerous debts. First, we would like to thank our respective departments at Loyola University Chicago and Purdue University for having provided generous support in the form of clerical help, photocopying, mailing, and telephone calls—all necessary when compiling a collection of essays whose contributors reside in various parts of the United States and in Italy. Our most heartfelt thanks also go to Fred Gardaphé as well as other friends and colleagues too numerous to mention here, for their support and encouragement along the way. Last but not least, our thanks go to Rosa Bellino-Giordano and Maria Donovan for their confidence, enthusiasm, encouragement, and infinite patience throughout the development of this project.

# Introduction

In our earlier collection of creative works and critical studies, *From the Margin: Writings in Italian Americana* (Purdue University Press, 1991), we opened our introduction with the following two paragraphs:

> Very few people have truly pondered the notion of Italian/American art, be it in literature, film, painting or any other art form to which Americans of Italian descent have contributed. Nor have many people specifically asked, what is Italian Americana and does it exist in America? While we do not pretend to answer this question within the parameters of this Introduction, we will consider it as well as a second question that is related, What role does the mysterious concept of *italianità* play in the creation of Italian/American Art?
>
> We would like these questions to reverberate in the ears and minds of those who read the stories, poems, plays, and essays included in this anthology. Only then, after a consideration of these and other works, and further intertextual recall, will readers be able to formulate for themselves answers to the questions.

Furthermore, when we compiled the Critical essay part of that book we realized how little theoretical and critical work had been done on Italian/American literature prior to the early 1980s.

The questions we posed in that introduction were taken up by our readers. During the nineties the writing and interpretation of Italian Americana has come out of its infancy and has blossomed, and certain members of the literary establishment came out of what we might label the *ethnic closet.*[1]

Before the 1980s, two studies are worthy of notice, because each in its own way is a ground-breaking volume. The first book-length study on Italian/American literature was Olga Peragallo's *Italian-American Authors and Their Contribution to American Literature* (New York: S. F. Vanni, 1949). Published posthumously, this annotated bibliography was a first attempt at identifying a widely dispersed body of literature that, save a few cases such as Pietro Di Donato's *Christ in Concrete*, had not received critical attention. Twenty-five years later, Rose Basile Green published *The Italian-American Novel: A Document of the Interaction of Two Cultures* (Cranbury, N.J.: Fairleigh Dickinson

University Press, 1974). In this book, the first attempt at a systematic analysis of Italian/American literature, Professor Green classified the history of Italian/American narrative into four stages, thus following the development of Italian/American narrative from the immigrants to third-generation Italian Americans: (1) "The need for assimilation"; (2) "revulsion"; (3) "counter revulsion"; and (4) "rooting."

About the same time of Green's book, an Italian/American literary critical voice was emerging sporadically in conference proceedings, especially those of the American Italian Historical Association's annual conferences. The 1980s, instead, proved to be most fruitful; 1981 marks the beginning of a sustained critical discourse with the appearance of Robert Viscusi's acutely original "*De vulgari eloquentia:* An Approach to the Language of Italian American Fiction."[2] As Viscusi continued to offer further readings of Italian/American literature, a sympathetic voice accompanied him along the way by William Boelhower's important studies: "The Immigrant Novel as Genre,"[3] *Immigrant Autobiography in the United States* (Essedue 1982), and *Through a Glass Darkly: Ethnic Semiosis in American Literature* (Helvetia 1984 [Oxford University Press, 1987]) helped validate to a certain degree a critical voice on Italian America. A seminal contribution to Italian/American literature was the 1985 publication of Helen Barolini's bestselling anthology *The Dream Book: An Anthology of Writing by Italian American Women* (New York: Schocken Books). Barolini's book is the first extensive anthology solely dedicated to Italian/American women writers that includes both creative and critical pieces. Her introduction, to be sure, is the first major piece not only dedicated to the gender issue, but also figured as a type of matrix for what followed. This decade, finally, was capped by a special issue of *MELUS* dedicated entirely to Italian/American literature (*MELUS* 14, nos. 3–4 [1987 (1989)]).

An Italian/American critical voice truly flourished with the onset of the 1990s. Two people of the later generation who have obviously profited from the lessons of Barolini and Viscusi include Mary Jo Bona and Fred L. Gardaphé. Mary Jo Bona's work has already proven itself indispensable for a rethinking of the gender issue, especially, in Italian/American literature. In her essay, "Mari Tomasi's *Like Lesser Gods* and the Making of an Ethnic *Bildungsroman*,"[4] Bona constructs a paradigm for the ethnic novel, here specifically Italian/American, similar but not identical to William Boelhower's paradigm of the immigrant novel. In another essay, "Broken Images, Broken Lives: Carmolina's Journey in Tina De Rosa's *Paper Fish*,"[5] Bona first contextualizes the novel within the broader scheme of Italian/American women writers, and, second, maps out Tina De Rosa's coding correlations which ultimately lay bare the novel's uniqueness in exploring the ethnic/gender dilemma. To this critical work, one must recognize, as with Barolini, her more personal *impegno* in her anthology of recent Italian/American women's fiction, *The Voices We Carry*.[6] Whereas Mary Jo Bona operates mostly within and around the literary text, Fred L. Gardaphé inhabits both the theoretical and textual worlds of Italian/American literature. His threefold Vichian division of the history of Italian/American literature is an excellent updated analog to Daniel Aaron's three stages of the "hyphenate writer."[7] Gardaphé proposes a culturally "specific methodology" for the greater disambiguation of Italian/American contributions to the United States literary scene. In his essay, he reminds us of Vico's "three ages and their corresponding cultural products: the Age of Gods in which primitive society records expression in 'poetry' [*vero narratio*,] the Age of Heros, in which society records expression in myth, and the Age of Man, in which through self-reflection, expression is recorded in philosophic prose." These three ages, Gardaphé goes on to tell us, have their parallels in modern and "contemporary [socio-]cultural constructions of realism, modernism, and postmodernism" (24). And, ultimately, the evolution of the various literatures of United States ethnic and racial groups can be charted as they "move from the poetic, through the mythic and into the philosophic" (25).

This decade also saw a more broad discussion on Italian/American literature and an engagement in methodological and theoretical strategies for a different reading of the texts in question, old and new. Anthony Julian Tamburri's *To Hyphenate or Not to Hyphenate? The Italian/American Writer: An* Other *American* (Guernica, 1991) provoked some discussion on how we might look at Italian/American literature through the eyes of a poststructuralist. Thomas Ferraro's work on ethnicity in general includes a revisionist look at Puzo's *The Godfather*.[8] In a similar vein, Fred Gardaphé's excellent study, *Italian Signs, American Streets: The Evolution of Italian American Narrative* (Duke University Press, 1996), maps out the development of Italian/American fiction through the lens of a New Americanist.

Along with these individual efforts one may also point to collections of essays in the form of conference proceedings and the like. Together with Viscusi in the 1980s one should not ignore two important essays by Robert Casillo and John Paul Russo on Scorsese and Coppola.[9] The 1990s have seen similar results. *La letteratura dell'emigrazione. Scrittori di lingua italiana nel mondo*, edited by Jean-Jacques Marchand (Edizioni della Fondazione Giovanni Agnelli, 1992) includes six essays on Italian/American literature. The proceedings of the American Italian Historical Association continue to include essays on literature and film.[10] In addition, the resumption of *Italian Americana*, the publication of journals such as *la bella figura* and *VIA: Voices in Italian Americana*, and the special issue of *Differentia* devoted entirely to Italian/American literature, all bear witness to the continued rise in interest in the critical study of Italian/American culture. Further still, after the appearance of *The Dream Book* and *From the Margin*, two more anthologies appeared in the mid-1990s: Mary Jo Bona's previously mentioned *The Voices We Carry: Recent Italian/American Women's Fiction* (Guernica 1994) and Maria Mazziotti Gillan's and Jennifer Gillan's *Unsettling America: An Anthology of Contemporary Multicultural Poets* (Penguin, 1994), a collection of writings from various ethnic groups, including Italian Americans. Finally, in the greater New York area, the Italian American Writers Association (IAWA), founded in 1991, holds monthly readings at various cafes to great public success and runs an Italian/American canon project that selects one title each month for its members to order from their respective book stores.

It has also been during this decade that the study of Italian/American culture has come into its own. Due to the work of numerous individuals who have invested time and money, interest in the literature and culture of Italian Americans has surged both among the public at large and within the university community. With the public at large this interest has manifested itself in an increased readership for Italian/American authors, while within the universities new courses on Italian/American literature and culture are offered successfully in such diverse settings as the University of Massachusetts at Lowell and Purdue University (where one may also choose Italian/American studies as a specialization at the graduate level in Comparative Literature), at Middlebury College in Vermont (where a graduate-level course is taught in Italian), and Columbia College in Chicago. In addition to such courses and programs, Professorships in Italian/American Studies have been established at Queens College of the City University of New York and The State University of New York at Stony Brook.[11] Further evidence of strong interest is also manifested in the fact that numerous young, talented second- and third-generation Italian Americans are writing and publishing poems, short stories, and novels on the Italian/American experience, thus continuing the tradition of Pietro Di Donato, Mari Tomasi, John Fante, and Mario Puzo, just to name a few.

A more recent phenomenon is the emerging awareness of a new poetic voice—that of Italian literature written in the United States. Today, several writers born and culturally trained in Italy live in the United States and produce a substantial amount of poetry and prose both in Italian and English. The list is long: Pier Maria Pasinetti, Franco Ferrucci, Joseph Tusiani, Giovanni Cecchetti, Giose Rimanelli, Peter Carravetta, Luigi Fontanella, Paolo Valesio, Luigi Ballerini, Rita Dinale, and Alessandro Carrera are some of the better known names. Through their writing a distinctive American voice in Italian literature—or an Italian voice in American literature—has begun to define itself. The recent publication of two important volumes dedicated entirely to Italian writing in the United States gives greater credence to this new emerging voice: *Italian Poets in America*, is a special edition of *Gradiva: International Journal of Italian Literature* 5 no. 1 (1993), edited by Luigi Fontanella and Paolo Valesio; *Poesaggio*, in turn, was edited by Paolo Valesio and Peter Carravetta (Pagus Edizioni, 1993). These two ground-breaking volumes give voice to the Italian Diaspora in the United States, and, by their form and content, recognize the fact that Italian America is not only not monocultural, but neither it is monolingual. Besides the introductions and postscripts of the two above-mentioned volumes, two essays on this topic include Paolo Valesio's "Writer Between Two Worlds: Italian Writing in the United States Today" (*Differentia* 3 no. 4 [1989]: 259–76) and Anthony Julian Tamburri, "Italian/American Writer or Italian Poet Abroad?: Luigi Fontanella's Poetic Voyage" (*Canadian Journal of Italian Studies* XVIII, no. 18 [1995]: 76–92).

★　★　★

Things have obviously changed since the appearance of *From the Margin: Writings in Italian Americana*. Our goal with this new project is to give a critical overview of where Italian/American literary and cultural studies are today. To this end *Beyond the Margin* includes three types of essays: the first type deals with notions and characteristics of Italian/American literature and culture in a general sense (Vitiello, Carravetta, Holub, Viscusi, Giordano, and Tamburri); the second type is dedicated to specific writers (Giunta, Domenichelli, Gardaphé, Livorni, Raptosh); the third type treats film (Hull, Viano, West).

Justin Vitiello's "Off the Road and Up the Creek Without a Paddle—or, Where Italian Americana Might Swim: Prolepsis of an Ethnopoetics" uses the creek imagery for the exploration of historical meaning and the cultural locus of Italian Americana, offering up a map to guide us through the interpretation of the historical, cultural, and aesthetic merits of Italian/American art. In so doing, Vitiello also renounces the "cultural McCarthyism" of right-wing intellectuals who are trying to perpetuate the notion of "a monolithic, monopolistic canon." In her essay, "Italian American Culturalism: A Critique,"

Renate Holub uses Gramscian concepts as set forth in his *La Questione Meridionale* to reflect on Italian/American culturalism in the current social and political American context. She further argues that Italian/American intellectuals, "could contribute in pioneering ways to contemporary critical, social, and political theory bent upon extending the register of democratic rights." In "Divine Comedy Blues" Robert Viscusi discusses the problem of Italian/American culture and literature when faced with the full richness of their Italian inheritance. In using the figure of the historical Dante, Viscusi crafts a wonderful metaphor for what ails Italian/American writers; he states: "Dante presents his case as desperate. No Italy exists. No Italian Power. No Italian language that all Italians understand. This case has a familiar ring to the writers of Italian America." Giordano's essay, "Emigrants, Expatriates and/or Exiles: Italian Literature in the United States," explores a new phenomenon in the ever developing cultural relations between Italy and America: that of the writer, born and culturally trained in Italy, who now lives in the United States or maintains residences in both countries and produces poetry and prose in both Italian and English. In "Rethinking Italian/American Studies: From the Hyphen to the Slash and Beyond," Tamburri examines the place of Italian/American literature in relation to ethnic studies in general and their place in the American cultural spectrum. Working with the different definitions that have been ascribed to Italian/American art forms, adhering to the notion of American culture as a "kaleidoscopic, social/cultural mosaic," not a melting pot, Tamburri proposes to [re]define and [re]categorize Italian/American literature and the Italian/American intellectual, stating that from this new perspective the roles will be altered from that of "raconteur of what took place—a role that may lead more toward nostalgia than analysis—to that of cultural examiner and, eventually, cultural broker."

The second type of essay looks at specific writers and their contributions to the literary discourse on Italian/American culture. With "Blending 'Literary' Discourses: Helen Barolini's Italian/American Narratives," Edvige Giunta investigates how Helen Barolini blends genres and her different writing personae—novelist, critic, translator, reviewer, and author of a cookbook—to articulate the "extremity of the Italian-American woman author's exclusion" and "her willingness to explore diverse strategies and embark on different routes" to be recognized as an author without qualifying labels. In "Sentences of Self and Blood and Sea: The Poetry of Sandra M. Gilbert," Diane Raptosh argues that Gilbert's poetic opus is an attempt at reconciling a woman's "exigencies of the species—her desire for stasis, her sense of ancestry, her devotion to the house in which she had lived" to the urgencies of her own, and that they are a metaphor for Gilbert's journey in search of roots and of a center. Mario Domenichelli turns his cultural energies toward a poet who is not read much today. An Italian emigrant, Carnevali chose English, his second language, as the true mode of expression for "his troubled muse." Although considered a minor poet, with "Emanuel Carnevali's 'great good bye,'" Domenichelli argues that in reading Carnevali, we are confronted with an individual who "willfully outlines his poetry, and life, as figures *in limine*, on some threshold, perpetually dangling between different dimensions, places, times." Ernesto Livorni's essay, "John Fante: The Saga of Arturo Bandini," gives us a fresh and original interpretation of Fante's major literary character, and his alter ego, Arturo Gabriel Bandini, as he is developed by Fante in four novels that span his writing career. Fred L. Gardaphé's essay, "(Ex)Tending or Escaping Ethnicity: Don DeLillo and Italian/American Literature," contends that the reason critics have not recognized an "Italian foundation" in De Lillo's later works is the result of the "Inability to construct a culture-specific sign code for reading Italian signs," that, though rare, appear in all of De Lillo's narratives and, according to Gardaphé, are "a vital basis of the philosophy upon which he contracts his narratives."

Finally, the essays on film by Stephanie Hull and Maurizio Viano, and Rebecca West, explore the works of three veteran directors (Coppola, DePalma, and Scorsese) and one recent, newcomer (Abel Ferrara), all of whom have on numerous occasions interpreted Italian/American culture in their works. Hull and Viano's essay, "The Image of Blacks in the Work of Coppola, DePalma, and Scorsese," examines the portrayal of race and racism as seen through the eyes of these three masters of film. Rebecca West's venture, "From Lapsed to Lost: Scorsese's Boy and Ferrara's Man," on the other hand, examines the fiction of masculinity in Martin Scorsese's early film *Who's That Knocking at My Door* and Ferrara's *Bad Lieutenant*. Concentrating on the main characters, West investigates the "representation of male subjectivity," as well as the "role of male-female relations, Catholicism, and Italian/American ethnicity in the shaping of these representations."

★   ★   ★

In closing our introduction, we leave our readers with some final thoughts before they embark on their interpretive journey. Ethnic studies in any form or manner—for instance, the use of ethnicity as a primary yardstick—do not necessarily constitute the major answer to filling in knowledge gaps with regard to what some may consider ethnic myopia in the United States. By now a cliché, nevertheless, we all know that the United States were born and developed along lines of diversity, at times with tragic results.[12] What is important in this regard is that we understand, or a least *try* to understand, the origins of the diversity and difference that characterize the many ethnic and racial groups that constitute the kaleidoscopic nature of this country's population. Accepting literature as, among many things, the mirror of the society in which it is conceived, created, and perceived, we come to understand that one of the many questions ethnic literature addresses is the negative stereotypes of members of ethnic/racial groups that are not part and parcel of the dominant culture.[13] In turn, through the natural dynamics of intertextual recall and inference, the reader engages in a process of analytical inquiry and comparison of the ethnic group(s) in question with other ethnic groups as well as with the dominant culture. In fact, it is precisely through a comparative process that one comes to understand how difference and diversity from one group to another may not be as great as it initially seems; indeed, that such difference and diversity can not only coexist but may even overlap with that which is considered characteristic of the dominant group. This, we believe, is another of the goals/functions of ethnic literature: to impart knowledge of the customs, characteristics, language, and so forth, of the various racial and ethnic groups in this country. Finally, partial responsibility for the validity or lack thereof of *other*[14] literatures also lies with the *critic* or *theorist*. In fact, the theorist's end goal for *other* literatures, perhaps, should not limit itself only to the invention of another mode of reading. Instead, it should become, in itself, a strategy of reading which extends beyond the limits of textual analysis; it should concomitantly, and ultimately, aim for the validation of the text(s) in question vis-à-vis those already validated by the dominant culture.

## NOTES

1. One example that comes to mind is Marianne De Marco Torgovnick's collection of disparate essays, *Crossing Ocean Parkway. Readings of an Italian-American Daughter* (Chicago: University of Chicago Press, 1995). Torgovnick herself admits to having abandoned her Italian Americanness only to recover it years later, once having established, we would add, a reputation as a scholar of English literature. For a provocative reading of Torgovnick's coming-out book, see Robert Masullo's review in the ultraconservative *Italic Ways* XXIV (1995): 1.

2. *Yale University Studies* 1, no. 3 (1981): 21–38.

3. *MELUS* 8, no. 1 (1981): 3–14.

4. *Voices in Italian Americana* 1, no. 1 (spring 1990): 15–34.

5. *MELUS* 14, no. 3 (1987 [1990]).

6. *The Voices We Carry* (Montreal: Guernica Editions, 1994).

7. Fred L. Gardaphé, "Visibility or Invisibility: The Postmodern Prerogative in the Italian/American Narrative," *Almanacco* 2, no. 1 (1992): 24–33.

8. See his first chapter, "Blood in the Marketplace: The Business of Family in the *Godfather* Narratives," in *Ethnic Passages. Literary Immigrants in Twentieth-Century America*, Chicago: University Chicago Press, 1993.

9. Robert Casillo, "Catholicism and Violence in the Films of Martin Scorsese" and John Paul Russo, "The Hidden Godfather: Plenitude and Absence in Francis Ford Coppola's *Godfather I* and *II*," both included in *Support and Struggle: Italians and Italian Americans in a Comparative Perspective*, ed. Joseph L. Tropea et al. (Staten Island, NY: AIHA, 1986).

10. The most recent proceedings from the 1994 conference, *Through the Looking Glass. Italian and Italian/American Images in the Media*, ed. Mary Jo Bona and Anthony Julian Tamburri, includes a number of essays on literature and film: Mario Aste, "Filmic Representations of Lucky Luciano in America and in Italy"; Mary Jo Bona, "Imaging of Italians and Italian Americans—A Critical Introduction"; Peter Carravetta, "Places, Processes, Perspectives in Italian-American Poetry and Poetics. Part I"; Mary Ellen Mancina-Batinich, "The Performers: Italian Immigrant Radio and Theater in Minnesota, 1900–1950"; Francesco Mulas, "Religion in John Fante's Novels"; Anthony Julian Tamburri, "Italian/American Cultural Studies—An Emergence[y]?"

11. The distinguished professorship at Queens College/CUNY is a permanent position held by historian Philip Cannistraro. The Stony Brook/SUNY position, instead, remains unfilled as we go to press. Finally, to our chagrin, we would be remiss to ignore the ill-fated, short-lived distinguished professorship of Italian/American studies that historian Dino Cinel held at the College of Staten Island/CUNY. While this position no longer exists as an Italian/American professorship, it has been retained, fortunately, as a distinguished professorship of Italian studies.

12. Of numerous historical cases, we have in mind the egregious examples of Native Americans and African Americans.

13. By ethnic literature, we mean that type of writing which deals, contextually, with customs and behavioral patterns that the North American mind-set may consider different from what it perceives as mainstream. The difference, we might add, may also manifest itself formalistically—i.e., the writer may not follow what has become accepted norms and conventions of literary creation, he or she may not produce what the dominant culture considers *good* literature.

14. We use the adjective *other*, here, in this essay, as an umbrella term to indicate that which either has not yet been canonized—that is, considered a valid category—by the dominant culture (here, read, for instance, MLA) or if already accepted, has been so in a seemingly conditional and a somewhat sporadic manner. Namely, when it is a matter of convenience on the part of the dominant culture.

# Beyond the Margin

# Part 1
# General Considerations

# 1

# Off the Boat and Up the Creek without a Paddle—or, Where Italian Americana Might Swim: Prolepsis of an Ethnopoetics

## JUSTIN VITIELLO

Having deliberately chosen a slightly off-color colloquialism for part of this essay's title, I do not intend to be glib or facetious. *Al contrario,* the creek image strikes me as germane to an exploration of the historical meaning and cultural locus of Italian Americana. As Lewis Mumford reminds us in *The City in History,* the river is more than a metaphor: "As a special organ of civilization, the city seems to have sprung up in a few great river valleys" (55–56). And along the Hudson, the Potomac, the Delaware, and the Chicago, the tributary of Italian American culture is cast in the shadows of negligibility where most of its representatives still thrash in trickles.

Before Italian Americana can ever (if ever) stake a serious claim as an ethos contributing conspicuously to the development of American civilization—via some miraculous upheaval of the empire that Italian *conquistadores,* among others, willy-nilly helped spawn, yet that, ironically, has relegated most Latin contributions to its hegemony to nether regions far removed from its citadels[1]—Italian Americans[2] themselves need to figure out where they belong (or not) in relation to the United States mainstream. In other words, *we* (Italian American writers, critics, scholars, and normal folk) have to decide where we flow in, with, or against today's mono- and multicultural currents—and where we might construct our own edifices or territories circumscribed by creeks, major rivers, or some other, fluvial, terrestrial, or even aerial conduits.

Perhaps we cannot, in all historicist honesty, enjoy the autonomy of "border" creativity heralded by the Native American Paula Gunn Allen in the face of the dominant culture ("they"): "having never lived in the master's house, we can all the more enthusiastically build

a far more suitable dwelling of our own. . . . It is no concern of ours
what 'they' say, write, think, or do. Our concern is what we are
saying, writing, thinking, and doing" ("'Border' Studies: The Inter-
section of Gender and Color," in Gibaldi, 313). Such noble, chthonic
detachment may be the mixed blessing of a few alternative and ethnic
cultures that have not been contaminated by assimilation or integra-
tion. We, like it or not, have been rooted in the villages, mostly urban,
transposed from "their" Europe. It is from such tendrils that we
must respond—polemically, critically, artistically—to contemporary
vortexes (vortices?) of margins and mainstreams.

Lashing and backlashing in this *corso* and *ricorso* are a pair of seemingly contradictory issues raised in two seminal essays of *From the
Margin*:

1.  Very few people have truly pondered the notion of Italian/
    American art. . . . Nor have many people specifically asked,
    what is Italian Americana and does it exist in America? . . .
    What role does the mysterious concept of *Italianità* play in the
    creation of Italian/American art? (Introduction, 1).
2.  It is now with an excellent corpus of works to refer to that we
    can look to the documents of Italian American literature as texts
    that address the universal human condition; it is now that the
    literary history of the United States can take fair account of
    Italian American literary production; it is now, as third-
    generation Italian Americans come of age socially, politically and
    intellectually, that Italian American literature can begin to have
    its due (S. J. Patti, "Recent Italian American Literature: The
    Case of John Fante," 337).

At one extreme, we ask ourselves an existential and sociocultural
question: Do we exist in terms of a unique ethos somehow creatively
expressed? (Apparently, perhaps to good effect this time, we are still
playing out the drama of the inferiority complex that migrated with
our folk families and *paesani* and seeking an alternative to the script
looming in Rose Romano's worst dreams: "If you say we don't have
poetry, aren't you saying we don't have a soul, that we don't exist as
a people, that we're just a bunch of individual wops who'd better get
American if we want to accomplish anything worthwhile?"—letter to
Justin Vitiello, 3 October 1991.) At the other edge, some of us are
espousing a position like Oscar Wilde's: "the one duty we have to
history is to rewrite it" (quoted in Kronik, 12)—a responsibility auda-
ciously shouldered by Fred Gardaphé: "Now the time has come for
the creation of a critical history of Italian American literature" ("Visi-

bility or Invisibility: The Postmodern Prerogative in the Italian/ American Narrative," *Almanacco*, 24). It is between these two poles that I intend to navigate *via* what Bibhuti S. Yadav has called the "tragic optimism" (163) of the poet's searching for "identity by placing questionability at the heart of Being, wondering whether even Being knows what it is, where it is and how it is" (139), rather than with the ontological cargo of interpreters presuming to "provide systematic understanding of what they have heard . . . , announce hermeneutical finality . . . , inaugurate schools of thought . . . (based on) scriptural text" (139–40).

Still convinced by what Sartre stressed in *What Is Literature?*, that is, that "we must take up a position *in our literature*, because literature is in essence a taking of position" (272–73), I want my prismatics to be clear from the outset of this excursus into the *ethnopoetics* of Italian Americana. I choose the word ethnopoetics as a key to the doors of perception in my prolepsis because, thanks to its Greek etymology and its modernist and postmodern adaptations, it generates a multiplicity of relevant meanings. *Ethnikos*, Werner Sollors reminds us (25–26), originally connoted "heathen," the concept of otherness (or, in its propagandistic function of rationalizing one's own barbaric behavior, "barbarism"). Only later, in the nineteenth century, did the significations of "ethnic" evolve to indicate the particularities of a racial or national group. The term, today in America, of course, preserves, in its nuances, this double sense of "universal inclusive peoplehood (shared by all Americans) and of exclusive otherness (separating ethnics from Yankee or mainstream culture)" (26).

The apparently contradictory semantics of *ethnikos* circumscribe the *locus* where the nuances of *Italianità* (or any other ethnic groups' ism) abide in creative tension and, contrary to Sollors's insistence, *can* reveal "authentically indigenous ethnic styles . . . (and) . . . historically authenticated . . . cultural content" (17 and 28). Such forms and substance can be peculiar to diverse peoples, no matter how overshadowed by the hegemonic culture, vis-à-vis their own *poetics*—a worldview that, if we recall Greek etymology once again and Platonic and Aristotelian thought as well, can embody individual talent, creative imagination, the making of a work of art as craft, aesthetic value and its political (as in *polis*) and ethical (cathartic) functions. In this context nowadays, employing ethnopoetics in literary/cultural work becomes what Michel Benamou called in "The Concept of Marginal in Ethnopoetics" an "activity in the cultural politics of marginal literatures" (Fisher, 152).

For Benamou, ethnic artists and their critics can perform the vital tasks of struggling to "reunify us with the human past . . . and the communal, ecological, and religious function of poetry . . . , reoralize the poem by performance . . . , reterritorialize language . . . , retotalize the human community" (152). With such an agenda, obviously entailing the rethinking of Western literary values for both artists and critics, we might not radicalize ourselves as totally as Franz Fanon (311–13) would have liked all ex-colonized cultures to do by eradicating all that is European and American in us since 1492. We could, nevertheless, develop imaginative and scholarly tools to assert and understand, in our literary activity (writing poetry, fiction, drama, criticism) the global (not only Western) universality of works where "ethnos does not mean the Other but the People" and where, at the same time, the textural (not sacred textual) expressions of our ethnopoetics enflesh "the vernacular of everyday speech, acts, songs, insults, toasts, boasts, etc." (Benamou in Fisher, 152).

Ethnopoetics extends our linguistic range beyond what is deemed worthy as art for art's sake to our many idioms, dialects, *volgari* in all their senses: sights (of our villages transplanted to ghettos), sounds (*'o sole mio!* and *mannagg'!* mixed with rock and blues), smells (yes, garlic and olive oil mingling with spaghetti and meatballs),[3] tastes (ditto), touches (tweaks, pinches, caresses, karate chops). Such concretely expressed forms of cultural valences can, as Gardaphé puts it, "bridge the gap between the Streets and the Academy, between the oral and literary traditions of Italian and American culture" by linking "present to past and memory to myth so well it's hard to tell them apart, and impossible to believe we're not listening to the original voice" ("From the streets to the academy," 24). Furthermore, voice, both contemporary and classical when achieved with craft, can resonate with what the editors of *From the Margin* have identified as "the characteristics of the *cantastorie* . . . who explain the quality of our life . . . , the story the illiterate told and lived but was never able to write" (5).[4] Thus recapturing the dignity of that folk culture in its anthropological and historical confrontation with our contemporary reality, we can gain the artistic consciousness necessary to reevaluate and articulate what Robert Viscusi in that same anthology characterizes as our "founding myth . . . , the memory of how the rich expelled the poor (from Italy) into a world invented for them by the great Amerigo . . . (but where) there was no chance that these new arrivals could identify themselves with the ruling peoples" ("A Literature Considering Itself: The Allegory of Italian America," 265 and 270). If this memory takes shape through research and imagination, we lay the cornerstones of a liberation based on a valid People's literary and political consciousness.

It is manifest that our creative/critical instruments already exist in part, for, after all, some of our intellectuals and artists have pondered their being/nonbeing in an anthology of Italian Americana like *From the Margin* (not to mention Helen Barolini's earlier one, *The Dream Book*). So the pressing questions for anyone interested in a serious united front of cultural emancipation now become:

1. How do we refine our artful use of these tools when we bear the immigrant stigma diagnosed by Gardaphé: "Italian Americans are invisible. . . . Not because people refuse to see us, but because, for the most part, we refuse to be seen; we are afraid of being seen" (*Almanacco*, 25)—yet when, under certain spotlights, we spew a bombast barely concealing our cultural illiteracy, prevaricating nostalgia, and terror of nonexistence, declaiming, for example, that "we are the people of Petrarch and Palladia (*sic* ?), of Michelangelo and da Vinci.[5] . . . Everything beautiful that you see (in America) has an Italian root. . . . We are the masters of Western Civilization" ("Italians Boot the Bias," 1)?
2. How do we face and overcome the danger entailed in the affirmation of ethnic pride, that is, the ahistorical and fascistic, if not blatantly racist chauvinism that has led the likes of a Frank Lentricchia to eschew dealing with his ethnicity: "When I saw the racist thing, it also made me see that cultural unity is purchased sometimes on the basis of exclusion and destruction and domination of other human beings. That made me not want to be a great rooter for Italian American ethnicity" (Bliwise, 7)?
3. How do we make a vision like that of Keats's Grecian urn ring true without falling into the old trap where Western universality is another name for the canon of a sycophantic intellectualist subclass serving the institutional violence of American elitist culture via media, the publishing world, and universities:

> Thou, silent form, dost tease out of thought
> As doth eternity: Cold Pastoral!
> When old age shall this generation waste,
>     Thou shalt remain, in midst of other woe
> Than ours, a friend to man, to whom thou say'st
> 'Beauty is truth, and truth beauty'—that is
> All ye know on earth, and all ye need to know?
>
> (289)

4. Via art and literary theory and criticism, how can we rethink, *always imaginatively*, the notion of *Italianità* so that we cut

through what Yadav (146) would call ontological illusions—like blood (Alfonsi, 26) or "a certain advantage in having come of Italian ancestry" (Green, 384)—and what Lemuel Johnson saw way back in 1971 as a fundamental defect in the ethnic pride movement, that is, identity "insistently defined not in terms of value and validity inviolate to itself but in opposition and contradistinction" to some Enemy and, therefore, "pathogenic" (173–74)?

5. How can we learn from other ethnic writers and scholars who are already on the frontlines of the battle to transform exclusive, repressive canons (of world as well as American literature) and to develop sensitive and probing apparati to evaluate new works of art created by non-Western, nonwhite, nonmainstream peoples for their integral truth and beauty?

6. In other words, politically as well as literarily speaking, how can we eradicate our own American tendencies toward Balkanization and plant and nurture a real multiculture of peace, the kind Mumford saw as the only hope for the survival of "Post-Historic Man": "the city . . . of 'One World Man' . . . as an essential organ for expressing and actualizing the new human personality . . . (where) the old separation of man and nature, of townsman and countryman, of Greek and barbarian, of citizen and foreigner, can no longer be maintained . . . (and) it is not the will of a single deified ruler, but the individual and corporate will of its citizens, aiming at self-knowledge, self-government, and self-actualization, that must be embodied in the city" (573)?

This last question merits further, deadly serious attention as linked to what John Berger considers "the most profound drama of our time"—which he sees as a result of the devolution of the abstract Western logic of progress cherished by transnational, global-consumerizing and consuming capitalism: namely, "the systematic oppression of those (peoples) who have a tragic view (of life) by those who have a technocratic and optimistic one" (xi–xii). Such an approach has already led to the genocide of Native Americans via the technological optimism of railroads, mining, and Manifest Destiny; but for Berger it will not cease till the last curtain drops on folk peoples. "This oppression *is* tragedy" he concludes—or I would hazard to say, *ethnocide*.

The cultural McCarthyism launched recently by media-championed right-wing "intellectuals" in this country to perpetuate the caducity of a monolithic, monopolistic canon[6] (I need not name names) aims at nothing less than stifling America's rainbow creativity and plunging its critics back into some dark age predating those schools of thought that D'Souza, in troglodytic knee-jerk fashion, judges to be our curse: "Formalism, hermeneutics, semiotics, structuralism, psychoanalytic criticism, Marxism, deconstructionism" (73). Moreover, the establishment pundits' blitzkrieg pseudodebates about the canon, true-blue to the false principle of naturalization whereby "a privileged social group will generalize its own interests so that they appear to be universal social goals" (Ohmann, 86), smacks of a version of racial superiority more lethal than ethnic chauvinism. Disturbingly, Saul Bellow, in his foreword to Allan Bloom's *The Closing of the American Mind*, fails to grasp the implications of his mentor's goose-stepping to "the *natural* rights inherent in our *regime*" and the lament, in this day and age, for "a poverty of living examples of the possible *high human types*" (21 and 30, emphasis my own). As any Native or African American would know so painfully well, this is the language of the master race all over again with its claim to naturalness barely clothing its cultural Manifest Destiny, one of the ultimate barbarisms rationalized by Platonic philosopher kings and Cartesian abstract logicians and enforced by its cannoneers[7] in our paleocybernetic age ushered in by technological fatalism and psychic numbness—an age when, as Mumford says, "never before had human blight so universally been accepted as normal: normal and inevitable" (474).

The stakes of doing ethnopoetics, then, comprehend our being-or-nothingness dilemma at the global level where unique cultures (or what is left of them) struggle to survive, preserve their integrity and nourish their vitality or sell out, shrivel, self-destruct, consume, and go the way of consumption—unless the masters come down harder and storm them more quickly toward extinction. So the survival or demise of cultures like the Italian American depends, at this *via crucis* of the New World Order—a pox *americana?*—on how well we can empathize with, grasp, adapt, and recreate, according to our own needs and values, a parable like the one, too poignant not to quote in full, with which Wole Soyinka concludes *Myth, Literature and the African World* (138–39):

As our Cartesian ghost introduces himself by scribbling on our black brother's—naturally—*tabula rasa*, the famous proposition, "I think, therefore I am," we should not respond, as the Negritudinists did, with "I feel, therefore I am," for that is to accept the arrogance of a philosophical certitude that has no foundation in the provable, one which reduces the cosmic logic of being to a functional particularism of being. I cannot image that our 'authentic black innocent' would ever have permitted himself to be manipulated into the false position of countering one pernicious

Manicheism with another. He would sooner, I suspect, reduce our white
explorer to syntactical proportions by responding: "You think, therefore
you are a thinker. You are one-who-thinks, white-creature-in-pith-helmet-
in-African-jungle-who-thinks, and finally, white-man-who-has-problems-
believing-in-his-own-existence." And I cannot believe that he would arrive
at that observation solely by intuition.

Not by intuition alone, but in the most cultured, intelligent, civilized, reasonable manner of a Gandhi's inviting the intruder to "quit
India," we Italian Americans might encourage our masters and their
sycophants, notwithstanding their superior weapons of destruction
and propaganda, to leave our young and still shaky cultural edifice
for us to redecorate, rehabilitate, redesign, or construct anew—for
ourselves *and* welcome guests (other ethnic groups!). Romano, in this
same spirit, even suggested that in the restoration we have a room
with our own presses: "for us to define ourselves by our standards
and to preserve our stories, we would not only have to do our own
writing, but our own printing and distribution as well"[8] ("Coming
Out Olive . . . ," 8). Keeping the issue of a people's self-publication
on the back burner for a bit, I want to reiterate here how essential
the seminal idea shared by Soyinka and Romano is to the past, present, and future of any culture that roots and grows via the intellectual
and imaginative valorization of its own artifacts, their forms and functions, truths and beauties, lies and ugliness—that is, vis-à-vis the
"apprehension . . . whose reference points are taken from within the
culture itself . . . , a continuing objective re-statement of that self-
apprehension, to call attention to it in living works of the imagination"
(Soyinka, viii, xi, and xii).

Practically speaking, this self-evaluation of a people's culture, history, and artistic creations (oral, literary; choral, individual; folk,
aulic) should take shape in the protean forms called disciplines of
human knowledge:

1. Literary, hopefully imaginative, criticism via what Gunn Allen
   designates "a . . . system that is founded on the principle of
   inclusion rather than on . . . exclusion . . . , a system that is
   soundly based on esthetics that pertain to the literatures we wish
   to examine" (Gibaldi, 309).
2. Ethnopoetics as an expression of people's creative *raison d'être*
   and explorations of nonbeing via storytelling (in prose or verse,
   *cantastorie* style)—which, Mario Vargas Llosa reminds us in *The
   Storyteller* is "something primordial, something that the very
   existence of a people may depend on" (94).

3. Sociopolitics, where Viscusi's argument in "Affirmative Action for Italian American Literature" (5) implies community in mutually productive values among peoples so that they can all enjoy what Mumford envisions as "the cultural resources that make for world unity and cooperation" in a New Human City that has, in its various actualizations, to some extent, "brought together . . . the diversity and variety of special cultures: . . . all races . . . can be found here, along with their languages, their customs, their costumes, their typical cuisines" (561).

Precisely by respecting the diversity of such Others, listening to their stories in their own languages and dialects, sharing the varieties that can be cultivated to produce ever better fruits of this earth, and nurturing our own existence in a creative relationship with other beings and cultures, we may feel at peace with ourselves and each other so we need not shout, stereotype, consume, invade, and rape-kill-convert-exterminate to try to prove we exist. Either we develop a culturally healthy being-and-becoming or we participate in the worldwide extinction of "old folks at home" and abroad, and most of the gods' children, by consuming the refuse of the most homogenizing forces ever devised in human history to cannibalize—not just metaphorically—other peoples.

My arguments here, not ideologically Marxist, dovetail with Marx's notion that "culture is not politically neutral" (see Katherine Ellis, "Arnold's Other Axiom" in Kampf and Lauter, 171). Furthermore, they are based on research articles recently published by the radically conservative Modern Language Association (MLA). For instance, Dennis Baron, in his "Language, Culture and Society," stresses that "literacy is a protean term, changing with the times and charged with political meaning" (Gibaldi, 40). Yet this point alone may strike many Italian American readers as far too radical precisely because they, uprooted from our immigrants' oral culture, still suffer a deficiency in cultural literacy that hampers them even when they try to read Italian American creative works. Viscusi states, "as far as literature is concerned, Italian Americans are where African Americans found themselves thirty years ago" ("Affirmative Action," 5)—that is to say, without enough of our own presses and readers, and without Bakers, Gateses, and Steptos.

This latter lack, that is, that of major literary critics, scholars, and theorists who study our works of imagination in depth and breadth, is now being addressed by volumes like the present one. But previously, with the few exceptions I have mentioned and will refer to later, *The Great Gatsby*'s final sentence—"so we beat on, boats against

the current, borne back ceaselessly into the past"—could be a motto
not only for first- and second-generation hyphenated Italian American
writers but also for many of our "intellectuals" and *cultori di cose
italiane* today. This is especially true in 1997, when cultural chauvinism, filial pietism and remystification of our history have undergone
a hyperventilating, often frantic resurgence.

There are so many cases of these Italian-American-style phenomena
currently in "the literature" (supposedly literary magazines, presumably academic journals, and even official media, where we have "made
it"—as buffoons one more time) that, for reasons of limited space
and my own wish to offend no one, I eschew citations. Instead, I
propose an exorcism of buffoonery and every other imaginable stereotype that boxes Italian Americans, whether it be at our habitual margins or in the mainstream still mostly foreign to us. To set this
essentially purgative (or purgatorial?) process in motion, we would
do well to consider the implications of Pietro Di Donato's confession
that "the Tony Macaroni writers are shot" (quoted in *From the Margin*, 9) and Lawrence Ferlinghetti's wistful dirge, "The Old Italians
Dying" (*From the Margin*, 147–50). After paying our respects, then
and only then, can we begin to disclose, as Joseph Tusiani perceives in
his story "La Velatura del Fico" (*From the Margin*, 122), "un'America
nuova, quell'America che non scoprì Cristoforo Colombo ma che ogni
emigrato scopre in sè ogni giorno, ogni momento della vita" ("a new
America, that America Christopher Columbus did not discover but
that every emigrant discovers within the self every day, every moment
of life"). In direct opposition to the abstract and the celebratory,
such a revelation of our specificities is the task at hand, a seemingly
Sisyphean labor that at least brings us toward that light of cultural
*coscienza* (consciousness and conscience) where our truth and beauty
can be unleashing.

Such a united front, in its individual, even iconoclastic and idiosyncratic forms of expressions (after all we Italians are supposed to be
a bunch of anarchists!), takes poetic shape in Romano's fine poem
"Vendetta." It is, first, an appropriately angry and radical rejection
of the stigmas and stereotypes regarding Italian Americans that, let
us face it, we ourselves have often helped to perpetuate, and even
mythify, but that, whatever their internal or external source, represent pretexts for our cultural oppression:

> I'm tired of being cute.
> I'm tired of being introduced to people
>     who think they're amusing me
>     by adding an a to the end of
>     every word they say . . .

> I'm tired of being stirred around
>     in a melting pot as though
>     I'm not a human being
>     but a plum tomato . . .
> I'm tired of being asked by insensitive fools
>     who get their news from movie star
>     gossip newspapers whether I know
>     anyone in the Mafia . . .
> I'm tired of not knowing anyone
>     in the Mafia.

(41–42)

Furthermore, this seminal work in Italian American and American literature, with its bitingly ironic, totally contemporary tone and idiom, demystifies the whole boatload of pious platitudes, the lies our forefathers, Italian as well as American, told us about the Dream we were supposed to have coming to us thanks to Columbus, Vespucci, the Bank of America, or Vito Corleone, that is, the entire crew of those who, once our old masters kicked us out of the Old Country, used us as their galley slaves, cannon fodder, indentured servants, cheap labor, and scapegoats for their many barbarisms. Our discovery of the "real America" where ex-Italians must struggle to stake out their own cultural presence and dignity (not property) via a development of a radical and radicalizing[9] artistic, literary, sociopolitical, and historical consciousness has now been made, *grazie*, due to publications like *The Dream Book, Voices in Italian Americana (VIA), From the Margin, malafemmina* press, and *la bella figura*. But this awakening also has bases, and historical, epistemological, and ethnopoetic precedents, in the multiculturalism, cultural studies and policentric, antiliterary-establishment criticism and theory (also called comparative literature) that have represented *for most of this century* various challenges to the "sacred untouchability" of mainstream culture and its literary canon.

Paul Lauter, more truly a believer in "the ideal of *humane* study" than the William Bennetts or E. D. Hirsches of the U.S. regime, has demonstrated with impeccable erudition that "canons are not handed down from Mount Olympus, nor yet from Mount Horeb, but are the products of historically specific conflicts over culture and values" (1991, 168). In the case of the American University literary canon—which for more than a century excluded American literature in favor of British letters—Lauter clarifies how, over seventy years ago, it underwent a major change in the name of certain standards determined by and determining the cultural valences of "the professors, educators, critics, the arbiters of taste of the 1920's." "Naturally" these predominantly "white men of Anglo-Saxon or northern European origins," given their cultural (and Protestant) prismatics, understandably were not equipped to appreciate the oral and written creative works of black migrants from the rural South, or Slavic, Jewish, Mediterranean, and Catholic immigrants from Europe. So these representatives of the dominant culture chose a battery of classics that they claimed as universally great, and "immortal," on the bastions of tastes dependent on their personal (therefore subjective), historical (therefore transient), and cultural (therefore relative) values. Little did they know that their very own destiny as *literati*, in the context of the debate about canons, would be put in its proper, culturally specific and mortal perspective: "the fate of words like *research* and *scholarship* . . . resembles the fate of words like *art* and *literature*, which have become open-ended categories whose meanings are continually redefined as new works and styles emerge" (Gerald Graff, "The Scholar in Society," in Gibaldi, 351).

My only quibbles with Graff's point are (1) as Lauter has shown, there is no such thing as fate or "naturalness" in the determination of human values related to the humanistic and scientific disciplines via which we develop knowledge of our world(s); (2) as Plato's banishment of Homer from the Ideal Republic versus Aristotle's revindication of the blind bard, Boccaccio's divinization of Dante's *Comedy* versus Bembo's preference for Petrarch, and subsequent reevaluations of classics over the centuries have shown *ad infinitum*, even the arbiters of Western cultural values have radically changed their standards over these last 2,300 years. So from a moderate point of view, there has been, over the ages, a constant "canon broadening" (Lauter, 21) and revisioning (where has Matthew Arnold gone?). After all is said against the overwhelming evidence that American literature comprehends works by immigrants and their children from every continent on this orb and when the smokescreen of the real political correctness, that McCarthyism demanding conformity to its institutionalized ethnocide, are undone, we can affirm with Gates that "we are . . . all ethnics in America, so that all the separate tributaries of what we might with great profit think of as comparative American literature are, in fact, 'ethnic' literatures" ("'Ethnic and Minority' Studies," in Gibaldi, 293).

If, to substantiate this moderate, balanced view, the existence of *MELUS*, a totally respectable academic journal, and the *Heath Anthology of American Literature*, two volumes of creative pieces selected by distinguished professors, is not enough, then nothing will ever mitigate the wrath of certain martinets. *Pace.* Our attention must be concentrated not on apologizing to them but on "opening the American mind" (see Simonson and Walker) by "opening up the canon" (Fiedler and Baker) to respond continuously and imaginatively in our artistic, humanistic, and scientific labors (indeed Herculean with so much good stuff that dreams are made on to read!) to the challenge Dexter Fisher posed in 1977: "At no other time than at present has there been such an urgent need to recognize that American literature includes a body of diversified writings previously unacknowledged by most literary scholars and critics, and that these writings are expressions of vital but neglected cultures within this society" (7). Only via such an approach, as David Dorsey recommends, can we develop our literary research to "have a more truthful and full history of . . . people of all hues (who) . . . have suffered America . . . (and) prevailed" and to understand the true complexities of American history and culture "through literature . . . produced by each side (or from many trenches—author's note) of the conflict" ("Minority Literatures in the Service of Cultural Pluralism," in Fisher, 19). In this potentially healthy struggle, moreover, true scholars and critics must employ new and old proven methods like "Marxism, psychoanalysis . . . , cultural studies, feminism . . . , the study of colonial and postcolonial discourse" (Jonathan Culler, "Literary Theory," in Gibaldi, 220) to "encompass things that have never been construed as 'literary' before—the experiences of women, or people of color, of . . . the poor, the illiterate, and the homeless, of ethnic minorities" (Giles Gunn, "Interdisciplinary Studies," in Gibaldi, 253)—*and of us wops too!*

Way back in 1956, Wellek and Warren's *Theory of Literature* provided a map with which to travel through any territory, or ghetto, of comparative literature. Like authentic cartographers, they made clear inroads into their terrain of knowledge. Their "extrinsic approach to the study of literature" placed a work of art in the contexts of biography, psychology, society, the history of ideas, other arts—and left room for their fellow-comparatists to add new relevant instruments like anthropology, structuralism, folklore, oral traditions, feminism, Marxism, or any other discipline or school of thought sharpening our skills of analysis of "the mode of existence of a literary work of art." Finally, for Wellek and Warren—two white males of Northern and Eastern European origin!—this work's value(s) could be elucidated by focusing, where appropriate, via "the intrinsic study of literature," on its euphony, rhythm and meter; its style; its imagery, metaphors, symbols, myths; its nature and mode of narrative; its genre; the aesthetic evaluation of it; and its place in literary history. To apply all these indicators via interpretation was, Warren told me and my classmates in the last course he ever taught on literary theory, the prerogative and responsibility of every new generation of scholars trying to understand what in the world our artists devise.

This set of tools can be, I submit, the key for critics and scholars toiling theoretically and analytically over Italian American literature. Let me suggest where such a *mestiere* (trade and profession) might be fruitfully plied by delving, once again, into "questionability"[10] as adjustable to any folk or literary artwork of whatever genre composed by an author who, while not necessarily sharing our "somatic structure" (see my review of Alfonsi), deals with Italian American reality or fantasy perhaps in the multi-linguistic forms of *Italianità* (as an ethnopoetic idiom) and with the multiconsciousness such forms might nourish to achieve a complex or profoundly simple artistic vision:

1. *In re* works written (or spoken/sung) in Italian or one of its dialects: How are they related to oral/folk/dialect works of artisanry/art in Italy vis-à-vis roots, cultural function, originality? How have emigration, acculturation, deculturation, assimilation and return to the original culture reshaped or distorted them? Do such works have anything to do with mainstream or avant-garde literary movements in Italy? Is art generated by migration still an Italian phenomenon? Do the form and content of works produced transatlantically, whether folk or literary, embody (a) a native Italian artistic sensibility and idiom, (b) a nostalgic, sentimental, or maudlin sense of a lost land and culture, or (c) a new hybrid valid as Italian American literature on its own linguistic terms of cross-breeding?

2. *In re* the Italian American works composed in English where traditions and linguistic peculiarities of the Old Country are deliberately preserved: Are they folk, folkloristic, sentimental, rhetorical—that is, authentic and functional and effective as art/artisanry or falsified and deadened by clichès? Are they alive as idiomatic hybrids or mere *maccheronismo*—that is, quaint but more interesting to folklorists and sociolinguists than to literary critics? Can Italian American literature with oral/folk consciousness and functions exist as an artistic phenomenon outside its community in a consumer society manipulated by media stereotypes and homogenizing technology?

3. *In re* Italian Americans' literary productions in one of the multifaceted styles of American literature: Do they, individually and idiomatically, rise or fall as valid works of art created by original artists or, in whatever currents they might flow, belong significantly to a school, movement, pantheon? To what extent do

these works preserve, transform, integrate, ignore, transcend a genuine ethnic consciousness—that is, do they render a coherent artistic/ethnic vision or not? Is the ethnicity of specific Italian American writers mere *coloratura* and embellishment or an integral fiber of their unique loom woven via a truly artistic voice? How can we interpret—with our tools of ethnopoetics, comparative studies, and contemporary schools of literary analysis—the ethnoliterary elements compounded or disintegrated in the transition from Italian to Italian American and, perhaps, to mainstream or avant garde forms of artistic expression? Can there exist bi- or multi-lingual/cultural writers (or *cantastorie*) who harmonize in convincing vocal strains the folk and literary aspects, the dialects and languages, the historico-cultural myths and visions of their original and new lands?

4. *In re* (1), (2), and (3), are they important works of art, speaking a profound truth with a beauty (or ugliness) appropriate to (=harmonious or cacophonous with) a vision that reverberates their voice (where voice equals vision and vice versa)?

Given the transiency of what some insist are universal values and tastes (as if our psychosomatological palates did not change!) and granted the dharma to be representative (and publish your living and dead friends), no anthology of literature—not even Oxford or Norton—has ever included a *corpus* of works whose "soul" is 100 percent everlasting in terms of (4). Nevertheless, this is not to deny the value of trying to interpret the historical, cultural, and aesthetic merit of individual art works, schools, movements, trends, examples of trendiness—not to speak of radical experimentation that might engender a deeper, higher, or broader conception of what we consider good or great literature. In this context, "the renaissance"—or just plain birth—of publications "devoted to critical thinking, analysis, and expression of Italian American culture and art" indicates that we are emerging "from the quagmire of cultural assimilation" (Lombardo, 3). Our anthologies and magazines previously mentioned are now asserting, via the fora given to our specific and diverse voices (*e pluribus unum* in microcosm?), the unique cultural and literary dignity of Italian Americana. We are watching and participating in the play and interplay of American literature as it evolves, regresses, and sometimes radicalizes in its history of the conflicts Barolini has felicitously identified as "literary hegemonies and oversights" (36f.) and cases of "literary apartheid" (40).

Barolini's *The Dream Book* is a crucial contribution in this drama that verges on cultural civil war because (1) generally speaking, it

establishes à la Soyinka that "redefining the self in one's own authentic
terms is essential for an integrated literary expression" (52); (2) it
responds head-on to the "pressure of pluralism" (41) in America from
the perspective of "recombining two cultures" to engender "a third
realm of consciousness and expression" with an Italian background
and an American foreground (34–35); (3) it challenges the pundits of
both American and Italian American studies by providing an artistic
vehicle of that "eternally" silenced, repressively archetypified creature Man called Woman, revealing that She (Pandora? Eve? Ave Maria?) is authentically many voices in many psychosomatic valences;[11]
and (4) it raises a question also posed by Robert Scholes in his fine
essay "Canonicity and Textuality" (148) about the relationship between literary judgments and ethical/political/poetic justice.

Sensitized, radicalized, and as Toni Morrison would say, "woman-
ized" by ex-Madonnas/whores/mothers, we can enter, with a more
complex awareness of the battle where, as Scholes notes, the lines are
drawn between "those who defend a universal standard of literary
quality" and "those who argue that standards are always relative,
local and political," and where the latter are further divided "into
champions of different excluded groups, seeking canonical status for
their own class of texts, and anarchists or absolute relativists, who
would undo all canons and standards if they could" (147). Like
Scholes, as I hope it is clear throughout this essay, I would hazard to
say (concerning our vindication of Italian Americana or any other
American cultural/literary phenomenon): "I do not see how anyone
can teach (or write or do scholarly research or criticism) without
standards, but I cannot find any single standard for determining the
worth of a text" (147). This is why it is urgent that we assume the full
responsibility to develop flexible, comprehensive standards beyond
*campanilismo, prominentismo, clientelismo, sciovinismo*, etc., etc., etc.,
in openly-frontiered realms of the aesthetically and ethically best of
what we, in self-apprehension and global awareness and maybe wisdom, are. For only with such a vision of interrelating territories and
resources in American literature will we ever be able to embrace, with
tragic optimism, the multiple truths that might be unified in a vision
like Keats's:

> A thing of beauty is a joy for ever:
> It's loveliness increases; it will never
> Pass into nothingness; but still will keep
> A bower quiet for us.
>
> (*Endymion*, I, 61).

Unfortunately, 1997 is no time to retreat into any quiet bower, for, while America is no ex-Yugoslavia, it is notorious for its Los Angeleses and its Bensonhursts, the dramatic explosions of *daily, systemic* problems that have to do, in considerable measure, with interethnic conflicts. This strife, in turn, is related to peoples' struggles to partake of the American Dream and the counteractions of those who already "have it" (or so they think) or compete with other "have-nots" for it.

While no ethnic group in its history of Americanization has a monopoly on suffering, Italians have suffered. Many of us, like Sandra M. Gilbert and her children, have to varying degrees, lost our linguistic, cultural, and historical roots: "What is *misterioso* to me is simply lost in mists of time to them" ("Piacere Conoscerla," *From the Margin*, 119). Nor is it an accident that it took Maria Mazziotti Gillan thirty-five years to write her fine poem, "Betrayals" (*Taking Back My Name*, 11–12)—because "by trying to erase my ethnicity, maybe I lost a part of myself" (Pofeldt, sec. C). That loss is tragic: traumatizing, debilitating, and pathological, for peoples as well as for individuals. Damned if you keep your heritage, damned if you don't.

I am not so naive as to believe that merely recapturing a cultural past is an instant recipe for ethnic health, or a cure-all for America's multiple social ills. Apropos, Scholes asks provocatively, "does the canon (even a revitalized one—author's note) make anyone wiser or more virtuous?" (149). The answer is any body of knowledge, any grand achievement of a civilization, especially in the abstract, is a double-edged sword, a force as potentially destructive as it is creative. And history has demonstrated, time and again, how once oppressed peoples can emulate or outdo their oppressors in brutalizing and exterminating a new scapegoat for the violence within them.[12]

Perhaps, then, the grounding of our ethnic awareness, ideally rooted in self- and mutual respect for diversity and otherness, could be the Gandhian principle of defense: We should protect our enemies against ourselves. Against ourselves, because the Los Angeleses and Bosnias are in us too. Only by recognizing that they lurk within us can we recreate a culture that is a truly life-giving alternative to hypes and bytes and stereotypes and scapegoatings and pseudo apotheoses. That would be a culture worthy of the name *coscienza*, the kind Manuela Bertone sees as evolving in *From the Margin* vis-à-vis a "richly compact set of responses to a common intellectual concern: the emergence of a sense of 'otherness,' the awareness of a shared cultural past, the need to express both of them in artistic terms" (29).

Thus, *Italianità* (a term unfortunately smacking of *Mussolinianismo*) might healthily embody "a new ability to historicize and reflect upon

the immigrant past . . . and ultimately to shape the national consciousness of cultural diversity via the multifaceted creativity of Italian
American culture" (Bertone, 29). At peace, and antifascist in a new
way, we could extend trust in selves and in peoplehood to all the
"Others" in a dialogue whose political ramifications could be as fruitful as the literary ones wisely recommended by Gates: "Perhaps it is
time for scholars to think of a comparative American culture as a
conversation among different voices—even if it is a conversation that
some of us were not able to join until very recently. Finally, it is
perhaps time for us to conceive of an ethnicity . . . without blood and
to reconfigure the complex relations among the texts that constitute
American literature" ("'Ethnic and Minority' Studies," 300).

While there are no panaceas to usher in a new age of continually
intelligent dissent, open and informed criticism, and cultural and
politico-economic democracy in America, at least we can, for the
moment, rooted in Italian Americana, enjoy the imaginative vision of
a rainbow culture that might arc for all of us. Here, we might just
be and seek, eschewing that great American Dream lie for which we
cannibalize one another. Here, with Joseph Papaleo, we can demyth-
ify the notion of heritage as somatic and bloody inevitability: "It's a
nice heritage we saw for a moment in *time* . . . I am saying it is only
history. History" ("Friday Supper," in *Almanacco* 73). Yes, history,
that by definition, can be rewritten, reclaimed, and changed in a
future where the choral dialogue Mazziotti Gillan initiates in "Growing Up Italian" (*Taking Back My Name*, 3) represents our potentiality
to envision and maybe to experience a life worth living every day in
our new houses and communities:

> I celebrate my Italian-American self,
> rooted in this, my country, where
> all those black/brown/red/yellow
> olive-skinned people
> soon will raise their voices
> and sing this new anthem
>
> Here I am
> and I'm strong
> and my skin is warm in the sun
> and my dark hair shines,
>
> and today, I take back my name
> and wave it in their faces
> like a bright, red flag.

I would venture to say that this is a potent example of poetry that is ethnic in texture and tissue and more than ethnic as it is understood in "native writing," that "basically descriptive reminiscence . . . , a way of making do with the charm and uniqueness of the face of the subject that is most familiar. And nothing more" (Papaleo, letter to J. Vitiello, 1 March 1992). For Mazziotti Gillan's form/content embraces two principles that in or outside any canon, beyond any mainstream or margin, are organically united in just plain good contemporary poetry: namely, (1) "the constant finding of the dual identities . . . that ebb and flow with the poet's sensibility and often make for that maddening ambiguity we call ethnic identity" via a distinctly timbered voice, an achieved poetic language that reflects in and of itself "how ethnic poetry can contain the respectfully rendered portrait of the details of the immigrant world and its soul and yet be filled with intellect, be modern in language and rhythm, sharp, quick, slashing in style and contain the modern pose and mode of irony" (Papaleo, ibid.); (2) that "indefinable" without which a poet abides only as a minor composer of some good works: that is, as Diane di Prima writes in "Rant" (*From the Margin*, 154–55), the ascending poetic vision of the artist who speaks, never self-consciously, for self, ethnic group, gender, class, humanity:

> You cannot write a single line w/out a cosmology . . .
> w/out imagination there is no memory
> w/out imagination there is no sensation
> w/out imagination there is no will, desire . . .
> history is the dream of what can be, it is
> the relation between things in a continuum
> of imagination
> What you find out for yourself is what you select
> out of an infinite sea of possibility . . .
> . . . you etch in light . . .
> Dig it.

Yes, dig it, and rage, rage against the dying of any lights, old or new, that might snuff out our creative expression, our ethnopoetics. These strengths of ours, in turn, can only be enriched by an enlightened reevaluation and reembracing of our Italian languages and dialects and literatures and culturopolitical histories. Such are the tools with which we can explore our literary/cultural/political territories in the late-twentieth-century American wilderness (city and country)— this time with respect for and in solidarity with those who have suffered and will suffer "the painful . . . double consciousness" (first recognized by W. E. B. DuBois in 1903) that might serve us, if we are *furbi* enough, as "double-voiced subversiveness and . . . multivalent aesthetic expressiveness born in the fecund dualities of oppression" (Lyne, 319). And if we are neither oppressed nor oppressive, our multi-consciousness can be our strength—shared with all the Others—to reach catharses of the tragic cultural dilemmas we might face with the passionate lucidity and classic/contemporary voice of a Mazziotti Gillan and with her dream of liberation:

> Without words, they tell me
> to be ashamed.
> I am.
> I deny that booted country
> even from myself,
>
> want to be still
> and untouchable
> as these women
> who teach me to hate myself . . .
> My anger spits
> venomous from my mouth:
>
> I am proud of my mother
> dressed all in black,
> proud of my father
> with his broken tongue,
> proud of the laughter
> and noise of our house.
>
> Remember me, ladies,
> The silent one?
> I have found my voice
> and my rage will blow
> your house down.
>
>         ("Public School No. 18: Paterson, New Jersey")

Our ethnogenesis as cocreators of American culture, coherent and harmonious not with its history of genocide, bigotry, racism, institutional violence, elitism, and vicious socioeconomic competition, but with the highest ideals we can remake and actualize, need not be a journey of "consent" (i.e., conformity to the mainstream) or "descent" (ethnic provincialism). *Pace* Sollors *et al.* As a viable alternative herein I propose, instead, *ascent* in our creative fire to the level of mutually productive cultural dignity to which liberated human beings and peoples deserve to aspire. Perhaps, if we get to the top of the mountain where we can best enjoy the rainbow, we may realize that it is a volcano! Then, as our Pompeiis and Herculanea are getting buried under the fire storms and their residue of soda cans, computer chips, and toxic waste, we will have to learn to flow together with the lava so that at least some fragments of our voices and cosmologies remain.

## NOTES

1. See chapters 1 and 2 of *The City in History* for an elucidation of the central role of citadels, both sacred and profane, in the founding of civilizations aspiring to hegemony.

2. I concur with A. J. Tamburri (*To Hyphenate or Not to Hyphenate*) that "Italian American should be written with a slash or nothing between the two terms of the composite." In this essay, however, I have respected those who punctuate as they choose.

3. I need not remind my *paesani* that this is an Italian American, not an Italian, dish.

4. See, also, Barolini, who, in defense of our folk heritage, writes: "We were told . . . of Italian illiteracy. But never that illiterate people have a culture and social systems" (19). I am indebted to her for demythifying the pseudo-cultural elitism of a Rose Basile Green, who insists that "a ditch-digger might have been illiterate, but he knew about Dante" (18).

5. Surely, the interviewee means Leonardo here and does not intend to stress the fact, indicated by "da Vinci" (i.e., "from the town of Vinci"), that the artist was a bastard.

6. I do not have the luxury of space to analyze the political history of canon formation. As a compromise, I refer readers to the excellent studies of this phenomenon in Fiedler and Baker; Fisher, Kampf and Lauter; Lauter; and Ohmann.

7. The pun is rooted in Greek etymology. See Robert Scholes, "Canonicity and Textuality" in Gibaldi, 139, where he explains that canon and cannon have common linguistic origins "connoting severity and imposition of power."

8. Romano, in fact, did her own printing and distributing of Italian American women's poetry via her *malafemmina* press and her monthly literary journal *la bella figura* (where male writers also appeared upon occasion).

9. My use of forms of the word *radical* is based on its Latin etymological meaning of "roots" (*radices*).

10. The following questions are elaborated from my review of F. Alfonsi's *Dictionary of Italian American Poets* that appeared in *Italica* 68, no. 1 (spring 1991): 60–62.

11. See also, Mary Jo Bona's review essay treating *The Dream Book* where she makes a fundamental point: "reforming the canon necessitates a reevaluation of the cultural ideology informing the dissemination of what has traditionally been called 'great' literature . . . often . . . solely based on the interests and passions of male critics, who claim their standards to be universal when often they are determined by their own race, class, and particular culture" (94).

12. The classic analysis of this phenomenon is found in Paulo Freire's *The Pedagogy of the Oppressed*.

## WORKS CITED

"Affirmative Action for Italian American Literature." Interview with Robert Viscusi. *John D. Calandra Italian American Institute* 6, no. 3 (spring 1991): 5–6.

Alfonsi, Ferdinando. *Poesia italo-americana/Italian American Poetry.* Catanzaro: Carello Editore, 1991.

*Almanacco 2,* no. 1 (spring 1992).

Baker, H. A., Jr. *Blues, Ideology, and Afro-American Literature.* Chicago: University of Chicago Press, 1984.

Barolini, Helen, ed. *The Dream Book: An Anthology of Writings by Italian American Women.* New York: Schocken, 1985.

Berger, John. Foreword. Danilo Dolci. *Sicilian Lives.* New York: Pantheon, 1981.

Bertone, Manuela. Review of *From the Margin. Harvard Book Review* (spring/summer 1991): 29–30.

Bliwise, R. J. "Putting Life into Literature." Interview with Frank Lentricchia. *Duke Alumni Magazine* (May 1988): 2–7.

Bloom, Allan. *The Closing of the American Mind.* New York: Simon and Schuster, 1988.

Bona, Mary Jo. "Voices of the Silent Ones: A Review Essay." *Voices in Italian Americana 2,* no. 1 (1991): 93–98.

Di Pietro, R. J., and E. Ifkovic, eds. *Ethnic Perspectives in American Literature: Selected Essays on the European Contribution.* New York: MLA, 1983.

D'Souza, Dinesh. "Illiberal Education." *The Atlantic* (March 1991): 51–79.

Fanon, Franz. *The Wretched of the Earth.* New York: Grove Press, 1968.

Fiedler, L. A., and H. A. Baker, Jr., eds. *English Literature: Opening up the Canon.* Baltimore: Johns Hopkins University Press, 1981.

Fisher, Dexter, ed. *Minority Language and Literature.* New York: MLA, 1977.

Freire, Paulo. *Pedagogy of the Oppressed.* New York: Continuum, 1987.

Gardaphé, Fred L. "From the Streets to the Academy." Interview with J. Vitiello. *Fra Noi* (January 1992): 24.

———. "(In)Visibility: The Cultural Criticism of Frank Letricchia and Don De-Lillo." Paper delivered at MLA Convention, San Francisco, 1991.

———. "Reclaiming one's heritage." Interview with Maria Mazziotti Gillan. *Fra Noi* (February 1992): 24.

———. "These Fish Tales Ring True." Review of J. Vitiello, *Vanzetti's Fish Cart. Fra Noi* (January 1992): 24.

Gates, H. L., Jr. *The Signifying Monkey: A Theory of Afro-American Literary Criticism.* New York: Oxford University Press, 1987.

Gibaldi, Joseph, ed. *Introduction to Scholarship in Modern Languages and Literatures.* New York: MLA, 1992.

Gillan, Maria Mazziotti. *Taking Back My Name.* San Francisco: *malafemmina* Press, 1991.

Green, Rose Basile. *The Italian American Novel: A Document of the Interaction of Two Cultures.* Rutherford: Fairleigh Dickinson University Press, 1974.

Hirsch, E. D. *Cultural Literacy: What Every American Should Know.* Boston: Houghton Mifflin, 1987.

"Italians boot the bias." *Philadelphia Inquirer* (7 October 1991): sec. E, 1f.

Johnson, Lemuel A. *The Devil, the Gargoyle, and the Buffoon: The Negro as Metaphor in Western Literature.* London: Kennikat Press, 1971.

Kampf, Louis, and Paul Lauter, eds. *The Politics of Literature: Dissenting Essays on the Teaching of English.* New York: Oxford University Press, 1990.

Kronik, J. W. Editor's Column. *PMLA* 107, no. 1 (January 1992): 9–12.

Lauter, Paul. *Canons and Contexts.* New York: Oxford University Press, 1991.

Lentricchia, Frank. *Ariel and the Police.* Madison: University of Wisconsin Press, 1988.

Lombardo, John. "The Power of the Press: Cultural Journals on the Rise." *Fra Noi* (February 1992): 3.

Lyne, William. "The Signifying Modernist: Ralph Ellison and the Limits of the Double Consciousness." *PMLA* 107, No. 2 (March 1992): 319–30.

Mumford, Lewis. *The City in History.* New York: Harcourt Brace Jovanovich, 1961.

Ohmann, Richard. *English in America: A Radical View of the Profession.* New York: Oxford University Press, 1976.

Papaleo, Joseph. Letter to J. Vitiello. 1 March 1992.

Pofeldt, Elaine. "Images from Poetry." Interview with Maria Mazziotti Gillan. *Lifestyle* (5 May 1991): sec. C.

Romano, Rose. "Coming out Olive in the Lesbian Community: Big Sister Is Watching You." Unedited. Compliments of the author.

———. Letter to J. Vitiello. 3 October 1991.

———. *Vendetta.* San Francisco: *malafemmina* Press, 1990.

Sartre, J. P. *What Is Literature?* Trans. B. Frechtman. New York: Harper and Row, 1965.

Simonson, Rick, and Scott Walker, eds. *Multi-Cultural Literacy: Opening the American Mind.* St. Paul: Graywolf Press, 1988.

Sollors, Werner. *Beyond Ethnicity: Consent and Descent in American Culture.* New York: Oxford University Press, 1986.

Soyinka, Wole. *Myth, Literature and the African World.* New York: Cambridge University Press, 1990.

Stepto, R. B. *From Behind the Veil: A Study of Afro-American Narrative.* Urbana: University of Illinois Press, 1979.

Tamburri, A. J., P. A. Giordano, and F. L. Gardaphé, eds. *From the Margin: Writings in Italian Americana.* W. Lafayette: Purdue University Press, 1991.

Tamburri, A. J. Review of F. Alfonsi, *Dictionary of Italian-American Poets. Voices in Italian Americana* 1, no. 2 (1990): 135–37.

———. *To Hyphenate or Not to Hyphenate.* Montreal: Guernica, 1991.

Vargas Llosa, Mario. *The Storyteller.* Trans. Helen Lane. New York: Penguin, 1990.

Vitiello, J. Review of F. Alfonsi, *Dictionary of Italian-American Poets. Italica* 68, no. 1 (spring 1991): 60–62.

Wellek, Rene, and Austin Warren. *Theory of Literature.* New York: Harcourt, Brace, and World, 1956.

Yadav, Bibhuti S. "Methodic Deconstruction." *Interpretation in Religion.* Ed. S. Biderman and B.-A. Scharfstein, 129–68. Leiden: E. J. Brill, 1992.

# 2

# Italian American Culturalism: A Critique

## RENATE HOLUB

### I. NONMONOLINEARITY OF THE MULTICULTURAL ACT

In one of his seminal essays, "The Southern Question," Antonio Gramsci makes reference to the so-called Sassari Brigade, which had been called in to "take part in the suppression of the insurrectionary movement at Turin in August, 1917."[1] The Boselli government and its supporters were certain that the Sassari Brigade, of an almost entirely provincial composition, would never fraternize with the Turin workers, on account "of the memories of hatred which every repression leaves with the people even against the material instruments of the repression, and which it leaves with soldiers, who remember their comrades killed by the insurgents."[2] To bring in troops from the provinces to combat urban insurgences was also the strategy deployed by Louis-Adolphe Thiers when determined, in the name of a Western European aristocratic-bourgeois alliance, to destroy the 1871 Paris Commune of workers, emancipationists, internationalists, artisans, and others. Since regionality appears to breed fraternity, in that it activates "innumerable threads of relationships, friendships, memories, suffering and hope," to again cite Gramsci, the defenders of state interests saw to it that neither the workers of Paris nor those of Turin were to meet up with their own "regional" kind. While the strategy worked in Paris, as we know from the historical record, Gramsci explains in the above mentioned essay why it did not work in Turin. The Sassari Brigade, welcomed by a crowd of Turinese ladies and gentlemen who "offered flowers, cigars and fruit to the troops" when they first arrived, was, a few years later, on the eve of the general strike of July 1919, suddenly removed from that city and at night. And "no 'elegant' crowd cheered them at the station."[3]

What Gramsci highlights among many other problems in his renowned essay is the specificity of the relation that obtained between

46

the Sassari Brigade and the Turin workers. I would like to define this relation as *nonmonolinear*. Since the brigade consisted mostly of peasants and only of a minute number of mining workers, the Boselli/ Orlando/Nitti/Giolitti governments had no reason to believe that the Sardinian peasants would bond with the Turin workers. However, some of the Turin workers were also Sardinians. They felt, spoke, and identified themselves as Sardinians and over a period conveyed that much to the brigade. So while in 1917 members of the brigade were still willing to shoot at striking Turin workers, whom they perceived as "gentrified other," by 1919 they no longer perceived the workers as "other" and consequently tried to avoid shooting at them in Turin. Many members of that brigade not only felt, spoke, and identified themselves as Sardinians, but also had begun to identify themselves as members of an oppressed class. As such the brigade consciously entertained relations not only with Sardinian workers in Turin, but with Turin workers of non-Sardinian origin as well. What the Sardinian peasants in the Sassari Brigade shared with the Turin workers of Sardinian and non-Sardinian origin alike, and what they did not share with the ruling class of Sardinia—the Sardinian peasants had, in fact, refused to enter into a political alliance with the Sardinian ruling class—was their oppression by an antipeasant and antiworker ruling class. The consciousness of this shared heritage of subordination had become a political liability for ruling class strategy. Since the state could no longer entrust this brigade with the suppression of working-class insurrections, it expeditiously removed it from Turin.

The Gramscian concept of nonmonolinearity of relations bears on my critical reflections on Italian American culturalism in more than one way. What I propose in this chapter is that this concept is useful for an assessment of the various functions of Italian American culturalism in the current social and political context in the United States. Since this concept, as many of Gramsci's analytical concepts, is the upshot of a specifically Gramscian philosophical approach to the phenomenal world, as such containing many elements of his method, analysis, and theory, I will also argue that the concept of nonmonolinearity is useful not only for describing the various functions of Italian American culturalism in particular, but also for developing criteria for a critique of multiculturalisms in general. Such a critique reflects on the relation of multiculturalisms to the political economies of power. Let me begin by stating that Gramscian nonmonolinearity implies, first of all, that there are more than simply two points to be connected by a line or a relation and second, that these points constitute forces that, similar to dynamic forces within a force field, magnetically engage with other points or forces. Relations are thus *in potentia* relations of differing strength or force, differing power sites or power relations.[4] As the example of the Sassari Brigades's conceptual shift indicates, there are more than two power sites or force fields in the Gramscian understanding of power relations. While subordination and domination are the terms that usually describe the status or relative strength of the position of each power site under certain conditions, these positions are changeable, and even exchangeable, at least temporarily. The brigade's refusal to shoot at workers empowers the brigade's members while simultaneously subverting the authority and the power of the Turin ruling class. Returning to Sardinia, the members of the brigade are in the position to further pursue philosophical ideas of self-determination and autonomous actions as they continue to be forced, as members of the peasantry and working class, into political and economic subordination. Their experiences as free or autonomous beings, or of social nonsubordination, will mark their philosophical reflection on their subordinate economic and political status, or their "conception of the world," to use Gramscian terminology, just as their lifelong experiences as members of a subordinate class with vis-à-vis the ruling class, next to their experiences or experiential encounters with Sardinian workers in Turin, had marked their structure of action. Though empowered to shoot at members of their own class, they were morally unable to do so once they recognized the position and the constitution of that class: its powerlessness vis-à-vis the ruling class, and their own rootedness in that class.

Gramsci's account of the brigade's dynamic relation with the Turin ruling class deploys a theoretical structure that examines the relations between experience, consciousness, and the ethics of sociopolitical action. This theoretical structure, generically known in contemporary social, political, and cultural theory as "Gramsci's theory of hegemony" is also at work when he examines, at another point in his essay on "The Southern Question," the lack of resistance of southern peasants to the emerging domination and hegemony of fascism.[5] Whereas the Sassari Brigade had shifted from a "conception of the world" that accepted the legitimacy of the uneven relation of power between the Turin ruling class and the Turin working class to a "conception of the world" that questioned that uneven relation of power and subverted its hegemony, the southern peasants, mostly due to the ideological mediations of their conservative intellectuals, continued to adhere to a "conception of the world" that spontaneously reproduced the consent to the status quo. Southern intellectuals, in Gramscian terms the teachers, priests, lawyers, doctors, and other professionals, disseminate and authorize conservative values and beliefs in the practices and structures of everyday social life of the peasants. As a result, the peasants did not question, but rather legitimated fascist hegemony, thereby producing and reproducing the structures of their own subordination. These two references to the "Southern Question," or more precisely, the many elements and issues involved in Gramsci's discussion of power as reflected in these two references are indicative of the complexity of Gramsci's theory of hegemony. Not dissimilar to Michel Foucault's seminal work on power, Gramsci's texts contain notions of hegemony that understand power not only in its repressive dimension, but also in its "productive" dimensions, as a mechanism or a force that produces itself in the practices of everyday life.[6] As we noticed earlier, in time the Sassari Brigade learned or rather became conscious of the origins and the conditions it shared with the Turin working class, and as a result, began to identify its class interests. Elsewhere, in his notes on "Americanism and Fordism," in the *Prison Notebooks*, Gramsci extends, similarly to Foucault, the operations of power from the public sphere, typically the sphere of economics and politics, to the private sphere, indeed, to the most private practices in everyday life, which includes sexuality.[7] In this sense, both Gramsci and Foucault critically restructured and expanded traditional theories of power—from Thomas Hobbes to Max Weber—who merely distinguished between legitimate and illegitimate forms and exercises of political power. This move allows them to concern themselves with the cultural sphere in the most broadest sense, where knowledge and norm production take place. Yet in contrast to Foucault's genealogical model of power description, which, in its desire to discover ever more fine-tuned apparatuses of administrating, surveilling, and controlling modern life, is ultimately unable to distinguish among differences in the quality of life of a wide range of social and cultural groups, Gramsci insists on a perspective that accounts for differences in the control and exercise of power. While the poorest farmers maintain some authority or power with respect to their children, they are themselves subject to political authority in most other practices of their lives. The poorest farmer is thus both subject and object of authority. Yet as the example of the Sassari Brigade illustrates, under certain conditions, the object-hood of the subordinate group can always potentially transform itself, at least temporarily, into subject-hood. When the brigade refused to obey orders to shoot, it challenged the authority or domination of the Turin ruling class, thereby, symbolically stripping it of what Weber called legitimacy. Objects and subjects are thus not stable objects and subjects in Gramsci's framework of power but capable of shifting position in relation to power. What they have in common is that they are both subject to the predicaments of space and time. In Gramsci's conceptual universe, geography and temporality endow power relations with precise if varying degrees of potentiality and impotence.

Against the background of these brief reflections on Gramsci's complex theory of hegemony, key metaphors of multicultural narratives, such as the polarity of "center" and "margin," or the juxtaposition of cultural hegemony and cultural repression, simply lose much of their empirical and critical edge. Italian American culturalism, conceptually and morally navigating the waters of multiculturalism, is no exception. Viewing the center as synonymous with power, domination, and authority and the margin as its unmediated opposite is a facile practice. And more so is the uncontested habit of universally endowing the center with a register of moral inferiorities and the margin with moral superiority. It is somewhat curious that a discourse that so rigorously insists on notions such as diversity and difference would unhesitatingly agree not only on the uniformity of its moral mission, but also on the identity of its political function. Yet recent research in France, Germany, and Great Britain on race relations, ethnicity, and multiculturalism, much of it carried out with Gramscian modes of analysis, has a good deal to suggest concerning the diversity of the function and application of the multicultural social act in different national contexts.[8] This research also speaks to the political use and manipulation of multicultural projects, by the right and the left alike. Precisely because it does not entertain a monolinear relation with either domination or subordination, multicultural action is not in and by itself antidomination, subversive, or free of power relations of its own. It can enter an alliance with undemocratic and democratic forces alike. In Germany, for instance, some multicultural projects, qua cultural activity, accompany the political struggles of non-German citizens living and working in Germany to gain German citizenship rights, that is, political and juridical rights, and economic security. In France and Great Britain, where many ethnic groups of respectively non-French and non-British origin enjoy citizenship rights or multiple citizenship rights, the multicultural or the plurality of cultural projects effects not only the rise of a picturesque pluralistic culture but also of new forms of racisms, including segregation.[9] It is this implicit "ambivalence of the multicultural model," to borrow a formulation of one of the foremost experts in European migration studies—Ursula Apitzsch—which is derived conceptually from Gramsci's notion of nonmonolinearity of relations, which I would like to highlight here.

## II. "Structures of Feeling" and "Universal Expressivity"

Like many multicultural projects, Italian American culturalism is based on what I would call an act of solidarity. Italian Americans fraternize or sororize with one another due to an apparently monolinear bond they share. They are Italian Americans, citizens of the United States with concomitant citizenship and property rights whose foremothers and forefathers arrived from Italy as immigrants. While this bond or shared inheritance is the most important enabling factor of Italian American culturalism, its formal content is specific not only to the Italian American community but also to other communities steeped in an immigrant tradition. One of the most dedicated Italian American cultural critics, Fred L. Gardaphé, has recently suggested to name this bond "intra-cultural."[10] I should note here that his term *intra-cultural bond* is as undifferentiated as are my terms *monolinear bond* or *monocultural bond*: Both potentially obfuscate class differences, social differences, and cultural-regional differences when assuming that Italian Americans relate in identical ways to Italian culture or to Italy as place of origin or that Italy is an identifiably single cultural unit. In light of recent political developments in some parts of Italy with strong regional overtones and accompanied by the celebratory formation of new populisms, the notion of "Italy" has increasingly taken on new and multiple meanings that forcefully question the stability of a unified Italian cultural unit. For these reasons, terms such as *intra-cultural bond* or *monocultural bond* deserve to be subjected to more scrutiny than I can offer here in the context of my argument. Suffice it to say in most general terms that the Italian American ethnic project is based on a shared inheritance of cultures that have their place of origin not in the United States but in the geography and history of Italy. In this sense the Italian American project is only somewhat monocultural, while simultaneously being multicultural. It is monocultural to some degree in its conception and its point of departure—the link with the Italian heritage, understood in the broadest sense—and it is clearly multicultural in its effects: It adds a new or particular cultural dimension to the apparently value-neutral "universality" of U.S. American standard culture. Thereby, Italian American culturalism participates in the celebration of currently evolving multiculturalist movements and contributes to their legitimation. While the multicultural benefits to standard U.S. American culture are discernible, the substance of the shared inheritance of the project is not. A closer look at Italian American cultural productions in literature and poetry written in *English* reveals, for instance, that Italy, or more precisely, Italian cultural traditions of everyday life, do not play a more significant role in the content of these works than the everyday life experiences of Italian immigrants in the United States. In this sense, the shared inheritance of Italian American ethnicity, Italian cultural traditions of everyday life, are not more important than the shared inheritance of "immigrant life in the United States."[11] And conversely, a look at recent Italian American cultural productions written in *Italian* reveals that the shared inheritances of Italian cultural traditions of everyday life and immigrant life in the United States play a subservient role to the desire to express elements of one's creativity in Italian.[12]

The structuration of Italian American culturalism has accommodated a certain evolutionary trajectory not dissimilar from various other ethnic cultural projects in the United States, and its pattern discloses now the following major elements: Its production component includes (a) literary writings in prose and poetry, (b) the canonization and typologization of these productions, according to phenomenological principles, and (c) philosophical assessments on the future, form, content, and meaning of Italian American culturalism. Its reception component includes (a) above all the Italian American community, (b) groups sympathizing with that community, such as teachers of Italian, and (c) to a minor degree, other ethnic projects sharing similar cultural politics. In addition, the structuration includes the continuous existence and, above all, the high prestige of a hegemonic culture and of dominant traditions, in this case U.S. American educational and cultural traditions controlled by a white elite, against which the Italian American culturalist project initially pursued its path, and without which it would undergo considerable transformations. The Italian American culturalist movement thus depends not only on active and passive agents (producers and consumers), on will and need, that is, but also on a certain context within which to articulate both will and need. Its ethnic activism is carried through by three types of interrelated agents: (1) the artists and writers, (2) the critics, and (3) the intellectual leaders, cultural workers, or philosophers. Often, their actions overlap. Gardaphé and Anthony Tamburri, writers, critics, intellectual leaders, and cultural workers in their own right, have been able to trace, for instance, a distinct phenomenology in the context of Italian American literature, which, similar to other ethnic literatures, moves from an expressive (or local) to a comparative (or contrastive) and ultimately to a synthetic stage in its relation to U.S. American dominant culture.[13] And conversely,

Robert Viscusi has recently reflected on the mission of the Italian American cultural project in a broader cultural framework. In his "Breaking the Silence: Strategic Imperatives for Italian American Culture," he discusses the ways in which Italian American historiography has worked and should continue to work to build a canon of the extraordinary Italian American contributions to U.S. American social, political, and cultural history.[14] One of the Italian American journals, *Italian Americana*, in part, fulfills Viscusi's suggestions. The journal *VIA (Voices in Italian Americana)* on the other hand, consciously practices the construction of an Italian American canon in the area of literary culture.[15] While one might argue that Viscusi primarily seeks to restore the past, or to enable a past to gain adequate historical representation, *VIA* tends to construct a present more adequate to the symbolic needs and desires, the poetic reality, we might say, of the Italian American community. What they, Viscusi and *VIA*, have in common is a categorical imperative in double reverse. To practice Italian American ethnicity not as an end in itself, but as a means to two ends: to legitimate Italian American ethnicity in the context of U.S. American culture, and to legitimate the desire of U.S. citizens to practice cultural plurality in its specificity. These are complex processes of legitimation of experiences specific not only to members of the Italian American community, but to other ethnic communities as well, attesting to desires for cultural survival and cultural self-determination amid, as they fuel it, a climate of culture wars waged in the name of diversity and antidiversity.[16]

For those familiar with Gramsci's texts, this insistence on cultural legitimation, as insisted on in the work of Gardaphé, Tamburri, Viscusi, and others, evokes an entire series of Gramscian reflections. The desire to be heard, to have a voice, to speak the places where one's body has been is a phenomenon that Gramsci touches on in his "notes on linguistics," his last notebook from prison, notebook 29. He also addresses cultural legitimation in his notes on philosophy, or rather "what constitutes a philosopher," and on folklore. It is apposite at this point of my discussion to add to the concept of nonmonolinearity, briefly explicated above, two more Gramscian conceptual tools: "structure of feeling" and "universal expressivity." In his notes on linguistics, Gramsci refers to the "linguistic" places where we are or have been, the linguistic experiences we have or have had with respect to dominant languages as well as to less dominant languages or dialects. These experiences leave a mark on our body, an entire register of feelings that latently structure our economies and that can be, but do not have to be, activated under specific circumstances.[17] Inspired by Raymond Williams's work on the workings of hegemony in predominant and residual cultural practices, I have called Gramsci's understanding of the existence of a multiple linguistic subject-hood due to experiences in multiple places relative to positions of power and subordination a "structure of feeling."[18] Precisely because Italian Americans have been in places in which non-Italian Americans have not been—through exposure to Italian dialects and languages, exposure to Italian cultural heritage and history, to traditions and cultures of everyday life originating in places far away from the United States; the history of Italian American social and cultural marginalization and discrimination in the U.S.—their "structures of feeling" by necessity consist of structures that are not shared with non-Italian Americans or other communities.[19] Moreover, the desire of Italian Americans for the right to speak some of these structures, and to explain these to others, and to express creativity in ways that are grounded in the body and to increasingly practice such rights in the wake of a vast multicultural movement in the United States is also evocative of Gramsci's concept of "universal expressivity." In his notes on the formation of intellectuals and on the study of philosophy, Gramsci speaks of cultural practices that are authentic precisely because they are not imposed from above but rise from below. These cultural practices occur and have always occurred historically, sometimes in the form of religion and folklore, because it is part of human nature to be creative, to think, and to judge.[20] Indeed, for Gramsci nonmodern expressivity, what we might call—against the background of modern cultural theory from Lukacs and Marcuse to Debord—nonalienated expressivity, still resides in folklore, in, however, a distorted fashion. Folklore contains a heritage of nonalienated expressivity.[21] So expressivity is for Gramsci ontologically grounded, and ethically as well. It is ontologically grounded in that authentic creativity responds to an inherent human need to engage in creative acts. What is fascinating here is that Gramsci relates this need to a human drive for freedom, an eternal principle of hope of sorts. He shares this ontological-liberational understanding of "universal expressivity" with another great philosopher of the twentieth century: Ernst Bloch.[22]

The two Gramscian concepts—structure of feeling and universal expressivity—loosely serve as metaphors for the many substantive affinities Italian American cultural practices reveal with respect to urgent issues in contemporary life and are, therefore, most relevant for a critical political and social theory. Let me point to some of the more striking affinities. Italian American cultural practices can be viewed, for instance, as acts of resistance to cultural domination of U.S. American mainstream culture, a resistance to the repression of one's "universal expressivity" as embedded in ethnicity. The need to

artistically, or otherwise, express oneself can involve expressing oneself not only in a single language, but in many forms of languages,
as Gloria Anzaldua in her "How to Tame a Wild Tongue," suggested,
since some ethnic experiences include many different linguistic systems layered by various communicative orders.[23] Anzaldua's call for
deliverance from "linguistic terrorism" echoes in Italian American
vindications of the right to speak one's languages. For this reason,
these practices are part of a liberational project, participants in the
struggle for cultural rights. Moreover, as "folklorist" work in the
Gramscian sense, the study of Italian Americana, of oral history, of
cultural practices of everyday life and the construction of a canon
thereof or what Viscusi in his above mentioned article called a "narrative," serves to preserve a history, a tradition, and forms of knowledge
that the "Americanization" of "Italianicity," however understood,
might efface. This actual recourse to tradition, as exhibited in some
ethnic practices, has also been the major subject of emerging mainstream philosophical, historical, and juridical discourses on what constitutes "authentic existence" in a "good society," on what constitutes
the "good life." In this context David Gross's *The Past in Ruins* (1992)
invites readers to reconsider the value of traditions for countering
meaninglessness and nihilism in contemporary postmodern life, while
Charles Taylor's *Multiculturalism and the "Politics of Recognition"*
(1992) makes an argument for including multiculturally traditioned
backgrounds in definitions of political and juridical subject-hood, and
therefore, in the definition of the extent and application of citizenship
rights.[24] Indeed, various scholars are already working on communicative models designed to dialogically accommodate already existing
heterogeneously traditioned communities, including ethnic and religious communities, for the purpose of producing consent to common
goals or objectives.[25] The exercise of cultural rights, as Apitzsch indicated in her essay "Antonio Gramsci und die Diskussion um Multikulturalismus," was also very much an issue of interest to Gramsci,
who looked at "cultures" in terms of their functions in the building
of a new civility, a new society, in which the particular and the universal would no longer clash.[26] As a final note concerning philosophical
contiguities of the Italian American cultural project, I would like to
add here that the right to cultural self-determination is surely a point
of contention in the responses to the division of the world in an
overdeveloped north and an underdeveloped south, recently sanctioned by the controversial NAFTA agreement and the GATT agreement under negotiation.[27] Mary Mellor and Maria Mies are among
those contemporary critical thinkers who pointedly connect the marginalization of indigenous cultures and ethnic heterogeneities in

underdeveloped global regions with the unwise application of western technological modes in the service of profitable proceeds for multinational companies of so-called postindustrial societies. In these scenarios, the right to cultural self-determination is part of the logic of resistance movements to ecological destruction and the demise of existing civilities occasioned by modernization and technologization drives of overdeveloped regions.[28]

No doubt, the vindication of cultural self-determination rights keeps the Italian American cultural project, as most ethnic projects, for the most part, in respectable company. This potentially humanitarian contiguity holds only, however, to the extent to which we choose to stay on philosophical grounds staked by libertarian principles. And even those grounds are not in themselves innocent. For they would have to grant rights to cultural self-determination even to those ethnically informed cultural projects whose self-understanding of ethnicity rests on claims to racial superiority. It is probably not insignificant in this context to remember that ethnic essentialism has historically harbored, and continues to harbor, pernicious layers of racial superiority claims and that the ideologues of Nazi Germany insisted very much on the ethnicity of their project, political and cultural alike, so much that cultural self-determination rights found their way into a *Blut und Boden* constitution. Yet it is not only by testing philosophical grounds that multicultural projects can run up against their liberatory and emancipatory limits. The cultural politics of identity, difference, and diversity feeding into the American discourse on multiculturalism will remain in the fangs of neoliberal Realpolitik and its unevenly divided global consequences, all liberational rhetoric to the contrary, to the extent to which it avoids addressing in any substantive manner the many functions, structures, and relations of multiculturalism in local, national, and global contexts. In light of recent global dynamics, such as massive increases in transnational migrations that have led to new politically and socially laden developments in race relations as the United States and other overdeveloped nations undemocratically relegate, as part of their New World Order, the larger economic burden to the underdeveloped world, any cultural project that has signed up for liberatory credentials in the ethnicity business needs to examine the democraticity of its designs. I see little reason to exempt Italian American culturalism from this exam. It is clearly an undertaking that would have to be carried out by a team of critical thinkers, and I am the least prepared, and perhaps also the least entitled, to engage in it. What I can suggest, nonetheless, are some questions to enter into the discussion by referring to two Gramscian analytical elements, one methodological and one conceptual, useful, from my point of view, for beginning to assess, quite in a Gramscian spirit, the function of "particular cultures" in the formation or structuration of a "new civility." From a Gramscian methodological point of view, such an examination would include an assessment of how much "particular cultures" are culturally particular or what other particulars—economic, social, political— that cultural particularity entails. And conversely, it would include an assessment, however, minimal, of the structures and relations in which the "new civility" is embedded. To further explicate the minimal contours, however reductive, of such questions, I find it most useful to briefly return to Gramsci's concept of a "structure of feeling."

## III. The Political Economy of Ethnicity Relations

The Italian American community in the modern United States, as producers and consumers of Italian American culturalism, does not exclusively speak the language of Italian American shared traditions and immigrant memory. Its "structure of feeling" is not and cannot be exclusively Italian American. Tamburri approaches this issue when he speaks of "several components of one's identity."[29] Yet while he emphasizes, against the background of Michael M. J. Fischer's work on ethnicity and memory, the significant fact that ethnicity "is something reinvented and reinterpreted in each generation," I would like to add to his well-founded view that the components of ethnic identity are part of or exist parallel to substantive components of nonethnic origin as well, such as class and political preference. After all, Italian Americans are United States citizens with citizenship and property rights, which they exercise. As such they are political subjects, take part in political and social institutions, and function not outside but within the systemic web of national and international economic structures. Italian Americans are producers of goods and ideas, disseminators, and consumers. As Gramsci would see it, their bodies are marked by all the places they have been and continue to be, while their unconscious and consciousness bespeak these experiences. The places where one's body moves do not lie outside geographies and temporalities, as Gramsci noted, but relate to distinct sites of power, domination, and subordination. For this reason I support the claim that the "question of cultural relations cannot be tackled without reflections on the question of hegemonic structures," as Apitzsch has put it.[30] Given the complexity of the "structure of feeling," namely, the net of social, civil, political, economic, institutional, organizational, and ideological relations within which citizens of a modern nation form their experiences, their "conception of the world," and accordingly engage in or disengage from specific actions, the notion of a powerful, single, and homogeneous center and a disempowered heterogeneous margin from which one reclaims positions of power does not squarely hold. This includes the parameters for claims for cultural power. A discourse on multiculturalism, I would like to propose, does not escape this predicament, since it neither has a monopoly on the location of hegemony, nor does it have the power to erect its structures or control its motions. Viscusi alludes to this bind in ethnicity politics when he notes that some Italian Americans surely enact the language of corrupt power and domination, and that some are conservative, right wing, and explicitly racist.[31] The politics of ethnicity relations are necessarily faced with the problem concerning how much culturally motivated liberational drives of any specific ethnic group can expand within the limits of a group that defines itself primarily in ethnic terms while ignoring the registers of its economic and political affiliations. In other words, it raises the issue concerning the specificity of hegemonic structures—economic, political, social—within which ethnic groups, who define themselves as culturally deprived, move both on a national and international level. It should be pointed out here in passing that in comparison with other immigrant groups in the United States, such as Scandinavian Americans and French Americans, Italian Americans have achieved a much higher level of economic success. Italian American households hold 107 percent of the U.S. average income, while Scandinavian Americans hold only 93 percent of the average income.[32] So the question of the relation of a "particular culture," "folklore," or the "culture of a subordinate group" as Gramsci would put it, to the "culture of the dominant class," while it can be handled, and legitimately so, as a vindication of cultural rights, it must from my point of view also be amenable to accommodate reflections on the possible elective affinities between "particular culture" and "predominant political culture," which in the case under consideration entails a political culture bent upon ideologically legitimating unequal distributions of economic rights both nationally and globally. Identity politics, the alpha and omega of the multicultural discourse, hardly escapes the dialectic of the political economy of cultural rights.[33]

The dialects that tie Italian American culturalism to its environment do not extend only to main stream politics and economics, however. Equally existent, if sometimes equally invisible or camouflaged, are relations that multiculturalism and their identity politics obtain with the culture industry. Cornel West highlights the problems connected to this relation when he writes: "How do we preserve critical sensibility in a market culture? In our churches, in our synagogues, in our mosques, they are often simply marketing identity. It must be a rather thin identity, this market. It won't last long. Fashion, fad. Someone benefiting, usually the elites who do the marketing and benefiting. How deep does one's identity cut? Most important, what is the moral content of identity? These are the kinds of questions that one must ask in talking about multiculturalism and eurocentrism."[34] Mid- to late-twentieth-century seminal mainstream theorists of the culture industry—from Adorno and Marcuse to Debord and Baudrillard—have held up little hope concerning the resistance capacities of cultural productions with respect to the commodification laws of a hegemonic market.[35] Conversely, alternative theorists have set up warning posts regarding the commodification vulnerability of even the multicultural project. As Marcia Tucker notes: "The vital, independent cultures of socially subordinated groups are constantly mined for new ideas with which to energize the jaded and restless mainstream of a political and economic system based on the circulation of commodities."[36] In other words, the vindication of multicultural rights with its concomitant identity politics runs the paradoxical gamut of being subsumed by an all-powerful culture industry as it contributes to that culture's hegemony. Are we then to presume that the Italian American cultural project is doomed to offer few redeeming features beyond its immediate redemptive value for the Italian American community? Does this project merely serve as an opium for the people or as a Band-Aid for a community now bent on attending to the *ressentiments* generated by white, elite, anglo-cultural imprints on two or more generations of immigrant lives?

The answers to these questions, I would contend, lie very much with the future directives the Italian American intelligentsia offer not only to their own community but also to intellectual communities at large. Italian American intellectuals, like other intellectual groups rooted in an ethnic community, apparently enjoy the advantage of defying the fate of unrootedness ascribed to modern intellectuals by an entire array of great sociologists from Weber and Simmel to Mannheim and Neumann.[37] Yet this advantage can easily evaporate if Italian American intellectuals shy away from rigorously addressing the centrally enabling element of their rootedness: their memory of migration experience. By rigorously addressing I mean, in a Gramscian sense, viewing migration not simply as Italian emigration to the United States, or everyday immigrant life in this country. Rather, a rigorous address views migration in as many relations as possible, including those that highlight the contrasts between the objectively different immigrant and ethnic histories in the discourse on multicul-

turalism. Unlike African Americans, Italian Americans did not arrive
in the United States as slaves but as immigrants, and they were not
systematically denied access to education, civil society, politics, and
economic prosperity as African Americans were. It behooves Italian
American intellectuals to weigh these fundamental differences and
to refuse to participate in their obfuscation in the name of facile
multiculturalisms. Moreover, as Italy, as many other overdeveloped
nations in Europe and elsewhere, under the impact of massive migration movements from south and east, turns from a country of emigrants into an immigrant society, Italian Americans have an
opportunity to rethink the social roots of their emigration, and to offer
to contemporary critical social and political theory their expertise and
knowledge concerning the predicaments of migration. This expertise
is surely also called for closer at home, in the context of the United
States, as vulnerable and unsturdy infrastructures, bent under pressures of increasing migration, solicit right-wing, xenophobic, political
solutions. Above all, Italian American intellectuals are in the position
to address what Gramsci so aptly recalls in his notes on migration: the
drama every emigrant lives before leaving his or her place.[38] Gramsci
mentions in this context that Italian intellectual elites remained re-
markably silent on the issue of emigration, although thousands of
Italians left and perhaps had to leave Italy for the United States and
countless other destinations. Critical thought today could only profit
from those intellectuals who are profoundly disinterested in repeating
the disinterest of elite intellectuals, and the civil societies they influence, in the face of the denial of a most basic democratic right to
millions of people worldwide: the right to stay in one's place of origin,
community, or choice.

Reflecting on the conditions necessary for the application of the
"rights to stay in one's location of choice" entails a rethinking of the
history of basic human rights. While Italian culture, similar to other
western nations, surely has no monopoly on a credentialled history
of democratic rights, it, nonetheless, has an unusual philosophical
trajectory to offer regarding their complexity. Italian American intellectuals could reassemble the elements of a democratic tradition that
countless political philosophers and activists have, over the past few
hundred years, indefatigably constructed in their struggle for authentic human freedom. Giambattista Vico, for instance, as Gramsci recalls in his *Quaderni del carcere*, refers to Solon's dictum "Nosce te
ipsum" in the *Scienza Nuova*.[39] I might add here that while Vico
refers to this dictum throughout the *Scienza Nuova* of 1744, it is more
to the point to look at his earlier 1725 edition, which is a politically
more radical version. Chapters 56–58 of this work discuss not only

the first principle of Vico's science, or his discovery, but also the application of that principle, and his science, in a political context.

Let me paraphrase Vico. Solon, he writes, advised the Athenians to reflect on the nature of their mind, which enables them to see that all humans are endowed with reason, which, in fact, is the true content of human nature; as a result, individuals are equal to one another in civil matters as well, a principle informing the political form of the republic, and above all popular republics (in modern lingo: parliamentary republics)."[40] When Gramsci comments on this passage, as Apitzsch rightly notices, he understands Vico as suggesting that Solon encouraged the plebeians to recognize the principle of equality underlying all human nature, such that it was their right to exercise civil rights equal to the ones enjoyed by the aristocracy.[41] Yet what Vico also suggests is that given that humankind created all there is, they can also create what there is not as of yet. A republic of equal rights for all determines, writes Vico, a state of perfection of a government, and it is to that end that Vico composed the *Scienza Nuova*.[42]

The equal rights Vico evokes were, at the beginning of the eighteenth century—when Naples and all of Italy for that matter was subject to feudal systems of governance and laws while England had already established a parliamentary monarchy—equal citizenship rights. They were primarily political and juridical. They were those fostered by the French revolution and pursued as major items on the agenda of the democratic wing of the Italian independence movement in the nineteenth century. When after Italy's almost completed unification in 1861, Italians assumed the status of free citizens of a modern sovereign state, in the form of a parliamentary monarchy, the citizenship rights Vico evoked in his utopia over a hundred years earlier were only in parts redeemed by the new constitution of the new Italian state. Women, illiterate social groups, and nonproperty owning groups were excluded from the political right to vote, and juridical equality with respect to women was also seriously impaired by that new constitution.[43] It was then that Anna Maria Mozzoni, one of the most brilliant nineteenth-century emancipationists, embarked on a long career as democratic activist. What is most insightful about her work is that she focused not only on a struggle for *political* and *juridical* equality, but also always framed that struggle as a struggle for *social* equality.[44] She was far ahead of her time when she understood in the early 1860s that access to political and juridical rights, citizenship rights, that is, was no carte blanche to equal social rights.[45] She was also far ahead of her time when she discussed in many of her essays, the need of alliances when fighting privilege, the necessity to ground her politics in a democratic philosophy of inalienable social rights.[46]

Minority movements in the context of nation-states in which minorities struggle for social rights while enjoying equal citizenship rights or multiple citizenship rights pay tribute, however indirectly, to Mozzoni's astute analysis of the complexity of rights, which includes social rights and the lack thereof. And they pay tribute to the thought of Antonio Gramsci, who extended the reflection of equal rights from the political and juridical to the economic and the *cultural*.

I think that Italian American intellectuals, by having privileged access not only to this extraordinary democratic tradition, but also to migration memory, could contribute in pioneering ways to contemporary critical social and political theory bent on extending the register of democratic rights to include, as part of basic human rights and as an expression of authentic human freedom, the "right to stay in the location of one's choice" and the "right to refuse to be forced into economic and political emigration." This, of course, entails a straightforward political program that opposes the unequal access to and distribution of resources and goods in the economies of the new world order. Avoiding such global visions is not of much benefit to most of us. For the intellectual progeny of immigrants, avoiding such global visions can only mean, it seems to me, the advent of yet another immigration: that of inner exile. In that case, the Italian American intelligentsia will share the fate of many intellectuals, as rooted as they may be in "particular cultures," and live as strangers in the memory of their own land.[47]

## NOTES

1. Antonio Gramsci, "The Southern Question," in *The Modern Prince & Other Writings* (New York: International Publishers, 1957, ed. 1987), 34. Originally written in 1926, shortly before Gramsci's arrest.
2. Gramsci, "The Southern Question," 34.
3. Gramsci, "The Southern Question," 35.
4. Gramsci's view of social forces and relations is philosophically tied to an Italian tradition of materialism inspired by Spinozism. See Paul Piccone's excellent discussion of this tradition in his *Italian Marxism* (Berkeley and Los Angeles: California University Press, 1983).
5. See Gramsci, "The Southern Question," 42–51.
6. For a very clear discussion of Foucault's concept of power see Nancy Fraser, *Unruly Practices, Power, Discourse and Gender in Contemporary Social Theory* (Minneapolis: University of Minnesota Press, 1989), 17–34 entitled "Foucault on Modern Power: Empirical Insights and Normative Confusions."
7. On the conceptual relation of Foucault to Gramsci see the last chapter "In Lieu of a Conclusion: Gramsci, Feminism, Foucault," in Renate Holub, *Antonio Gramsci: Beyond Marxism and Postmodernism* (London: Routledge, 1992), 191–205.
8. I would like to thank Ursula Apitzsch (Frankfurt) for sharing many of her

insights on the multicultural in Germany and Western Europe. I am also greatly indebted to her "Antonio Gramsci und die Diskussion um Multikulturalismus," *Das Argument* 191 (1992): 53–62, which led me to the work of Etienne Balibar and Alain Finkielkraut on race relations in France. Of equal importance for me was a recent international conference "Nation, National Identity, Nationalism" at University of California-Berkeley, where scholars discussed the multicultural issues in an international context, in particular with respect to the war in former Yugoslavia and with respect to ethnic tensions in the former Soviet Union. For a recent critique of facile multiculturalisms here in the United States see Todd Gitlin, *The Twilight of Common Dreams. Why America is Wracked by Culture Wars* (New York: Henry Holt and Company, Metropolitan Books, 1995).

9. See Alain Finkielkraut, *The Undoing of Thought*, trans. Dennis O'Keeffe (London and Lexington: The Claridge Press, 1988). Org. French ed. *La défaite de la pensée*.

10. Personal communication, May 1993.

11. Gardaphé's *Italian Signs, American Streets. The Evolution of Italian American Narrative* (Durham, S.C.: Duke University Press, 1996) discusses the major literary productions. I would like to thank Fred Gardaphé here for providing me with a prepublication copy of his study.

12. See *Poesaggio*, ed. Peter Carravetta and Paolo Valesio (Treviso: Pagus, 1993).

13. See Anthony Julian Tamburri, *To Hyphenate or Not to Hyphenate. The Italian/ American Writer: An* Other *American* (Montreal: Guernica, 1991), and his "In (Re)cognition of the Italian/American Writer: Definitions and Categories" in *Differentia* 6 (1994): 9–32.

14. Robert Viscusi, "Breaking the Silence: Strategic Imperatives for Italian American Culture," in *VIA, Voices in Italian Americana* 1, no. 1 (spring 1990): 1–15.

15. *VIA, Voices in Italian Americana*, ed. Anthony J. Tamburri and Paolo A. Giordano, review editor Fred L. Gardaphé.

16. For a discussion of this culture war in the United States, see James Davison Hunter, *Culture Wars. The Struggle to Define America. Making Sense of the Battles over the Family, Art, Education, Law, and Politics* (New York: Basic Books, HarperCollins, 1991), in particular pp. 197–224.

17. See notebook no. 29 "Note per una introduzione allo studio della grammatica," in Antonio Gramsci, *Quaderni del carcere* 3, ed. Valentino Gerratana (Turin: Einaudi, 1977), 2341–51.

18. See Raymond Williams's discussion of the field of hegemony, including cultural hegemony, in his *Problems in Materialism and Culture* (London: Verso, 1988), 31–39. *Resources of Hope. Culture, Democracy, Socialism*, ed. Robin Gable, intro. Robin Blackburn (London: Verso, 1989), 74-76. See also discussion of this concept in Renate Holub, *Antonio Gramsci, Beyond Marxism and Postmodernism* (London and New York: Routledge, 1992), 155–64.

19. Tamburri has invoked the multiplicity of subjecthood in his *To Hyphenate or Not to Hyphenate. The Italian/American Writer: An* Other *American*, 20–21.

20. See Gramsci, "The Study of Philosophy and of Historical Materialism," in "The Southern Question," in *The Modern Prince & Other Writings*, 28–51, and pp. 58–75 of *The Modern Prince & Other Writings*; "The Formation of Intellectuals," "The Southern Question," in *The Modern Prince & Other Writings*, 118–25. These sections are also available in the standard English cultural selections from the prison notebooks, *Selections from Cultural Writings*, ed. David Forgacs and Geoffrey Nowell Smith, trans. William Boelhower (Cambridge, Mass.: Harvard University Press, 1985. For a critical discussion of Gramsci's theory of the intellectual, commonly but

incorrectly understood as a theory in which two groups, the organic intellectual and the traditional intellectuals are pitted against each other, see Renate Holub, "Gramsci's Theory of the Intellectual in the U.S. Today," in *Working Papers in Cultural Studies* No. 17, pp. 1–39 (Massachusetts Institute of Technology, Cultural Studies Project, 1991). For a more detailed discussion of Gramsci's complex notion of intellellectuals see Renate Holub *Antonio Gramsci*, 151–91.

21. I am indebted to Lucia Chiavola Birnbaum's research program based in large parts on Gramsci's view of folklore. See her *liberazione della donna. feminism in Italy* (Middletown, Conn.: Wesleyan University Press, 1986) and *black madonnas. feminism, religion, and politics in Italy* (Boston: Northeastern University Press, 1993).

22. See Renate Holub, "Gramsci's Theory of Consciousness: Between Alienation, Reification and Bloch's 'Principle of Hope,'" in *Antonio Gramsci*, 93–117. See also Georg Lukacs, *Die Seele und die Formen. Essays* (Neuwied and Berlin: Luchterhand, 1971. Orign ed. 1911), who relates this creativity need to the "transcendental homelessness" of modern individuals.

23. Gloria Anzaldua, "How to Tame a Wild Tongue," in Russell Ferguson, Martha Gever, Trinh T. Minhha and Cornel West, *Out There. Marginalization and Contemporary Cultures* (New York: The New Museum of Contemporary Art, and Cambridge: The MIT Press, 1990), 203–11.

24. See David Gross, *The Past in Ruins. Tradition and the Critique of Modernity* (Amherst: The University of Massachusetts Press, 1992) and *Telos* 94 (winter 1992–93) for a critical discussion of the wide-ranging implications of Gross's thesis on the need of traditions in modern or postmodern life. See also Charles Taylor, *Multiculturalism and the "Politics of Recognition"* (Princeton: Princeton University Press, 1992) and his *Ethics of Authenticity* (Cambridge: Harvard University Press, 1992).

25. I am referring to research currently being conducted by a diverse group of scholars (Robert Bellah, Lewis S. Mudge, Adam Seligman, Charles Taylor) on the notion of community and communicative action. See also my analysis of the concept of "differential pragmatics" in this context in *Antonio Gramsci*, 151–90 as well as Renate Holub, "Feminismus und Differenzpragmatik," unpublished lecture (University of Zurich, May 1993) and Renate Holub, "Differenzpragmatik," unpublished lecture (University of Basel, Switzerland, June 1993), and "Gramsci und Differenzpragmatik," unpublished lecture (Humboldt University Berlin, Germany, June, 1993).

26. Apitzsch, 60.

27. The GATT agreement under negotiation threatens culturally specific modes in the production, modification, and purchase of seeds in subsistence cultures, by legitimating attempts on the part of transnational corporations to monopolize seed—thus far a local common resource—in the form of assuming all property rights to seed and thus to the seed's biodiversity. See Vandana Shiva, "Biodiversity and Intellectual Property Rights," in *The Case Against Free Trade. GATT, NAFTA, and the Globalization of Corporate Power* (San Francisco and Berkeley: Earth Island Press, North Atlantic Books, 1993), 108–20.

28. See Maria Mies, *Patriarchy and Accumulation on a World Scale. Women in the International Division of Labour* (London: Zed Books, Ltd., 1986) and Mary Mellor, *Breaking the Boundaries. Towards a Feminist Green Socialism* (London: Virago Press, 1992).

29. Tamburri, "In Re-Cognition of the Italian/American Writer: Definitions and Categories," 12 and see his *To Hyphenate or Not to Hyphenate*, 21-22.

30. Apitzsch, "Antonio Gramsci," 59.

31. Viscusi touches on the racisms underlying the Bensonhurst incident in his

"Breaking the Silence." I am thinking of high-ranking Italian American judges with right-wing propensities.

32. See Christopher Jencks, *Rethinking Social Policy: Race, Poverty, and the Underclass* (New York: Harper Perennial, 1993), 38.

33. For a poignant critique of the tendentially apoliticality of many multicultural projects in a postmodern key, see Henry A. Giroux, *Schooling and the Struggle for Public Life: Critical Pedagogy in the Modern Age* (Minneapolis: Minnesota University Press, 1988).

34. Cornel West, *Prophetic Thought in Postmodern Times. Beyond Eurocentrism and Multiculturalism*, vol. 1 (Monroe, Maine: Common Courage Press, 1993), 19–20.

35. Max Horkheimer and Theodor W. Adorno, "The Culture Industry: Enlightenment as Mass Deception," in *Dialectic of Enlightenment*, trans. John Cumming (New York: Continuum, 1972, org. German ed. 1944), 120–68; Herbert Marcuse, *One-Dimensional Man: Studies in the Ideology of Advanced Industrial Society* (Boston: Beacon Press, 1964); Guy Debord, *Society of the Spectacle* (Detroit: Black & Red, 1983, Org. French ed. 1967); for Jean Baudrillard, see, for instance, his *The Mirror of Production*, trans. Mark Poster (St. Louis: Telos Press, 1975, org. French ed. 1973).

36. See Marcia Tucker, "Introduction: Invisible Centers" in *Out There. Marginalization and Contemporary Cultures*, ed. Russell Ferguson, Martha Gever, Trinh T. Minhha, Cornel West (New York: The New Museum of Contemporary Art, and Cambridge: The MIT Press, 1990), 7–14.

37. Max Weber, "Science as a Vocation," in *From Max Weber: Essays in Sociology*, H. H. Gerth and C. Wright Mills, ed. (New York: Oxford University Press, 1946), 129–59; Georg Simmel "Exkurs über den Fremden," in his *Soziologie. Untersuchungen über die Formen der Vergesellschaftung*, vol. 2 (Frankfurt: Suhrkamp, 1992), 764–71; org. ed. 1908; Karl Mannheim, "The Utopian Mentality," in his *Ideology and Utopia: An Introduction to the Sociology of Knowledge* (San Diego, New York, London: Harcourt Brace Jovanovich, 1936), 192–263; and, finally, Franz L. Neumann, "The Intelligentsia in Exile," in *Critical Sociology. Adorno, Habermas, Benjamin, Horkheimer, Marcuse, Neumann*, Paul Connerton, ed. (London: Penguin Books, 1976), 423–41.

38. See Gramsci, *Quaderni del carcere*, vol. 3, 2253–54.

39. I am also indebted to Apitzsch's essay for reminding me of the inordinately rich Gramsci/Vico connection in this context.

40. Giambattista Vico, *Opere Filosofiche*, ed. Paolo Cristofolini, intro. Nicola Badaloni (Florence: Sansoni Editore, 1971), 255.

41. Cited from Apitzsch, 56.

42. Vico, *Scienza Nuova*, 256.

43. Peasants did not gain their right to vote until 1911, and universal suffrage—all citizen's right to vote, including women—was not instituted until 1945. The juridical struggles of women continue to this day.

44. For an introduction to Anna Maria Mozzoni's work, see her *La liberazione della donna*, ed. Franca Pieroni Bortolotti (Milan: Mazzotta, 1975) and above all Franca Pieroni Bortolotti, *Alle origini del movimento femminile italiano (1848–1892)* (Turin: Einaudi, 1963). For an introduction into the specificity of the Italian emancipationist movement (Belgiojoso, Mozzoni, Kuliscioff, Aleramo), see part 1 "Second Wave Feminism, First Wave Feminism, and Beyond" (chapters 3–7) in Renate Holub, *The Feminist Paradigm in Italy* (forthcoming).

45. Her major essay is entitled "La donna e i suoi rapporti sociali," in Mozzoni, *La liberazione*, 33–91.

46. Mozzoni entertained philosophical relations with great democratic thinkers of

the eighteenth and nineteenth century, such as Beccaria, Filangieri, Fourier, and John Stuart Mill. Indeed, she translated the latter's *The Subjection of Women* into Italian. Vico also figures in her political program, when she opposes positivism—and the "natural" place some positivists assign to women in the order of things—on the grounds that it cannot reflect on the political and moral dimensions of its projects due to the presumed scientificity of its foundations. Vico's notion of philosophy or of his "new science" as keeping the natural sciences accountable with respect to their social function is used throughout her essays on women, positivists, and education.

47. As this article goes to press, I have had the opportunity to familiarize myself with the work of extraordinary social scientists dealing with Italian migration from a critical point of view. While their positions on migration cannot be integrated into this article at this late point, I would very much like to refer the reader to their names: Donna Gabaccia, Phylis Martinelli, and Paola Sensi-Isolani. The latter two presented excellent papers on Italian migration issues in the context of the conference *Italians, Americans, Italian Americans: Cultural Interfaces of Migrations*, which took place on September 7–9 at the University of California, Berkeley. The conference papers, edited by Renate Holub and Anthony Tamburri, the coorganizers of this conference, will be forthcoming in a volume. An International Conference with the title "For Us There Are No Frontiers: Global Approaches to the Study of Italian Migration and the Making of Multi-Ethnic Societies, 1800 to the Present" took place in Tampa, Florida, on April 3–5, 1996. It was organized by Donna Gabaccia and Fraser Ottanelli.

# WORKS CITED

Anzaldua, Gloria. "How to Tame a Wild Tongue." In *Out There. Marginalization and Contemporary Cultures*. Edited by Russell Ferguson, Martha Gever, Trinh T. Minh-ha, and Cornel West, pp. 203–11. New York: The New Museum of Contemporary Art and Cambridge: The MIT Press, 1990.

Apitzsch, Ursula. "Antonio Gramsci und die Diskussion um Multikulturalismus." *Das Argument* 191 (1992): 53–62.

Baudrillard, Jean. *The Mirror of Production*. Translated by Mark Poster. 1973. Reprint, St. Louis: Telos Press, 1975.

Birnbaum, Lucia Chiavola. *liberazione della donna. feminism in Italy*. Middletown, Conn.: Wesleyan University Press, 1986.

———. *black madonnas. feminism, religion, and politics in Italy*. Boston: Northeastern University Press, 1993.

Bortolotti, Franca Pieroni. *Alle origini del movimento femminile italiano (1848–1892)*. Turin: Einaudi, 1963.

Carravetta, Peter, and Paolo Valesio, ed. *Poesaggio*. Treviso: Pagus, 1993.

Debord, Guy. *Society of the Spectacle*. 1967. Reprint, Detroit: Black & Red, 1983.

Finkielkraut, Alain. *The Undoing of Thought*. Translated by Dennis O'Keeffe. London and Lexington: The Claridge Press, 1988.

Fischer, Michael M. J. "Ethnicity and the Post-Modern Arts of Memory," in *Writing Culture. The Poetics and Politics of Ethnography.*, James Clifford and George E. Marcus, ed. Berkeley, Los Angeles, London: California University Press, 1986.

Fraser, Nancy. *Unruly Practices. Power, Discourse and Gender in Contemporary Social Theory*. Minneapolis: Minnesota University Press, 1989.

Gardaphé, Fred L. "Whose Culture Is It." *VIA* 1, no. 1 (spring 1990): 149–55.

———. *Italian Signs, American Streets. The Evolution of Italian American Narrative.* Durham, S.C.: Duke University Press, 1996.

Giroux, Henry A. *Schooling and the Struggle for Public Life. Critical Pedagogy in the Modern Age.* Minneapolis: Minnesota University Press, 1988.

Gitlin, Todd. *The Twilight of Common Dreams. Why America is Wracked by Culture Wars.* New York: Henry Holt and Company, Metropolitan Books, 1995.

Gramsci, Antonio. "The Southern Question." In *The Modern Prince & Other Writings.* 1926. 10th reprint, New York: International Publishers, 1957.

———. *Selections from Cultural Writings.* Edited by David Forgacs and Geoffrey Nowell Smith. Translated by William Boelhower. Cambridge, Mass.: Harvard University Press, 1985.

———. *Quaderni del carcere.* Vol. III. Edited by Valentino Gerratana. Turin: Einaudi, 1977.

Gross, David. *The Past in Ruins. Tradition and the Critique of Modernity.* Amherst: Massachusetts University Press, 1992.

Holub, Renate. "Gramsci's Theory of the Intellectual in the U.S. Today." In *Working Papers in Cultural Studies* No. 17, pp. 1–39. Massachusetts Institute of Technology, Cultural Studies Project, 1991.

———. *Antonio Gramsci: Beyond Marxism and Postmodernism.* London and New York: Routledge, 1992.

Horkheimer, Max and Theodor W. Adorno. *Dialectic of Enlightenment.* Translated by John Cumming. 1944. Reprint, New York: Continuum, 1972.

Hunter, James Devison. *Culture Wars. The Struggle to Define America. Making Sense of the Battles over the Family, Art, Education, Law, and Politics.* New York: Basic Books, 1991.

Jencks, Christopher. *Rethinking Social Policy. Race, Poverty, and the Underclass.* New York: Harper Perennial, 1993.

Lukács, Georg. *Die Seele und die Formen. Essays.* 1911. Reprint, Neuwied and Berlin: Luchterhand, 1971. Original ed. 1911.

Mannheim, Karl. "The Utopian Mentality." In *Ideology and Utopia. An Introduction to the Sociology of Knowledge.* Pp. 192–263. San Diego, New York, London: Harcourt Brace Jovanovich, 1936.

Marcuse, Herbert. *One-Dimensional Man. Studies in the Ideology of Advanced Industrial Society.* Boston: Beacon Press, 1964.

Mellor, Mary. *Breaking the Boundaries. Towards a Feminist Green Socialism.* London: Virago Press, 1992.

Mies, Maria. *Patriarchy and Accumulation on a World Scale. Women in the International Division of Labour.* London: Zed Books, Ltd., 1986.

Mozzoni, Anna Maria. *La liberazione della donna.* Edited by Franca Pieroni Bortolotti. Milan: Mazzotta, 1975.

Neumann, Franz L. "The Intelligentsia in Exile." In *Critical Sociology. Adorno, Habermas, Benjamin, Horkheimer, Marcuse, Neumann.* Edited by Paul Connerton. Pp. 423–41. London: Penguin Books, 1976.

Piccone, Paul. *Italian Marxism.* Berkeley and Los Angeles: California University Press, 1983.

Shiva, Vandana. "Biodiversity and Intellectual Property Rights." In *The Case Against*

*Free Trade. GATT, NAFTA, and the Globalization of Corporate Power,* Pp. 108–20. San Francisco and Berkeley, Calif.: Earth Island Press, North Atlantic Books, 1993. Pp. 108–20.

Simmel, Georg. "Exkurs ueber den Fremden." In *Soziologie. Untersuchungen ueber die Formen der Vergesellschaftung.* Vol. 2. 1908. Reprint, Frankfurt: Suhrkamp, 1992.

Tamburri, Anthony Julian. *To Hyphenate or Not to Hyphenate. The Italian/American Writer: An* Other *American.* Montreal: Guernica, 1991.

———. "In (Re)cognition of the Italian/American Writer: Definitions and Categories." In *Differentia, review of italian thought* 6 (1994: 9–32).

Taylor, Charles. *Multiculturalism and the "Politics of Recognition."* Princeton: Princeton University Press, 1992.

———. *Ethics of Authenticity.* Cambridge: Harvard University Press, 1992.

Tucker, Marcia. "Introduction: Invisible Centers." In *Out There. Marginalization and Contemporary Cultures.* Edited by Russell Ferguson, Martha Gever, Trinh T. Minha, Cornel West. Pp. 7–14. New York: The New Museum of Contemporary Art and Cambridge: The MIT Press, 1990.

Vico, Giambattista. *Opere Filosofiche.* Edited by Paolo Cristofolini. Introduction by Nicola Badaloni. Florence: Sansoni Editore, 1971.

Viscusi, Robert. "Breaking the Silence: Strategic Imperatives for Italian American Culture." In *VIA* 1, no. 1 (spring 1990): 1–15.

Weber, Max. "Science as a Vocation." In *From Max Weber: Essays in Sociology.* Edited by H. H. Perth and C. Wright Mills. Pp. 129–59. New York and Oxford: Oxford University Press, 1946.

West, Cornel. *Prophetic Thought in Postmodern Times. Beyond Eurocentrism and Multiculturalism.* Vol. 1. Monroe, Maine: Common Courage Press, 1993.

Williams, Raymond. *Problems in Materialism and Culture.* London: Verso, 1988.

———. *Resources of Hope. Culture, Democracy, Socialism.* Edited by Robin Gable. Introduction by Robin Blackburn. London: Verso, 1989.

# 3

## *Divine Comedy* Blues

### ROBERT VISCUSI

The past does not exist, some people say, but Italians go on trying to resurrect it. Rebirth has been a major pastime in Italy since the thirteenth century. Ancient Rome has frequently returned to life at the urging of some politician or some poet. Nowadays, Italians specialize in restoring works of medieval and Renaissance art to a condition better than new. Nowhere has this Italian taste for bringing old things back to life shown itself more violent, and more hopeless, than in the hinterlands of the Italian diaspora.

Some prefer to call it a migration. As if the Italians knew where they were going when they left Italy forever. They didn't know. No one knew. Not even the people who *thought* they knew knew. No one *could* know where those people were going, because the place did not exist. All that existed for the Italians was a vast map of inhabitable space in the other hemispheres, much of it practically empty, thanks to search and destruction of indigenous peoples. The Italians went out into the world thinking they were going to make money and come back to Italy. Instead they were going to find themselves planted in these empty places, lunar wastes from which they would never return. Italy became the object of dreams, and diaspora grew upon the Italians like a chronic condition.[1]

Once they knew their expulsion was permanent, the Italians began, gradually, living as peoples do in diaspora. They invented a cult of Italy Outside Italy. Let us call it Orthodox Italian Americana. It was a simple cult, comprised of a handful of songs (*O sole mio, Torna a Sorrento, Funiculì funiculà*), one dance (the tarantella), a parade (Columbus Day), a feast (varied from place to place), *mamma, pappà famiglia*, a bill of fare (red wine, pizza, checkered tablecloth, spaghetti and meatballs—and upstairs, for the *cognoscenti*, handmade *gnocchi alla puttana*), and one poet (Dante Alighieri).

After a few generations, Diaspora Italians began to complain that this cult of Italy Outside Italy made all the demands but offered few of the consolations that one expects from a narrow orthodoxy. Writers as varied as Pietro di Donato, Richard Gambino, Helen Barolini, and Rose Romano have all protested the constrictions that Orthodox Italian Americana imposes upon its young.

Since 1969, when Mario Puzo published *The Godfather*,[2] Orthodox Italian Americana has known itself to be in crisis. Puzo had built a critique on something he learned from *The Brothers Karamazov*: "Fathers and teachers, I ponder 'What is hell?' I maintain that it is the suffering of being unable to love."[3] *The Godfather* follows the failure to love through all the levels of life in Italian America. Its publication coincided with the culmination of the ethnic politics of the 1960s, showing Italian Americans protective of "our thing" (*cosa nostra*). *The Godfather* painted Italian America as an underground cult, a people living inside a bunker of fear, hatred, greed, suspicion, and repressed lust. Incest and fratricide filled the boring and tortured Sunday afternoons. Betrayal and murder filled the restaurants by night.

"But we are not criminals!" the Italian Americans cried. Joe Colombo started the Italian American Civil Rights League to protest. At a demonstration in 1971 under the Statue of Columbus in Columbus Circle, someone shot Colombo. Whoever did that was saying to the Italian Americans, "Yes you are."

To this day, Italian Americans have not succeeded in freeing themselves from this picture. Why? Could it be that their own cult includes this picture? Italian Americans frequently cry prejudice, at the same time insisting "we *never* cry prejudice the way all these other groups do." Could this practice of complaint and denial be enclosing the Diaspora Italians yet deeper into the Puzo bunker with its walls of poured paranoia?

Italian American writers have long known what only Puzo has succeeded in demonstrating perfectly: that the orthodox religion of the Italian Diaspora is too constricting, too weak, too poor, too angry, too stiff, too buried under the leaden cloak of its own formidable respectability. Don Corleone, father or son, is remarkable for his puritan sexuality. In Puzo's erotic arithmetic, his adds up to murder. The inability to love is hell.

What Puzo has demonstrated, others have attempted to remedy. Italian American writers have been trying to do for the Italian Diaspora what Dante did for Italy. To give it access to its own cultural inheritance. To breathe life into a larger and richer past.

This implies breaking through the walls of a constrictive orthodoxy by using its own weapons against itself. For Dante, where he sits in the pantheon of Orthodox Italian Americana, remains enclosed in the family silence of what we revere because we do not dare to understand it. Italian American writers have been attempting to break this silence. It is not the only thing they have been doing, but it is the most immediately necessary. In this essay I follow some of the devices, ancient and modern, that Diaspora Italians have been using in the United States to break the law of *omertà*. They mean to tell the truth, and they mean to know what it might mean to call oneself *Italian* with the freedom of a full inheritor, an ease of access to all the riches of thought and reflection that the name might imply.

They know it is hopeless. *Blues*: the Diaspora Italian writes Divine Comedy Blues because, the more the full richness of the Italian inheritance reveals itself, the longer and harder seems the project of ever producing anything able to stand against it. The blues are universal.

There are those who sing the blues unconsciously, unwillingly. For example, some remain on their knees in a niche before the Madonna, even as they admit their incapacity to deal with l'America and all its challenges. Others march boldly in the parade, even as they sign themselves into the Affirmative Action Ward at Bellevue. Most writers, however, who sing Divine Comedy Blues do so on purpose.

Why? The historical record provides one sort of explanation. Dante is the poet of the migration, its prophet and its exemplary figure, its sign of all that is missing. Nothing is more written across the page of Italian American letters than the *Comedia*. Whatever its own intrinsic virtues may be, the *Comedia* achieved this preeminence by a historical logic of considerable beauty. First, Dante had imagined the New World long before its discovery, a fact perfectly evident to Amerigo Vespucci, who quoted the opening lines of *Purgatorio* to introduce the new astronomy he was discovering.[4] Second, Dante was the distant ancestor of the diaspora. He had imagined a single Italy five centuries in advance of the Risorgimento, which brought his fantasy to life as a nation that discovered itself much richer in population than in nonhuman resources. After its final success in 1870, the Risorgimento soon began exporting Italians all over the world with calendar pictures of Dante for their walls and a myth of Dante for their conversation. And they believed in it. Everyone did, from the liberal Italophiles who founded the Dante Society of America at Harvard in 1880, the very year that the mass immigration of Italians began in earnest, to these wandering Italians themselves, who founded one Circolo Dante Alighieri after another.

Another reason has more to do with Dante's own project. Dante presents his case as desperate. No Italy exists. No Italian power. No Italian language that all Italians understand. This case has a familiar ring to the writers of Italian America.[5]

Of all the virtues Dante exhibits, none stands out more plainly as an example to Italian America than does his stupendous honesty. Here speaks a poet willing to give up the land of his youth for his beliefs. Here judges righteous judgment a pilgrim who wanders through the world willing to live and die for his truth.

Italian America has need of such witness. Nothing can matter more in this gloomy cave than a poet who risks all to speak truth. The mafia with its law of silence only reflects on a large scale a cultural system in love with evasion and concealment. Louis Forgione, John Fante, Mari Tomasi, Gay Talese, Rose Romano: These writers have specialized in telling everything. Talese has gone so far as to claim that the Law of Silence has stifled most Italian American writers.[6]

It certainly has not helped. Silence imposes lies and half-truths. And what is even worse than lies, Silence imposes Caution, which strangles writing in its cradle. Caution imposes itself like a glum policeman in front of every door in the mind. Behind that door a chaos reigns. A pathless forest grows right to the sill of that door. Outside, pilgrimage begins, seeking meaning in chaos.

Dante left Caution behind. Puzo likewise entered a moral darkness from which no easy exit has yet revealed itself. Italian American writing has rarely accomplished such acts of absolute determination against the doors of Caution and the powers of Silence. But it dreams, it aims, it improvises blues for its epic, its voice of untrammeled truth telling, its pilgrimage of clarification, its remorseless comedy.

Blues Dante? Most readers know the poet by some other sobriquet. Vergil Statius Dante, Plato Augustine Dante, Bertran de Dante, Chartres Dante, Aquinas Dante (and his grandsire Dante Aristotle), Leopardi Manzoni Dante: All these characters have inspired formidable bibliographies. But their very proliferation implies unexpected roles yet to play. The Dandy Dante of the late-nineteenth century in England, for example, signifies a social order seeking its own lost coherence,[7] Dandy Dante replaces social order with a self-portrait, rendering the whole human universe as a mirror of his own carefully constructed shape, thus resolving in a single stroke the problem of coherence, reducing the cosmic to the cosmetic.

Blues Dante mates American poetic expression—blues—with Dante, which it treats as an encyclopedia of Italian history and culture.

## I'VE GOT YOU UNDER MY SKIN

Blues, for Italians in the United States, signifies the creole of languages and styles that they learned in the vaudeville of American

popular expression.[8] Italians learned to sing what the subject peoples
next door were singing. They became aware of their darkness, they
learned to think of themselves on the wrong side of the color line.
Frank Sinatra's versions of "That Old Black Magic" and "I've Got
You under My Skin" express in a thousand tiny ways the deep famil-
iarity that Italians learned to feel inside the skins of dagoes and guin-
eas and wops—that is, darkies with a language problem—skins they
began wearing the minute they stepped off Ellis Island.

Blues offers two great advantages to the Italian American poet.
First, blues systematically induces artistic liberation. Blues frees a
singer to improvise meanings in the spaces between words. Blues
builds an art out of that free play that we use when first learning, or
inventing, a language. It provides powerful forces of rhythm and
rhyme and repetition to drive the freedom of play. Second, blues
assumes desolation. Desolation, social death, slavery: Any one of
these terms describes the precondition for blues. This makes for a
hard-edged honesty that lies beyond the reach of counterfeit.

Among Italian American poets who write with a blues freedom, we
can name Ferlinghetti, Corso, di Prima, and Rose Romano, who has
written the resonant Silence Blues she calls "Mutt Bitch":

> It's not easy being an angry poet
> when you come from a culture
> whose most profound statement of anger
> is silence.
> No one knows
> what you're talking about.
> No one knows
> what your problem is.
> No one believes you.
> A poem needs a lot of explaining
> but refuses to do it itself.
> It expects the culture
> to back it up.
> If I have no culture
> I can say nothing;
> therefore, if I
> say nothing,
> I have no culture.[9]

This poem outlines its desolation with a blues logic comprised of
vicious circles that repeat themselves in infinite ways while the rhythm
keeps the thing alive: when performing, Romano bounces these lines
in a syncopated Brooklynese we rarely hear these days in Boro Park,

where she grew up, except if we are listening to tapes of Jimmy Durante, who may not be her model but is certainly her precursor. That is, with her perfect ear Romano recognizes this Brooklyn voice as pure Italian American spoken music, and she writes her poetry for that instrument.

The tune, however, she learns from another Italian American blues artist, Maria Mazziotti Gillan. Here is the opening of her blues "Growing Up Italian":

> When I was a little girl,
> I thought everyone was Italian,
> and that was good. We visited
> our aunts and uncles,
> and they visited us.
> The Italian language smooth
> and sweet in my mouth.
>
> In kindergarten, English words fell on me,
> thick and sharp as hail. I grew silent,
> the Italian word balanced on the edge
> of my tongue and the English word, lost
> during the first moment
> of every question.
>
> It did not take me long to learn
> that olive-skinned people were greasy
> and dirty. Poor children were even dirtier.
> To be olive-skinned and poor was to be dirtiest of all.[10]

The fall into knowledge comes, as it should in a song, with a change in the music, from the smooth and sweet "I thought everyone was Italian / and that was good" to the harsh and painful "English words fell on me / thick and sharp as hail. I grew silent." She falls into a blues knowledge: "To be olive-skinned and poor was to be dirtiest of all."

Blues knowledge gives blues authority. Blues knowledge can tell you how poor, how dark, how dirty. Blues admits to it all, and from its honesty comes its authority. Even the most skeptical epistemologists admit the truth of pain. Pain, grief, rage, and shame, honestly expressed, give blues authority. Romano and Mazziotti Gillan speak with blues authority. They have *Italian,* all its grimmest meanings thick upon it, under their skin.

## Lasciate Ogni Speranza Voi Ch'entrate

Blues Dante. So far we have only pieces and fragments to examine. *Divine Comedy* Blues exists as a project, not a building. I am sketching a literary enterprise still very much in process of formation.[11] This enterprise stands on testimony. The blues artist *witnesses* and *testifies*.

Dante's motto for the Gates of Hell, "leave every hope, ye that enter" [lasciate ogni speranza, voi ch'entrate], records the price the poet pays for opening the door of caution and breaking the law of silence. But it only suggests the richness of the poet's reward. Dante's pilgrimage through the howling underworld of hate earns him visions of Purgatory's mountain and of the love that moves the stars. This redemptive logic, set before you as a journey, becomes the loom on which Dante weaves a complex portrait of all the universes—physical, human, metaphysical, divine—seen at once, all of them together, at every step along his articulated path.

Dante's loom, of course, shows itself rich with suggestion and with accomplished vision. All these good things to the contrary notwithstanding, however, the *Comedia* has also the power of a negative sample. For the Diaspora Italian, the *Comedia* encircles all the secret motives of the Diaspora. It tells not only why one wished to stay. It also tells why one decided to leave. That is, Dante's poetry much more richly accommodates despair than his political theorizings can do.

Blues reads *Comedia*, as we now say, from a *position*. The Blues Italian—poet of the Italian Diaspora—measures the distance from Diaspora back to Italy without necessarily attempting to make the passage. Indeed, the Blues Italian may travel to Italy strictly to demonstrate the *error* of return. "Return?" the Blues Italian sings, "return *where*? Sorrento?" Hardly. Sorrento, once you start living in it, seems like a particularly cramped and curlicued version of life in the northeast Bronx, the only difference being that the food is still better in Italy, but the social services in New York are such as Marcus Aurelius dreamed of but no one has ever seen in Rome. Blues reads *Comedia* fully cognizant of the worst picture of how Dante's great imaginary Italy actually turned out.

A catastrophe from day one. Italy the pompous. Italy where is your next meal. Italy of policemen. Italy of dogs. Italy of horses. Italy of the cardinal's nephews. Italy of the count's boyfriends. Italy of the Pope's children. Italy of abbeys and convents and hospitals and title deeds as long as human written recollection. Italy of what conspires to stay in control no matter what revolutions be consummated in the newspapers. This Italy has always possessed inheritances in lands and money and culture and language—all the tools of substance and prestige it has needed to keep itself in place. Dante's Italy, once it was realized, added yet another weapon to the armory. A decisive weapon, from the position of the Blues Italian writing in Diaspora. This was the weapon that enabled the Italy of the rich to drive out so many who did not manage ever to come back.[12]

*Divine Comedy* Blues measures what they lost. Visit the small-town Circolo Dante Alighieri. It may not prove easy to remember who exactly the poet was, but one will see how it happened he found himself stranded outside the Earthly Paradise. Dante, like Columbus, long ago in diaspora became a totem. Not a historical actor nearly so much as a processional divinity, what we carry in the parade when reinventing some fable of what we are.

Who writes *Divine Comedy* Blues? One sort of *Divine Comedy* Blues consists of reading Dante as the poet of diaspora, hailing in his text the familiar exile's preoccupation with inheritance.[13] Another sort sees in diaspora the desolation of universal exile, regno doloroso.[14]

Another sort of *Divine Comedy* Blues picks up fragments of the larger fabric and reassembles them into a new confection. This *arte povera* has its most famous exemplar in the Watts towers. In writing, its best example is the prose poetry of Pietro di Donato, in such works as *Christ in Concrete* or *Three Circles of Light*,[15] whose very titles suggest the absolutely Gothic imagination that produced them, as if di Donato himself had been shot from a cannon straight out of the middle ages to spend his life wandering brokenly about in Brooklyn and Hoboken, where one might find him in the bus station tacking up a picture of his mother, or Mother Cabrini, or, late in life, the Mount of Venus.[16]

A third consists of laying down American jive on an Italian line. John Ciardi's translation renders the *Comedia* about as blue as English can get.

> They turned along the left bank in a line;
>     but before they started, all of them together
>     had stuck out their pointed tongues as a sign
>
>     to their Captain that they wished permission to pass
>     and he had made a trumpet of his ass.[17]

(Cf. Sinclair: "he made a trumpet of his rear" and Singleton "he had made a trumpet of his arse." Only Ciardi touches the blues vernacular).

One finds a more leisurely blues Dante in Lawrence Ferlinghetti's jazz poem "The Old Italians Dying,"[18] which makes the opening terzina of *Paradiso* the theme for forty lines of variations.

## BLUES COMEDIES

Diaspora Italians are writing Blues Comedies. Divine comedies are the most recognizable: they wear the label on the outside, as it were. But Italian comedies of all sorts survive into the expressive repertory of the diaspora. Sometimes this is in the eye of the beholder. Frank Lentricchia has been called Dirty Harry, hero of a Spaghetti western. That's one sort of Italian comedy. Another sort, *commedia dell'arte*, often used as a barker a loud buffoon called Strawman or Pagliaccio. Pagliaccio speaks crudely, offending everyone in the cast and the audience. Camille Paglia does a Blues Pagliaccio, who depends for her coherence on themes of peasant wisdom that, as she reminds the reader, she learned from strong Italian women in a matriarchy. Her buffoneria depends upon deep roots in the Italian comedy. Paglia has painted herself in blunt terms, has worn primary colors, and has offended pretty much everyone in sight, in order to gain a hearing. Street comedy.

Blues Dante, if it is worthy of Dante, will be impolite and will tell secrets too long kept close. Not only for the sheer hell of telling the angry truth in a society that teaches anger to be silent, but, and more richly, to loose the tongue of the Diaspora Italian.

Till recently, the loosing of tongues has remained a dream in the Italian Diaspora. Puzo adopted an elaborate allegory to tell a little bit of truth. This has earned him the unremitting hatred of Diaspora Italians unwilling to meet the challenge of ugly realities, unwilling to speak against the ancient injunction to silence. *State zitto*, my grandmother would always say. For years the only Italian sentence I could speak was this one that means *be quiet*. This single commandment encompassed political and poetic *educazione* for her, as for so many children of Southern Italy, that land for so many centuries part of the Spanish Empire, and of the French and German and Saracen and Roman Empires. Dominated peoples teach their children the *omertà*, which means *don't tell anyone anything*. Southern Italians also teach their children *bella figura* which means *when you must tell something, be sure it's a lie*. These injunctions to silence have muted the Diaspora Italians, reducing them to a narrow dialect of complaint and denial.

Only by the determined loosing of their tongues can this millennial
regime of lies be brought to a close.

## NOTES

1. An excellent parallel to this argument, outlining the structural production of
a diasporic condition, is Stephen Castles, "Italians in Australia: Building a Multicultural Society on the Pacific Rim," *Diaspora* 1, no. 1 (spring 1991): 45–66. Castles
emphatically conveys the massive scope of the movement of peoples: "Altogether 25
million Italians emigrated between 1876 and 1965—which is roughly equivalent to
the whole Italian population at the time of reunification in 1861!" (p. 50).
2. (New York: G. P. Putnam's Sons, 1969).
3. Puzo cites this in the epigraph to his first novel, *The Dark Arena*.
4. Amerigo Vespucci, "Lettera a Lorenzo di Pierfrancesco de' Medici, 28 luglio
1500," in Mario Pozzi, ed., *Il mondo nuovo di Amerigo Vespucci* (Milano: Serra e Riva
Editore, 1984), 59.
5. See Robert Viscusi, "*De vulgari eloquentia*: An Approach to the Language of
Italian American Fiction," *Yale Italian Studies* 1 (winter 1981): 21-38, for a prelimi-
nary topology of these parallels.
6. The present essay was delivered on 12 October 1992, at Yale University. I had
previously heard Talese speak of the law of silence during a meeting at the Istituto
italiano di cultura in New York City. The following spring, Talese published his
opinion on this matter, and several other matters as well, in his famous essay, "Where
are the Italian American Novelists?" The *New York Times Book Review*, Sunday, 14
March 1993. The essay produced rejoinders by Rita Ceresi, Albert Di Bartolomeo,
Thomas De Pietro, Richard Gambino, Dana Gioia, Daniela Gioseffi, and Eugene
Mirabelli in *Italian Americana* 12, no. 1 (fall/winter, 1993): 7-37, to which Robert
Viscusi replied in "Where to Find Italian American Literature," published with a
response by Dana Gioia in *Italian Americana* 12, no. 2 (summer 1994): 267-77.
7. Robert Viscusi, *Max Beerbohm, or the Dandy Dante: Rereading with Mirrors*
(Baltimore: Johns Hopkins University Press, 1986).
8. Houston A. Baker, *Blues, Ideology, and Afro-American History: A Vernacular
Theory* (Chicago: University of Chicago Press, 1984) theorizes the blues as the ground
of a critical position.
9. From Rose Romano, "Mutt Bitch," in *Vendetta* (San Francisco: *malafemmina*
Press, 1990).
10. From Maria Mazziotti Gillan, "Growing Up Italian," in *Taking Back My Name*
(San Francisco: *malafemmina* Press, 1991), 1.
11. This paper, written for a meeting of Italian and Italian American poets at the
Yale Whitney Humanities Center on 12 October 1992, reflected the preoccupations
of that moment and forms a part of a larger conversation. Many people took part,
and it turned out that there was a great deal to say. At day's end, some conferees
repaired to Naples Pizzeria, downstairs from the offices of the the Yale Italian Department (yes). We fell to reciting poetry. I recited a three-line poem I had written for
the quincentenary: "i found christopher columbus hiding in the ashtray. / what are
you doing there, if you please? / noone smokes, he said, leave me, alone." The Italian
poets at the table said they did not understand this poem. So the next day I wrote
the long poem *An Oration upon the Most Recent Death of Christopher Columbus* (West
Lafayette: Bordighera, Inc., 1993), partly to explain it to them, partly to demonstrate
how a "*Divine Comedy* Blues" might work.

12. I have attempted to address this complex heritage in *Astoria* (Toronto: Guernica Editions, 1995).

13. Giuseppa Mazzotta, *Dante, Poet of the Desert* (Princeton: Princeton University Press, 1979); Teodolinda Barolini, *Dante's Poets* (Princeton: Princeton University Press, 1984).

14. Paolo Valesio, *Il regno doloroso* (Milan: Spirali, 1978).

15. Pietro di Donato, *Christ in Concrete* (Indianapolis: Bobbs-Merrill, 1939); *Three Circles of Light* (New York: Julian Messner, 1970).

16. Fred Gardaphé edited an extremely valuable tribute to Di Donato in *Voices in Italian Americana* 2, no. 2 (fall 1991): 1–76, which gives Gardaphé's overview of Di Donato's achievement, as well as sample of his work in different periods.

17. John Ciardi, *Dante Alighieri, The Inferno: A Verse Rendering for the Modern Reader* (New York: New American Library, 1954), XXI, 136–41. I am indebted to my colleague the poet Vinnie-Marie D'Ambrosio for this insight into Ciardi's translation.

18. Lawrence Ferlinghetti, "The Old Italians Dying," in Anthony Julian Tambirri, Paolo A. Giordano, and Fred L. Gardaphé, ed., *From the Margin: Writings in Italian Americana* (West Lafayette, Ind.: Purdue University Press, 1991), 147–50.

# Part 2
## Reading Literature

# 4

# Emanuel Carnevali's "great good bye"

## MARIO DOMENICHELLI

> I'm here for. . . .
> what am I here for?
> Oh, to wail
> a great
> good bye![1]

Emanuel Carnevali, more than a poet, seems to be the embodiment of the late-Romantic myth of the poet in which life and poetry, as in the *bohème* or in the *scapigliatura*, take one and the same shape. Carnevali's life and poetry combine into reciprocal figures under the Rimbaudian sign of a sort of heroic fury searching into darkness, to wring out of darkness the secret it covers: its very paradoxical light. Carnevali's Rimbaudian juvenile fury is the fury of a hurried man, of a doomed youth urged by the sense of an impendent death, by the sense of an end. Carnevali's poet, like Rimbaud's, is the thief, the darkness-breaker of light haunted by the ghost of disease and corruption, by syphilis, like Baudelaire and Rimbaud; like Thomas Mann's fictional embodiment of the *maudit* Adrian Leverkuhn in *Doktor Faust;* like Nietzsche, or Dino Campana. Carnevali's life trajectory is exemplar, under this point of view, also in the cold fury that gives color to the certainty of loneliness, to his destiny of incomprehension and oblivion, to his scandalous presence, first, and then to his discreet removal from the American literary scene.[2] Carnevali wilfully outlines his poetry and life as figures *in limine*, on some threshold, perpetually dangling between different dimensions, places, times.

His inspiration, his dark muse combines clear symbolist roots with the brief and yet violent shake he gave the American poetic *milieu* at the very outstart of Modernism.[3] Carnevali lived his life very *in limine*, between a small town in Italy, where he came from, and New

York, where he spent the early years of his writing life. His language too was a threshold language. He chose American English, his second language, his language of exile,[4] as the true, strange, peculiar, irregular, abnormal, unfamiliar, and displaced mode of expression of his dark and atrocious sweet muse. American English was his *viaticum* into darkness, as he journeyed beyond the threshold, visited darkness, and knew her blackness and brightness, just as Baudelaire had: "Je reconnais ma belle visiteuse, / c'est elle noire et pourtant lumineuse."[5] An Italian immigrant, Carnevali wrote poetry with a clear French symbolist bent in American English[6]; an Italian immigrant in New York and a New York poet, part of the poetic city *koiné*, but, as it were, always from the margins. Carnevali always kept on the threshold, never really belonging to anywhere, a guest everywhere, a stranger, and a perpetual outsider. *(Non)* belonging (to anywhere) is the first condition, the *prima ratio* and persistent feature of his muse.

The "great good bye," therefore, and the lines of our epigraph, taken from Carnevali's *Marche funèbre* (section 2), identify the sense, the direction of his will, as well as his necessity of non-belonging, of not being included ever, and of his utter estrangement. It is the sense and direction of a *nostos*, a journey back home to a poetic *patria*, the poet's true homeland in the mind, the *civitas poetica* in imagination and the place of a perfect coincidence between words and emotions, words and things. That was the place in the mind, the place of authenticity, Carnevali kept indefinitely journeying back to. That is the reason why Carnevali's poems seem to be the announcement of a perpetual departure on a never achieved *nostos*, a never-ending journey in the mind to the imaginary homeland of some *Ursprache*, where he could hear and speak and write the impossible poem in some unheard perfect language.[7]

Carnevali arrived in New York in 1914, when he was seventeen (he was born in 1897). He lived the poor life of an immigrant, always looking for any job at hand to survive in a New York he describes in the pages of his autobiographical novel, *Il primo Dio*,[8] in the terms, more or less, of Crane's Bowery, or Céline's American section of *Le voyage au bout de la nuit*[9]—an urban landscape of endless misery, of starvation almost, continual search for food, squalid rooms. In the meantime, however, Carnevali, who had had a few years of high school education in Italy, in one of the best schools in Venice, learned English, and his poems began to be known among the New York poets, and also in Chicago, among the poets publishing their poems in *Poetry*, Harriet Monroe's famous magazine. The New York poets too had their magazine, *Others*, whose last issue was published in July 1919 and was officially dedicated to Carnevali. Carnevali had attacked

*Others* with a violence, rooted in his own utter, real, otherness. The point of Carnevali's attack was, very simply, authenticity. The attack hit home sharply. The "others" (William Carlos Williams, Maxwell Bodenheim, Alfred Kreymborg, Lola Ridge) considered Carnevali right, and dedicated the last issue of their magazine to him.[10]

Williams signed the thankful dedication. Carnevali, who boldly maintained that he was a pair of eyes forever open into a darkness that could not close them, had also acted as an eye opener for the *Others*. He made them understand that their otherness was false when compared with his own. They, the "others," were technicians, and, therefore, forgers, because only forgers need technique, which Carnevali defiantly rejected. They were refined, certainly, and they possessed the truth of refinement but not the whole truth, just splinters of it.[11] Williams agreed completely and thanked Carnevali for the righteousness of his attack: "for you," says Williams addressing Carnevali, "I'll begin a dance." Carnevali, according to Williams, is right in rejecting technique. It is true that he, Carnevali, writes bad poems, ugly poems; it is true since Carnevali is the one poet who deals with death, with truth, and refuses the cage of technique, and, unprotected by technique, directly faces death and ugliness. And his poetry is an act of desperate courage, and heroism.[12] In March 1919 Carnevali published an article in *Others* on Rimbaud. With the barbarous *enthousiasmos* mentioned by Ballerini in his postfaction to *Il primo Dio*, Carnevali, talking about Rimbaud, defined his whole philosophy of composition. Through Rimbaud, Carnevali found that the achievement of poetry is the achievement of life that consists in knowing the ego and possessing it. In Rimbaud, the perfect image is the perfect life. Rimbaud is the poet who achieved that beauty that enabled him to strike the world with his absolute judgment.[13] This term *absolute* is quite relevant and meaningful. It entirely defines and summarizes Carnevali's ideas on poetry and beauty. *Ab-solutus* means unbound, it means free, it means, very simply, not belonging to anyone, or anywhere, at any time.

Rimbaud, says Carnevali, is a prayer to things of beauty, perfectly lifeless things, things that bear witness to eternity. And the poet must pray to be sunk into the vision of youth, in order not to turn again to fornication and oblivion. And he must accept his vision, even at the cost of madness. The poet must accept the "atrocious death of the faithful and the lovers."[14]

Authenticity, sincerity, truth, are all. Pound, too, said that,[15] not very convincingly, however, in Carnevali's opinion. In his review of *Pavannes and Divisions*,[16] Carnevali accuses Pound of insincerity, and strongly attacks Pound's modernist idea of impersonality. Only a most personal emotion gives validity to a man's artistic theories. Pound's "personal emotion," this is the point, is only concealed, not subtracted, and the whole book is a series of masks (Pound's idea of the poetic *persona*), a series of *poses*, and an indecent manifestation of willful self-desertion, and a lie, in the end.

The problem, with Carnevali, must be that, in a sense, he seems to have lived burning the candle at both ends. Such a hurried man had no time for paraphrase, lies, masks, and inauthenticity. He was possessed with the ultimate truth of death, as Williams said,[17] and lived each of his days as if it were the last. His poetry bears witness to a sort of unconditional trust in words, words of truth, heroically coherent to their true meaning. Words must, therefore, be absolute; they must be free, they must be let free, and they are not to be trapped in the lie of technique, of poetic *personae* and fashions. Sincerity is the first, and almost unique poetic principle. Kept at a distance from life, poetry contradicts this principle and is, therefore, a lie, and consequently the negation of poetry, not the new poetry Carnevali was looking for, with his eyes forever open into darkness, possessed as he was by the absolute truth of death. Under this point of view, *Colored Lies* (January 1918)[18] is a sort of implicit manifesto. The poem is impressionistic and shifts its focus from external appearance to the interior, so to speak, of the red faces of the houses in a long row, hiding and yet revealing the old spinsters at the window respectably trying

> To smile
> A red lie
> For a while
> In a long row

The second section moves accordingly from the blue, black, and gray dresses of men to what is hidden beneath them, beneath the three-colored lie, a lie colored "with the colors of the sky."

The double, repeated movement defines the intrusion perpetrated by poetry: "the intrusion" that

> Would put confusion
> Into the chests of men
> Who crawl away
> Armored in lies of black and blue and gray.

As a matter of fact, poetry coincides with that uncovering, as we also read in a 1919 poem, *Chanson de Blackboulé*[19]:

> I have today again uncovered the sky and have found it
> ever so cool and ever so new, under,
> I wait for no answer, and no thing
> to ask, and no thing
> to say, besides what you know and I know
> and that which
> to the end of days
> will have one and an only
> meaning
> and no meaning
> and all meanings and
> the meaning.

The uncovering movement is radical indeed. The meaning being uncovered, the one, the only meaning, which is no meaning, and all meanings, which is the meaning, is death. The uncovering movement is also the movement of negation (no answer, no thing to ask, no thing to say) clearly outlined in the peculiarity of the splitting between the privative "no" and the quintessential "thing." Thus the world itself, all its voices and colors and shapes, is erased into the silent opaqueness of death, and negation, into, as it were, paradoxically enough, its perfect transparence, its perfect silence. Only through opaqueness and silence can the poet see, hear, write, there is no music since without pause, and there is no light, no color, no transparence without opaqueness and blackness. No poet worth the sheet of paper he writes on can call himself a poet unless he shares that secret and is willing to pay for that knowledge with his own life. There are poets of a different kind, certainly, but Carnevali describes them as grotesque shop girls combing their hair and painting their lips, powdering their faces dry:

> I imagine them
> before their mirrors
> trying to produce a poem
> (*Ad maiorem gloriam poesiae*, February 1920)[20]

Poets, indeed, deal with vanity in any case. Some poets, however, deal with the ordinary vanity of their mirror, with the mask they paint over their faces at the mirror. Some other, fewer poets, instead, deal with the vanity of life, with the "no thingness" of death. The difference between the former and the latter is a peculiarity of the sight, since there are eyes only good for the surface of the mirror, and there are other, different death-and-darkness adapted eyes. The difference of eyes also marks the difference between truth and forgery.

To Carnevali there seems to be no possible compromise. Poetry is truth, naked truth, to be stared at with undaunted eyes. *Procession of Beggars* (February 1919)[21] is exactly a statement of this truth-and-death obsessed, and possessed poetry. "Eyes" like "keen cries"; "Bright eyes [. . .] burning away / the little bit of my soul"; "dead eyes / in the dead faces / in the crowd" calling "insistently— / like abysses." The poet's eyes uncover death's quintessential truth everywhere. That is why poetry is a never ending, continually repeated good-bye, a great good-bye, like some uninterrupted prayer of the dead.

> I have learned to be
> all hushed
> with a faith,
> waiting
> when from everywhere
> Death was rushing
> hurriedly onward.

These lines come from *Utopia of the men who come back from the war* (July 1919).[22] The poem is not about the subject described by the title. It is a poem on poetry, again, as a great, serial good-bye announcing the departure for a no longer existing place, the never-ending return to an ever-vanishing home country beyond some undefined border between here and there, between now and forever. Section 2 bears the title of *No return*, which is exactly the point:

> No return
>
> For those who live
> with their old things
> in their old houses:
>
> To go to war
> is to go very far from this world,
> to go beyond it.
>
> The veterans
> never come back.
> And the dead also
> have gone beyond this old world
> forever.

The war, the battle, is turned into the poet's *psychomachia*, his war with the shadow. And there is no return since neither the veterans, nor the dead come back, ever, and yet they journey back forever, and their never-ending journey is poetry itself.

> Hesitating everywhere, hesitating fearfully
> The few poets, they who weigh with delicate hands,
> Walk in the unfrequented roads,
> Maundering,
> Crying and laughing
> Against the rest.

These lines written in September 1919 (*The Day of Summer: To Waldo Frank*, "Noon"[23]) articulate the whole metapoetic bent of the sequence structured on the *topos* of the "day of life." The last lines, of course, deal with death, and a possible, perhaps wished for, renunciation to poetry:

> What would you want, O death,
> Face-of-character,
> With a faceless man like me!
> Without you, Death,
> I am dead.
> [. . .]
> Now I will walk with the marionettes
> Now I'm dislocated enough and my mouth is clogged.
> I'll go talk to them
> Now I'm dumb enough.

"Without you death / I am dead," indeed, since poetry coincides with the sense of death, and, lacking death, there is yet another kind of death-in-life, the poet's walk with the marionettes, the dumb ones. In *Neuriade* (December 1921),[24] the poet's death wish, his flirting with Death brings him to the encounter with Death as a

> Little grey lady sitting by the roadside in the cold,
> My fire is to warm you, not to burn you up.
> Little grey lady in your little grey house in the warmth,
> Your warmth is to loosen my frozen arms and tongue,
> Not to drowse me.

There must be some unkind secret in Carnevali, some unknown pact with darkness. And it is as if he could prewrite his destiny; it is as if he came to know in his nightmares what his life was to become. His "Invocation to death," the last part of *Neuriade*, is a sort of prayer beginning with these lines:

Let me
Close my eyes tight,
Still my arms,
Let me
Be.

To die and to be are found with the same movement, a powerful movement of union, indeed, through which Being and Nonbeing coincide. It is a movement defined as "The yearning for peace," "just not to fear any longer / The landlady." And a kind of peace Carnevali found at last, going back to Italy, broken by syphilis and a connected lethargic encefalitis, with his "head no longer beating the stars," as he was to say in *The Return*[25] in May 1924. His book, *A Hurried Man*, an almost forgotten and yet very memorable book, was published in 1925 by Contact Editions.[26] Carnevali had already returned to Italy after a brief experience in Chicago, during which he was, for a time, a riotous and rebellious associate editor of Harriet Monroe's *Poetry*.[27] His time was quickly over. In 1922, in Chicago, he was badly struck by his disease, and was found almost naked kneeling in the snow, with his terrible intelligence completely annihilated.[28] He recovered but was never the same, he was forgotten, and cast away, sent back to Italy, where he spent the remnants of his life in hospitals. He continued to write beautiful poems, but all the enthusiasm was gone, and Carnevali's chords were not those of hopeless quiet, of stillness, and of contemplation.

Ballerini is probably right in considering Carnevali a lesser poet, perhaps not even a poet, properly speaking.[29] Yet it seems that it may be a bit reductive to consider Carnevali's experience of stars and abysses little more than naive poetry. Carnevali had "no thing" to say, "no thing" to ask, a meaning and no meaning and all meaning to look for, and he had no time for anything else. His mirror was not *a table de toilette* mirror. He saw *per speculum in aenigmate*,[30] he saw as through a glass darkly, trying to capture the magic of shadows and the essence of things in the space of that mirror.

We can read in Aristotle's *Politics* that the philosopher does not belong to the *polis*. The philosopher is *a-polis*, he is an *a-polites*. And yet it is thanks to his eccentric marginal position that the philosopher can see the truth the gods inspire him with. That is why, from the margins, *ab-solutus* as he is, the philosopher can speak the absolute Truth his ears only have heard as the very paradigm of the laws of the *polis*.[31] This reminds me of Stephen Dedalus's rules on pronouncing his final *non serviam* in Joyce's *A Portrait of the Artist as a Young Man*: cunning, silence, and exile, tracing the path to beauty and truth. Exile, or simply keeping out of place, not *polites*, but *a-polites*, is not only the philosopher's strategy, it is also the poet's, since the poet is in any case a border creature, a creature of the threshold, only surviving at the edge of things as a marginal creature. Whenever he goes beyond the threshold, he enters a dangerous orphic dimension. There is a warning at the threshold, the same enigmatically given in English, at the end of Campana's *Orphic Songs* (1914):

> They were all torn
> and cover'd with
> the boy's
> blood[32]

A boy's sacrifice to the poetic Furies is needed in the night of the soul to wring out of the night its secret, the magic ring, "le noveau" searched for by the symbolists; or, to put the question in Modernist terms, some boy's sacrifice is needed "to make it new." Rimbaud, Campana, Carnevali . . . names in the martyrology of poets, "voleurs de feu." Affected as we still are by the Modernist subtraction of the ego in poetry, we like the martyrs' poems, perhaps, but we don't seem to understand the price they paid for them. We don't seem to understand the strict connection between the price paid for poetry and poetry itself. Their lines were written in blood.

| | |
|---|---|
| *Mephostophiles* | Then, Faustus, stab thy arm corageously [. . .] |
| *Faustus* | Lo, Mephostophiles, for love of thee |
| | I cut mine arm, and with my proper blood |
| | Assure my soul to be great Lucifer's, |
| | Chief Lord and regent of perpetual night. |
| | View here the blood that trickles from mine arm, |
| | And let it be propitious for my wish. |

(Marlowe's *Doctor Faustus*, I, v)

## NOTES

1. E. Carnevali, *Il primo Dio*, ed. Maria Pia Carnevali (Milano: Adelphi, 1978), 178.
2. See *The Autobiography of William Carlos Williams* (New York: New Directions, 1967), 269.
3. See Luigi Ballerini, "Emanuel Carnevali tra autoesibizione e orfismo," in *Il primo Dio*, 420–24.
4. On poetry and the language of exile, Pound, and Carnevali, see ibid., 416–17; 428. See also my "Pound esule nel fascismo" in *Fascismo ed esilio II. La patria lontana: testimonianze dal vero e dall'immaginario*, ed. Maria Sechi (Pisa: Giardini, 1990). Carnevali continued to write in English also after his return to Italy in 1922.

5. *Les ténèbres* in *Les fleurs du mal*, ed. Jacques Crépet, Georges Blin, Claude Pichois (Paris: Corti, 1968), 85.

6. In his 1919 attack against *Others*, Carnevali mentions Italian writers such as Papini, Soffici, and Croce, of course, but the polar star in his poetic constellation is Rimbaud.

7. See Walter Benjamin, "Über Sprache überhaupt und über die Sprache des Menschen," in *Schriften* (Frankfurt: A.M., Suhrkamp, 1955), 401 ff. On *Ursprache* and Modernism see my "Implosion, Hyperreality and Language," in *Finnegans Wake in myriadmindedman, jottings on joyce*, ed. R. M. Bosinelli, P. Pugliatti, R. Zacchi (Bologna: Clueb, 1986), 277 ff.

8. *Il primo Dio*, Carnevali's autobiographical novel, has been reconstructed by David Stivender. Kay Boyle had used it with other materials (letters, poems, passages from *A Hurried Man*) to compile the *Autobiography of Emanuel Carnevali* (New York, Horizon, 1967).

9. Stephen Crane published *An Experiment in Misery* in *The New York Press* (22 April 1894). In 1893 he had already published *Maggie, A Girl of the Streets*. As for Céline's New York, see *Voyage au bout de la nuit* (Paris: Gallimard, 1952), 237 ff.

10. Carnevali's article on "Maxwell Bodenheim, Alfred Kreymborg, Lola Ridge, William Carlos Williams," was published in *A Hurried Man* (Paris: Contact Editions, 1925), 247–68. See also *Il primo Dio*, 353–69, and Ballerini postfaction, 421–24.

11. See *Il primo Dio*, 366 (technique), 369 (refinement).

12. Williams, however, notices a contradiction. Rimbaud, La Forgue, Corbière Carnevali's poetic constellation are not free from technique. On the contrary, their vision of perfection is reduced and completely limited, shaped by technique. Which is to say that no poetry is possible without technique, that poetry itself can only be forgery, and that there is no way out. This is also Williams's perspective later, for instance, in *Paterson*:

> Rigor of beauty is the quest.
> But how will you find beauty when
> It is locked in the mind past
> All remonstrance?

or in *The Fool's Song*, in which the whole question is summarized in the following terms:

> I tried to put a bird in a cage.
> O fool that I am!
> For the bird was Truth
> Sing merrily, Truth: I tried to put
> Truth in a cage!
> And when I had the bird in the cage,
> O fool that I am!
> Why, it broke my pretty cage.
> Sing merrily, Truth. I tried to put
> Truth in a cage!
> And when the bird was flown from the cage,
> O fool that I am!
> Why, I had nor bird nor cage,
> Sing merrily, Truth: I tried to put
> Truth in a cage!
> Heigh-Ho! Truth in a cage.

The very modernist problem here is that the difference between words and things keeps Truth out of the question. Words themselves are lies since they can only represent what they are not, the things words are not. Truth cannot be where it is being spoken, or written. Beauty itself always remains beyond words, it is unspeakable.

13. See *Others*, March 1919, 22.
14. Ibid., 24.
15. See my "Pound, esule nel fascismo," 142–46. See in particular Pound's definition in *Pavannes and Divisions* of what *The serious artist* should be. The article was published for the first time in *The Egoist* in 1913. Pound often repeated this idea of the strict link, almost an identification between sincerity and poetry, later attached it also from Confucius and the theory of the redefinition of all names.
16. *Poetry*, 15, no. 4 (January 1920): 211-21.
17. *Others*, July 1919, 3 (See Ballerini, 423).
18. *Il primo Dio*, 162-65.
19. Ibid, 214–17.
20. Ibid, 218.
21. Ibid, 176–81.
22. Ibid, 190–91.
23. Ibid, 194–213.
24. Ibid, 221–29.
25. Ibid, 232-39.
26. *A Hurried Man* (Paris: Contact Editions, 1925). Owing to censure problems, the book had practically no diffusion in the United States.
27. See *Il primo Dio*, part 4, 111 ff.
28. Sherwood Anderson in his *Memoirs* (University of North Carolina Press, 1969) gives his version of that terrible night (402–04). Carnevali gives a different version, saying that Anderson politely showed him the door (*Il primo Dio*, 128–31).
29. See Ballerini, 425–28. Carnevali's *Enthousiasmos* "finisce con l'esistere solo come quantificazione tautologica di se stesso affidata al ritmo dell'anafora e dell'esclamativo [. . .] saprà solo esibire, in una parola, la propria presenza. . . . il bandolo di una perenne inconseguenza, alta sugli strepitosi regesti del mistico, abissale nei sorrisi della demenza [. . .] Carnevali non fece che accentuare una sua sempre fortissima tendenza all'esuberante per seguire la quale egli finì col rinunciare all'auscultazione e alla transcrizione dentro il linguaggio e verso un linguaggio ulteriore. [. . .] delle sue pulsioni profonde." Ballerini is right in talking about orphism in Carnevali. It is strange, unless I am mistaken, that Ballerini never mentions Campana's orphism, considering the astonishing analogies between Campana and Carnevali, both in destiny and in approach to poetry.
30. *Corintii*, I:12–13.
31. See, on Aristotle's *Politics*, Mario Vegetti, *Il coltello e lo stilo* (Milano: Il saggiatore, 1979), 144.
32. Writes Campana to Emilio Cecchi in 1916: "If you were to occupy yourself with me again, either dead or alive as I might be, I pray you not to forget the last words, *they were all torn and covered with the boy's blood*, which are the only important words in the whole book." (See Dino Campana, *Opere*, ed. Sebastiano Vassalli, Milano: Editori Associati, 1989, viii.) The quotation comes from Whitman's *Song of Myself*, 34, "the murder in cold blood of four hundred and twelve young men," "the glory of the race of rangers." In the above-mentioned letter to Cecchi, Campana connects these lines to the book's subtitle of *I canti orfici*: "*Die Tragoedie des letzen Germanen in Italien.*" The German is taken—writes Campana—not in the naturalistic

sense, but as the representative of moral superiority like Dante, Leopardi, Segantini. As a further explication Campana adds: "I was ideally seeking a homeland, since I had none." The tragedy of the last German, therefore, becomes the tragedy of the last poet in Italy. And the ideal Fatherland sought for is what may be called *civitas poetica*. Of course, the quotation from Whitman may also be linked to the orphic myth and the sacrifice of the *pharmakos*.

# 5

# John Fante, "The Saga of Arturo Bandini"

## ERNESTO LIVORNI

*To Graziano and Riccardo*

In the book *The Italian-American Novel*,[1] Rose Basile Green ends the chapter "Counterrevulsion" with a consideration of the literary work of John Fante. By "Counterrevulsion" she intends that period "When they discovered both the inadequacy and the distortion in the themes that represented our national literature, [so that] American writers of Italian descent returned to Italian-American subjects for their fictional materials."[2] She opposes this concept to that of "Revulsion," which she describes as follows (p. 91):

> According to Webster's Dictionary, revulsion is a sudden, violent change of feeling. Such a change occurred in Italian-American themes when the writers reached the plateau of introspection. This turnabout, however, had its model in the national literature. In their effort to make homes for themselves in a new environment, the pioneers of America expanded their narrations to include discussions of their political, social, and religious problems. Like other pioneers, the Italian-Americans reached the inevitable point in assimilation when, in the attempt to achieve identity, they experienced a sudden revulsion from the crudities of their new environment. Unlike the national pattern, however, the design in the development of this revulsion in the Italian-American writers went through two distinct, subsidiary phases. During the first phase these writers of fiction abandoned Italian-American themes; during the second phase, the younger group had a counter-revulsion, a return to the old sources, reiterating the Italian-American themes from a more highly developed integration with the native culture.

John Fante's literary career is one of the most important instances of this dialectic between "revulsion" and "counterrevulsion," as his character Arturo Bandini must first rescue and deal with his Italian heritage, before being able to move on in the underground literary world in the new land in which he was born. Only now that many unpublished manuscripts have appeared in print after Fante's death in 1983 is it really possible to consider this curve of his literary career. Among his projects published posthumously[3] there appears *The Road to Los Angeles,* a further contribution to "The Saga of Arturo Bandini,"[4] which is fully developed in four novels: *Wait Until Spring, Bandini* (1938), *The Road to Los Angeles* (1985), *Ask the Dust* (1939), and *Dreams from Bunker Hill* (1982). In his last years, then, Fante was still working on his epic character Arturo Bandini, who begins and ends the author's literary parabola. Fante died before being able to revise *The Road to Los Angeles,* the novel that presumably was the most troublesome to him: it was, in fact, the first one on which he started working, yet it must have never appealed to the author as fully accomplished.[5]

It appears, then, that the character Arturo Bandini in Fante's writing is an obsessive presence throughout his career and for evident autobiographical reasons. This consideration is important to appreciate fully both Green's interpretation of the work of this writer and his own reflection on self-identity as an Italian-American writer. The change in perspective from *The Road to Los Angeles* to *Wait Until Spring, Bandini* is the result of Fante's broader consciousness of his literary enterprise: To be able to narrate the first attempts Arturo makes at his own literary career (the self-reflecting enterprise that seems at first to imply a moving away from his own cultural roots: Thus, *The Road to Los Angeles* embodies what Rose Basile Green calls "revulsion"), Fante realizes that he must surrender to the call of his cultural and ethnic tradition (the "counter-revulsion" of *Wait Until Spring, Bandini,* which finally prevails over the repressive attempts). The different approach to writing that Fante takes when he abandons the former novel and starts afresh with the latter finds its *trait d'union* in Fante's alter ego Arturo Bandini, already born in *The Road to Los Angeles.* Before offering a necessary overall interpretation of the saga with a focus on the protagonist, a consideration of the four novels that constitute "The Saga of Arturo Bandini" ought to trace first the rationale that led Fante to abandon *The Road to Los Angeles* in favor of *Wait Until Spring, Bandini.*

Arturo Gabriel Bandini makes his first appearance in the alleys of Los Angeles Harbor, where rather than searching for a steady job he is desperately trying to define his own identity in literary, philosophical, political, and ethnical terms. His name has an immediate literary echo, as he himself will admit:[6]

Arturo Gabriel Bandini.
A name to consider in the long roll of the immortal: A name for endless

ages. Arturo Gabriel Bandini. An even better-sounding name than Dante Gabriel Rossetti. And he was an Italian too. He belonged to my race.

This proud reference, however, combining both the literary and the ethnic background of the character,[7] will occur only at the end of the narration of Bandini's frustrating journey from a suffocating family routine to the physical anguish of labor survival: Even when struggling with the oppressive necessity of a job, Arturo is always sustained by an insatiable hunger for intellectual life. The experience recounted in *The Road to Los Angeles* takes its departure with at least two important considerations: the loss of the natural father and the acquisition of a literary father. "I had a lot of jobs in Los Angeles Harbor because our family was poor and my father was dead."[8] This is the initial sentence of the novel and it is also an important sign of the stylistic manner employed by Arturo Bandini to present his economic conditions: in that statement the relationship between cause and effect is subverted by the concluding clause. In other words, the search for a job is rationalized by the condition of poverty in which the Bandini family lives, but the connection between poverty and death escapes even the syntactic structure, organizing itself according to the simplest paratactic level. Furthermore, the manipulation of the syntax is Arturo Bandini's only chance to control his destiny: the condition of having "a lot of jobs" is indeed due to an economic system, but even such imponderable factors as the death of the father play a primary role in mastering Arturo's existence: the only chance left to him is the act of writing. Bandini uses his language to turn upside down the results of the chain of events in which he is caught: It is plausible to suppose that the presence of his father would have meant a more stable economic condition for the family, would have made unnecessary Arturo's frustrated and unhappy wandering from one job to the next, and would have allowed him to dedicate his time to study. By making himself the subject (not only in the syntactic sense of the word) of the situation and announcing obliquely his primary role— at least within his family—now that his father is dead, Arturo Bandini is already revealing the philosophical influence that has actually replaced the paternal figure: Friedrich Nietzsche. *Man and Superman* and *Thus Sprake Zarathustra* are, in fact, the two books that Arturo reads with great interest. Indeed, in one of his first attempts to write, Arturo Bandini is able to scribble only a few reveries from his readings, and aphorisms by the German philosopher emerge naturally:[9]

I wrote: Friends, Romans, and countrymen! All of Gaul is divided into three parts. Thou goest to woman? Do not forget thy whip. Time and

98 ERNESTO LIVORNI

tide wait for no man. Under the spreading chestnut tree the village smithy
stands. Then I stopped to sign it with a flourish. Arturo G. Bandini. I
couldn't think of anything else. With popping eyes they watched me. I
made up my mind that I must think of something else. But that was all.
My mind had quit functioning altogether. I could not think of another
item, not even a word, not even my own name.

The references to Nietzsche are numerous throughout the book,[10]
much more than Bandini's mentions of Spengler and Schopenhauer
(whom he often associates with the author of *Thus Sprake Zarathustra*). Nietzsche's aphorisms on women, especially, are so thorough
that they even conduct (as a sort of *leitmotif*) Arturo's erotic experiences and his debates with his sister on the existence of God and the
social function of religion:[11]

> I got up on the divan and yelled, "I reject the hypothesis of God! Down
> with the decadence of a fraudulent Christianity! Religion is the opium of
> the people! And that we are or ever hope to be we owe to the devil and
> his bootleg apples!"

These statements are repeated later to Uncle Frank, his mother's
brother, who proposes himself as a possible father figure for Arturo
and is evidently rejected on the philosophical level, although accepted
on that of economics. It is, in fact, Uncle Frank who is finally able
to assure him a steady job, and it is to that economic world that we
now turn. "Religion is the opium of the people!" screams Arturo to
his mother and sister first (in the passage quoted above), and then to
his own uncle. However, this apparently Marxist-Leninist consciousness at times conflicts with the Nietzschean fascination lived by the
character until he would be able to reach a balance between the two
poles: The ethnic issues arise during the humiliating labor experience
in the cannery where Arturo finds himself working beside Filipinos
and Mexicans.[12]

Before his conversation with his boss, Shorty Naylor, Arturo never
refers to his Italian name and background; actually, in one of his
daydreams he imagines himself carrying out a secret mission for
Franklin Delano Roosevelt. His new boss as well considers him an
American, unlike the other people working in the cannery
(pp. 56–57):

> "I don't like Americans in my crew," Shorty said. "They don't work
> hard like the other boys."
> "Ah," I said. "That's where you're wrong, sir. My patriotism is univer-
> sal. I swear allegiance to no flag."
>     . . .

"Remember: the work is hard, and don't expect no favors from me either. If it wasn't for your uncle I wouldn't hire you, but that's as far as it goes. I don't like you Americans. You're lazy. When you get tired you quit. You fool around too much."
"I agree with you perfectly, Mr. Naylor. I agree with you thoroughly. Laziness, if I may be permitted to make an aside, laziness is the outstanding characteristic of the American scene. Do you follow me?"

Nevertheless, Arturo's rhetoric fades in his first encounter with a Filipino worker, who is initially addressed by Bandini as "nigger," then as "a damn Filipino, which is worse," before suffering Arturo's final violent rage (p. 65):

"You feel better now?" he asked.
I said, "What do you care? You're a Filipino. You Filipinos don't get sick because you're used to this slop. I'm a writer, man! An American writer, man! Not a Filipino writer. I wasn't born in the Philippine Islands. I was born right here in the good old U.S.A. under the stars and stripes."
Shrugging, he couldn't make much sense out of what I said. "Me no writer," he smiled. "No no no. I born in Honolulu."
"That's just it!" I said. "That's the difference. I write books, man! What do you Orientals expect? I write books in the mother tongue, the English language. I'm no slimy Oriental."
For the third time he said, "You feel better now?"

Being "born right here in the good old U.S.A. under the stars and stripes" is the psychological pivot that, mixing with the literary ambitions of our character, leads him to dangerous patriotic feelings: The racist statements are founded on literacy and birth rights, so much so that the fact that he was born "right here" pushes Bandini to forget his ancestors' routes.

The same treatment is reserved for three Mexican girls immediately after this episode. Arturo's puzzling attitude toward the other ethnic groups in the cannery reveals two different strategies. Two are the moments engaging an ironic demolition of the false consciousness Arturo has developed in the New Deal era: The first is the peaceful and resigned behavior of the Filipino worker, *vis-à-vis* Bandini's proclaimed superiority in the name of his social status and his perfect American pedigree ("I'm a writer, man! An American writer, man!"); but the second, and climatic, moment concerns the concentration of the two racist episodes—that is, the one with the three Mexican girls and the other with the Filipino worker—so that their accumulation increases the tension between Arturo and the outside (working, but also ethnic) world as well as within his own (self-identical) consciousness. In fact, his assumption of being a writer precedes even his pale attempts at writing, whereas his patriotic statement dramatically contradicts not only his conversation with Shorty Naylor, but also the ideological consciousness he has apparently possessed in his family confrontations. It is Arturo himself that alerts us to the deep reasons that instinctively push him toward the harassment of the Filipino worker:[13]

> His skin was a nut brown. I noticed it because his teeth were so white. They were brilliant teeth, like a row of pearls. When I saw how dark he was I suddenly knew what to say to him. I could say it to all of them. It would hurt them every time. I knew because a thing like that had hurt me. In grade school the kids used to hurt me by calling me Wop and Dago. It had hurt every time. It was a miserable feeling. It used to make me feel so pitiful, so unworthy. And I knew it would hurt the Filipino too. It was too easy to do that all at once I was laughing quietly at him, and over me came a cool, confident feeling, at ease with everything. I couldn't fail. I walked close to him and put my face near his, smiling the way he smiled. He could tell something was coming. Immediately his expression changed. He was waiting for it—whatever it was.

The master-slave dialectics[14] receives an extraordinarily powerful actualization in this episode that calls for a phenomenological, rather than sociological, interpretation. It is in the recognition of his own and his fellow workers' alienated existence that Arturo finds a new opportunity to reflect on his identity. He comes to admit for the first time his belonging to that social condition also because of his ethnicity:[15]

> My uncle was right about the work, all right. It was work done without thinking. You might just as well have left your brains at home on that job. All we did through the whole day was stand there and move our arms and legs. . . . Nobody liked that machine. It didn't matter if you were a Filipino or an Italian or a Mexican. It bothered us all.

However, Arturo Bandini is unable to go further, trapped in an ideological eclecticism and confusion typical of the Thirties: his attempts to raise a political consciousness in the workers ("Why don't you pull this cannery down and demand your rights? Demand shoes! Demand milk! Look at yourself! Like a boob, a convict! Where's the milk? Why don't you yell for it?" pp. 98–101) fail miserably. Arturo is unable to sympathize completely with either the workers themselves ("Dynasty of slaves! Dynasty of slaves! You want to be a dynasty of slaves! You love the categorical imperative! You don't want milk, you want hypochondria! You're a whore, a slut, a pimp, a whore of modern Capitalism!") or with "Shorty the boss" (addressed as "you capitalistic proletarian bourgeois") "who knew nothing about Hitler's Weltanschauung." In these oscillating sympathies for political extremisms are some of the reasons why the novel was never published: Fante never seemed to worry about the subject matter being too provocative so that we may suppose that even in later times *The Road to Los Angeles* remained among his papers, unlike other material, because the author was still looking for a way of reconciling the ambiguities of that novel.

Fante must have sensed he could overcome the ideological impasse by searching in Arturo Bandini's childhood rather than adolescence: *The Road to Los Angeles* had forced the writer, if not his alter ego character, to face his heritage. John Fante himself supports such a suggestion in his "Preface" to *Wait Until Spring, Bandini*, where he writes: "I am fearful, I cannot bear being exposed by my own work. I am sure I shall never read this book again. But of this I am sure: all of the people of my writing life, all of my writing characters are to be found in this early work." In this novel, the first evidence of that attempt at focusing on his own heritage comes through two stylistic devices: the elimination of the narration through the eyes of the main character, as it was used in the previous novel, with the consequent affirmation of a flexible impartial perspective; and the use of the past tense, this time immediately affirming the elegiac tone of an epic recounting of a period of life forever lost. Furthermore, the role of the main character is equally shared by the child Arturo Bandini and his father Svevo, who actually is first to appear on the scene:[16]

> He came along, kicking the deep snow. Here was a disgusted man. His name was Svevo Bandini, and he lived three blocks down that street. He was cold and there were holes in his shoes. That morning he had patched the holes on the inside with pieces of cardboard from a macaroni box. The macaroni in that box was not paid for. He had thought of that as he placed the cardboard inside of his shoes.

Fred Gardaphé,[17] quoting this very passage and following Ong's theory formulated in *Orality and Literacy*, has related the simple sentence structure widely used by Fante in this novel to the sentence structure of oral stories. Presenting examples from other texts of the Italian-American experience, the critic points out at least two other important stylistic devices: the use of repetition and that of formulaic language in Italian.

Indeed, Fante superbly employs both means to portray first Svevo

Bandini and then his family (especially his wife Maria and his first son Arturo) even before they actually appear. The passage quoted earlier and the following not only form the initial page of the novel but give us important information about the character (pp. 11–12):

> He hated the snow. He was a bricklayer, and the snow froze the mortar between the brick he laid. He was on his way home, but what was the sense in going home? When he was a boy in Italy, in Abruzzi, he hated the snow too. No sunshine, no work. He was in America now, in the town of Rocklin, Colorado. He had just been in the Imperial Poolhall. In Italy there were mountains, too, like those white mountains a few miles west of him. The mountains were a huge white dress dropped plumblike to the earth. Twenty years before, when he was twenty years old, he had starved for a full week in the folds of that savage white dress. He had been building a fireplace in a mountain lodge. It was dangerous up there in the winter. He had said the devil with the danger, because he was only twenty then, and he had a girl in Rocklin, and he needed money. But the roof of the lodge had caved beneath the suffocating snow.

Through the sudden and quick mention of Svevo Bandini's name— as though it were only a matter of anagraphic information—through that definition ("a disgusted man") that even precedes the nomination, and above all through the obsessive repetition of the personal pronoun that, in fact, opens the novel, the icastic presentation of the character is sculpted in the snow with which he struggles as he walks home. Svevo Bandini is Everyman since his first apparition, and his quotidian journey has already assumed epic echoes in the immobile social condition[18] that keeps dominating his life "in America now, in the town of Rocklin, Colorado" as it did "When he was a boy in Italy, in Abruzzi."

Only "the suffocating snow," the perennial natural element with which Svevo has been fighting throughout his life, is needed to communicate the character's relationship with the world. The insistent reference to the snow, always present in Svevo's life, instead of conforming to a stereotype of magic landscapes, indeed transmits that sense of suffocation.[19]

These concentrated elements of repetition find their counterpart in other instances in this chapter: I will only mention the description of Svevo's eyes followed by that of his wife's and the sudden departure of Svevo from the house at the end of the chapter, which balances his arrival at the beginning of it.

Interestingly, the first instance of formulaic language in Italian appears as well in these first pages of the novel and it is strictly related to the snow and the passages just quoted:

*Dio cane. Dio cane.* It means God is a dog, and Svevo Bandini was saying it to the snow. Why did Svevo lose ten dollars in a poker game tonight at the Imperial Poolhall? He was such a poor man, and he had three children, and the macaroni was not paid, nor was the house in which the three children and the macaroni were kept. God is a dog. (p. 13)

Besides the repetition of the elements (already observed in the initial paragraphs) which gives emphasis to Svevo's economic situation and justify the opening blasphemous expression, it is that very sentence that is the key element of the paragraph. The Italian formula is a timid approach to interior monologue that soon becomes a simple instance of reflection on language with one of the several allusions to Joyce in this novel.[20]

But Svevo Bandini is not the only protagonist: next to his wife there is the first of his three children, Arturo Bandini.[21] That Arturo is supposed to function as his father's deuteragonist is evident since the first references to the boy (33–34):

Breakfast for three boys and a man. His name was Arturo, but he hated it and he wanted to be called John. His last name was Bandini, and he wanted it to be Jones. His mother and father were Italians, but he wanted to be an American. His father was a bricklayer, but he wanted to be a pitcher for the Chicago Cubs. They lived in Rocklin, Colorado, population ten thousand, but he wanted to live in Denver, thirty miles away. His face was freckled, but he wanted it to be clear. He went to a Catholic school, but he wanted to go to a public school. He had a girl named Rosa, but she hated him. He was an altar boy, but he was a devil and hated altar boys. He wanted to be a good boy, but he was afraid to be a good boy because he was afraid his friends would call him a good boy. He was Arturo and he loved his father, but he lived in dread of the day when he would grow up and be able to lick his father. He worshipped his father, but he thought his mother was a sissy and a fool.

Again, the return of the same formulas in the presentation of father and son ("His name was Svevo Bandini" versus "His name was Arturo"; "He hated the snow" versus "he hated it"; "he had a wife named Maria" versus "He had a girl named Rosa")[22] marks the parallel between the two characters in such a way that not only similarities, but differences as well are stressed. The most evident signal is another syntactic structure based on the obsessive repetition of the adversative conjunction and revealing the different perception Arturo has of his own heritage. Whereas wandering in the snow allows Svevo to establish a dialogue with his reveries about childhood in Italy and thereby feel continuity between then and now, his son Arturo—with no memories yet to refer to—lives in his present time the dichotomy

ERNESTO LIVORNI

between reality and dream. His daydreaming starts with the reference to a new and truly American name, refuting his mother's and father's *italianità*. However, another kind of daydreaming will lead Arturo toward the rescue of his ethnic identity: It is the imagined love story with Rosa that leads the young protagonist to recognize himself as Italian. In his repeated interior monologues about Rosa, Arturo insists not only on his desire to become a baseball star,[23] but also on their being Italians: "I am an Italian too, Rosa" (p. 116), "Rosa, me and you, a couple of Italians" (p. 118), "he was an Italian too, like Rosa Pinelli" (p. 133).

Finally, father and son will be reunited in a silent understanding after Arturo tracks Svevo down at Mrs. Hildegarde's house and convinces him to come back home. Only at that moment, when his father stands up against the angry woman and defends his son, reconciliation and the return home will be possible. The relationship that Svevo establishes with Mrs. Hildegarde presents again the master-slave dialectics already considered in *The Road to Los Angeles*. Svevo and the woman start a relationship that only at first may appear, in its dynamics, simpler than that between Arturo Gabriel Bandini and the Filipino, but is indeed much richer in implication, given not only the social context in which the father's situation evolves, but also the relevance that sexuality acquires, the only aspect that makes Svevo feel in control of a woman who is otherwise his master in economic and cultural terms. Thus, Fante exploits again the master-slave dialectics. Yet, this time the pattern is complicated by a psychological twist that runs throughout the episode, and reaches its climax in Svevo's considerations of the adultery:[24]

> She with her wealth and deep plump warmth, slave and victim of her own challenge, sobbing in the joyful abandonment of her defeat, each gasp his victory. . . . And when he left her sobbing in her fulfillment, he walked down the road with deep content that came from the conviction he was master of the earth.
> . . . Thou shalt not commit adultery. Bah. It was the Widow's doing. He was her victim.
> *She* had committed adultery. A willing victim.

Only Mrs. Hildegarde's mistreatment of his own son—accused of being a foreigner like his father—can shake Svevo: The end of Svevo's sojourn at Mrs. Hildegarde's service is stressed by the imprecations in Italian hurled at the woman ("'*Bruta animale!*' he said. '*Puttana!*'")[25] and the affirmations of Arturo's identity: "'Mrs. Hildegarde,' he said. 'That's my boy. You can't talk to him like that. That boy's an American. He is no foreigner'" (p. 265).

In this statement, Arturo comes to a double understanding of his identity: On the one hand, his *Telemachia* has been successful insofar as he has voluntarily embarked in his search for the father. The final reunion sanctions Arturo's coming to terms with his heritage without feeling ashamed of it any longer. On the other hand, however, he receives his baptismal ceremony in the very last words his father addresses to the American woman, representative of that new world in which Svevo came "Twenty years before" (p. 12) and Arturo had dreamed about and wanted to belong to since the beginning of the novel.

Only after writing the novel of Arturo's childhood can Fante go back to the project attempted with *The Road to Los Angeles;* but this time that road has been already walked and Arturo is in the City of Angels, trying to make it as a writer. In the same place, Bunker Hill, he sojourns for the length of two novels, as the last work of the saga is titled *Dreams from Bunker Hill.* The obsessive characterization of this section of town is offered through dust: When it appears, it blackens the whole landscape, especially in chapters six and seven, where it gives an apocalyptic tone to the narrative, as Arturo, walking "up the dusty stairs of Bunker Hill" surrounded by "Dust and old buildings and old people sitting at windows, old people tottering out of doors, old people moving painfully along the dark street," discovers the "dust of Chicago and Cincinnati and Cleveland on their shoes" (p. 45).[26]

The dust carries indeed an apocalyptic meaning when Los Angeles is shaken by the earthquake. It is an episode worthy of a close consideration, for the natural phenomenon not only confirms the infernal connotation of the dust, but also the ethical interpretation of the speaker, whose sense of guilt merges in the tumbling down landscape:[27]

The stone bench fell away from me and thumped into the sand. I looked at the row of concessions: they were shaking and cracking. I looked beyond to the Long Beach skyline; the tall buildings were swaying. Under me the sand gave way; I staggered, found safer footing. It happened again.

It was an earthquake.

Now there were screams. Then dust. Then crumbling and roaring. I turned round and round in a circle. I had done this. I had done this. I stood with my mouth open, paralyzed, looking about me. I ran a few steps toward the sea. Then I ran back.

You did it, Arturo. This is the wrath of God. You did it.

The rumbling continued. Like a carpet over oil, the sea and land heaved. Dust rose. Somewhere I heard a booming of debris. I heard

screams, and then a siren. People running out of doors. Great clouds
of dust.
You did it, Arturo. Up in that room on that bed you did it.

The earthquake is the overwhelming realization of that "tinge of
darkness in the back of my mind" (p. 95) felt by Arturo as he left
Vera Rivken's house and considered the consequences of the act of
adultery just committed. The cataclysm shakes the landscape as well
as Arturo's conscience: The earthquake shifts the references to the
physical "sand" of the beach into the metaphysical "dust" rising over
the character's thoughts. By the same token, "a booming of debris"
tears Arturo's behavior as well, as he waves his body back and forth
on the beach toward that sea that "is back there, back in the reservoir
of memory."[28] Arturo's footsteps on the sand are stamped by the self-
accusation that beats the rhythm of his hearty life.
This episode is pivotal to an understanding of the novel's ethical
grain, not so much for Arturo's assessment of his Catholic heritage
(this decision being the immediate effect on his conscience of the love-
making episode with Vera Rivken followed by the earthquake), but
especially for the literary portrayal it offers of the protagonist. In fact,
that act that will afterward be cataloged as adultery is instead, in
its actual development, praised as Arturo's affirmation of his
superhomistic conquest.[29] The visit to Vera Rivken is indeed his
chance to espouse living and writing experiences, as he dreams of
doing since the beginning of the novel: A telling episode is Arturo's
encounter "with Los Angeles prostitute" (p. 23). After refusing to
join her, the aspiring writer is somewhat pleased with her acknowl-
edgement of "him as a man" and starts fantasizing: "Man about town
has universal experience. Noted writer tells of night with woman of
the streets" (p. 23). The passage acquires a grotesque tone, when a
few lines later Arturo imagines himself interviewed before receiving
the Nobel prize; yet, his poetic statement lives in the interstices of
episodes like this one (p. 23):

Bandini (being interviewed prior to departure for Sweden): "My advice
to all young writers is quite simple. I would caution them never to evade
a new experience. I would urge them to live life in the raw, to grapple it
bravely, to attack it with naked fists."
Reporter: "Mr. Bandini, how did you come to write this book which
won you the Nobel Award?"
Bandini: "The book is based on a true experience which happened to
me one night in Los Angeles. Every word of that book is true. I lived
that book, I experienced it."

Bandini's imagined book, in other words, claims to be "based on a true experience" in the very moment in which Arturo refuses "to live life in the raw" (i.e., to accompany himself with the prostitute) and embarks on a fantasy trip that promises to be more rewarding.[30] Thus, this further episode confirms the necessary tie between writing and truth, on the one hand, writing and eroticism, on the other: Issues of ethics and aesthetics, as they are faced time by time, intertwine in the name of writing as creation. There is enough evidence of this both in this episode and in the previously discussed one about Vera Rivken. After all, this perspective has already been set at the end of the first chapter, when he writes to the editor Hackmuth (p. 17):

> the old zip is gone and I can't write anymore. Do you think, Mr. Hackmuth, that the climate here has anything to do with it? Do you think, Mr. Hackmuth, that I write as well as Faulkner? Please advise. Do you think, Mr. Hackmuth, that sex has anything to do with it, because, Mr. Hackmuth, because, because, and I told Hackmuth everything. I told him about the blond girl I met in the park. I told him how I worked it, how the blonde girl tumbled. I told him the whole story, only it wasn't true, it was a crazy lie—but it was something. It was writing, keeping in touch with the great, and he always answered.

Even though at this point Arturo's writing is depending too much on unreacheable models, such as Faulkner, and exterior excuses, such as Mr. Hackmuth, it is important to stress the implicit assessment of writing on at least three levels: Writing *per se* is a sort of mental exercise that one needs to cultivate regularly; yet, as the *locus* in which the beauty of the page unfolds like an erotic embrace, writing needs the experience of the Other as effacement rather than assertion[31]; finally, writing as "the whole story" shakes itself from the narrow links and limits of truth and falsity in order to solve its own ambiguity as self-reflection. Arturo seems particularly aware of this last difficulty when he considers the reasons why he wants to write (p. 20):

> So you walk along Bunker Hill, and you shake your fist at the sky, and I know what you're thinking, Bandini. The thoughts of your father before you, lash across your back, hot fire in your skull, that you are not to blame: this is your thought, that you were born poor, son of miseried peasants, driven because you were poor, fled from your Colorado town because you were poor, rambling the gutters of Los Angeles because you are poor, hoping to write a book to get rich, because those who hated you back there in Colorado will not hate you if you write a book. You are a coward, Bandini, a traitor to your soul, a feeble liar before your weeping Christ. This is why you write, this is why it would be better if you died.

Arturo's attempt at running away from his past (the Italian heritage of which his father is the icon; the sense of guilt for his social condition; poverty as mark that has to be erased by economic success) is dramatized in one of the rare dialogues within his self: It is interesting that Arturo's wish to write is first related to his desire of fulfilling the economic dream, and then somehow punished by the accusing words of cowardice, betrayal, and falsity; that is, Arturo's awareness of the false consciousness leading his writing career is presented in a sort of quick and scattered trial of reasons that the character acts upon himself.

In light of these last considerations in *Ask the Dust*, it is eerie to find such a detail at the beginning of *Dreams from Bunker Hill*, the last novel of the saga of Arturo Bandini, which was published almost half a century later:[32]

> As I studied my reflection in a long mirror I could not help remembering that in all my Colorado years my people had been too poor to buy me a suit of clothes, even for the graduation exercises in high school.

Self-reflection, this time typically dramatized in a phenomenological gesture, is again combined with memories of a social condition from which Arturo is running away. Indeed, the dreams of the title are essentially two: Arturo's attempt at economic success by becoming a writer and the world of sports (although this time baseball has been replaced by wrestling).[33] By no chance, the two novels that never fulfilled Fante's requirements—that is, the two published at the end of his life—are those dealing with the use of writing as a social weapon able to open more comfortable means of living. This particular aspect exemplifies the distance between the last and the first two novels that launched him in the years 1938–39. It must be said, however, that *Dreams from Bunker Hill*—besides its passionless description of Hollywood lifestyle, full of tempting tricks and miserable delusions—is first of all a strenuous attempt, on Fante's part, at ending the cycle by allowing Arturo to return to Boulder. Yet, that very cycle is left open again by granting the character a departure from his native town that, this time, appears to be definitive. After all, if the mother is still the sweet and comforting presence felt since the appearance of Bandini, the father Svevo (never mentioned by his first name in this novel) is depicted without the pervasive empathy of *Wait Until Spring, Bandini*. Now, Svevo is in the background, most of the time oblivious of the family events.[34] Even the issue of *italianità* has disappeared or, which is even worse, has been relegated to color the episodes with a touch of folklore: Thus, Edgington can scornfully call Arturo "a miserable, disagreeable dago dog" (p. 95) without causing any immediate reaction. More important is the grotesque appearance of "Mario, Duke of Sardinia" (p. 108)—Arturo angrily addressed him "you no good peasant wop!" (p. 112)—in the unlikely customs of a wrestler completes the ambivalent relationship with Arturo's own heritage: The embrace enlighting the first novel of the saga of such a vital struggle for the survival of the identity of the character has been now deflated by the American dream.[35]

## NOTES

1. Rose Basile Green, *The Italian-American Novel: A Document of the Interaction of Two Cultures* (Madison, N.J.: Fairleigh Dickinson University Press, 1974). The critic justifies John Fante's adherence to this particular moment of the literary Italian-American experience by discussing three of his books: *Dago Red* (New York: Viking Press, 1940); *Wait Until Spring, Bandini* (New York: Stackpole Sons, 1938; now Santa Monica, Calif: Black Sparrow Press, 1983); *Full of Life* (Boston, Mass.: Little Brown and Company, 1952; now Santa Monica, Calif.: Black Sparrow Press, 1988).

2. Rose Basile Green, *The Italian-American Novel*, 128: She adds that "This phase corresponds more exactly to Robert E. Spiller's third division in which the settler, homesick for his racial past, went back to the 'old sources of wisdom and beauty' in order to improve his condition." The following quotation is from p. 91.

3. These are the books published posthumously: *The Road to Los Angeles* (1985), *The Wine of Youth: Selected Stories of John Fante* (1985), *1933 Was a Bad Year* (1985), *West of Rome* (1986), all published by Black Sparrow Press.

4. This is the title used by the editors of Black Sparrow Press, as they published all the novels and short stories by Fante.

5. The tormented story of this manuscript is outlined in the *Editorial Note* to the novel:

> In 1933, John Fante was living in an attic apartment in Long Beach and working on his first novel, *The Road to Los Angeles*. . . . Fante had signed a contract with Knopf and received an advance. However, Fante didn't finish the novel in seven months. Sometime during 1936, he reworked the first 100 pages, shortening the book somewhat, and completed the novel. . . . The novel was never published probably because the subject matter was considered too provocative in the mid-1930s.

6. J. Fante, *The Road to Los Angeles* (Santa Rosa, Calif: Black Sparrow Press, 1985), 130. To this reference one may add those sympathetic to Hemingway (p. 118) and Keats (p. 133). Compare it with Svevo's ignorance of D'Annunzio in *Wait Until Spring, Bandini*, (New York: Stackpole, 1938; Santa Rosa, Calif.: Black Sparrow Press, 1983), 177, in a passage that starts indeed with Mrs. Hildegarde's praise of Svevo's heritage. In *Ask the Dust*, instead, literary echoes are called for a reaffirmation of Arturo's *italianità*: in that novel, the grateful and proud attitude of feeling American ("Thank God for my country. Thank God I had been born an American," p. 44; "I'm an American," p. 49) is soon replaced by an embrace of the Italian heritage in the name of that literary tradition ("I think about a few other Italians, Casanova and Cellini," p. 90). See also the list of "the books that had changed my life: Sherwood Anderson, Jack London, Knut Hamsun, Dostoevsky, D'Annunzio, Pirandello, Flaubert, de Maupassant" in *Dreams from Bunker Hill*, p. 139.

7. Arturo Gabriel Bandini, like his creator, is from Abruzzi, that very region from whence Dante Gabriel Rossetti's father had moved to England. The similarities with the Pre-Raphaelite poet, however, seem to end here: They rather mark Bandini's posture than a true vocation as a writer and a conscious voice of his ethnic group.

8. J. Fante, *The Road to Los Angeles* (Santa Rosa, Calif.: 1985), 9.

9. Ibid., 71.

10. Nietzsche's occurrences from these two books begin already in the first chapter, when Bandini first takes time off "a job as a grocery clerk" to read "Nietzsche, memorizing a long passage about voluptuousness" (p. 11), and then—after quitting that job—runs to the library to get *Man and Superman*. A fine instance of Bandini's posture, which emphasizes what already suggested about the reference to his name and Dante Gabriel Rossetti, is the monologue ending the third chapter (p. 24):

> And they [the girls in the magazines] all smiled like whores. It all got very hateful and I thought, Look at yourself! Sitting here and talking to a lot of prostitutes. A fine superman *you* turned out to be! What if Nietzsche could see you now? And Schopenhauer—what would he think? And Spengler! Oh, would Spengler roar at you! You fool, you idiot, you swine, you beast, you rat, you filthy, contemptible, disgusting little swine!

Other Nietzschean traits surface in Bandini's projects: Thus, the sketch of "A Moral and Philosophical Dissertation on Man and Woman" ends with an invocation to Zarathustra. To complete the pantheon of philosophers mentioned by Arturo, however, one must mention also Bergson (p. 42), Kant (p. 44), Plato (p. 45), Comte (p. 85), and Marxist statement such as "Religion is the opium of the people" (pp. 23, 39). It is also noteworthy that these references are assembled in the first chapters of the novel, destined to disappear later on with the exception, of course, of Nietzsche and Spengler.

11. Ibid., 23. See also *Ask the Dust*, p. 22: "I have not read Lenin, but I have heard him quoted, religion is the opium of the people. Talking to myself on the church steps: yeah, the opium of the people. Myself, I am an atheist: I have read *The Anti-Christ* and I regard it as a capital piece of work."

12. About Fante's political views and his return to Catholicism, see *John Fante & H. L. Mencken: A Personal Correspondence 1930–1952* (Santa Rosa, Calif.: Black Sparrow Press, 1989).

13. J. Fante, *The Road to Los Angeles*, 64–65. A reflection on this episode recurs in *Ask the Dust*, 46–47, in which Fante stresses Arturo's painful consciousness of otherness, mixed with both a sense of proud and angry identity toward those who used to deride him, and shame for his offensive treatment of Camilla. For a sense of the different approach taken in *Wait Until Spring, Bandini*, which also mirrors the younger age of the protagonist, see pp. 37, 48–50. The reflection on epithets recurs also in "The Odyssey of a Wop," the short story inserted in the collective volume *Dago Red*, now included in *The Wine of Youth: Selected Stories* (Santa Rosa, Calif.: Black Sparrow Press, 1985).

14. The allusion is naturally to Hegel's *Phenomenology of Mind*, later elaborated by Marx in his own speculation on the dialectics of history. Further important studies of the concept are in Alexandre Kojève, *Introduction à la lecture de Hegel* (Paris: Gallimard, 1947); Georg Lukacs, *Der Junge Hegel* (Berlin: Europa Verlag 1948); Herbert Marcuse, *Reason and Revolution* (London–New York: Oxford University Press 1955). In *Wait Until Spring, Bandini*, the master-slave dialectics acquires a psychological twist when Svevo is hosted by Mrs. Hildegarde.

15. J. Fante, *The Road to Los Angeles*, 86–87. Also cfr. ibid., 45: "Labor conditions in the machine age, a topic for a future work."

16. J. Fante, *Wait Until Spring, Bandini*, p. 11. It is possible to draw the following division of chapters, according to the perspective taken toward the characters on whom the narrator focuses time by time: Chapters 1–3 revolve around Svevo; chapter 4 the mother Maria; chapters 5–7 Arturo; chapter 8 Svevo's recounting and life with Hildegarde; chapters 9–10 Arturo's experience of Rosa's death and his rescue of his father.

17. Fred Gardaphé, "From Oral Tradition to Written Word: Toward an Ethnographically Based Literary Criticism," in Anthony Julian Tamburri, Paolo A. Giordano, Fred L. Gardaphé, eds., *From the Margin: Writing in Italian Americana* (West Lafayette, IN.: Purdue University Press, 1991), 294–306. See also, in the same volume, Samuel J. Patti, "Recent Italian American Literature: The Case of John Fante," 329–37, which deals primarily with the novel in question and *The Brotherhood of the Grape* (Santa Rosa, Calif.: Black Sparrow Press, 1977).

18. The dry statement on poverty that opened *The Road to Los Angeles* here is effused in the insistence on consumption: first there appear the "holes in his shoes" and even the remedy ("pieces of cardboard from a macaroni box") only amplifies the real entity of Svevo's poverty.

19. However, its function does not end there: In the next paragraph the snow is associated with Svevo's wife in a simile (p. 12):

> It harrassed him always, that beautiful white snow. He could never understand why he didn't go to California. Yet he stayed in Colorado, in the deep snow, because it was too late now. The beautiful white snow was like the beautiful white wife of Svevo Bandini, so white, so fertile, lying in a white bed in a house up the street. 456 Walnut Street, Rocklin, Colorado.

20. The most conspicuous is perhaps the father-son relationship, but one should not underestimate the reflection on language (especially through a loose adaptation of the interior monologue) and on religion. To be true, the latter aspect helps to understand the different narrative strategy developed between *The Road to Los Angeles* and *Wait Until Spring, Bandini*. See also the ironic reference to Joyce in *Ask the Dust*, 19.

21. Although the title may in fact refer to both father and son, it is used by Arturo's friends, to invite him not to be so anxious to play baseball even during the winter (p. 230).

22. The quotations regarding Svevo and Arturo are taken, respectively, from pp. 11–13, 33–34. See also the presentation of Svevo's wife: "Her name was Maria" (pp. 13, 16, 22, 24, 32), "Her name was Maria Bandini, but before she married him her name was Maria Toscana" (p. 21). About the mother-figure in Fante's novels, Basile Green writes: "John Fante, for example, became absorbed in a Freudian search for an ideal, which he eventually identified with his mother."

23. The name Arturo chooses as he imagines himself as a baseball star is Banning (p. 49), that is, the name of the character of Bandini's own book as it appears in *The Road to Los Angeles*. By no chance, *Ask the Dust* opens with the protagonist Arturo Bandini, now in Los Angeles engaged in the fulfillment of his dream as a writer, who "noted with satisfaction that Joe DiMaggio was still a credit to the Italian people, because he was leading the league in batting" (p. 11). For the importance of baseball as a means of overcoming a poor environment and ethnic difference, see *1933 Was a Bad Year* (Santa Rosa, Calif.: Black Sparrow Press, 1985).

24. J. Fante, *Wait Until Spring, Bandini*, 199–200. The theme of adultery as "a mortal sin" and cause of "the warm even rhythm of my guilt," against which no reading of Nietzsche or Voltaire can help, is faced in the Vera Rivken episode in *Ask*

*the Dust*, 96. For another instance of the religious undertone assumed by the episodes in that novel, cfr. ibid., 144.

25. The shaky spelling of the first expression is worthy of further consideration: In fact, the wrong agreement of the adjective (in the feminine form with a masculine noun) may be justified by its being addressed to Mrs. Hildegarde; the misspelling of *"bruta"* for *"brutta,"* however, evokes a heavier offense, as though Svevo accused the lady of brutal behaviour toward the child. It must be said, however, that Basile Green reads this line as "Brutta Animale!" (p. 160).

26. For other instances of the efficacy of the all-pervasive coat of dust in this novel, cfr. pp. 48, 50–52, 94, 125, besides Fante's own prologue.

27 Fante, *Ask the Dust*, p. 98. For other instances of this kind of metaphoric meaning for the dust, cfr. p. 104 ("The world was dust and dust it would become": A sentence by no chance followed by Arturo's recounting of his decision to go to church every morning).

28. Ibid., p. 97. The rest of this passage is telling for a full understanding of the mythical and psychological dimensions of the sea imagery:

> The sea is a myth. There never was a sea. But there *was* a sea! I tell you I was born on the seashore! I bathed in the waters of the sea! It gave me food and it gave me peace, and its fascinating distances fed my dreams! No, Arturo, there never was a sea. You dream and you wish, but you go on through the wasteland. You will never see the sea again. It was a myth you once believed. But, I have to smile, for the salt of the sea is in my blood, and there may be ten thousand roads over the land, but they shall never confuse me, for my heart's blood will ever return to its beautiful source.

29. Arturo tries to suffocate his sense of guilt again by reminding himself of the readings of Nietzsche, beside Voltaire, he has done. Furthermore, his sadistic game with Vera pushes him so far as to superimpose Camilla on his occasional lover: "She was Camilla, complete and lovely. She belonged to me, and so did the world. . . . She wasn't Camilla anymore. She was Vera Rivken, and I was in her apartment and I would get up and leave just as soon as I had some sleep" (p. 95). The scene loosely recalls that in D'Annunzio's *Il piacere*, in which Andrea Sperelli imagines Elena while making love with Maria. The outcome for the two heroes, however, is different and such difference depends on the critical ridge set between ethics and aesthetics, or, to put it in Fante's terms, between "experience" and "writing."

30. Two considerations necessarily occur at this point: the first concerns a further episode which immediately follows (the imagined arrest for stealing milk, justified in the following terms: "you see, I've really got plenty of money, big sales of manuscripts and all that, but I was doing a yarn about a fellow who steals a quart of milk, and I wanted to write from experience," p. 31); the second regards Fante's writing as a necessary literary antecedent of the Beat Generation writers (by no chance, Charles Bukowski wrote a short, but significant preface to the Black Sparrow Press edition of *Ask the Dust*).

31. This statement does not necessarily mean that writing is required to experience the Other: Fante's conviction is quite the opposite, as this letter to Hackmuth as well as the prostitute and, *a contrario*, the Vera Rivken episodes support the necessity of writing to take over experience. In other words, the syntactically oblique "experience of the Other" is able to avoid the ineluctability of the categoric imperative "experience the Other." In this respect, the episode of the risked drowning by Arturo and Camilla (p. 67) is also exemplary: "So this was the end of Camilla, and this was the end of Arturo Bandini—but even then I was writing it all down, seeing it across a page in a typewriter, writing it out and coasting along the sharp sand, so sure I

would never come out alive." When Arturo by chance reaches the beach, "wondering if I could perhaps make a poem out of it," he has the unpleasant surprise to learn that Camilla had been faking drowning all along.

32. J. Fante, *Dreams from Bunker Hill*, 10. See also Arturo's remembrance of his father at the beginning of chapter three: "I remembered my father in Colorado at the kitchen sink on a bright spring morning, singing with happiness as he shaved. *O Sole Mio.* I stood before my bathroom mirror and sang it too. Oh God, how good I felt!" (p. 23). Here, the reflection in the mirror, significantly undertaken in the act of shaving, suggests a transparent imitation of the father figure.

33. To feel the different attitude toward writing, one may just consider Arturo's enthusiasm when he took possession of the shack on the beach: His affirmation that he "became a writer once more in the world" (p. 98) only apparently picks up after the dialectical understanding of "writing" and "experience" as presented in *Ask the Dust*. Furthermore, among other motifs of *Dreams from Bunker Hill*, there is, of course, the love motif, intertwining with branches of eroticism and sex: the relationship with Mrs. Helen Brownell is paradigmatic and seems to concentrate it all. It is obvious that through her Fante wants to stress the mother motif as well, as it becomes apparent both in the chapters in which Arturo receives letters from "my poor innocent mother" (p. 59) and those of his temporary homecoming.

34. In fact, he is in action only twice, with two gestures that balance each other: Svevo first offers his coat to his son, just arrived from warmer places; then, he is quick and abrupt in asking money from him for the family. More tender moments, such as his pride for the interview Arturo receives in the local paper, are mentioned as oleographic details.

35. This chapter first appeared as an article in *VIA* 6, no. 1 (1995): 52–73.

# 6

# Blending "Literary" Discourses: Helen Barolini's Italian/American Narratives

## EDVIGE GIUNTA

> Though she didn't know how to read or write, when it came to cooking she knew everything there was to know.
> Laura Esquivel, *Like Water for Chocolate*

> One could read the progress of her life in the spills of mysterious substances that now obliterated her favorite recipes. . . . this dripping and this dribbling had been Helen's way of making history.
> Louise DeSalvo, *Casting Off*

> If books did not tell me who I was, I would write those that did.
> Helen Barolini, "Becoming a Literary Person Out of Context"

The scarcity of writings by Italian/American women in 1979, the year of publication of Helen Barolini's *Umbertina*, places this novel in a problematic position with regard to issues of tradition, genre, and authorship.[1] In *The Dream Book*, an anthology of writings by Italian/American women edited by Barolini and published in 1985, Barolini, assuming the role of the critic rather than the fiction writer, explores the issues underlying her own emergence as an Italian/American woman author. In the long introduction to this book, she indicts a literary market that is blind and hostile to Italian/American women:

> That Italian American women have been underpublished is undeniable; just as exclusionary, however, is that the few who are published are not kept on record and made accessible, even bibliographically, in libraries and in study courses. Not only do Italian American women writing their own stories publish with great difficulty . . . but once in print, they must confront an established cadre of criticism that seems totally devoid of the kind of insight that could relate to their work. (44–45)

114

Although she does not include her own work in this anthology meant
to legitimize the writings of the authors included, posing as a critic,
Barolini adds another feature to the authorial persona that she has
been painstakingly constructing.

In "Becoming a Literary Person out of Context," an autobiographical essay published in 1986, Barolini refers to *The Dream Book* as an
*"apologia pro vita mia"* (BLP, 267), and maintains that "an Italian
American woman becomes a writer out of the void. She has to be
self-birthed, without models, without inner validation. . . . She is
perceived as a stranger both to literature and in literature" (BLP,
263). Barolini's defiant claim that, in the absence of books that would
tell her how she was, she would "write those that did" (BLP, 265),
becomes especially poignant when one tries to define exactly what
kind of writer Barolini is and to identify what niche she has created
for herself in the literary market. Examining the interconnections
between textual experience and extratextual elements in Barolini
sheds light on the ways in which gender, genre, and ethnicity intersect
in the process leading to the creation of her authorial voice. An intertextual analysis of Barolini's works, that weaves fiction and life, poetry
and criticism, recipes and autobiography, will identify the forces shaping her development as an author while also pointing to the role that
discourses on ethnicity play in the process of authorial self-fashioning.

A search for books by Barolini in a large bookstore in the Northeast
proved fruitful, to my delight, since, besides Barolini's *Festa*, only
one other book by an Italian/American woman author was kept in
stock (Dorothy Bryant's *The Kin of Ata Are Waiting for You*). But as
I made my way to the Fiction and Literature section, the bookseller
competently steered me towards another part of the bookstore, a more
exotic one: "Cooking." Even bookstores, I thought to myself, have
managed to keep Italian women in the kitchen. As I browsed through
Helen Barolini's *Festa: Recipes and Recollections of Italian Holidays*
(1988), I could not help thinking that there was something subversive
about the presence of this book in a bookstore that had exiled Italian/
American women. Had she not written *Festa*, Barolini would not have
entered this place.[2] And wasn't Dorothy Bryant's book kept in the
Science Fiction section? Could it be that this was a decoy, a strategy
for survival devised by Italian/American women writers? Could it be
that to survive Italian/American women authors did not have to revise
only the male literary tradition, as Adrienne Rich astutely advises *all*
women writers to do,[3] but also to "revise" themselves—to hide, to
disguise under Anglo-sounding names or to turn to genres that seemingly have no direct connection with their ethnic tradition (science
fiction) or that have more acceptable connections with that tradition?[4]

Criticizing Scorsese's *Italianamerican* (1974), Barolini argues that this autobiographical documentary offers yet another stereotypical representation of Italian Americans:

> the scene opened on his mother and father at the food-laden table, eating; then he [Scorsese] directed his mother to go into the kitchen and show him how she did the tomato sauce. Doing the sauce, of course, is *the* metaphor for being an Italian American woman. (BLP, 272)

Barolini rejects this oversimplified view of Italian Americans, alert to the fact that such a view is deeply ingrained in American culture.[5] Yet she writes *Festa*, a book of recipes that presents her as *the* Italian/American woman "doing the sauce" rather than attempting to become a literary person. However, the title of her autobiographical essay, "Becoming a Literary Person Out of Context," clarifies the literary and autobiographical nature of *Festa*. "Context" is the key word. Barolini creates herself as an author "out of context," that is, because she has no context, she utilizes diverse spheres, even nonliterary ones, as spaces for authorial expression. As domestic texts, cookbooks have always been an accessible genre to women, even Italian/American women. This is one genre in which they are authorized: Marcella Hazan, Cathy Luchetti, Anna Del Conte, Biba Caggiano, Anne Casale, Viana La Place—women with Italian names make it in this specialized section of the publishing market.[6] And *Festa* fits the genre: the recipes are there to initiate aspiring cooks and refine the skills of experienced ones. But *Festa* speaks in other voices and languages that are at least as important, if not more, than the dominant voice of the experienced cook: From the autobiographical introduction to the introductory sections that combine accounts of the customs and festivals of Italy with more autobiographical tidbits, *Festa* strives to create a language and a story, moving beyond the declared purpose of the cookbook.[7]

The genre of *Festa* is not new. Other cookbooks are complemented by subtexts, such as photographs, cultural histories, and biographical anecdotes.[8] Viewed in the "context" of Barolini's literary work, however, this book further problematizes her status as an idiosyncratic author—one who does not specialize. She is a novelist, a critic, a translator, a reviewer, an anthologist—*and* the author of a cookbook. Writing of a time when she had "receded in the shadowy recesses of translation and . . . camouflaged [her] voice with another's," Barolini recalls the fragility of her "hold" on her work and the fear of being pushed "into the morass of self-doubt" (SDS, 555). Recounting her emergence as an author, Barolini herself calls attention to the variety

of her literary production, which is linked to her struggle towards
authorial self-creation:

> I wrote about the Italian poet, Lucio Piccolo, and about *Giacomo Joyce;*
> I wrote stories about displaced Americans in Rome and this time the
> displaced people were Anglo-Americans, not Italian Americans.[9] (*BLP*,
> 269)

Fascinated by displacement, Barolini writes about that experience in
her fiction and in her criticism, and vicariously examines the implications of existing on the margins. The heterogenous quality of her
"literary" production sheds light on the displacement of Italian/
American women authors in the literary market, which is directly
linked to their absence from the curriculum.[10] In his discussion of
Barolini's literary production, Gardaphé argues that the autobiographies of Italian/American women are characterized by "an intense
politicization of the self . . . [which] emerges in combative voices,
representative of the intense struggle Italian American women have
waged in forging free selves within the constraints of a patriarchal
system" (20–21).[11] Barolini's blending of genres and writerly personas
articulates the extremity of Italian/American women authors' exclusion and their willingness, as a result, to explore diverse routes in
order to become authors. Through a process of self-authorization,
Barolini fashions a multiplicity of voices, all participating in the creation of a decentered authorial voice. Trying to establish her "voices"
in canonical genres in which her gender/ethnicity is absent, such as
fiction and criticism, Barolini resorts to a subversive transformation
of the genre in which her gender/ethnicity *is* present.[12] Opening *Festa*,
one reads, "Other Books by Helen Barolini," with *Umbertina, The
Dream Book,* and *Love in the Middle Ages* listed below. Facing the
title page of *Festa*, this list defies the circumscribed literary space that
the genre of *Festa* may seem to ascribe to its author. At the same time,
adding *Festa* to these titles, Barolini sanctions her diverse authorial
experiences, which both reflect and challenge cultural definitions of
Italian/American femininity. Indeed, as Gardaphé puts it, Barolini
transforms the stereotypical image of the Italian woman by turning
"the woman's room, the family kitchen, into an embassy of cultural
tradition" (24).
  Food as a literary subject matter is a staple of Italian/American
literature. In the writings of women, this topic takes on an especially
poignant significance, as it articulates both a perception of the domestic space as oppressive and an awareness of the ways in which women
empower themselves within that space. Not only does food provide

a language through which to express such an ambivalent view of the
domestic space, it also becomes a vehicle through which to articulate
ethnic identity. In Louise DeSalvo's novel, *Casting Off*, the Italian
background of the overtly Irish Helen MacIntyre emerges through
the lavish descriptions of food and in the use of the recipe as an
autobiographical text of sorts:

> She thought about how one could read the progress of her life in the spills
> of mysterious substances that now obliterated her favorite recipes, the one
> for pecan pie in an old Good Housekeeping cookbook that was now out
> of print and that she held together with rubber bands. (28–29)

The "dripping" and "dribbling" that covers Helen's cookbooks represents her "way of making history," while through the "splotches" and
"spills" she inscribes her signature on the text of her life, a life from
which she feels disconnected (29–30). In a similar fashion, the poet
Rose Romano proclaims that she can "write" her "life/story with different shapes in/various sizes in limitless patterns of/pasta laid out to
dry on a thick, white/tablecloth" (*The Wop Factor*, 57). While both
DeSalvo and Romano do not turn to the cookbook as a genre, they
demonstrate the interconnectedness of food writing and life writing,
Writers such as Romano and DeSalvo, and also Tina De Rosa, Sandra
M. Gilbert, Phyllis Capello, and Kathy Freeperson, to mention just
a few, have variously turned to food as the necessary ingredient to
subvert popular views of Italian/American ethnicity pervasive in
American culture. For these writers, ethnicity, as Romano puts it, is
not something to "drag out/of a closet to celebrate quaint holidays/
nobody heard of" (*The Wop Factor*, 57). Barolini turns to the cookbook, the text that American culture deems the recognized token of
Italian/American women's identity, to create a much more complex
story, one that the reader must learn "to read."[13]
    The intersection of gender and ethnicity magnifies the conditions
that stifle the authorial voice and restricts the genres available for
the creation of Italian/American women's literary discourses. This
shrinking of the literary space replicates the narrowing of the walls
of the domestic space that have historically circumscribed and shaped
female creativity. Exploring the ambiguities of the domestic space,
many women writers endow the language of domesticity with a poetical function, and thus fashion an aesthetics of domesticity. Barolini
herself draws from domesticity an arsenal of literary strategies, paral-
leling the strategies employed by other women authors who inscribe
the narratives and objects of domesticity in their works.[14] Gender,
genre, and ethnicity all play a role in Barolini's creation of a poetics

of domesticity. The cookbook represents a literary occasion for Barolini to explore her relationship to each of these cultural forces. By asserting the author's "cultural specificity" and "ethnic difference," a cookbook "provides the self with authority to speak" (Goldman, 179). As a "form of writing," a recipe is a "culturally contingent production" (Goldman, 172): *Festa* thus functions as a narrative through which Barolini negotiates her position between American and Italian culture, but also as a text that furthers her authorial assertion as a woman who cooks *and* writes. Like a ventriloquist, Barolini speaks through her "recipes." The introductions to each month/ "chapter" in *Festa* rely on subtitles such as "Strambino: In My Italian Kitchen" (*F*, 115), and intertwine memories of the Festival of Spoleto and descriptions of menus, quotations from *Childe Harold* and prices of food, conversations with artists *and* with cooks. "Mother, parents, family—they all merge in the festas that are so much a part of Italian life" (*F*, 260), writes Barolini, and in a similar way, disparate elements "merge" in *Festa* to forge the author's voice and authorize her stories.

*Festa* is much like the "feast of tongues" in Sandra Mortola Gilbert's poem, "Still Life: Woman Cooking" (*Emily's Bread*, 65). Even in the title, Gilbert reverses the paralyzing implications of the domestic space by turning it into art—"a still life"—but she also critiques the creative paralysis caused by the rhythms of domestic life. Barolini's own literary transformation of domesticity involves a re-vision of *the* domestic genre *par excellence,* the cookbook. Such a re-vision challenges the criteria that define "literary" texts and "'fine literature'" (Ling, 742) and critiques the conditions that limit access to the literary space—as a public space—for groups that are victims of social and cultural discrimination. Discussing the possibility of defining a female poetic, Jane Marcus focuses on a "model of art, with repetition and dailiness at the heart of it, with the teaching of other women the patient craft of one's cultural heritage as the object of it" ("Still Practice," 84). Marcus argues that this is "a female poetic which women live and accept. Penelope's art is work, as women cook food that is eaten, weave cloth that is worn, clean houses that are dirtied. Transformation, rather than permanence, is at the heart of this aesthetic" (84). And "transformation" is "at the heart" of Barolini's *Festa*, a book that transforms recipes and cooking into a newly created literary experience. Susan Leonardi argues that in a literary text a recipe can function as "embedded discourse" and "narrative strategy" (340): "Like a narrative, a recipe is reproducible, and, further, its hearers-readers-receivers are *encouraged* to reproduce it and, in reproducing it, to revise it and make it their own" (344). Thus the recipe simultaneously empowers the author and the reader, erasing hierarchical distinctions between the two. And through *Festa* Barolini gives "a version of the Italian American house" that, as Gardaphé suggests, presents the "kitchen" as the space for female storytelling (26).

Barolini resorts to a wide spectrum of creative vehicles and models to empower herself to speak different languages and tell different stories. In *Festa*, she writes of a book of recipes she has inherited from her husband's grandmother, written "in her own beautiful hand" (*F*, 12). A recipe indeed works as "an apt metaphor for the reproduction of culture from generation to generation" and "the act of passing down recipes from mother to daughter works as well to figure a familial space within which self-articulation can begin to take place" (Goldman, 172). Barolini entitles her anthology of Italian/American women writers after an actual "dream book" that Italian immigrants consulted and shared:

> On a front page, in awkward uphill handwriting was the Italian notation of one Angela Zecchini who, with many misspellings and an incorrect date for the inception of World War I, recorded this terse account of her life. . . .
> It was . . . a book the Italian women of Telluride [Colorado] used constantly, the Baedeker of their dreams. . . .
> The original tattered and much-thumbed dream book was the companion of those displaced women. (*DB*, xii–xiii)

These writings, produced within a culturally constructed private space, deprived of access to the realm of "public" discourse, and seemingly addressing a self-selected, "private" audience, represent the cultural heritage of marginalized groups. They are indeed literary artifacts, women's early literary production, formulating notions of art, authorship, and audience not sanctioned as "literary."[15] *Festa* subversively crosses the bounds of female privacy and speaks in a "politicized" voice (Gardaphé, 20), claiming an authorial space that legitimizes its narratives. In *The Languages of Patriarchy*, Jane Marcus questions traditional methods of literary history and claims that

> in the case of Virginia Woolf, very often the drafts and the unpublished versions seem "truer" texts. . . . Perhaps it would be true of all women writers. Perhaps it would be true of all oppressed people's writings, of blacks and lesbians, that the published text is *not* the most interesting book. (xii)

Marcus contends that the ways in which different forms of censorship intervene on texts often camouflage the authorial voice. Thus, constructing the literary history of "oppressed people" necessitates a search for unofficial texts and sources.[16] Women's autobiographies, letters, memoirs, and other non-"literary" texts, such as cookbooks— and "dream books"—represent a repertoire the critic must draw on to construct a marginal author's history.

The process of authorial self-birth (BLP, 263) lies at the core of Barolini's literary production. Her entire opus aims at the creation of an "autobiography as piecework" (Gardaphé, 19), a fragmentary and discontinuous narrative that nevertheless brings forth the author's voice. Barolini's novel, *Umbertina*, self-consciously examines the history of its creation as an ethnic female bildungsroman *and* kunstlerroman.[17] Questioning the conventions of these genres, the novel traces the Italian roots of Tina Morosini, an aspiring scholar of Italian literature. As Anthony Tamburri argues, *Umbertina* departs from traditional representations of Italian/American femininity: "The novelty of *Umbertina* lies precisely in Barolini's treatment of women as individuals, who, at one point or another in their lives, become aware of their true plight—the duality of gender and ethnic oppression—and . . . attempt to free themselves from the prison-house of patriarchy" ("Gender/Ethnic," 42–43). By telling the stories of Tina's mother's (Marguerite's) lifelong and seemingly unsuccessful search for a talent, Tina's decision to become a scholar of Italian literature, and Tina's "encounter" with her great-grandmother Umbertina's bedspread, Barolini examines the diverse routes leading to, or thwarting, the creation of an Italian/American woman author. From an autobiographical perspective, Barolini portrays herself both as Marguerite, the unrealized artist who dies pregnant with an unwanted child, a metaphor for her aborted artistic creativity, and as Tina, who succeeds in becoming a literary scholar. Marguerite's tragic death captures Barolini's perception of the fragility of her position as an aspiring artist. Marguerite's suicide, an event the narrative hints at without ever asserting it with certainty, emblematizes Barolini's own self-doubt.

Marguerite's unfulfilled search for her artistic talent emerges in her "restlessness" (*U*, 181), her moving from place to place, and her inability—or unwillingness—to define a "domestic" space.[18] Marguerite's houses are characterized by "this visible edge of impermanence, of things falling apart" (*U*, 304). "I don't care where I live" (*U*, 305), she used to say, but her daughter knows that "she did care. She cared enormously for place, and each one they came to and claimed, she worked at to make beautiful. And then moved on" (*U*, 305). Tina thinks how "curious" was her mother's attachment to "drawers and boxes and to the idea of having everything contained, in place; she who tore it all apart so readily, ready to move on, sending them winging like birds of passage on the flights of her inquietude" (*U*, 306). Marguerite's "care" for "place" represents her search for her space "in the world" (*U*, 182), but she cannot find this space because she focuses her intellectual energy on her husband's professional and personal success (Tamburri, "Gender/Ethnic," 33). The juxtaposition between personal "place" and public "world" articulates the author's critique of the historical dichotomy between private and public and of the effects of such a dichotomy on an author's self-fashioning. Similarly repressed in her artistic aspirations, Lily Bart, the protagonist of Edith Wharton's *The House of Mirth*, dwells on her unrealized aspiration to redecorate her aunt's drawing room, which would provide an ineffectual outlet for her creative talent.[19] Like Lily, Marguerite is displaced, and her displacement is illustrated through her relationship to places: constant moves, attempts to mark the places with her presence, simultaneous attachment to and disregard for the domestic space.

Marguerite's displacement figuratively reflects Barolini's own awkward position on the Italian literary scene, in which her husband, Antonio Barolini, much like Marguerite's husband, found himself perfectly "at ease":

> He was supremely at ease with the fact of his calling as an Italian poet and author, confident of being a literary person without having to question his right to be one, or whether he was odd to be one. Literature was his unquestioned patrimony and privilege. (BLP, 267)

In an oblique exploration of her own conflicting and ambiguous relationship to the literary world, Barolini portrays Marguerite as muse, translator, spectator, amateur artist striving to articulate a speech for which she finds no words. After hearing of Marguerite's death, her mother wonders, "What did she want? What was she looking for? . . . All that moving around. All those homes she set up and then tore down. And moving those girls around so they had no normal life at all . . . What was it all for? To punish us?" (*U*, 286). Marguerite's expatriation and marginality are linked to and express her cultural and historical entrapment as a third-generation Italian/American woman raised in America in the 1950s, a period that did not encourage the emergence of either female or ethnic voices.[20] Thus Marguerite remains on the margins, a spectator even of her own life. However, her daughter will begin to articulate the cultural disconnection from which they both suffer.

Both Marguerite and Alberto Morosini, Tina's poet father, influence the professional direction taken by Tina. In many ways, they legitimize her literary career by establishing precedents for her: Marguerite through her struggles, and Alberto through his confidence in his position as an Italian poet. Tina's ambivalent attitude towards Italian culture—and specifically Southern Italian culture—becomes apparent while she is travelling in Calabria and feels torn between being a tourist and being a traveler. The image of Tina as a "tourist" of her "heritage" (BLP, 270), a phrase Barolini elsewhere uses to refer to herself, is recalled in the description of Tina's visit to the Museum of Immigration. Tina's role as a passive spectator seems to undergo a change when she stops in front of Umbertina's bedspread:

> Tina stood before the glass drinking in the beauty and warmth of the old spread. Its colors irradiated her spirit; the woven designs of grapes and tendrils and fig leaves and flowers and spreading acanthus spoke to her of Italy and the past and keeping it all together for the future. It was as if her old ancestor, the Umbertina she had fruitlessly sought in Castagna, had suddenly become manifest in the New World and spoken to her. (U, 407–8).

Tina intuitively understands the poetical language spoken by the bedspread, both a domestic artifact and the epitome of her past. The bedspread contains its own kind of writing, "woven designs" that speak to Tina in a language that she begins to comprehend. The history of the bedspread, its acquisition, its loss through sale, and its donation to the Museum of Immigration by a Northern Italian woman symbolically capture the turbulent history of Italian/American—specifically southern Italian—ethnicity. The artifact that represented Umbertina's connection with her heritage is deviously appropriated by Anna Giordani, the Northern Italian social worker whose name enters the annals of immigrant history at the cost of erasing Umbertina's. The unspoken story of the bedspread raises the question of the need for corrective stories and histories that will trace, reclaim, and record the life stories of marginal figures such as Umbertina.

Tina's search for her great-grandmother represents her search for a poetical subject, though this search does not actualize into a life choice. By taking a Ph.D. in Italian Tina begins to write *about* Italian authors, but she has not yet learned the language to articulate her own *italianità*. The bedspread, an embodiment of the ethnic subject matter, remains in many ways inaccessible, displayed in the Museum, not revivified in poetical language. But if Tina does not become a poet, Barolini becomes a writer. The novel thus captures the struggle of the authorial voice of one Italian/American woman, trying to extricate itself from cultural paradigms that prevent it from being born.

Barolini's work provides an account of her experimenting with different mediums for artistic expression. Although fiction and criticism appear as mutually exclusive in Tina's career, Barolini's entire literary production expresses a struggle to reconcile and "merge" the two as well as other genres. "Becoming a Literary Person Out of Context," for example, compresses the undertakings of the critic, the fiction writer, and the autobiographer. In that essay, the third-person pronoun, used in reference to the Italian/American woman writer as a figure whose creation in process risks being aborted, is soon replaced by the first person pronoun, an "I" voice that, though "besieged by doubts" (BLP, 263), speaks confidently, telling a story—*her* story—that claims its right to be heard.

A history of disguises, male pseudonyms, unrecognized collaboration with male partners, and censorship characterizes the emergence of nineteenth- and early twentieth-century women authors. The illegitimate status of the woman author caused emerging authors to experience an all-consuming "anxiety of authorship," a gender-determined "disease" which Sandra Mortola Gilbert and Susan Gubar juxtapose to Harold Bloom's "anxiety of influence" (51):

> In comparison to the "male" tradition of strong, father-son combat . . . this female anxiety of authorship is profoundly debilitating. Handed down not from one woman to the other but from the stern literary "fathers" of patriarchy to all their "inferiorized" female descendants, it is in many ways the germ of a dis-ease or, at any rate, a disaffection, a disturbance, a distrust, that spreads like a strain throughout the style and structure of much literature by women. (51)

Gilbert and Gubar find that the anxiety of authorship does not afflict with equal intensity twentieth-century women authors who, having become legitimate creators of literary discourses, free themselves from that form of anxiety and embrace the anxiety of influence.[21] Conversely, the absence of literary foremothers and the unrecognized—and thus illegitimate—status of Italian/American women authors places them in a position in which they are still stifled by the "anxiety of authorship." Italian/American authors experience a sense of belatedness, which is magnified by their connection with the celebrated literary tradition of Italy,[22] and various ethnic, multicultural "renaissances," including Jewish/American, African/American, Chicana, and Asian/American among others.[23] Mapping out the territory inhabited by Italian/American authors, especially women, one finds the names of small publishing houses and unknown literary magazines, and titles that quickly go out of print—which brings us back to Barolini's comment on writing "out of the void" (BLP, 263).[24]

Barolini's work captures the position of Italian/American women authors who, rather than benefiting from the debates on multiculturalism and gender issues, find themselves still on the fringes. Ironically, even their marginalization has not yet entered fictional or critical discourse.[25] A letter from a reader of *Umbertina* comments directly on the absence of Italian/American "literary" women, both as the creators and as the created: "I've never seen the name of an Italian woman on a book cover before, so I had to buy your book" (BLP, 271). Have things changed over the last fifteen years? The publication of Mary Jo Bona's *The Voices We Carry: Recent Italian/American Women's Fiction* (1994), a special issue of *VIA: Voices in Italian Americana* (1996) devoted to women, several books by authors such as Rita Ciresi, Louise DeSalvo, Marianna De Marco Torgovnick, Diane di Prima, Maria Mazziotti Gillan, Daniela Gioseffi, Cris Mazza, Carole Maso, Christine Palamidessi Moore, and Agnes Rossi, and also the reprints of Tina De Rosa's *Paper Fish* (1996) and three of Dorothy Bryant's novels by the Feminist Press (1997), and Diana Cavallo's *A Bridge of Leaves* by Guernica (1997), represent a step forward in the making of a tradition of Italian/American female authors. However, there has been no concerted effort on the part of the literary market and the academic world to allow the "dream book" to enter the realm of literary reality. The placement of Barolini's and Bryant's books in the Cooking and Science Fiction sections reflects the still-existing displacement and marginalization of Italian/American women authors, women who might be relegated to the kitchen or forced to travel to utopian lands to achieve recognition. But while the terrain remains still largely uncharted, Barolini's and other authors' subversive strategies forge alternative territories that have begun to legitimize Italian/American women's voices.

## NOTES

1. The author acknowledges the Purdue Research Foundation for granting permission to reprint this article. An earlier version was first published in the *Romance Languages Annual 1994*, vol. 6, ed. Jeanette Beer, Ben Lawton, and Patricia Hart (West Lafayette: Purdue Research Foundation, 1995), 261–66. The following abbreviations of Barolini's works will be used in parenthetical documentation in the text: *F: Festa; DB: The Dream Book: An Anthology of Writings by Italian American Women;* BLP: "Becoming a Literary Person Out of Context"; SDS: "Shutting the Door on Someone"; *U: Umbertina.* On the use of the slash instead of the hyphen, see Tamburri, *To Hyphenate or Not to Hyphenate.*

2. Significantly, as of March 1996, *Festa* is the only book by Barolini still in print.

3. "Re-vision, the act of looking back . . . of entering an old text from a critical direction, is for women . . . an act of survival" (Rich, 35).

4. Dorothy Bryant is the author of many books, some of which focus on Italian/American ethnicity, such as *Miss Giardino* (1978). While science fiction is only one of the many genres Bryant has turned to, it is significant that *The Kin of Ata Are Waiting for You* is, among her many books, the one that can be easily found in bookstores. In "Where Are the Italian American Novelists?" Gay Talese speaks of the pressure to anglicize Italian names to gain access to the literary market (29). Unfortunately, this is a familiar story that many, besides Talese, can tell. For example, Francesca Vinciguerra, a popular Italian/American author of the 1940s, anglicized her name and called herself Frances Winwar (*DB*, 6). Sandra M. Gilbert reduces her Italian name, Mortola, to an "M," a cipher that captures the diminutive status of Italian/American ethnicity: "I am really Sandra Mortola Gilbert," Gilbert wrote to Barolini, "and my mother's name was Caruso, so I always feel oddly falsified with this Waspish-sounding American name, which I adopted as a 20-year old bride who had never considered the implications of her actions!" (*DB*, 22).

5. Barolini writes of the response of the students at Sarah Lawrence College, where the screening took place: "Viewing Ms. Scorsese's life as spectators, they could indulge in sentiment and nostalgia for a life they'd never have to live. Being liberated from imposed roles, they could romanticize the heart-warming Italian Americans who were represented as living confining roles. And so it is in literature: Italian American characters serve the function of picturesque peasants for the tourist-reader who doesn't have to be them" (272).

6. "Write an Italian cookbook, author Nives Cappelli was told when she tried to market an ethnic novel, but don't write about Italian Americans because they don't read" (*DB*, 44–45).

7. For an analysis of the cookbook as a cultural and literary text, see Leonardi and Goldman. On food in Italian/American culture, see Gardaphé, "Linguine and Lust: Food and Sex in Italian/American Culture."

8. A recent book by Gabriella De Ferrari, *Gringa Latina,* contains recipes to accompany the autobiographical narrative.

9. *Giacomo Joyce* must have been an especially significant text for Barolini, because of its idiosyncratic nature and thinly disguised autobiographical subject. Barolini must have also been intrigued by its author's self-imposed exile, reminiscent of all those "displaced" figures who fascinated her, as well as of her own displacement. Joyce's creation of an Italian persona also captures Barolini's own struggle between two cultures.

10. For a discussion of the historical exclusion of Italian/American authors from the canon see Chiavola Birnbaum, "red, a little white, a lot of green, on a field of pink: a controversial design for an Italian component of a multicultural canon for the United States" in Tamburri et al. eds., *From the Margin* 282–93. See also Barolini's introduction to *The Dream Book* (3–56). For a broader critique of the canon, see Robinson and Lauter.

11. See Louise DeSalvo's memoir, *Vertigo.* Also Diane di Prima's *Memoirs of a Beatnik* and *Recollections of My Life as a Woman.*

12. Sandra Mortola Gilbert's reputation as an established critic of English literature contrasts with her reputation as a poet who writes about Italian/American topics. In an interview, Gilbert comments: "I don't feel myself to be a tremendously established poet. In fact, I'm always interested when people even know that I write poetry" (Hongo and Parke 99).

13. In the concluding line of "Ethnic Woman," after claiming that her life is written in "limitless patterns of/pasta laid out to dry" on her bed, Romano challenges the reader," "Must I teach you/to read?" (*The Wop Factor* 57).

14. See Geyh's analysis of Marylinne Robinson's *Housekeeping*. The poetry of several Italian/American women abounds with domestic imagery. For example, Gilbert's "The Dream Kitchen," "Parable of the Clothes," "Still Life: Woman Cooking" (*Emily's Bread*, 19–20, 26, 65) and "Doing Laundry" (*DB*, 349–50), Anna Bart's "Ravioli" (*DB*, 326), and Kathy Freeperson's "Italian Bread" (*DB*, 303–4).

15. It is through the consideration of what Homi K. Bhabha described as a "cultural hybridity that entertains difference without an assumed or imposed hierarchy" (4) that the multicultural discourse can shape a cultural space in which "the 'right' to signify. . . . is resourced by the power of tradition to be reinscribed through the conditions of contingency and contradictoriness that attend upon the lives of those who are 'in the minority'" (Bhabha 2).

16. Many feminist critics have rewritten literary history, embracing wider criteria that validate the specificity of female literary experience. In *Women of the Left Bank*, for example, Shari Benstock recovers the work of the women who participated in the creation of Modernism in ways that are not recognized as legitimately literary.

17. See Tamburri's two essays on *Umbertina* (one of the essays appears in Tamburri et al. eds., *From the Margin*, 357–73). See also Beranger, and Gardaphé, "Autobiography as Piecework" as well as the section on *Umbertina* in "The Later Mythic Mode: Reinventing Ethnicity through the Grandmother Figure" in *Italian Signs. American Streets*, 123–31.

18. Tina thinks of her family as "campers on the move, vagabonds with aristocratic baggage and topnotch pots and pans to drag behind them as they traveled" (*U*, 305).

19. On Lily Bart's role as an artist figure see Dittmar.

20. "Marguerite is prototypical of Lopreato's 'second-generation' (i.e., third-generation) family, which he considers to be the first 'to make the big cultural break between the old society and the new" (Tamburri, *Margin* 359). Tamburri points out that Marguerite represents the rebellious type who even through her "mode of dress and behavior at school" expresses her "contempt for imposed roles" (*Margin* 359).

21. See Rosdeitcher's interview with Sandra M. Gilbert and Susan Gubar, 23–24.

22. See Chiavola Birnbaum in Tamburri et al., *From the Margin*.

23. Italian/American women writers have creatively responded to the questions raised by multiculturalism. See Giunta, "Reinventing the Authorial/Ethnic Space: Communal Narratives in Agnes Rossi's *Split Skirt*."

24. See Giunta, "'A Song from the Ghetto': Tina De Rosa's *Paper Fish*."

25. See Giunta, "Crossing Critical Borders in Italian/American Women's Studies."

# WORKS CITED

Barolini, Helen. "Becoming a Literary Person Out of Context." *Massachusetts Review* 27 no. 2 (1986): 262–74.

——, ed. *The Dream Book: An Anthology of Writings by Italian American Women.* 1985. Reprint, New York: Shocken, 1987.

——. *Festa: Recipes and Recollections of Italian Holidays.* New York: Harcourt Brace Jovanovich, 1988.

——. "Shutting the Door on Someone." *Southwest Review* 75 no. 4 (autumn 1990): 555–61.

——. *Umbertina*. 1979. Reprint, Salem, N.H.: Ayer, 1989.

Benstock, Shari. *Women of the Left Bank: Paris 1900–1940.* Austin: University of Texas Press, 1986.

Beranger, Jean. "*Umbertina* d'Helen Barolini: Une odyssee italienne de Castagna a Cape Cod." *Annales du Centre de Recherches sur l'Amerique Anglophone* 15 (1990): 153–67.

Bhabha, Homi K. *The Location of Culture.* London: Routledge, 1994.

Bona, Mary Jo ed. *The Voices We Carry: Recent Italian/American Women's Fiction.* Montreal: Guernica, 1994.

Bryant, Dorothy. *Miss Giardino.* Berkeley, Calif.: Ata Books, 1978.

Cavallo, Diana. *A Bridge of Leaves.* New York: Atheneum, 1961.

Ciresi, Rita. *Mother Rocket: Stories.* Athens: University of Georgia, 1993.

De Ferrari, Gabriella. *Gringa Latina: A Woman of Two Worlds.* New York: Houghton Mifflin, 1995.

DeSalvo, Louise. *Casting Off.* Brighton, U.K.: Harvester, 1987.

———. *Vertigo: A Memoir.* New York: Dutton, 1996.

di Prima, Diane. *Memoirs of a Beatnik.* 1969. Reprint, San Francisco: Last Gasp of San Francisco, 1988.

———. *Recollections of My Life as a Woman.* New York: Viking, 1996.

Dittmar, Linda. "When Privilege Is No Protection: The Woman Artist in *Quicksand* and *The House of Mirth.*" *Writing the Woman Artist: Essays on Poetics, Politics and Portraiture.* Edited by Suzanne W. Jones. Pp. 133–54. Philadelphia: University of Pennsylvania Press, 1991.

Esquivel, Laura. *Like Water for Chocolate.* Translated by Carol Christensen and Thomas Christensen. New York: Doubleday, 1992.

Gardaphé, Fred L. "Autobiography as Piecework: The Writings of Helen Barolini." In *Italian Americans Celebrate Life, the Arts and Popular Culture: Selections for the 22nd Annual Conference of the American Italian Historical Association.* Edited by Paola A. Sensi Isolani and Anthony Julian Tamburri. Pp. 19–27. Staten Island: American Italian Historical Association, 1990.

———. *Italian Signs, American Streets: The Evolution of Italian/American Narrative.* Durham, N.C.: Duke University Press, 1996.

———. "Linguine and Lust: Food and Sex in Italian/American Culture." Lecture given at Union College. Schenectady, N.Y. 19 May 1995.

Geyh, Paula. "Burning Down the House? Domestic Space and Feminine Subjectivity in Marylinne Robinson's *Housekeeping.*" *Contemporary Literature* 34 (spring 1993): 103–22.

Gilbert, Sandra. *Emily's Bread.* New York: W. W. Norton, 1984.

———. *The Ghost Volcano.* New York: W. W. Norton, 1995.

——— and Susan Gubar. *The Madwoman in the Attic: The Woman Writer and the Nineteenth-Century Literary Imagination.* New Haven: Yale University Press, 1979.

Gillan, Maria Mazziotti. *Where I Come From: Selected and New Poems.* Toronto: Guernica, 1995.

Giunta, Edvige. "Crossing Critical Borders in Italian/American Women's Studies." *Proceedings of the National Conference of Italian American Studies.* New York: John D. Calandra Italian American Institute, 1995. Forthcoming.

———. Reinventing the Authorial/Ethnic Space: Communal Narratives in Agnes Rossi's *Split Skirt.*" *Literary Studies East and West. Constructions and Confrontations: Changing Representations of Women and Feminisms, East and West.* Vol. 12 (1996): 90–102.

————. "'A Song from the Ghetto': Tina De Rosa's *Paper Fish*." Afterword. Tina De Rosa. *Paper Fish*. 1980. New York: The Feminist Press, CUNY, 1996. 123–57.

Gioseffi, Daniela. *Word Wounds and Water Flowers*. *VIA* Folio 4 West Lafayette, Ind.: Bordighera, 1995.

Goldman, Anne. "'I Yam What I Yam': Cooking, Culture and Colonialism." In *De/ Colonizing the Subject: The Politics of Gender in Women's Autobiography*. Pp. 169–95. Minneapolis: University of Minnesota Press, 1992.

Hongo, Garrett and Catherine Parke. "A Conversation with Sandra M. Gilbert." *The Missouri Review* 9 no. 1 (1985–86): 89–109.

Lauter, Paul. "Race and Gender in the Shaping of the American Literary Canon: A Case from the Twenties." *Feminist Studies* 9 (fall 1983): 435–63.

Leonardi, Susan J. "Recipes for Reading: Summer Pasta, Lobster à la Riseholme, and Key Lime Pie." *PMLA* 104 no. 3 (May 1989): 340–47.

Ling, Amy. "I'm Here: An Asian American Woman's Response." In *Feminisms: An Anthology of Literary Theory and Criticism*. Edited by Robyn Warhol and Diane Price Herndl. Pp. 738–45. New Brunswick, N.J.: Rutgers University Press, 1991.

Marcus, Jane. "Still Practice, A/Wrested Alphabet: Toward a Feminist Aesthetic." In *Feminist Issues in Literary Scholarship*. Edited by Shari Benstock. Pp. 79–97. Bloomington: Indiana University Press, 1987.

————. *Virginia Woolf and the Languages of Patriarchy*. Bloomington: Indiana University Press, 1987.

Maso, Carole. *The American Woman in the Chinese Hat*. Normal, Il: Dalkey Archive Press, 1994.

Mazza, Cris. *Your Name Here:* ————. Minneapolis: Coffee House Press, 1995.

Rich, Adrienne. "When We Dead Awaken: Writing as Re-vision." In *On Lies, Secrets and Silence: Selected Prose 1966–1978*. Pp. 33–49. New York: Norton, 1979.

Robinson, Lillian. "Treason Our Text: Feminist Challenges to the Literary Canon." *Tulsa Studies in Women's Literature* 2 (spring 1983): 83–98.

Romano, Rose. "Where Is Nella Sorellanza When You Really Need Her?" In *New Explorations in Italian American Studies: Proceedings of the 25th Annual Conference of the American Italian Historical Association. Washington, D.C., November 12–14 1992*. Edited by Richard N. Juliani and Sandra P. Juliani. Pp. 147–54. Staten Island, N.Y.: American Italian Historical Association, 1994.

————. *The Wop Factor*. Brooklyn/Palermo: Malafemmina Press, 1994.

Rossi, Agnes. *Split Skirt*. New York: Random House, 1994.

Rosdeitcher, Elizabeth. "An Interview with Sandra M. Gilbert and Susan Gubar." *Critical Texts* 6 no. 1 (1988): 17–38.

Talese, Gay. "Where Are the Italian American Novelists?" *New York Times Book Review*, 14 March 1993, 1, 23, 25, 29.

Tamburri Anthony Julian, Paolo A. Giordano, and Fred L. Gardaphé, eds. *From the Margin: Writings in Italian Americana*. West Lafayette: Purdue University Press, 1991.

————. "Helen Barolini's *Umbertina*: The Gender/Ethnic Dilemma." In *Italian Americans Celebrate Life, the Arts and Popular Culture*. Fra Noi (February 1992): 29–43.

————. *To Hyphenate or Not to Hyphenate. The Italian/American Writer: An Other American*. Montreal: Guernica, 1991.

Torgovnick, Marianna De Marco. *Crossing Ocean Parkway: Readings by an Italian American Daughter.* Chicago: University of Chicago Press, 1994.

*VIA: Voices in Italian Americana.* Special Issue on Women. Guest Editor Edvige Giunta. 7, no. 2 (fall 1996).

Wharton, Edith. *The House of Mirth.* 1905. Reprint, New York: Charles Scribners, 1969.

# 7

# (Ex)Tending or Escaping Ethnicity: Don DeLillo and Italian/American Literature

## FRED L. GARDAPHÉ

> Bill was not an autobiographical novelist. You could not glean the makings of a life-shape by searching his work for clues. His sap and marrow, his soul's sharp argument might be slapped across a random page, sentence by sentence, but nowhere a word of his beginnings or places he has lived or what kind of man his father might have been.
>
> Don DeLillo, *Mao II*

Don DeLillo has kept an almost eerie silence about his Italian/American past. In the few interviews he has granted, DeLillo has given up precious little information about his Italian/American upbringing. Once, when asked why there is so little information available about his personal life, he replied, "Silence, exile and cunning, and so on. It's my nature to keep quiet about most things" (*Anything Can Happen*, 80). One interviewer tells of being handed "a business card engraved with his name and [the sentence] 'I don't want to talk about it'" (*Anything Can Happen*, 79). The "it," I believe, does not refer so much to his work, as the interviewer suggests, but to DeLillo's name and all that goes with it. In that 1979 interview, DeLillo constantly refers to his desire to "restructure reality," to "make interesting, clear, beautiful language," and to "try to advance the art" (82). These desires, combined with the pressures that many ethnic/Americans face to assimilate into mainstream American culture by erasing all but the most acceptable signs of their culture, can help us understand the absence of obvious self-referential ethnicity in all but DeLillo's earliest writing.

This absence of literary reference to DeLillo's own ethnic background both in his interviews and in his writing has been discussed

131

132    FRED L. GARDAPHÉ

by only a few critics. In his essay, "How to Read Don DeLillo,"
Daniel Aaron writes,

> I think it is worth noting that nothing in his novels suggests a suppressed
> "Italian foundation": hardly a vibration betrays an ethnic consciousness.
> His name could just as well be Don Smith or Don Brown. His ethnic
> past does not serve for him as an "intoxicant of the imagination" (Allen
> Tate's phrase) in the way New England Puritanism did for Hawthorne
> and Emily Dickinson or the experience of being Jewish did for several
> generations of Jewish writers. DeLillo can be very funny, but unlike black
> and Jewish writers who have sucked humor from their humiliations,
> there's nothing particularly "ethnic" about his dark comedy unless we
> imagine that traces of the uneasy alien or of ethnic marginality are discern-
> ible in his brand of grotesque parody, his resistance to the American
> consensus, and his sympathy and respect for the maimed, the disfigured,
> and the excluded people in his novels. (68–69)

I argue that there is, indeed, an "Italian foundation" in DeLillo's
work that becomes a vital basis of the philosophy upon which he
constructs his narratives. This Italian foundation is more obvious in
his earliest narrative. That it rarely surfaces in his later work can be
attributed to DeLillo's growing mastery of the writer's craft and his
ability to mask it by using WASP protagonists. That this masquerade
has rarely been acknowledged by critics is the result of an inability
to construct a culture-specific code for reading the Italian signs that
appear rarely, yet consistently, in nearly all his published narratives.
While Aaron has identified a visible absence of DeLillo's Italian
Americaness, and while he points to places where we might find it,
he makes no attempt to read the ethnic "traces" that can be located
in DeLillo's work. This is what I do through a discussion of the
Italian signs that appear in two of his earliest published stories and
in his first novel. I conclude my discussion of DeLillo by pointing
out the Italian signs that appear in a number of his later works and
show how awareness of these signs can generate new readings of De-
Lillo's writings.

Of the little that DeLillo has revealed about his personal life, we
know that he was born in 1936 to Italian immigrants and left his
working-class Italian/American home to attend college at Fordham,
a Catholic university in New York.[1] His early life was spent in the
urban settings of the Bronx and Philadelphia, where he most likely
experienced the type of neighborhoods he writes of in a few of his
early stories. Of his entire body of published work, only two of his
earliest stories are set in Little Italy and these are the only works that
use Italian/American subjects as protagonists.

The Italian/American signs that do emerge in DeLillo's later writing are almost always relegated to the margins of his narratives in the same way his characters are relegated (or relegate themselves) to the margins of their societies. Out of the ten novels DeLillo has published to date, seven contain characters that can be identified as Italian Americans. However, DeLillo's novels contain any number of ethnic characters who have traits that DeLillo suppresses and at times even erases (or has characters who try to erase).[2] As Frank Lentricchia reminds us, "DeLillo's heroes are usually in repulsed flight from American life" ("American Writer," 5). Indeed, there is almost always an obvious ethnic character in his narratives whose very presence undoes or attempts to undo the knot of American identity. A consistent thread that runs throughout DeLillo's work is the posing of the question, "what does it mean to be American?" It is often through the ethnic characters that DeLillo delivers his most biting social criticism. Lentricchia is one of the few critics to read the ethnic signs in DeLillo's work.[3] However, Lentricchia makes no reference to any of the Italian/American traces in DeLillo's works.[4] In his essay, "*Libra* as Postmodern Critique," Lentricchia perceptively points to DeLillo's characterization of Jack Ruby as "an escape hatch back to the earth of the robust ethnic life" (212). Ruby's private world remains "outside the subterranean world of power . . . whose only exit is blood" (213). Counter to Ruby's self, which is found in the private world of ethnicity, is Lee Harvey Oswald, whose historical self is lost in the public world of political action. America can make us all Librans, as Lentricchia suggests (210), because it enables us to constantly re-form our selves. For DeLillo, ethnicity and a loyalty to it represents the maintenance of an autonomous selfhood, to maintain a strong ethnic identity is to remain in the ghetto, on the margins of society.

DeLillo is one of the most prolific American writers of Italian descent. Indeed, an entire book could be devoted to analyzing the ethnic signs in his ten novels. To demonstrate the effect that his ethnic sign production has on his narrative development I present readings of two of his earliest short stories and of his first novel and include brief references to aspects of his later work to demonstrate the possibilities of new readings that can be generated when those narratives are contextualized within an Italian/American literary tradition.

As is the case with so many writers, the content of DeLillo's earliest stories comes from his own ethnic "home" as evidenced in stories such as "Take the 'A' Train" and "Spaghetti and Meatballs." In later stories and in his first novel, the content comes from the homes of "others." The primary home in these later works is that of the white, Anglo-Saxon Protestant American that we find as the protagonist of his first novel, *Americana* (1971). On a formalist level, DeLillo's writing moves from an experience centered to a language centered focus, from creating a single, modernist version of truth to the depiction of versions of truth. Accompanying this is a freedom to be what we want by having the ability to reinvent one's self. By not writing a typical *bildungsroman*, DeLillo, working in the tradition of High Modernism, is able to avoid the burden of history, of one's personal and social histories, which lead to a reification of tradition, the propensity for repetition and the enshrinement of forms. DeLillo, by asserting his individuality through art, moves away from the family and the identity one gains from it. This movement toward assimilation (certainly a de-centering experience) out of Little Italy and into Big America, expands the possible artistic horizons for DeLillo and enables him to fashion an escape from the bonds of loyalty often demanded by one's filiation. Free from the burden of his own personal tradition, DeLillo can more easily affiliate with the works of Joyce (who interestingly also used the Jew to represent social alienation) for example, than with those produced by such Italian/American writers such as Pietro di Donato. In the eyes of mainstream American readers, this affiliation with Joyce is by far a richer intertextual relationship. In the eyes of many marginal readers this may be read as "selling out." It is not known whether or not DeLillo was familiar with the narratives of earlier Italian/American writers, but a look at his earliest stories reveals that he shares much with them.

His earliest short stories, such as "Spaghetti and Meatballs" and "Take the 'A' Train," are heavily loaded with Italian/American geography and time and are focused on the burdens both history and family place on the Italian/American individual. These burdens, as these early stories suggest, hinder successful participation in American society. Much of DeLillo's work, as Judith Pastore has noted, is colored by his ethnic heritage, even as it reveals his movement away from it.[5] In her discussion of DeLillo's attitude toward marriage, Pastore never gets specific about how DeLillo's heritage affects or "colors" his narrative presentations. While she perceptively observes that DeLillo uses divorce to present the decay of a family centered society in America—equating the strong family with Italian/American culture, and while she points to the central role that food plays in Italian/American culture, Pastore never gets beyond these two stereotypical "ideals" of Italian/American culture in her analysis. Thus, while she is on the right track in hunting down the Italian signs in DeLillo's work, she never gets to a culture-specific reading of their significance. While many of the self-specific signs of ethnicity found in his earlier work disappear in DeLillo's later fiction, this early work can be read as rehearsal for some of the more interesting aspects found in his later work. In "Take the 'A' Train," published in 1962 when DeLillo is twenty-six years old, the author portrays the inability of a son to be a son in the traditional Italian way. Angelo Cavallo is a man on the run like the horse that his surname means in Italian. Cavallo leaves the Little Italy where he was born and raised because he is in debt to loansharks for his gambling. At the opening of the story he is told by his landlord, to whom he owes rent money, that "two men was here to looka for you. Tree times they come today" (9). Knowing that he is a dead man if he stays, Cavallo leaves his "garlic-and-oil Bronx tenement" and hits the streets of a "dead" neighborhood. He sees a subway entrance and heads underground where he plans to "stay . . . and sleep" (10). Angelo is an angel cast out of the world that was the paradise his parents had come to from Italy. It is his pride that keeps him from going to his father for help. His only alternative is to spend his time in exile, riding the New York subway system. This scene, in miniature reappears as the opening scene in DeLillo's *Libra* (3–4), his most controversial novel and the novel that as Lentricchia points out, helped to draw DeLillo out of his earlier obscurity ("American Writer," 3).

For days, Cavallo rides the underground trains, knowing that it is only a matter of time before he becomes a "bum sleeping on the subway like the bums you see all the time in bars and in the street sprawled like dead men" (10). Cavallo must "stay down . . . down in the dark" (10) where "a man could live his entire life . . . in this compact civilization beneath the earth" (14). Cavallo, in an interesting way prefigures the characterization of Lee Harvey Oswald that De-Lillo creates in *Libra*. Like Cavallo, Oswald believes, "There was nothing important out there." The language and the imagery created in this section of the story create obvious allusions both to the fall of Lucifer and to the fall of Adam and Eve. Banished from his life in Little Italy, Angelo is able to, for the first time, really think about his life there. No matter what he encounters on the trains underground, he is reminded of his life in the old neighborhood. When he awakens the next day during rush hour, the people going to work remind him that he can never return to his job as a maintenance man in a Bronx department store because his salary "wouldn't even begin to get him out of the hole" (11). The sight of a blond woman reminds him of his ex-wife Helen, the non-Italian, non-Catholic woman he met in 1945 while he was a soldier stationed in England. Angelo married her, much to the dismay of his father who makes life miserable for the couple whenever they visit. And one day, after nine years of marriage, Helen leaves him for another man. While on the train his thoughts shift back to his wedding reception, which he recalls as "a smiling snapshot of everything he wanted his life to be: a good big slow meal with the wife, then maybe some of the family coming over to play lotto or cards or something; good wife, good family, lots of laughs, lots of beer. . . . No, he would never forget that night. It was one of the few things left to remember" (12–13). Once Cavallo enters the underground, all that he has left are memories like this one. Throughout this short story, his thinking shifts in and out of consciousness of his present degraded condition and reveries of his past. In an attempt to connect his present condition to the origins of what led him to this state, he speculates that it might have all begun with his father. "Maybe his father was the beginning of sleeping on trains, and he was saving thinking about him until now, until he had something to hate him for" (15). First of all, Cavallo's father never welcomed his wife, and would taunt them both when they'd come over for dinner: "For why you come here. . . . For you mama's spaghetti because your wife no can cook? Or for your old man's money because you no can find good job? Some son, my Angelo. This country big country. Lots jobs. Even carpenter like me make so much money in one week that in old country I dropa dead joost to look at it" (15).

In this exchange DeLillo captures the failure of the son to take advantage of what father came to America for and suggests that while the meaning of America changes with each generation, the earlier generation has a tremendous influence on the way later generations live their lives. As much as Angelo fears his father, he tolerates the old man who sits "at the head of the table, the throne" (16) because he needs to borrow money from him. It is Helen who can not take the old man's criticism:

> She a stranger, that woman. She is not of us. She no belong here. Why she no give you kids? A woman is to give you kids. She no give kids, she no woman. She no even smell like woman. A bar of soap you are married to, Angelo. She is to wash hands with, that woman. Where you find her; on shelf in English supermarket? I do not make joke. You want to come-a this house anymore, you leave her home. (16)

No matter what he does, Cavallo cannot gain his father's approval. He stays away from his parents for three years and tries to forget his father, but he can't.

> How do you forget the man who is your father? This was the thing he thought about more than any other during the time of not seeing him; this was the thing he could not do, the forgetting, because too many years

went into the making of the memory, too many times of love and hate and fear and love again. This is a turning away that some people can make, he though . . . a turning away that starts when they are six and sent to some camp on some mountain every summer until they are thirteen when they are sent to something called prep school which lasts until it is time to be sent to college and then to the army and then to marriage; and this is why they never have a mother or father, only a two-headed thing called parents who are only to write letters to, never to touch. There is no love without touching and feeling, he thought. (17)

Cavallo cannot turn away from his parents, just as he can not deny his dependency on touch even when it hurts. Cavallo recalls his thirteenth birthday, when his father's present was a strange dramatization of the facts of life: "In this country they read it to their young ones from books with long words. No book I need to tell you this. Take down your pants. . . ." His father took the boy's organ in his coarse hand. It hurt. "This is what makes you man. It is not just to go to bathroom with. It is to put into woman. When you are close to woman and touch her and move your hands over her, it will get hard as fist, and burn red like torch. That is all you must know. . . . Remember this day, Angelo. It is the day of your becoming man. It is the day your father made you man (18).

Cavallo's relationship with his parents is based on a sensuality that his wife is unable to share and that she eventually begins to deny him. After she refuses to make love one night, he returns to his parents' home, and a year later Helen leaves him. The overwhelming presence of the father, the patriarch in an oppressive culture that needs no books to transmit knowledge, follows Cavallo through his marriage like a shadow and accompanies him into his flight underground. Cavallo's past tortures him into contemplating suicide, but he can't do it: "For Angelo. Kill myself and I kill them all, all forever, the ones who danced one night for me. No, he could not die that way" (22). He surfaces for a brief period and joins the Saturday night street crowd in Times Square only to realize that he cannot fit in with them. Cavallo by leaving his past finds that there is nowhere he can go; he is a man out of place above ground and so returns to the subway. The story ends on "Sunday: the end of the world" (24) with Cavallo recalling the realization he had come to long ago that he could no longer have sex with his wife "without knowing that the old man was coming in too" (25). The presence of his father is so strong that he can never run away from it. DeLillo ends the story with Cavallo on the wrong train, one that moved out of the underground and into the sunlight. Frantically, Cavallo runs through the cars toward the rear with, "an immemorial desolate shriek unbending in his chest. As he ran, his right arm was stretched forth, high in the air. The hand was open, fingers straining, as though he were trying to seize one final handful of a darkness black as the universe" (25).

DeLillo reduces Angelo to "nothing but a mind thinking" (24), a man reaching for darkness. Angelo Cavallo, literally an angel on the run, is a man who belongs nowhere, who must remain in perpetual motion, like many of the characters who permeate DeLillo's later fiction. As critic Charles Molesworth notes:

> Don DeLillo's novels begin, again and again, with a solitary man being propelled headlong in a sealed chamber. . . . Many of his characters find their destinies shaped by or expressed not only in place—a room, a hole— but in movement. One way to read a typical DeLillo agent/scene ratio is to see the encasement of young Oswald [Lee Harvey in *Libra*] as that of a bullet that will eventually smash through the dark of America's nightmare. ("Don DeLillo's" 143–44).

In running away from the burden of his father-haunted past, Angelo Cavallo is doomed to spend the rest of his life hurtling forward into the light while he gropes for the darkness that grants him the safety of anonymity in the security of belonging somewhere. But what DeLillo suggests in this story is that one can never remove the impact that the past has on the mind, no matter how one physically removes one's self from the environment that has shaped that mind. Read alongside *Libra*, "Take the 'A' Train" can help us to unmask the characters of DeLillo's later American masquerade.

In "Spaghetti and Meatballs," published in 1965, DeLillo paints a classic Italian/American still life out of a conversation between two Italian immigrant men. The story opens with Rico Santullo, age fifty-five, sitting out in the street among his belongings. He has been thrown out of his apartment and his wife has gone off to live with her cousin. Old man D'Annunzio, age seventy-nine, comes upon Santullo and the two sit and talk. D'Annunzio recounts the story of Mazzoli the chestnut man who faced a similar situation and tried to kill himself only to be saved by the police. Santullo laments the fact that there is no privacy no more: "Whatever you try to do there's a priest or a cop to save you" (245). The issue of privacy is one that will continue to appear in DeLillo's later work, but in this story Santullo is the man who has nothing, the man who sits without a home, in public among his material goods. Santullo has no plans but to "smoke my guinea stinker" (245). When lunchtime rolls around, they hail a neighborhood kid and send him to a grocery store to fetch salami, cheese, pickles, and olives. As they wait for the boy to return with their food, they discuss food, and Rico asks D'Annunzio, "What would you eat if you could only have one thing to eat for the rest of your life" (248). The old man responds with bread, cheese, and wine, "It's simple and yet it is everything. That is all I would need" (248). Rico says his choice would be spaghetti and meatballs and wine mixed with soda. Their choices of typical Italian and Italian/American meals, reveals both their unfamiliarity with the other foods of America and their dependency on their own culture to sustain them. They, like the father of Angelo Cavallo, remain trapped in their culture of origins, which, while continuing to offer people like Santullo respect even when he has been dispossessed of his home, does not prepare them for life outside their ghetto.

As they eat their lunch, Santullo remarks, "Is this happiness or is this happiness" (249). But as Santullo turns on a portable radio to soft music his attitude toward this all changes as evidenced in his remark, "But this kind of beauty never lasts" (249). D'Annunzio tells him to "Think of the present. Of now" (249), and not to worry. Santullo continues his lament and D'Annunzio urges him to, "Eat the lunch, enjoy" (249). When Santullo asks what is to become of him, D'Annunzio responds, "Is too complicated. Don't think about it. Eat, eat" (249). But Santullo doesn't take his advice. Instead he offers, "Life is politics. It's politics and no money" (249), to which D'Annunzio adds, "And being alone" (249). Through this interaction DeLillo reveals that these men are trapped by a mentality that was formed by the reality of the politics that kept them poor in Italy, which forced them out of their native country; that the difference between being poor in Italy and being poor in America is that in America the poor are alienated even from each other. Despite America's offering them a greater opportunity to earn a living, it still offers them hardly any opportunity to control their destiny. D'Annunzio, content to enjoy the moment, is juxtaposed to Santullo, stops enjoying it once the radio has been turned on.

As they talk about their lunch, D'Annunzio says it was good until the end, meaning until Santullo brought out his worries, which happens after he turns on the radio. They smoke a cigar and the old man falls asleep. The music stops and the stock market report comes on. The story ends with Santullo's smoking a cigar as he listens to the announcer summarize the market's action for that day. DeLillo offers no resolution to the story, no Maupassantian twist that points to a moral of the tale. Instead, he leaves his characters trapped at the end, like Cavallo in the subway train. The trap portrayed at the end of "Spaghetti and Meatballs" displays a great juxtaposition of the Italian man of the old world sitting still and smoking with the disembodied voice of technology in the new world proclaiming the status of the stockmarket which represents the mechanism created by those who control the forces that evicted Santullo and sent him onto the streets. Against the forces that control his destiny, Santullo can only sit still. By ending the story in this way, DeLillo is suggesting that a clash of two different cultures has occurred and that the culture of the new world has Santullo worried.

In both these stories, DeLillo characterizes the old world shaped Italians as unable to connect to the world outside their culture. They are limited in their abilities to control their own destinies and thus change their position in society. The only hope for the immigrant and the immigrant's children is to leave that world behind and forge a new identity that will enable them to thrive in a modern society. Cavallo, who escaped the labyrinth of a Little Italy, finds his only option is to remain alone in the maze of the New York subway system. Santullo, who has realized that the reality of the life he has lived is "politics and no money," is unequipped to challenge the world that comes to him from inside the radio and so must remain a listener. These Italian characters, unable to actively make their way in the world outside their ghetto, remain frozen in the past. And so, it is no wonder that DeLillo abandons the Italian prototypes of these earliest stories for those more American characters who are able to achieve the power to shape the content disseminated by the media. This then becomes the major theme of his first novel, *Americana*.

Prior to the appearance of his first novel, DeLillo published a number of other stories that reveal his movement away from his ancestral culture and toward the larger, mainstream American culture. In "Coming Sun. Mon. Tues.," published in 1966, DeLillo sketches the antics of a 1960s couple who run away from home and set up house. "In Baghdad Towers West," published in 1968, tells the tale of a man whose wife left him to "run off with an enforcer for the Mafia" (205). The man sets up house with three women, a sculptress, a model, and an actress, in an apartment complex called Baghdad Towers West. "The Uniforms," published in 1970, features a gang of terrorists who kill, among others, a group of WASP golfers; this story reappears as the opening of DeLillo's *Players* (1977), and in "In the Men's Room of the Sixteenth Century," a story that appeared the same year as his first novel, DeLillo creates an undercover cop who, disguised in drag and known on the streets as "Lady Madonna," attempts to bring law and order to the Times Square nights. These stories suggest DeLillo is moving away from his Little Italy and out onto the streets of mainstream America. Yet while he has abandoned the "foreign" protagonist, he has retained the philosophy that underscored that protagonist's presence in his work.

As Tom LeClair points out, while he does not write an obviously autobiographical first novel, he, nevertheless, is drawing from his experience as an ethnic American in his art.

> If first novels, especially family novels, are commonly autobiographical, a seemingly "natural" form, *Americana* is intentionally detached from De-Lillo's own experience as the son of Italian immigrants living in the Bronx. Rather than offering an account of ethnic assimilation, DeLillo composes a narrative of mainline "desimilation," an account originating in leisure and alienation, a life that stands for American middle-class values. (34)

The American middle-class values that DeLillo infuses in his protagonist David Bell are the very values that become goals for the ethnic who wishes to become American. By exploring the other, DeLillo presents a warning to those who would covet Americaness and attempt to remake themselves in the image and likeness of the stereotypical American. DeLillo uses the WASP protagonist to deconstruct the media made and controlled myth of the American dream. The natural move for the child of immigrants, evidenced in the works of Fante, Mangione, and di Donato, is away from the world of the parents and toward the larger world of mainstream America. As De-Lillo takes these natural steps away from the immigrant world, he turns his attention away from the past and toward the present and future. By concentrating his creative and critical sensibilities in this direction, he becomes involved in the choices and challenges that face the ethnic self faced with the dilemma of abandoning the old world of his or her ancestors for an accepted place in the new world. Unlike John Fante, DeLillo does not wholeheartedly embrace the possibilities of the American dream. More like Pietro di Donato, he scrutinizes it carefully. In a move that takes him beyond di Donato's outright rejection of the American dream by the Italian immigrant's child, DeLillo, through his American protagonists dramatizes the effects of living life the American way. He also redefines America through what he presents as the most American of protagonists. Unlike earlier novelists who present the dangers of assimilation, such as Garibaldi La-Polla (*The Grand Gennaro*, 1935), Guido D'Agostino (*Olives on the Apple Tree*, 1940), and Michael DeCapite (*No Bright Banner*, 1944), DeLillo makes the same point more effectively by using a mainstream persona. By suggesting that becoming/being American is destructive for the WASP, DeLillo implies that the idea of the ethnic's desire to assimilate into American culture is ludicrous.

LeClair perceptively identifies DeLillo's invisible ethnic background as contributing to his ability to both capture and to analyze the effects of contemporary American culture:

> Although no ethnics have central roles in DeLillo's fiction, the social distance of his upbringing contributed, I believe to his double view of American life, its promises and mythologies, an appreciation of its rich potentialities and an ironic sense of its excessive failures. Raised in a world of work and family, DeLillo is in his novels fascinated by the seductions of American leisure and privacy, the needs of entertainment and connection produced by these "achievements," the violence and secrecy that fill the voids of needs unmet. American success for DeLillo also means education in abstraction and technology, preparation for a highly mediated and digitalized life, producing . . . methods for wide understanding and for floating alienation. DeLillo's early social distance may also be partly responsible for his split attitude toward literature: his self-confessed obsession with writing and his recognition of its punishing isolation, his desire to reach a general audience and his suspicion of any entertainment's effect, his need to insert himself into yet remain alien from American life. (14)

The idea of a double view that the American ethnic brings to his experience is one that Jerre Mangione, in 1981, analyzed with particular attention to the Italian/American writer in his essay "A Double Life: The Fate of the Urban Ethnic."

> Cultural pluralism means, of course, a quest for identity, a way of resolving problems of duality. But it also has economic implications—that is, the effort of the poor trying to get their fair share of the capitalistic pie. . . . To a greater degree than their parents, the children of the immigrants were truly victims of circumstances, born to life a double life, caught between two sharply differing cultures—that which their parents had brought with them from the Old World and that which was thrust upon them outside the home. (171–72)

That DeLillo does not use Italian/American characters to make his point, does not necessarily disconnect him from an Italian/American literary tradition. In fact, his philosophy of America, as expressed through his WASP protagonist, David Bell, is as critical as any of those works produced by Italian/American writers using Italian/American characters and reflects a similar approach to the question of American identity that was employed by earlier American writers of Italian descent. DeLillo manifests this sense of a double life as a struggle between the private and the public, the mob (meaning crowds) and the individual, personal anarchy and public culture, in nearly all of his novels.[6]

*Americana* is David Bell's record of a journey in search of an

America other than New England WASP society into which he was born. Bell is very much at home in mainstream America in which the power structure is populated by WASPS. He is able to rise to a position of power at a young age because he has always fit in with mainstream Americans like those "nice people" who would come to his parents' parties, those who "had no scars or broken noses. They dressed more or less the same. They talked the same way and said the same things, and I didn't know how dull they were or that they were more or less interchangeable. I was one of them, after all. I was not a stranger among them" (189).

While the WASP world might be dull, it represents the realm of success that everyone seems to aspire to. The pressure of fitting into this WASP society is presented through a number of minor(ity) characters in the novel. At a party near the opening of the novel, the host, Quincy, entertains his guests by "telling a series of jokes about Polish janitors, Negro ministers, Jews in concentration camps and Italian women with hairy legs" (5). "Enlightenment is demonstrated by how loud one laughs. It was meant to be a liberating ethnic experience. If you were offended by the jokes in general, or sensitive to particular ones which slurred your own race or ancestry, you were not ready to be accepted into the mainstream" (6). At the same party, a non-drinking Pakistani Moslem holds a glass so that others not "think me too solemn and undeviating an individual" (8). The only people free to be individuals are WASPs like David Bell, who became a high school sports star by "being first in scoring, last in assists" (91), i.e., by being an individual.

David has been groomed for success by his father, Clinton Harkavy Bell, a success in the world of advertising, himself the son of Harkavy Bell, "one of advertising's early legends" (132) who knew how to take advantage of "a good American name" (197). David's father studies television commercials at home with his children. It is through him that David learns of the "American Dream," which requires that "You save, you finagle, you invest. You work yourself up to x-amount of dollars and if you plan well and get lucky in the market you can begin to build something for your family. That's what makes a democracy worth all the sweat and corruption. Security for your wife and children after you're gone. . . . That's your job as head of a family in a free republic" (152).

But the world his father lives in keeps him alienated from much of America. Clinton cannot understand why his train home from the office is attacked by Puerto Rican, Negro kids from Harlem and Italian kids from the south Bronx, who pelt the train with rocks. He asks, "What did we ever do to them?" His daughter answers simply,

"You moved to the suburbs" (155). What Clinton does not realize is that he represents what those kids have been conditioned to want and what they are kept from having by the very system he has helped create. As Ken Wild, David's friend from college says later in the novel, "Systems planning is the true American artform" (265). David reconstructs the key to the system of electronic media in the section of the autobiographical film he scripted that represents his father. The actor tells the camera that advertising and TV create a system that makes a person "want to change the way he lives" (270): "It moves him from first person consciousness to third person. In this country there is a universal third person, the man we all want to be. Advertising has discovered this man. It uses him to express the possibilities open to the consumer. To consume in American is not to buy; it is to dream. Advertising is the suggestion that the dream of entering the third person singular might possibly be fulfilled" (270). America's greatest achievement, as David's script reads, is that it has "exploited the limitation of dreams" (271).

Upon his graduation from a California college where he studied film, David is offered the choice of three jobs arranged by his father: two in advertising and one in the mailroom of a television network. David chooses the mailroom job to avoid "following too closely in his footsteps" (34). He leaves the mailroom in near record time and enters a work environment that is populated by employees with hyper-Anglo Saxon names like Weede Denney, Richter Janes, Quincy Willet, Grove Palmer, Jones Perkins, Reeves Chubb, and Theodore Francis Warburton. This monolithic crew of WASPs controls the programming of the network where David works. David is the creator of "Soliloquy" a network television show that "consisted very simply, of an individual appearing before the camera for an hour and telling his life story" (24). After the show is canceled without reason, David prepares to produce a documentary about the Navajo Indians. On his way out to meet the film crew, David gathers a woman sculptor, known only as Sullivan, an alcoholic Jack Wilson Pike, whom Sullivan describes "as American as a slice of apple pie with a fly defecating on it" (47), and Bobby Brand, a Vietnam Vet who is trying to eliminate the slang from his vocabulary because "It's insidious. It leads to violence. . . . I want to be colorless" (113). Bell is drawn to these people because he wants to become an artist. However, David learns that Brand is a "novelist" who has written nothing but talks of a novel-in-progress called *Coitus Interruptus*, which features a WASP ex-president who's turning into a woman. The new president is black, "hip and magical." "The theme is whatever you want it to be because appearance is all that matters, man. The whole country's going to puke blood when they read it" (205).

The group halts its westward trek in Fort Curtis, a midwest town in which David begins to make an autobiographical film using the town's residents as actors. David gets so caught up in the enterprise that he fails to meet the network's television crew and is subsequently fired. From here he begins hitchhiking west and is picked up by Clevenger, a Texas entrepreneur who drives a lavender Cadillac. Clevenger drops him off near a "sci-fi oriented" (357) community consisting of white kids who refuse to become "part of the festival of death out there" (355) and so live near eleven Apache Indians who are, "exiles from an Apache tribe, who refused to become ranchers like the rest of their people" (355). The group has no idea what the Indians do other than play poker. The group's founder is a tall white man with blue hair called The Incredible Shrinking Man, who describes their philosophy as conservative: "We want to cleave to the old things. The land. The customs. The words. The ideas. Unfortunately wilderness will soon be nothing but a memory. Then the saucers will land and our children will be forced to embrace the new technology" (358). Clevenger returns to pick up David and carry him back to civilization. David is offered a job test-driving tires for Clevenger, whose company organized so that "the Mexicans did most of the driving, the blacks most of the tire changing, the whites most of the balancing and measuring . . ." (370). David tells him he wants to drive and change tires and Clevenger just looks at him "in anger at all dumb-ass northern guilt and innocence" (370). David leaves Texas after witnessing a drunken orgy performed by Clevenger and two of his white assistants with three Mexican women. After a series of strange rides he uses his American Express card to fly back to New York.

*Americana* is a novel about language and its role in representation that on the one hand conditions as it creates consumers and on the other hand, when analyzed carefully can be used to deconstruct ruling myths that create, organize, and control mass realities. The same country that makes the David Bells enables him to remake himself in the likeness of those who are different. In this novel, DeLillo may have abandoned the use of Italian/American characters to talk about such themes as alienation, difference, relationship to family, and history, but he has simply found a different way of presenting the same issues he worked with in those early stories. In *Americana* we find two representations of Italian Americans who, while both minor characters, set up ways of being that challenge the WASP experience in David's America. The first is Tommy Valerio, Bell's best friend, whose "mother would squeeze my cheeks and rub her knuckles on my head." This touching behavior "embarrasses" him and makes him uncomfortable around them so that he "soon found excuses to stay away" (134). Later, when David tries to contact him, he learns that Tommy was killed in the Viet Nam War and that his family has accepted the death and are impressed by a letter the president sent to Tommy's mother. Tommy introduces David to the police chief's daughter, "who was available for experiments of all kinds" (134). The two "take turns" with her in the backseat of Tommy's car. Tommy appears in one other scene in which he hits fly balls for David. The experience, David recalls, was one of being "nobody. I was instinct and speed and a memory that extended back for no more than seconds. That was all" (199). At the end of the novel, a similar scene occurs in which David plays catch with an Indian boy, an experience of which he says "I could not recall feeling this good in many years" (359).

The second representation of an Italian American comes to us in Arondella, a mysterious character who could be a racketeer (the likes of which Richard Conte plays in the film *Cry of the City*), with whom his sister runs away from home. Arondella, as Mary tells David, is a hit man whom she met in Boston. She is running off with him because "there are different kinds of death. . . . And I prefer that kind, his kind, to the death I've been fighting all my life" (163). Mary encourages David to leave home because the place is "haunted" and their mother, who is deathly ill, will "try to take you with her" (164). Arondella is recreated in David's autobiographical film through Mary, who is played by Carol Deming, a local Fort Curtis woman. His sense of insult was overwhelming.

> If someone used an obscene word in my presence, he demanded an immediate apology. He always got it, of course, his reputation being what it was. He was prepared to kill, quite literally to kill, to avenge the honor of someone he loved. He was always swearing on his mother's grave. In his company of men, there was no great promise or proof of honor than to swear on your mother's grave. . . . He told me about a friend of his called Mother Cabrini. Cabrini got a lot of mileage out of his mother's grave until it was learned that his mother was not dead. Telling this, he managed to be both outraged and amused. They were all children, of course, but not in the same way the rest of us are children. We have learned not to be afraid of the dark, but we've forgotten that darkness means death. They haven't forgotten this. They are still in the hills of Sicily or Corsica, wherever they came from. They obey their mothers. They don't go into a dark cellar without expecting to be strangled by a zombie. They bless themselves constantly. And us, what do we do? We

watch television and play Scrabble. So there it is, children of light and darkness. (278)

What the two have in common, despite their different upbringing, is the "instinct that death is without meaning unless it is met violently" (280). Arondella, represents a world that is dark and full of superstition, an in-your-face world that knows how to deal with death and thus with life. Through both these Italian/American characters, David creates identities that serve as alternatives to his WASP world. They represent the sensual "other" whom David moves toward as he "de-similates." These characters, like the other non-WASPS that David encounters, offer alternative philosophies. Like the Indian Black Knife who Sullivan speaks of, Dr. Hiroshi Oh, David's college professor of Zen, and the Mediterranean woman he and Brand run into at an A&P (206–7), they represent salvation to the systemized American. As Sullivan says, "America can be saved only by what it is trying to destroy" (256).

By the end of the novel, David believes that by turning away from corporate America and toward art he has achieved his ultimate goal of becoming "an artist as I believed them to be, an individual willing to deal in the complexities of truth. I was most successful. I ended in silence and darkness, sitting still, a maker of objects that imitate my predilection" (347). Thus, the solution for Bell lies in creating art and through the process recreating a self that can be separated from the past. DeLillo, as we will see in Sorrentino, sees becoming an artist as a way out of the history that has attempted to shape his protagonist's personality.

Signs of *italianità* and references to identification with other cultures surface in some way in nearly all of DeLillo's later work, more often than not it is through minor characters. In *Great Jones Street* there's a writer named Carmela Bevilacqua, and Azarian, who is into soul music and the Black experience (a version of Norman Mailer's "white nigger"?). In *Ratner's Star* there are the characters Consagra, Lepro, who uses a word that means both "why" and "because" (which the Italian word *perchè* does), and Lo Quadro. In *Running Dog* there is a cop named Del Bravo and the Talerico brothers: Paul and Vinny the Eye, who as members of organized crime belong to families and "Families know where they belong" (220). This identification of Italians with families and the CIA with organization replicates the dilemma presented in *Americana* of the system versus the family. In *The Names*, Volterra is a artist/filmmaker who serves as the protagonist's alter-ego. In *White Noise* there's Alfonse "Fast Food" Stompanato, the head of a college's Popular Culture department and Grappa, both of whom represent assimilated Italian Americans. In *Libra* there's the mafioso Carmine Latta and again DeLillo refers to the CIA as the company, and the Mafia as the family. DeLillo uses these minor characters, who often appear more as caricatures, as foils against which an identity is created for his protagonist. However, by the time we reach his latest novel, *Mao II*, while the Italian American signs seem to have disappeared altogether, he continues to present the struggle between the private and the public, the individual and collective life, as the great challenge that faces every American.

In much of DeLillo's writing there is reference to the breakdown of family and the subsequent cultural fragmentation that forces people to forge identities out of materials presented to them from outside the family. The Italian American is able to become a cultural chameleon outside the family, affiliating with whatever he or she chooses.[7] In terms of Italian American culture, DeLillo's abandonment of the Italian American as a subject of his writing suggests the decline of a distinct *italianità* that has assimilated into the larger American culture that in the Vichian scheme of nationalism is in decay; it is a culture that leads nearly all of his protagonists to search for a better life in the margins of society. Though DeLillo has successfully left the old world and the myths they have created in the new world (for as Lentricchia says, "Writers in DeLillo's tradition have too much ambition to stay home" ["American Writer" 2]), his departure is guided, if not haunted, by proverbs such as *chi lascia la via vecchia sa quello che lascia ma non sa quello che trova* (Who leaves the old way for the new, knows what is left behind but not what lies ahead), and he may belong more to the old world than one might think, especially when we recall some of the proverbs that guided public behavior in southern Italian culture: *A chi dici il tuo segreto, doni la tua libertà* (To whom you tell a secret, you give your freedom); *Di il fatto tuo, e lascia far il fatto tuo* (Tell everyone your business and the devil will do it); *Odi, vedi e taci se vuoi viver in pace* (Listen, watch and keep quiet if you wish to live in peace). When looked at in this light DeLillo's writing is perhaps more closely aligned with the traditional southern Italian idea of keeping one's personal life to one's self, an idea that Dante proposes when he writes in his *Convivio* that speaking of the self is improper.[8] Strategically, DeLillo avoids breaking a personal and an ancestral *omertà* by employing the narrative strategy of speaking through the persona of the other, by creating a masquerade in which his ethnicity can enter the mainstream without detection. Though DeLillo has successfully avoided being identified as an "ethnic writer," he may belong more to the old world than one might think, especially when we read his work in the context of southern Italian culture. When looked at in this light, the work of Don DeLillo is quite possibly extending the literary tradition of Italian American culture into a postmodern world.

## NOTES

An earlier version of this essay appeared in my book, *Italian Signs, American Streets*.

1. Author Giose Rimanelli has discovered that DeLillo's parents come from Montagano, a small town near Casacalenda (Rimanelli's home town) in the region of Molise. Rimanelli believes that DeLillo's surname was originally DiLillo and was most likely changed upon DeLillo's parents' entry into the United States.

2. While his second novel, *Endzone*, lacks an identifiable Italian American presence, there is a strong ethnic presence in Anatole Bloomberg, a Jew who believes that "History is guilt" (45) and therefore attempts to "unjew" himself. Bloomberg describes this process—really a recipe for assimilation, which requires (1) geographic relocation to "a place where there aren't any Jews," (2) the elimination of linguistic markers of ethnicity, and (3) acquiring a new way of thinking (46). Later, Bloomberg defends this process by saying:

> I don't want to hear a word about the value of one's heritage. I am a twentieth-century individual. I am working myself up to a point where I can exist beyond guilt, beyond blood, beyond the ridiculous past. Thank goodness for America. . . . I reject heritage, background, tradition and birthright. These things merely slow the progress of the human race. They result in war and insanity. (77)

3. For an interesting reading of DeLillo's work: Judith Pastore's "Marriage American Style: Don DeLillo's Domestic Satire" and "Pirandello's Influence on American Writers: Don DeLillo's *The Day Room*."

4. What Lentricchia has been working toward in his theory and practice of American literary criticism, is precisely what DeLillo does with American literature, that is, he keeps "readers from gliding into the comfortable sentiment that the real problems of the human race have always been about what they are today" ("American Writer," 6). For a more detailed analysis of the role *italianità* plays in the development and practice of the cultural criticism of Frank Lentricchia and for a discussion of Lentricchia's reading of DeLillo, see my article "(In)visibility: Cultural Representation in the Criticism of Frank Lentricchia."

5. As Pastore notes:

> If we look at what DeLillo is saying about marriage and divorce American style, we find that beneath his sophisticated postmodern format, his satiric vision is fairly conventional, moving away certainly from his Italian-American, Catholic origins, but still retaining enough of that heritage to color his presentation. ("Marriage American Style," 2)

6. This is especially the case with *Mao II*, the novel that earned DeLillo the prestigious Pen/Faulkner award in 1992.

7. For a more detailed analysis of DeLillo's use of the family in his fiction see, Judith Pastore's "Marriage American Style."

8. "The established canons of rhetoric forbid anyone to speak of himself except for some compelling reason. The ground of this prohibition is that one cannot speak

of someone without either praising or blaming him, and to let either of these pass one's lips in regard to oneself would be to show a want of urbanity" (*The Banquet* 14).

# WORKS CITED

Aaron, Daniel. "How to Read Don DeLillo." In *Introducing Don DeLillo*. Edited by Frank Lentricchia. pp. 67–81. Durham, NC: Duke University Press, 1991.

Aligheri, Dante. *The Banquet*. Translated by Christopher Ryan. Saratoga, Calif.: Anima Libri, 1989.

DeLillo, Don. *Americana*. 1971. New York: Penguin, 1989.

———. "Baghdad Towers West." *Epoch* 17 (1968): 195–217.

———. "Coming Sun. Mon. Tues." *The Kenyon Review* 28, no. 3 (June 1966): 378–94.

———. *End Zone*. 1972. New York: Penguin, 1986.

———. *Great Jones Street*. New York: Houghton Mifflin, 1973.

———. "In the Men's Room of the Sixteenth Century." *Esquire* 76, no. 6 (December 1971): 174 + .

———. *Libra*. New York: Viking, 1988.

———. *Mao II*. New York: Penguin, 1991.

———. *Pafko at the Wall*. *Harper's* (October 1992): 35–70.

———. *Players*. New York: Alfred A. Knopf, 1977.

———. *Ratner's Star*. New York: Houghton Mifflin, 1976.

———. "Spaghetti and Meatballs." *Epoch* 14 (1965): 244–50.

———. "Take the 'A' Train." *Epoch* 12 (1962): 9–25.

Gardaphé, Fred L. "(In)visibility: Cultural Representation in the Criticism of Frank Lentricchia." *Differentia* 6–7 (spring–autumn 1994): 201–18.

———. *Italian Signs, American Streets: The Evolution of Italian American Narrative*. Durham, N.C.: Duke University Press, 1996.

———. "Visibility or Invisibility: The Postmodern Prerogative in the Italian American Narrative." *Almanacco* 2, no. 1 (primavera 1992): 24–33.

Gardaphé, Fred L. Anthony J. Tamburri and Paul Giordano. "Introduction." *From the Margin: Writings in Italian Americana*. pp. 1–11. West Lafayette, Ind: Purdue University Press, 1991.

LeClair, Tom. *In the Loop: Don DeLillo and the Systems Novel*. Champaign: University of Illinois Press, 1987.

LeClair, Tom, and Larry McCaffery. "An Interview with Don DeLillo." In *Anything Can Happen*. Pp. 80–90. Urbana, Il: University of Illinois Press, 1983.

Lentricchia, Frank. "The American Writer as Bad Citizen." In *Introducing Don DeLillo*. Edited by Frank Lentricchia. Pp. 1–6. Durham, N.C.: Duke University Press, 1991.

———. "Introduction." *New Essays on White Noise*. Edited by Frank Lentricchia. Pp. 1–14. New York: Cambridge University Press, 1991.

———. "*Libra* as Postmodern Critique." In *Introducing Don DeLillo*. Edited by Frank Lentricchia. Pp. 193–215. Durham, N.C.: Duke University Press, 1991.

———. "Tales of the Electronic Tribe. In *New Essays on White Noise*. Edited by Frank Lentricchia. Pp. 87–113. New York: Cambridge University Press, 1991.

Molesworth, Charles. "Don DeLillo's Perfect Starry Night." In *Introducing Don DeLillo.* Edited by Frank Lentricchia. Pp. 143–56. Durham: Duke University Press, 1991.

Pastore, Judith Laurence. "Marriage American Style: Don DeLillo's Domestic Satire." *Voices in Italian Americana* 1, no. 2 (1990): 1–19.

———. "Pirandello's Influence on American Writers: Don DeLillo's *The Day Room.*" *Italian Culture* 8 (1990): 431–47.

Tamburri, Anthony Julian, Paolo A. Giordano, and Fred L. Gardaphé, eds. *From the Margin: Writings in Italian Americana.* West Lafayette, Ind.: Purdue University Press, 1991.

# 8

# Sentences of Self and Blood and Sea: The Poetry of Sandra M. Gilbert

## DIANE RAPTOSH

In "A Fine White Flying Myth," an essay in *Shakespeare's Sisters—Feminist Essays on Women Poets,* Sandra M. Gilbert as critic poses the following question: "How does a woman reconcile the exigencies of the species—her desire for statis, her sense of ancestry, her devotion to the house in which she has lived—with the urgencies of her own self?"[1] Gilbert sees as the paradox of Plath's life (and by extension that of any woman's life) and of the Plath myth that "even as she longs for the freedom of flight, she fears the risks of freedom—the simultaneous reactivation and disintegration of the past it implies."[2] That these questions bear direct critical urgency in relation to Plath cannot be denied. Helen Barolini took up some of these same questions as well in an introductory exposé on Gilbert in *The Dream Book—An Anthology of Writings by Italian American Women* for their representational usefulness in that context;[3] indeed, the statement posits the terms of what is for many Italian/American women writers a linguistic, aesthetic, and psychic bind. These critical excerpts, provocative in their varied general applications, are especially so for the light they cast on Gilbert's own poems.

A majority of Gilbert's poems in her first three collections (*In the Fourth World, Emily's Bread,* and *Blood Pressure*) are attempts at reconciliation of just such urgencies. In these works, women's reckonings with the concept of *stasis* in all its (and her own) derivative possibilities—*standing, stoppage, station*—take place. In their unravelings of these issues, Gilbert's poems necessarily come to terms (or at least attempt to) with stopping's opposite: leaving, flying, fleeing, call it what you will. We find written into these poems impulses of women who, feeling trapped in scripts they did not write, in homes and other constructs they did not build, looking inward and outside themselves for routes to freer lives. Often the women speaking through these poems seek to live a quest plot much the same way as men's stories and poems have permitted.[4] The way the poet most often "lights out" is when she decides to put her self's exigencies before those of species and house (though we will find they are on the most fundamental— and paradoxical—level, inextricable, one from the next). This brand of fleeing most often involves tapping topographical and ancestral roots. The strongest poems in the collections look hard and unflinch-ingly at what and who is there. The topography is usually mountain-ous: ranges out of southern California and southern Italy. At times the terrain is that of the female body, turned to, again, with the end in mind (or in body) of tapping the depths of self. Ancestors, almost without fail Italian or Italian American, are often brought to full view as well. Such figures serve to both mirror and distort the self; by turns, they assuage and haunt, denounce and withdraw. And return. The poems in the first section of her first collection, *In the Fourth World*, attend to these issues of women's mixed longings and loyalties. Many of the poems here take as their setting the interior of a house. The speaker in most of the poems preoccupies herself with emerging from the four walls and, thereby, presumably, becoming closer to a self unsheathed. This close to unencumbered self is often bodied forth, in this book anyway, in some strangely alluring, often anony-mous figure at least a few times removed from the speaker herself. This interior but exteriorized being makes its first major appearance in a poem entitled "The Intruder." Initially, we find,

> . . . he's only a breath in the dark,
> measuring himself out like a heartbeat,
> discreet as the blood that flows and coils in places
> we never bother to remember.

$$(8)$$

But of course the poet must and does remember, *re-member*. The speaker is herself a bit discreet in the poems in this first section; she tends to keep a distance from both the face and place she needs to meet. But only for a while. As the darkness deepens and the self widens to embrace the "intruder" self and allows herself to be strengthened by that presence, the speaker steps into the night and probes the dark more assiduously. Doing so, she continues trying to tap the self, in Plathean fashion, clean to its most ferocious, most tenacious roots. In the poem just after "The Intruder," the poet finds she is bolstered by such an interloping presence. She walks into the night and goes through the following motions of body and mind:

I crouch like a bald rock at the edge of the meadow,
I become a naked coat, a shell,
I play dead.

Will they find me in the morning, seething with flies?
The great owl swoops by, hooting.
I shiver in the grass, I kiss cold stones.

Between cracks in the ground I see
the deep earth cellar where
fierce roots move.

(9)

The poet hovers over such fierce early burgeonings awhile, still in search of some root, of some rooted self. Again, the poet's search of the stuff of earth storehouses has as its end a locale in which place and pulse merge, a place paradoxically both real and mythical. As is true of the figures in "The Intruder," those in "The Fear of the Night" come forth as emblematic of blood-link alongside, if not simultaneously within, images of the land. In one of the last poems in the first section of *In the Fourth World*, the poet yet another time invokes the figure of the highly charged, affective, interloping self—this time in the persons of Frank Costello and others of his ilk:

. . . eating spaghetti in a cell at San Quentin,
Lucky Luciano mixing up a mess of bullets and
Al Capone baking a sawed-off shotgun into a
huge lasagna—
                    are you my uncles, my
only uncles?

          O Mafiosi,
bad uncles of the barren
cliffs of Sicily—was it only you
that they transported in barrels
like pure olive oil across the Atlantic?
. . . . . . . . . . . . .
[O]nly half a dozen Puritan millionaires stood on the
    wharf,
in the wind colder than the impossible snows of the
    Abruzzi,
ready with country clubs and dynamos

to grind the organs out of you.

(22)

In this piece too we have a couple of recurring components at work: a self or selves enclosed (this time in prison) and references to southern Italian mountainsides. And implicit in the last two stanzas is the suggestion that there exists some vestige of purity, like that of pure olive oil, in these brazen-seeming Mafiosi. Borne of some Sicilian precipice, this boldness looks preferable to the Puritan millionaires' apparent code of respectability. The Puritan figure can be seen as having the same effect on the beings in the poem as do the four walls of the house in poems earlier. The religious millionaires are attempting to impose some framework of decorum on a pair of selves impelled largely by bellows of tissue and blood.

Again we have the poet's attempt at getting at a self that has sloughed a bulk of societal expectations—like the figure of the flowing and coiled intruder, this time in the skin of the "bad uncles." These figures embody a "badness" the poet seems to be emboldened by. Such representatives of the untrammeled self serve as nothing less than figures of desire.

As we have seen before, such figures are, more often than not, inseparable from the terrain from which they've sprung. With the poem "1/1/76" we step into a "rotten night in N.Y." The air is thick as Times Square prepares to ring in the bicentennial New Year:

> . . . the house of misrule! the sacred pipes erect!—
>
> till the egg bursts
> and the Bicentennial New Year comes with screams:
> 200 dead Indians, 200 Christs in concrete,
> 200 slanty-eyed skulls in the Rockies
>
> all rising inscrutable to say—to say—
> well, what is there to say?—
> and on the California coast gulls spin and squeal,
> sentinels over Drake's Bay,
>
> where the great Queen's ship once hung
> shining and unself-conscious as a golden egg.

(23)

The Indians, the Japanese, the Chinese—all figures on the transcendent—are nearly indistinguishable from the earth from which they rise. And the elastic syntax here allows the spirits of these dead, in conjunction with the coast gulls, to live as sentinels. They are those who keep guard, to be sure, but perhaps more importantly these figures act as those who watch, who perceive, as those who've dropped to the root of the verb beneath the sentinels: *to feel*.

The first section of *In the Fourth World* ends with a poem entitled "Shell Collecting." The setting is Black Point, again off the California

coast. We find here cliffs reminiscent of those from which blossomed
the "bad" Sicilian uncles. We find wild, at times bodiless presences,
half visible extrusions and bald beings seeking a place adjacent to
rock:

> On the cliff the raw grass
> winds around itself,
> tangling, untangling.
> In the gray sea a thousand
> storms are drowning.
>
> Beside a cave at water's edge I find
> an immense sea anemone,
> almost invisible, packed in sand.
> It quivers to the touch.
> It is so naked I want to kill it.
>
> Stirring still water with a stick,
> I see, now, everywhere
> anemones without shells
> clinging to sand and rock,
> silent, enigmatic, . . .

(24)

The speaker here is moved and maddened by what seems to be the
supersentience of the stuff and lives in the natural world. What most
allures in these stanzas in the mood of exquisite misrule in combina-
tion with what is the ultimate susceptibility of presences in the natural
world. It is as though the speaker here is striving to merge with both
wind and windblown, in a manner resembling the Romantics.

It is not surprising that in the poet's stirrings of self (with a stick!),
the self that surfaces is informed at varying levels by Italian and
Italian American ancestry. Nor is it surprising that the poet should
turn to actual, invented, and reinvented images suggestive of her
mother's place of birth, Sicily. These images often emerge in craggy
and agonizing forms, like the "tough little kernels [that] enter your
bloodstream" (from "Five Meditations on One Who Is Dead"). Sift-
ing through such stuff the poet begins to come to terms with blood
presences—aspects and reflections of the self.

In the second section (entitled "Voices") of *In the Fourth World*, the
poet speaks in the lucidly defined characterization of "Grandmother."
The poem is remarkable for the multileveled mergings that take place,
foremost among which is physiognomy with physical surroundings.
I quote the poem in full:

Each night I see myself in the white
mirror of sleep—

(is it myself
I see?)

—a face vast and wrinkled as the sea
at evening,

a vague face
withdrawing. . . .

Other faces, small and white and round as
peeled apples

fall from the long dark
face I wear:

my round grandchildren!
One is taking my nose away,

another my lips, a third my cheeks. . . .
In the morning

I find they've moved to California
with all my features intact

And only my eyes are left in
a face that is no longer mine.

                                                                (31)

What this recounting amounts to is the step-by-step "Californiaca-tion"/effacement of the self, a nullification of ancestry.

The third section of the book (titled "The Dream Work") in which each poem appears in the form of poetic reverie or fable) abounds with topographical imagery. Still more slopes and precipices appear alongside and at times suffuse with imagery of kin and body. In "The Milk Dream," for example, we find

My breasts are full of milk.
They tower above me like peaked rocks
(though no one sucks).
Warily I touch the left nipple.
It's red as a strawberry, feels like rubber,
but rises from a white and stony
promontory.
This is the Not-Me

I think (calm, philosophical).
This hard white wall conceals some valley
tough with its own life.

Yet I long to enter,
to walk into the center of these mountains,
to find the little secret spring where warm milk wells,
not me but mine.

I rise, I start on the journey.
. . . . . . . . .
The air is cold near the peaks.
There are few houses.
Already the sun has set
and blue winds flow by like tides.
Everywhere doors are closed,
windows made fast for the night.
All closed, all locked against me.

Lonely, I camp among the rocks
at the edge of my body.

(44)

Once more the poet attempts to have at the "I" within and without
the hard, white wall; to do so she walks wistfully into the center of
"these mountains," her breasts. And once more the poet attempts to
reconcile the seemingly oppositional forces of statis with flight. In her
consciousness she climbs from her own familiar house of flesh, from
the state of motherhood, from the current state of the self, with the
goal of entering the very tough and edgy quick of things. She aims
to find the "secret spring," to walk past "me" to find "mine." This
state of "mine-in-me" she discovers in ancestry. It is the same state
that Hélène Cixous describes as that which is got to

> through the same opening that is her danger[.] [S]he comes out of herself
> to go to the other, a traveler in unexplored places; she does not refuse,
> she approaches, not to do away with the space between, but to see it, to
> experience what she is not, what she is, what she can be.[5]

Mountains and their preternatural interiors serve to embody similar
states of fusion and potentiality. So, too, do these peaks appear in the
form of juttings and pulsations in the vicinity of heart. In the surreal
poem "The Dream of the Red Chamber," the heart figures as the
poet's actual living room:

> It is the chamber in which I live:
> thick red-brown walls, walls the color of liver

and a system of pumps and valves
I'm too simple to understand.
I sit on an oriental rug in the middle of my heart.
The rug has beautiful markings, red and brown,
like the shell of a rare turtle.
I sit cross-legged and meditate, while
the walls of my heart say *doom-om, doom-om.*

But the beating of my heart distracts me.
Will this motion never stop? This dull symmetry
(first *doom,* then *om*), this bloody earthquaking?
I dream of calm: the cold grey plush of the brain,
the dry white crevices of the spine.

Days pass as I sit in my heart,
bored and alone, wondering how to get out.

(46)

Similar tensions ripple here as in poems before: The heart's unrelenting beat admonishing *move on*; the potentially ruinous ennui of domestic life, even when oriental and exotic; the ever-present hankering for a toehold somewhere else—in this case perhaps one of the steepest pitches of all: the axis of the central nervous system.

The sense of impending doom present in the above poem increases as the book nears its end (there are a few exceptions). The final poem in the dream series, "The Grandmother Dream," seems especially suffused with that mood. Here the poet finds her dead Sicilian grandmother, a midwife whom she's never met, sitting at the edge of her bed. The language the grandmother speaks is "a tangled river of Italian: / her Sicilian words flow out like dark fish, slippery and cold / her words stare out at me with blank eyes." Are these eyes what are left of the grandmother we heard from earlier whose flesh and bones and uprooted darkness too few had bothered to remember? The poet seems at this point to want to meet herself at the ancestral river.

Nevertheless, here, as before, the poet ends up trapped. In her bedroom she watches her grandmother/midwife pluck tools from her black bag: "heavy silver instruments / polished—misshapen, peculiar— / like the knobs of an invisible door." The door, invisible, beckons like some inscrutable intruder. Note, though, that the poet does not yet enter the room onto which the door opens; the poet here has not accepted and assimilated what is her own.

Nor does she completely see her way clear in the final section of the work, also titled "In the Fourth World." Here, domestic necessities are the norm: the homelife she attends to with care and the overall busy-ness of one called to the duties of home distract the self of these poems to such a degree that she can no longer even sneak off, sit cross-legged and muse. If the home is indeed a haven in a heartless world, then the self in one particular poem, "Doing Laundry," has decided to go about her duties as pure heart:

> I pound and I pound
> the shirts disappear
> the brassieres dissolve to nothingness
>
> I am a heart doing laundry
> and I beat and I pound
> until I no longer remember
> the color of dirt.

(59)

All work and no play makes this heart a dull thud.

In Gilbert's next collection, *Emily's Bread,* the poems look hard at women's place, which notion here has underlying it considerations of *terrain* and *estate;* among the voices speaking out are the two pioneering Emilys—Dickinson and Bronte. The poems speak to the hopes and hopelessness of the domestic woman's life, who takes her place at the kitchen table, at the writing desk and at points in between. Often the senses of beatitude and demonism to be had in such places fuse, as in a poem like "The Dream Kitchen." In this poem, where all seems redolent of happy homelife, an unidentified "she," whose eyes glowing "pale as radium," seems to set things slightly off:

> . . . "Well?"
>             and I followed her
> through the tall door,
> and the dream kitchen
>
> with its pulsing ovens
> rose round us like a mountain range, . . .

(19)

The stark, irradiated eyes recall again the penetrating gaze of the poet's Grandmother in a couple of earlier poems.

Still, the overriding tone of this as well of most of the other poems in this collection suggest that there is perhaps less doom and more Ohm in the home than we might have expected in *In the Fourth World.* For example, later in the above poem, we find that the dream kitchen "rocked us, stroked us, / steaming with syrups and creams." This poem also looks ahead to another piece that relies for its effectiveness again on mirror imaging. Entitled "Evening/Mirror/Poem," the poem ushers in

Evening. Drop by drop of darkness,
the empty hall drains into the mirror

as if misty lips were sucking it in,
or as if the cold glass were really a cliff edge

over which every image must fall
in a sweet slow motion tumble—

. . . [until]

Midnight. Darkness. The pure
threads shred, the colors falter:

and the drowned eyes of the weaver
stare into the space where the mirror was, . . .

(25)

Particularly notable in this and other poems in this collection are pieces that exemplify the ways in which the exigencies of self and house and species merge; we need really only refer to the title of the above poem, in which merge cliff and looking glass and poet. Also the poems entice for their brand of a Keatsian "motionless flight"; more often than not fleeing becomes just another way of returning home. For instance, in part four of a four-part series entitled "Her House," the poet calls out

Dear God! One day she opened
the pantry door and saw
the sea beating among the cupboards,
its webs of brine tangled
like fine white linen
where the cups once were.

(28)

And in another poem similar unions take place, this time of the poet's self with her long-lost would-be sister from the hills of Tuscany. This sister's patronymic, nevertheless, means *ennui*. Entitled "Anna La Noia," the poem is quoted here in full:

She was the sister I never had,
a pale Italian girl from the dry, olive-gray
hills of Tuscany—
    *Anna La Noia*
    *Anna Ennui*
with eyes like seeds
focusing hard and sharp
on a darkness I couldn't see.

At dawn she appeared
in a white shift like a novice, a nurse's aide
beside my bed:
    high milkless breasts, high child's voice,
    cool skin, indifferent wrists. . . .

We gossiped in the early heat,
made up old stories, poems, lies:
in the half-light
that leaked around the shutters
she held out a shining hand—

    *Anna La Noia*
    *Anna Ennui.* . . .
I pressed my lips against small
knuckles cold as pebbles.

What was it I remembered then?
Now, what have I forgotten?

All morning, straying, whispering
under the hard green olives
she led me on:
    her tender neck, her rosy vulnerable
    schoolgirl knees!

At noon in the simmering vineyard
we embraced,
we became one woman.

                                                    (50–51)

Some quite remarkable doublings take place here: The speaker satisfies her wish to rove, she strays and unites herself within the rosy girl.
What is more, she somewhat paradoxically celebrates domestic ennui.

Again in another poem this vision of merging comes up. The poet
returns to Black Point Beach. Someone beckons her in:

    She said, *The Door is open.*
    She said, *You can go through.*

    Sitting on the hot stairs, half down to the beach,
    I see it for a moment—

    No door at all but a wide
    bright space, and beyond it

    the place where something lives
    that I must name:

                    two steep
arms of land relinquishing

a giant motion, a drumming and fretting
that leaps, shines, spends itself

in halos of desire
that still are never spent, never done

shining or fretting
at the cliffs that

try to give them up
but can't.

                                                              (98)

In her third book Gilbert gives fullest rein yet to the visceral, adventuresome streak that has brought these women thus far. It is in *Blood Pressure* that the speaker comes closest to arriving at this "place" where something lives that must be named. Here, the muse who returns (intrudes) is, the poet says, "part of the bargain. / He'd always be there like a blood relative, / a taciturn uncle or cousin, / if you didn't love him." In a number of some of the most finely wrought poems yet, the poet faces such places and kin squarely. She does so in one titled "In the Golden *Sala*":

Son of Sicilian hillsides,
heat of poppies opening like fierce
boutonniéres of Apollo,
light of Agrigento, fretting the sea and the seaside
    cliffs—
light of the golden *sala*,
the great *sala* of the ruined *palazzo*
where my Sicilian grandmother and her nine children
camped outside Palermo.

                                                              (53)

The poet goes directly to the source, the Sicilian hill itself, and she surveys it in all its difficult resplendence. The poppies are fierce. The light (of Agrigento) frets the sea and cliffs in a multitude of senses of that verb; the light can be seen as devouring, gnawing, making rough; it can be seen as being disturbing or vexing. We have also a couple of other senses of "fret" to bear in mind as well, which denotations involve ornamenting with interlacing lines or furnishing with frets— the lateral ridges (originally rings of gut) on a guitar's fingerboard. The poet looks long and unflinchingly at this *sala* and sees the place for all its plays of light and terrors. I'll jump now to the last stanza:

When a new baby slid out in a splash of water
he must have looked up, dazed,
toward the black eyes of the midwife
and the black eyes of the midwife's nine blackhaired
  children
would have looked quizzically down,
as if from a high cliff by the sea
hot and yellow with new poppies.

(54)

This stanza as well evidences the poet's looking hard and clearly. And though she's at least one lifetime removed from the would-have-been birth, she sizes up the event with a set of eyes new as the baby's themselves. And they won't turn away; this time the eyes are unafraid of the black eyes of the grandmother/midwife. This seeming fearlessness insinuates itself at almost every level imaginable here. Syntactically the two stanzas are revealing for the way they employ the long periodic sentence. In the stanza just above, which has as its center a conjunctive joining two sets of black eyes and two phrases verbatim plus "nine blackhaired children," all without taking (or letting the reader take) a breath, all, presumably, without the poet's looking away, until the sentence and stanza ends in an *as if* by the sea in a batch of new poppies.

In poems immediately following this, the poet continues indefatigably toward what she calls in the poem "Beets" that "somewhere that there was still a secret / procession of blood, / under the ground." She keeps going places where the necessary faces are: to "The Summer Kitchen," to see Zia Petrina, who, "as the damp / New World sunrays struggled to rise / past sooty housetops," would "look suddenly up / with eyes black as the grapes. . . ." Or to her Genoan grandfather in "Grandpa," "only now in Queens, pining for the old farm, / the hills above the sea. . . .": Or to pay a visit to her mother in "Jackson Heights": "Each day, 'Thank God for Queens,' my mother said. / Sicily was what she tried to forget— / the stony village, the farmyard, the donkey shit." And to pay her respect to a couple of her old teachers in "For Miss Lewis and Miss Newton." "How youthful you look now," the poet says,

and how old I've grown!
Adult as a briefcase, I'm carried
over the Rockies by TWA.

(80)

To visit—one might presume?—the young girl that once she was,
whom she explores in "Low Tide":

> I know
> you're somewhere still, still keeping house
> under the sea, under the bitter waters.
>
> Low tide. I pick my way among the pilings
> down the long rotting pier
> to the ocean beds where you huddle
> among slippery stones.
>
> I'll find you, I'll pluck you out
> though the claws of silence
> skin my fingers
> and my knuckles turn to salt.

(81)

It may well be the girl she plucks and cannot live fully without is
both part herself and part emanation of the poet stepping forth in
the future. She meets this girl in a poem titled "2085":

> It's 2085, you're walking on a dirt road
> in Sicily, you're my blood-
> kin, a seventeen-year-old girl
>
> with black curls and a faint smudge of
> shadow on your upper lip.
>                     Have you
>
> come from New York to find lost ancestors,
> or have you always been here?
> Dry hills, stacks of heat,
>
> tower around you; nearby, there are goats, donkeys,
>     chickens,
> a smell of dung simmering,
> and smoke, grain, *rosmarino;*
> in the sky, a track of supersonic light—
> but you don't look up, you're reading, thinking
> trying to imagine the past,
>
> and my sentences won't help you, though they
> brood in you like chromosomes:
>                     I can't
>
> tell you who I was, in my queer custome,
> with my modern ideas.
>                     My words

stand in the fields beside you—
stones, dead trees—the way
the land you walk through

stood behind me, an unknown monument.
And now the road unfolds and shines ahead
like the history neither of us understands.

It turns you
toward the sea, toward
the inarticulate Aegean.

(113–14)

It looks to be a hill-lined road with blood and sea at one end and a history of *her* waiting to be turned to word at the other.

This poem's speaker insists at once that her sentences "won't help" the girl from 2085 and that those same sentences "brood in you like chromosomes." So despite the speaker's playful protestations to the contrary, it is exactly this composition process—turning histories of self and blood and sea to word—that allows the Italian American woman writer a primary means for flight. Such a woman as the poem portrays may fear the risks of freedom, even downplay the importance of her "sentences." Nevertheless, the act of writing and rewriting her history remains an essential way out of stasis, a way into what she is, into what she is not, into what she can be.[6]

## NOTES

1. Sandra M. Gilbert, "A Fine White Flying Myth: The Life/Work of Sylvia Plath," in *Shakespeare's Sisters—Feminist Essays on Women Poets,* eds. Sandra M. Gilbert and Susan Gubar, 245–60 (Bloomington: Indiana University Press, 1979).
2. Gilbert, "A Fine White Flying Myth," 259.
3. Helen Barolini, ed., *The Dream Book—An Anthology of Writings by Italian American Women* (New York: Shocken Books, 1985), 23.
4. Carolyn G. Heilbrun, *Writing a Woman's Life* (New York: Ballantine Books, 1988), 48.
5. Cixous, Hélène, and Catherine Clement, *The Newly Born Woman,* Theory and History of Literature, vol. 24 (Minneapolis: University of Minnesota Press, 1986), 86.
6. This chapter first appeared in the *Romance Languages Annual 1996,* vol. 8, ed. Ben Lawton, Jeanette Beer, and Patricia Hart (West Lafayette, Ind.: Purdue Research Foundation, 1997), 297–302.

# Part 3
## Reading Film

# 9

# The Image of Blacks in the Work of Coppola, De Palma, and Scorsese[1]

STEPHANIE HULL
MAURIZIO VIANO

As we opted for a self-conscious textuality, it may be useful to preface that the introduction is at once written by Maurizio, who was first contacted with the offer to contribute to this anthology, and by both of us. Whereas section 2 (by Stephanie) and section 3 (by Maurizio) had an easier birth, the introduction and the conclusions became the site of constant rewriting. Even during the last proofreading session, we could not help reworking the margin(s) of our discourse.

## I. Introduction (Maurizio Viano)

As an Italian living in the United States since 1977, I have often had the chance to observe instances of racism within the Italian/American communities with which I have come into contact. My introduction to the United States was mediated by a first year tucked away within one of the many Italian/American communities in Louisiana. An hour and a half from New Orleans, the small town of Hammond often surprised me for the virulence of racial prejudice among the third-fourth-generation Italian Americans living in the environs. Later, I discovered that racism is by no means confined to those living in southern states. Several of the people that I have come across in the North End, Boston's predominantly Italian neighborhood, are, if not openly racist, at least nostalgic for the times when their community enjoyed racial purity—on July 1992, for example, a tenement building, in which a black woman and her son live(d), was spray-painted with racist epithets.

There are, of course, sound sociohistorical explanations for the rac-

169

ism of Italian Americans. Italian immigrants often found themselves
next to Blacks in the labor market. After the Civil War, large groups
of people from the poorest regions in Italy were recruited to replace
the slaves in the plantations. In some of the big cities of the northern
United States, the urban territories inhabited by Blacks and Italian
Americans have often been adjacent, equally on the margin, so they
engender the typical friction between underdogs.

Aware though I was of such extenuating circumstances, I proudly
remained on my pedestal. After all, I was coming from a country that
took pride in its being immune from racism against Blacks—while
conveniently forgetting that between Italy's North and South prejudice was rampant. I found Italian Americans embarrassing in their
staunch display of racist attitudes, and I even reproached them for
failing to understand the structural homology existing between them
and Blacks, a homology that should have made them feel close to one
another against the dominant WASP group. But those were the days
of idealism.

During the 1980s, racism has exploded in Italy as well. For the
first time in history, instead of the usual emigration of Italian men and
women as cheap labor force, Italy has been confronted with massive
immigration, mostly from Africa. Now that the socioeconomic tables
are turned, now that Italy has become a rich country tantalizing the
South of the world with the promise of a consumer paradise, Italians
have proven that they can be racist, *all'Italiana*, in a nice way, just
as they were "nicer" Fascists than the Nazis: *con anema e core*, but
racist, nonetheless. So much for my pedestal.[2]

Racism is everywhere; it affects all groups and—Rodney King *do-
cet*—is deeply entrenched in the U.S. system. As a point of fact,
racism (tribalism, ethnicity) turns out to be *the* issue for an explosive
and potentially fascist decade such as the 1990s.

By making racism a human trait, the recognition of the ubiquity
of prejudice alters the image that I had of prejudice among Italian
Americans. I asked myself whether my observation of their racism
was not perchance influenced by the cinema. These were the days of
Spike Lee's powerful ascension as a Black filmmaker. Two of his
films in particular matter here, the ones having white protagonists
together with Blacks: *Do the Right Thing* (1989) and *Jungle Fever*
(1991). In both cases, the Whites are Italian Americans and, for the
most part, also racist. Superficially, as the many protests in the Italian
Americans' publications testify, Lee's films have no doubt contributed
to the (mis)perception that Italian Americans are the racist Whites
*par excellence*. On a closer look, however, I find that his films send
out a much more complex message.

*Do the Right Thing* contains the justly famous sequence in which virtually all of the ethnic groups badmouth one another, making it clear that Lee knows all too well that racism forms the core of the melting pot. I would argue that Lee's choice of Italian Americans for his interracial films may also be seen as a tribute to the fact that, after all, Italian Americans and Blacks have a certain relationship, however conflictual. It must be noted that *Jungle Fever* portrays *two* interracial couples, both of them involving a black person, respectively Flipper (Wesley Snipes) and Orine (Tyra Farrell) with an Italian/American partner, Angie (Annabella Sciorra) and Paulie (John Turturro). Although Lee's film criticizes the relationship between Flipper and Angie, which takes up most of the narrative space, as the outcome of a culturally induced "fever," it also seems to suggest that something substantial may be happening between Paulie and Orin. *Jungle Fever* does not really develop this subtext, but whispers it, as it were, in half words, leaving us to wonder what may indeed happen when a Black and a well-read, politically aware Italian American come together for reasons other than "jungle fever."

My contention is that, all things considered, Lee chose Italian Americans not only because of their racism but also because of a certain similarity existing between them and Blacks. In my American experience I have often remarked that these two groups have more things in common (the taste for theatrical clothing, for example) than, say, Anglo-Saxons and Blacks.[3] Lee's films would then be symptomatic of a friction that nonetheless means contact between the two groups. Unlike many other films of the 1980s celebrating an improbable "buddy-buddy" situation, Lee's cinema does not idealize race relationships, but shows them at their worst, with the pessimism of a nineteenth-century realist.

I can only admire the honesty with which Lee implicates himself in the films, even when that means playing the role of Mookie, the most controversial character in *Do the Right Thing*. After the police murder Raheem, Mookie does something that has aroused endless controversy among critics and viewers of both races: he throws a garbage can through the window of Sal's pizzeria, thus initiating the riot that will destroy it. It is worth noting that, by all accounts, Sal (Danny Aiello) is not stereotyped as a racist Italian American, but on the contrary, ends up being one of the most human and reasonable characters in the film. Instead of either idealizing race relations or showing that all evil is on one side, Lee's films show the inevitability of an explosion in which the good and the bad are not divided in accordance with the color line.

When asked to contribute to the present anthology, I felt I wanted to know more about the depiction of race relations in the work of the major Italian/American directors—Coppola, Scorsese, and De Palma. Of course, the history of Italian/American cinematography in relation to Blacks does not start nor end with these three directors. Frank Capra, for example, is praised in Donald Bogle's excellent study of Blacks in American cinema for his sensitive handling of the actor Clarence Muse in films such as *Rain or Shine* (1930), *Dirigible* (1931), and *Broadway Bill* (1934).[3] Likewise, Bogle finds that "under the sensitive direction of Vincente Minnelli, Eddie 'Rochester' Anderson accomplished something in an era his predecessors never approached: he touched his audience."[4] And among contemporary directors, one ought to look more closely at the subtle racism of Cimino's films or at the Catholic sensationalism of Abel Ferrara's. Still, I thought, a first contribution to a totally unexplored field of inquiry might well profit by an examination of the three directors who, in the eyes of the public opinion, exemplify contemporary Italian/American cinematography.

To enrich and counterbalance my perspective, I then asked Stephanie, a black colleague equally interested in the practices of the imaginary, whether or not she would be interested in collaborating with me: she was. We watched films and talked about them, often finding ourselves in disagreement and learning from it. After debating the pros and cons of the different modes of collaboration, we decided to keep our work separate so that the reader would not be tricked into believing in a unitary argument. There is no "Italian/American cinematic-treatment-of-Blacks" as such. There are only relationships between some texts on the one hand and sociohistorically situated viewers, who bring the wealth of their passions to the films, on the other. May the gaps and breaks that exist between Stephanie's analyses and mine offer a surplus of textuality, an invitation to the brain dance to the readers of this essay.

## II. Images of Blacks in the Work of Coppola and De Palma (Stephanie Hull)

While I was convinced by our early discussions that it would be impossible to find common ground with Maurizio on this project, the idea itself was too intriguing to dismiss. I have a long-standing interest in the study of culture through cinema, especially through "period" films and literary adaptations. What was perhaps most compelling about this topic was that Maurizio and I started with a clear idea of the sort of conclusions we expected to draw and ended with far more questions than we'd had when we began. The format of this essay seemed appropriate in that it paralleled our approach: we both watched all the films, then "specialized" in our respective directors. We wrote, discussed (argued), and revised; our small patch of common ground is documented in the last section of the paper.

My project in this section is to discuss the images of Blacks presented in a group of films selected from the work of Italian/American directors Francis Coppola and Brian De Palma. I stress the selectivity of this analysis. Although I have attempted to choose a broad range of examples, the result is a series of observations on, as opposed to an exhaustive accounting of, these directors' positioning of black characters in their films. To some extent, the films chosen lend themselves to thematic grouping: for example, the Vietnam War in Coppola's *Apocalypse Now* and *Gardens of Stone* and De Palma's *Casualties of War* or literary adaptation in Coppola's *Rumble Fish* and *The Outsiders* and De Palma's *Bonfire of the Vanities*. But while groupings of this sort are helpful in comparing the possible presentations of Blacks in these films, they are apt to lead to generalizations about the directors that must not be permitted to overshadow our conclusions.

In De Palma's *Sisters* (1973), *Dressed to Kill* (1980), and *Wise Guys* (1986), the black characters are confined to stereotypical roles and settings that are reinforced by the white characters with whom they interact and who are peripheral to the action and plots of the films. The opening scene of *Sisters* shows a black man appearing on a television game show entitled *Peeping Toms*. Although the notion of the peeping tom is culturally autonomous and is supported thematically by the voyeuristic games played by the fictional contestants, De Palma's placement of a black character in this role evokes a shift from peeping Tom to Uncle Tom, a concept with equally established connotations. Evidence that this is not an arbitrary judgment of De Palma's intent is provided when, as a prize for his participation on the program, the black man receives an evening of dinner and dancing at the "African Room." This invites speculation about whether all prizes won on De Palma's fictional game show would be equally racially inspired. De Palma presents the "African Room," decorated with gorillas and staffed by shirtless black waiters, as a desirable social setting for the contestant. In so doing, he perpetuates two stereotypes: the first is that the black man has only recently, if at all, surmounted his jungle origins; the second is the notion that, however removed he may be from these origins, the connection to the jungle and to Africa remains stronger than any apparent assimilation with mainstream white American culture.

When this man becomes the first victim of a psychotic, white female murderer (Margot Kidder), the police investigator dismisses a neighbor's report that she witnessed his stabbing. He immediately assumes that the murderer is also black since, as he explains, "these people are always stabbing each other." He is not interested in the investigation of "race murders." After sufficient time has passed for the murderer to remove all traces of the incident, two detectives reluctantly and perfunctorily search her apartment, making it clear as they do so that they have no interest in finding evidence or in hearing witnesses' testimony. Although the neighbor, an investigative reporter, has found witnesses to attest to the existence of "the colored guy," the police choose not to allow an investigation. The crime committed against the black man is left unresolved despite the continued efforts of this neighbor, who is subsequently depicted as having a tendency toward sensationalistic journalism and thus an attraction to exploitable themes such as racially motivated violence. In thus detracting from the credibility and motivation of the only character interested in vindicating the dead man, De Palma's message becomes further complicated: Does his portrayal of this incident condemn both the apathy of bigoted, white law enforcement officials in multicultural neighborhoods and the exploitation of racial difference in the media's reporting of violence and crime? And if so, can the exaggerated stereotypes of the social construction of this victim be read as part of De Palma's intent to show the injustice of such stereotypes? Because the issue of this murder is never again raised in the film, the implicit message is, instead, that this young woman was fortunate to have chosen an expendable member of society as her victim. The police are not disturbed by the loss of this man; the only interest the reporter has in the story is as a means of advancing her career and retaliating against the establishment. Rather than use the stereotypes he depicts as a commentary on such depictions, De Palma sets up a scenario that has the potential to convey such a message and then abandons it, leaving viewers to conclude that the images of the Uncle Tom in the jungle are, in fact, De Palma's last word on race relations in this film.

*Dressed to Kill,* thematically similar to *Sisters,* provides another opportunity for De Palma to explore and exploit negative stereotypes of Blacks. A white woman who has witnessed a crime asks her neighbor, a black woman, if she may use her phone. The black woman refuses. Suspecting that this white woman is actually involved in the crime, the black woman identifies her to a black police officer, who then calls a white officer to speak to the white woman. Later, this accused white woman is harassed by a group of five black men (equipped with the requisite portable-but-enormous stereo) in the subway. Apparently because the subway guard to whom she reports this incident is also black, he neither reacts verbally to her request for help nor intervenes. Instead he gets off the train, leaving the five men free to chase her through the cars until they, in turn, are frightened by the sight of another potential attacker (Michael Caine), intending to assault their victim with a straight razor; none of the five men makes an attempt to defend the woman against this white man. De Palma's message here is more subtle than in *Sisters*: it appears here that there can be no positive interaction between Blacks and Whites, only the separatism that prevents communication in the apartment building, the police station, and the subway. The segregation that divides the society he portrays has infected the sense of humanity and creates boundaries that are not transgressed by the senselessness of the violence or of the loss of life he depicts.

In *Wise Guys*, De Palma moves away from the themes of violence and murder. In this film, Blacks do not find their status improved; it is only taken slightly less seriously. The only appearance made by Blacks in this film is as guests at a birthday party to which the main character's dangerous Italian/American acquaintance has not been invited. The explanation that the omission occurred because "just the immediate family" was getting together seems to satisfy the mob boss until he notices a black couple among the guests. Although it is clearly used for comic effect, we do not forget that this "immediate family" joke operates both on the anger this potentially dangerous man will feel at having been not only excluded, but also placed beneath the black couple on the guest list, and on the implication that the two Blacks are the absolute last people one would expect to see at an intimate, Italian/American family gathering. Here again De Palma perpetuates rather than questions the stereotypes that determine the interaction of the races in his fictionalized society.

In foregrounding the conflict between American and Vietnamese characters, the three films *Apocalypse Now* (1979), *Gardens of Stone* (1987), and *Casualties of War* (1989) achieve a partial effacement of racial issues among Americans of different backgrounds. However, the question of negative portrayal of Blacks is never completely absent. In Coppola's *Apocalypse*, Captain Willard (Martin Sheen) begins his journey down the river by describing the men on board the boat; two of these men, Clean (Lawrence Fishburne) and Phillips, are black. As Willard explains in a voice-over, "Clean was from some South Bronx shithole and I think the light and the space of Vietnam really put the sap on his head"; Phillips, the "Chief," is the pilot and poses somewhat of a threat to the authority Willard tries to assume:

"It might have been my mission, but it sure as hell was the Chief's boat." Clean, a seventeen-year-old from a disadvantaged family, generally behaves as though he were not especially bright. When the crew of the boat meet Captain Kilgore (Robert Duvall), who commands the troops who will escort them into the river, Kilgore completely ignores Clean, preferring to talk with a young, white soldier. The pain and anger are clearly visible in Clean's facial expression, yet he soon becomes a member of the majority again, yelling "Run, Charlie!" as Kilgore's men open fire on the Vietnamese from their aircraft. In depicting Clean as an undereducated, inner-city, black teenager and Phillips as a well-spoken, intelligent, and authoritative black man, Coppola creates human types as opposed to stereotypes. Although Clean's lack of positive qualities makes him resemble the stereotypical ignorant black, these qualities do not seem exaggerated, given the carefully constructed context; further support of this interpretation is provided by Phillips's character, which is free of any of the stereotypical qualities, as would perhaps be expected given his role and authority.

As the action progresses, there is a night scene in which Willard stops to question two anonymous black soldiers who are arguing and calling each other "nigger"; one wears several apparently African beaded necklaces and no shirt. These men are fighting a single Vietnamese man they hear but cannot see, attempting to kill him before his bombs come any closer to their hiding place. Willard, out of a simple desire for information, asks who their commanding officer is; the man with the necklaces replies, "Ain't you?" When Willard, having ignored this first response, again asks if these men know who is in command, the same man answers simply, "Yeah." This exchange between Willard and the men is left open to interpretation. At face value, it is simply either a symptom of the confusion of this situation or the disrespect for army discipline shown by a man who, having lost his commanding officer and facing death in the darkness and mud, is having difficulty sustaining his will to continue being a soldier. However, the racial issue complicates this apparently simple explanation of the soldiers' arguing and flippant replies. Their inability to make decisions without arguing with each other, coupled with their use of racial slurs in the process of arguing, seems to indicate an ethnic motivation to their inability to handle the situation effectively without a superior officer. When Willard arrives, it is ostensibly his superior rank but possibly his skin color that provokes the soldier to assume that Willard is or will be in charge. The disrespectful attitude and improper uniform of the soldier demonstrate his rejection of the rules of this game. Yet the fact that he expresses this rejection with

African beads and ethnic slurs against his own people show Coppola's intent to leave this man completely alienated, unable to separate himself fully from the social and military hierarchy he is clearly attempting to abandon.

During the first fighting scene, the only soldier badly wounded is a black man. He screams in pain as he is carried into a helicopter; a Vietnamese woman throws a bomb into the open door, and the aircraft explodes into flames. The next casualty among the major characters is Clean, who is shot during an ambush as they continue up the river; as he is wounded and dies, a tape sent to him by his mother, wishing for his safe return, continues to play in the background. Finally, when Willard forces Phillips to continue their journey in spite of fog so dense that navigation is impossible, Phillips is killed by a spear thrown from the riverbank; he tries to strangle Willard as he falls. There is a clear imbalance in the depiction of Blacks following this final death that continues to the conclusion of the film: effectively, all identifiable black characters are killed before the boat reaches its destination and the climax of the film begins. Although the relations between Blacks and Whites are not foregrounded in this film, the statement made by this gradual process of segregation by death is hardly subtle and effectively undermines the positivity of the original establishment of the characters of Clean and Phillips. The strong statements made in conjunction with the deaths of these two characters, first that Clean, while a member of a disadvantaged minority, is not by analogy expendable, and second that blind obedience to [a white] authority despite his superior judgment is clearly the cause of Phillips's death, in the end are not integral either to the climax of the plot or its resolution.[5]

Coppola's *Gardens of Stone* again relegates the issue of race relations to a subcurrent, also after establishing its main black characters without racially motivated, stereotypical attributes. Goody Nelson (James Earl Jones) is the sergeant major who acts as a stabilizing force and source of experience and wisdom, yet who has a very human tendency to use scandalous language when among his men; "Slasher" Williams (Dick Anthony Williams) is extremely tough on all of his men without exception, thus without racism. Within the plot, which deals mainly with the private lives of the Arlington National Cemetery Honor Guard and only peripherally with the difficulties of fighting the Vietnamese, two minor episodes recall the tension that exists between Whites and Blacks. The first occurs during the initial interview between the main character, Willow, and Sergeant Hazard (James Caan): When Willow tells him he is a basketball player, Hazard comments,

"We could use another good player, especially a white one"; Willow does not respond.

The second episode occurs off-camera at a bar, as Nelson explains what makes the Vietnamese soldier difficult to defeat in spite of his inferiority in terms of manpower and technology: it is the difference in what this soldier is fighting for that makes him continue a fight he knows he will lose. Completely unmotivated by this conversation, a loud discussion begins between two men whose voices reveal that one is black and the other white. As this argument escalates into physical violence, the song on the jukebox, the Doors's "Break on through to the Other Side," segues into the Temptations's "I Heard It through the Grapevine." This provides a musical accompaniment to the racial issue evoked by the fighting as well as by Nelson's comments, which take on relevance outside the American-versus-Vietnamese context. The cause of this fighting is never developed; the importance of this interruption seems to be that even among army personnel, a setting in which race should not be at issue, there is an awareness of difference that arguably motivates a certain degree of anger and frustration, if not actual physical conflict. Coppola's depiction of black characters in this film, while it represents a subcurrent, is essentially no different from that of his white characters. Here, he has developed character types as opposed to stereotypes. He has dealt with racial difference as would the characters he has created, without arbitrary additions on the level of the plot (that, in fact, focuses on the life of a young, white soldier) or avoidance of the issue of difference (insofar as it becomes an issue, given the basic narrative).

De Palma's *Casualties* begins with a sequence set in a streetcar in which people of several different nationalities ride together but for the most part do not interact. The attention of the main character, a white man named Ericksson (Michael J. Fox), is focused on a young Vietnamese woman seated across from him, but he does not speak to her. This image reverts to one of the past, in which American troops in Vietnam walk through a village together. Brownie, a somewhat loud-mouthed black man who expresses his distrust of the apparently friendly villagers, is the only black soldier with a speaking role and the only soldier to receive a serious injury when his suspicions prove to be correct and the troop is attacked. Ericksson is part of a field unit that illegally kidnaps, rapes, and murders a young Vietnamese girl; because of his refusal to participate he is threatened by these men, who fear he will report their behavior. The superior officer to whom Ericksson must first take his case is a black man, Captain Riley, who in response to the information he hears relates an anecdote about the treatment of Blacks in the American South: his wife, when refused access to a segregated hospital despite the emergency, gave birth to their first child on the reception room floor. Riley concludes that "[w]hat happened is the way things are, so why try and buck the system?" Ericksson is dissatisfied with this response and continues to tell his story until the men are brought to justice, in spite of the threats to his personal safety that continue as he repeatedly confronts bureaucracy and indifference. What is noteworthy here is that Brownie and Captain Riley are not only stereotypical black character types, Brownie because of his boisterousness, amusing commentary, and obvious lack of education and Riley because of his origins in the post-slavery, deep South, but also take responsibility for their own inferior status. The ideas and words that keep them subseparate from white culture are not imposed on them by Whites in the context of the film but are instead ideas they have internalized and words they themselves speak. Brownie's distrust of the Vietnamese echoes preconceived notions of his own race: one cannot predict the behavior of Blacks or Vietnamese, since they are much more like desperate animals than people. Riley, having been jailed by a presumably white authority following his fury at seeing his wife mistreated, is kept imprisoned long enough to "realize" that the incident itself was unimportant and that his concern should be for his new baby. These men not only internalize the statements that have taught them to accept inferiority, they also recite their lessons to others.

In attempting to recreate the historical atmosphere of the Vietnam War era, Coppola's depictions question race relations after the characters have been established on a relatively equal basis, whereas De Palma's vision denies even this basic equivalence and, further, forces the characters to speak their own subjugation. Paradoxically, Coppola's depiction of an ignorant, black, teenage soldier becomes a more positive image than does De Palma's depiction of Captain Riley, a superior officer and authority figure who claims for himself inferiority and helplessness.

Coppola's *The Cotton Club* (1984) and De Palma's *The Untouchables* (1987) expand the exploration of historical subject matter. *The Cotton Club* generated a large amount of publicity and criticism for its avoidance of what was ostensibly its major topic, Blacks in Harlem during the late 1920s and early 1930s, in favor of a vignette of the life of a white cornet player, Dixie Dwyer (Richard Gere).[6] Rather than repeat the almost unanimous judgments of the film's failings, I will focus on one statement made by the character Lila (Lonette McKee), a woman who is of mixed racial background and is, therefore, able to perform both at the Cotton Club, which allows only black performers and has an all-white clientele, and later at a club that bans black performers as well as patrons. Confronted by Sandman (Gregory Hines), a black dancer, about the morality of "passing," she replies, "I'm not black; I'm not white. I'm a human being and that's the way I like it." Interestingly, following this conversation there is a sequence of headlines reporting rampant violence: the first victims are two boys, one white and one black. This simultaneous murder reinforces Lila's view that the lives of human beings, not blacks or whites, are at risk in this social climate; it also serves to bring Coppola's film further from its supposed topic. In declaring, as well as demonstrating, her freedom from the segregation that should be the central issue of this film, Lila questions the simplistic judgment of positive and negative imagery.[7] Although her character is still criticized as a continuation of a Hollywood tradition that confines the mulatto woman to roles with a tragic conclusion, the implication that she feels guilty in accepting her successful career seems more to be a projection of the guilt Sandman tries to inspire in her than to be any real remorse on her part. Her success is only tragic if viewed either with regret for the mediocre career she leaves behind with the black half of her ethnicity, or with resentment that such a choice must be made. Lila, in avoiding Sandman's persistent efforts to spend time with her, continually makes it clear that she is capable of separating her professional life from her private life, thus assumedly of utilizing her cultural backgrounds to maximum effect in various situations. Far from confining her to a tragic role, Coppola's depiction of Lila implies that, if further developed, her character's ability and willingness to choose would ultimately be empowering.

In *The Untouchables* images of Blacks are almost completely absent. This in itself is not surprising because the film deals primarily with the Italian/American underworld and the American government's attempts at regaining power: Blacks would not logically be found in either of these bastions. The first shot sequence of the film begins with the back of the head of a black man who kneels at Capone's feet, shining his shoes; the second and final image of Blacks in this film is, in fact, a non-image: Eliot Ness (Kevin Costner) and his wife listen to the *Amos 'n' Andy* show on the radio. Given the setting of Chicago in 1930 and the exclusivity of the milieu frequented by the mobsters and the government men, the absence of black characters in these settings is plausible. However, rather than allow this total absence, De Palma chooses to include two images that, although arguably historically valid, are at the origin of extremely negative stereotypes of Blacks. As documented in Hollywood film of the era, Blacks were largely confined to roles as servants (Bogle, 35–38), thus, the black bootblack character could be viewed as intended to lend the film a certain 30s Hollywood flavor. The *Amos 'n' Andy* radio show, which later became a television show, has long been a source of conflict for its portrayal of Blacks as exaggeratedly ignorant and lazy people, an image that extended far beyond its originally fictional context. The two depictions of Blacks in *The Untouchables*, because they do not serve to advance the plot in any way, leave the impression that De Palma's film could very well have excluded all images of Blacks rather than incorporating only these two highly controversial and demeaning stereotypes.

Cinematic adaptations of literature, especially popular literature, are widely believed to have accountability to their sources. It is through such adaptations that the motivation behind a director's interpretation of characters can be most obvious. In Coppola's adaptations of S. E. Hinton's *The Outsiders* and *Rumble Fish*[8] (both 1983) and De Palma's adaptation of Tom Wolfe's *Bonfire of the Vanities*[9] (1990), the images of Blacks are not always consistent with those found in the original texts. While Hinton's *The Outsiders*, published in 1967, does not mention Blacks at all, Coppola inserts Blacks to reinforce Hinton's message of social equality. When two of the boys, involved in a murder, spend a week living in the small town of Windricksville as fugitives, their carelessness causes a fire in an abandoned church where some small children have apparently been brought on a school field trip; they rush in to save the children, at least half of whom are black. The adults present treat them equally and, as in Hinton's text, are more than willing to forget the juvenile delinquency of the boys who risk their lives to save them. Coppola's intent seems to be to show that in this particular situation, both ethnic and social differences are erased; the addition of black children compounds and makes more impressive this erasure.

In *Rumble Fish*, Hinton deals to some extent with Blacks as a population living in the lower-income section of the already low-income town, "downtown [. . .] across the bridge [. . .] where the lights were" (*Rumble Fish*, 66). Blacks appear in one chapter only, when the main narrator Rusty James (Matt Dillon), his brother the Motorcycle Boy (Mickey Rourke) and his friend Steve decide to enter this neighborhood to escape the monotony of their lives. The boys encounter Blacks first in a pool hall: "The place was smoky and dark and full of black people. This didn't bother me, and it didn't seem to bother Steve either" (Hinton, 82). They encounter a black man later in the street as Rusty James and Steve, both drunk, try to find their way back home: "Two live shadows stepped out of the dark ones to block the alley. One was white. One was black. The black one had something in his hand that looked like a tire tool" (*Rumble*

*Fish,* 85). Coppola takes this interaction, which is segregated in its confinement to a single chapter in the novel, and spreads it throughout his story, beginning the film with a traveling shot of a black man (Lawrence Fishburne?) who walks down a street past a pool hall window, entering to speak the first lines of the film. While these lines are taken from Hinton's novel, she describes the character who speaks them without defining his ethnic origin, which, in her work, generally permits the assumption that he is white. Coppola chooses to film his adaptation in black and white and emphasizes the dichotomy not only by adding this black character but also by superimposing his original speech with an image in which Rusty James misses his shot at pool, causing the white cue ball to go into a pocket while only the black-and-white eight ball remains on the table. The black man moves to the side of the frame and comments, "You cats are constantly arguing and fighting amongst yourselves," implying a contrast in behavior and thus a difference in customs between Blacks and Whites. Notably, while all the other main characters appear to be teenagers and are dressed in undershirts, jeans, sneakers, and denim or leather jackets, the black character is visibly older and wears a light-colored suit with a shirt and tie and a fedora.

Following a fight in which Rusty James receives a serious knife wound, a dream sequence reveals his somewhat delirious thoughts in which he sits in a classroom, being lectured by the black character, who takes the role of teacher, and looking at his girlfriend, who sits on top of a high bookcase in the corner, dressed in a flowing black robe. This dream shifts to another in which he and the same black man are working next to each other in what appears to be a shop class. When he awakens and goes to school late, the secretary is a black woman who knows Rusty James is an alcoholic; although she is not unkind to him, she does not seem to acknowledge him except to send him into the principal's office. The discrepancy in status between the dream world, where a Black could be an educator, and the real world, where a black woman does not make an effort to help a white teenager in trouble, is all the more powerful for the fact that these images of Blacks are entirely interpretive and not indicated in the original text.

In the predominantly black neighborhood it becomes obvious that the Motorcycle Boy is equally at ease among Blacks or Whites. These scenes are filled with dancing, laughing, music, and occasional fighting, yet the actual interaction between people is limited to Blacks: even though the presence of the Whites is not challenged, they are clearly spectators here. When the boys are mugged, Coppola makes use of an interesting comment made by Steve in the novel—"Progressive country: integrated mugging" (*Rumble Fish*, 86)—to emphasize the point that this violence can have no origin in prejudice. While Rusty James, having presumably died in the fight, looks down on the scene in an out-of-body experience, the black man drinks a toast: "To Rusty James, a very cool dude." Similarly, when the Motorcycle Boy is killed at the film's conclusion, the crowd that gathers begins with this black man and a black woman and grows as a number of other Blacks and a few Whites approach his body, already expressing their regret at losing such a man.

The main difference between the images of Blacks in the two novels, which is defined by their absence from *The Outsiders* and their selective presence in one chapter of *Rumble Fish*, and in Coppola's adaptation is the strategic nature of their placement in the films. The juvenile delinquents in *The Outsiders* are humanized by their willingness to risk their lives for these children regardless of race, and become by this act acceptable to mainstream society despite their own minority status in the community. The presence of the main black man in *Rumble Fish* "corrects" the segregation of Blacks in the novel and justifies not only interaction between members of the two communities (both positive and negative) but, as evidenced in the dream sequence, increased possibility for the eventual advancement of black people. Still, their positive nature does not necessarily make these arbitrary manipulations an asset to the cinematic adaptations. Hinton's original statement, whether it excluded or limited Blacks, held its own relevance and instructive value for society prior to the corrections made by Coppola's adaption.

De Palma's *Bonfire of the Vanities*, although it follows Tom Wolfe's novel of the same name relatively closely, also operates a number of major changes that affect the depiction of Blacks in his film. The plot revolves around a relatively brief sequence of events in which Sherman McCoy (Tom Hanks), while driving back to Manhattan from the airport with his mistress Maria (Melanie Griffith), makes a wrong turn and ends up in the Bronx; in trying to get back onto the expressway, he comes upon a tire blocking the road. When he leaves the car to move the tire, he is confronted by two black teenagers. Maria, taking the wheel in an attempt to rescue Sherman from the fight that ensues, inadvertently backs into one the boys, Henry Lamb (Patrick Malone). Their subsequent failure to report the incident, coupled with the fact that the boy ends up in a coma (and in the novel, dead) leads to the involvement of the three remaining characters: Reverend Reginald Bacon (John Hancock), who mobilizes the black community to demand that the hit-and-run be investigated. District Attorney Weiss, who is eager to comply since the offenders are identified as a

184      STEPHANIE HULL AND MAURIZIO VIANO

white man and woman; and Judge White (Morgan Freeman), who presides over the Bronx County Court where the case is brought to trial.

In depicting the incident, De Palma makes a number of significant changes from the text, beginning with Sherman's and Maria's initial entry into the Bronx. When a fight between a prostitute and a pimp in front of their car prevents them from driving forward, Sherman notes with surprise that in "a $48,000 Mercedes roadster . . . in the middle of the South Bronx . . . Miraculous! No one pays any attention to them" (Wolfe, 81). In De Palma's version Maria, having asked Sherman, "Where are all the white people?" is frightened by an old drunken man who yells at her through the closed window; Sherman drives off recklessly to protect her from this man. The actual confrontation between Sherman and the teenagers, which describes Sherman's sense of danger despite the neutrality of the dialogue between him and the boys, is depicted in Wolfe as primarily instigated by the larger boy. The smaller boy, as Wolfe described him, had "a delicate face . . . eyes wide open . . . startled . . . he looked terrified" (Wolfe, 86). De Palma depicts Henry Lamb as more wary than reluctant: Lamb hesitates slightly in his approach toward Sherman but holds his hands as if ready to fight. Although here as in the novel his only involvement in the fight is to stand and shout instructions to his partner, his gesture of readiness to participate detracts from the sympathy engineered by Wolfe's description.

De Palma replaces Wolfe's Judge Myron Kovitsky, "about sixty, short, thin, bald, wiry, with a sharp nose, hollow eyes, and a grim set to his mouth," with a black man, paradoxically renamed Judge White. The opening scene of the novel as well as the introduction to the character of the judge are marked by confrontation between the black and Jewish communities of the Bronx. In Wolf's prologue the Mayor is jeered as he speaks before an assembly of Blacks who he realizes too late are supporters of the Reverend Bacon, a community leader engineering unrest among the peoples of Harlem. Wolfe's introduction to Judge Kovitsky shows him infuriated but undaunted by anti-Semitic epithets directed at him by prisoners in a Department of Corrections vehicle outside of his court. The ability of this character to effectively maintain control of situations involving the criminal element of his community is reproduced in De Palma's Judge White.

De Palma also differently envisions Wolfe's characters Bacon, who is "a tall, black man . . . looking like ten million dollars" (Wolfe, 189), capable of intimidating the assistant DA's with whom he meets by his presence alone. De Palma's interpretation is a poorly dressed, overweight man with a tendency to preach rather than to speak and an entourage of women in choir robes, singing or humming gospel music as he walks through the streets ahead of them. De Palma's Bacon is much more a parody than a threat, despite his marked ability to mobilize the people. The people themselves are a stereotypical crew of loud, unruly, and impetuous black men and women, arguably inspired by Wolfe's description of the angry crowd in his prologue, yet interpreted visually by De Palma and thus to some extent defined by his depiction. While the Bacon of the novel is clearly an impressive and imposing figure, De Palma's version of the character casts doubt on the judgment of those who would support him.

In another exaggeration of the text, De Palma recasts the scene in which Weiss forces his staff to take on the McCoy case. The employees of the DA's office stand around a television set that shows a black woman reporting the Department of Motor Vehicles' finding that although there is no official investigation in progress, there are fewer than two hundred Mercedes with the license plate numbers the hit-and-run victim was able to identify; a black staff member named Howard is present and smiles insipidly through Weiss's racist tirade when in response to this journalist's accusation of police apathy he declares, "We're gonna prove to these black motherf——s—pardon my language, Howard—we're gonna prove to these niggers that this administration loves them!" This black staffer is not only arbitrary, but also willing to smilingly endure the slurs of the DA, presumably because he is no longer "one of" the people targeted by the racism, not being a member of the poor or the criminal element with which the DA is concerned. Nor, presumably, is the black woman journalist, who reports this information professionally and impartially. These two black characters, both added by De Palma, are completely external to the issue and thus display neither the ignorant boisterousness of the crowds, nor the tempered fury of the judge.

In the conclusion of the film, Sherman is tried before a courtroom filled with Bacon's unruly supporters. In Wolfe's version the chaos that ensues at the judge's dismissal of the case is mainly confined to one man's outburst: this man is removed from the court and the other occupants fight the crowds to leave the building. De Palma's conclusion also revolves around one man's outburst, but with a different conclusion: a black man from the audience accuses Judge White of being a "racist pig" and receives in response a lengthy, yet eloquent, speech about the nature of justice and decency, the culmination of which is that decency is the cross-cultural common denominator of civilization. Whereas Judge Kovitsky is challenged for his verdict, he is not required to justify his perspective as is Judge White.

De Palma's film is a commentary of a different nature than that of

Wolfe's original text. With the reinterpretation of the Reverend Bacon and Henry Lamb, additional dialogue such as that which affects the also-additional character of Howard-the-lawyer, and Judge White's racial transformation from Jewish to black, the cinematic text becomes a highly self-conscious reflection on the roles of Blacks in the novel as well as in society. Characters such as Howard and the Reverend Bacon seem to have only negative stereotypical qualities and motives, Howard being clearly more interested in keeping his job than in defending his honor and Bacon having more satirical characteristics than leadership ability. The possibility of Henry Lamb's innocence is de-emphasized, making the consequences of his actions seem less unfortunate and more appropriate. Judge White's motives are never accepted by the black community for whom he is obviously a strong, though unconventional, advocate. The people, impressed by display and sensationalism rather than by discipline and wisdom, instead support Bacon, leaving White entirely alone in his good judgment. The film audience is left to question both the initial racial transformation of the character and the choice of name, both of which suggest that there is only one possible origin of the wisdom he represents.

To summarize my observations on these examples of the directors' representation of Blacks, I look at these films in a comparative mode, considering the directors in relation to each other in terms of genre in addition to the works of each director separately. Clearly, each director finds different means of introducing historical perspective and notions of authenticity; their approaches to adaptation also differ considerably. However, while Coppola's imagery has an experimental quality to it, resulting in his creation of strong, positive images of Blacks in his films as well as a number of negative images, De Palma only rarely presents a thought-provoking portrayal of Blacks. Where he does, he almost immediately undermines its useful qualities. Because both Coppola and De Palma are still directing and because this analysis by no means includes all their work to date, the limited selection of films discussed here precludes either a stronger praise of Coppola or a harsher criticism of De Palma. However, given the chronological scope and the diversity of genre of the selections, these films are, indeed, sufficiently representative of the directors' treatment of Blacks in their films to justify their being held accountable for any tendencies that become evident through this analysis.

### III. The Advantages of Scorsese's
### Realism (Maurizio Viano)

I have argued elsewhere that Scorsese's ethnic films (*Who's That Knocking at My Door?* [1968], *Mean Streets* [1973], *Raging Bull* [1980], and *GoodFellas* [1990]) exemplify Scorsese's reworking of the realist tradition.[10] In these films, Scorsese succeeds in portraying a certain reality (e.g., the Italian/American neighborhoods) without the pitfalls of conventional realism, first of all the myth of objective and impartial representation. By making viewers aware of the director's subjective involvement in the material, Scorsese's cinema represents a most interesting case of expressionist realism, a film style that, in a sense, reunites the two strands that are commonly detected as forming the backbone of the history of cinema, namely, expressionism and realism. One of the most immediate consequences of Scorsese's innovatively realist attitude is the filmmaker's "honesty," his desire to give voice and image to a positional truth, the truth of and from a particular position. It comes as no surprise, then, that Scorsese's cinema, when compared with Coppola's and De Palma's, is the most sensitive to racial issues, reaching moments that are unique in the history of Italian/American filmmaking. For all the difficulties inherent in conclusive judgments—so eloquently pointed out herein by Stephanie— I do have a general sense of what these directors do or do not do when portraying race relations. In my view, De Palma tends to avoid sociological reflections on ethnicity per se and lacks any intention to make clear statements about race: his interests lie elsewhere. Conversely, Coppola seems to be concerned with racial inequality in general (that is, *not* in the Italian/American community), as a good liberal would; he has the tendency to correct this situation by idealizing race relations or by avoiding the subject of racial tensions altogether; and he never questions (at least in his films) *his own* racism. Unlike these two directors, Scorsese often brings the racial problem to the fore, revealing his concern with, and his awareness of, racism in the Italian/American community. What follows is a brief analytical description of the role played by Blacks in Scorsese's films.[11]

In 1972, in keeping with the rebellious spirit of the times, Scorsese made *Boxcar Bertha*, an antiestablishment film loosely based on the "autobiography of Bertha Thompson as told to Dr. Ben L. Reitman," then published under the title *Sister of the Road*. The book documents Bertha's vagrant life during the Depression, relates her growing political awareness, and features her as the only major character. It should be noted also that the book has no black characters at all and only mentions "Negroes" six times, usually as part of some statistical observations on the problematic, unjust features of a society with which Bertha is at odds. Scorsese's film gives Bertha (Barbara Hershey) one steady lover instead of the many she has in the book, namely Big Bill Shelley (David Carradine); and two buddies, Rake Brown (Barry Primus) and Van Morton (Bernie Casey). Together, the four make up an anarco-criminal gang whose Robin Hood-like adventures the film gleefully narrates. In a post-*Bonnie and Clyde* mode, Scorsese's film gives its audience the thrill of an action-packed pic, the sensational spectacle that producer Roger Corman expected from his directors.

If Big Bill Shelley and Rake Brown are reminiscent of figures encountered in the book, then Van Morton, who is black, is totally the film's invention. Van Morton is a key figure in *Boxcar Bertha*, somebody who crosses the race line in the safe companionship of marginals and politicos. Significantly, he appears in the film from the very beginning, in the tragic opening sequence in which Bertha's father dies in an airplane accident. The text first introduces Bertha to us in three close-ups and then suddenly cuts to a shot of her full figure. Van Morton's importance is visually underscored because we see him next to her in the frame, on the left, playing the harmonica. The somewhat stereotypical image of a black man with a harmonica only serves the purpose of measuring Van Morton's progress in the narrative and is punctually subverted by the film's end. In the last sequence, after the railroad police have literally nailed Big Bill Shelley's hands to a train car, his outstretched arms suggesting the image of the crucifixion, Van Morton becomes the black angel of revenge: He shoots them all and provides us with the satisfaction of a much-hoped-for retribution. With Van Morton's passage from harmonica to gun, with his movement from the initial corner-of-the-frame to center frame in the end, *Boxcar Bertha* contains an oblique statement in favor of the armed struggle that Black Panthers were then considering as a viable political strategy. Wishful and totally within the rhetoric of the times though this statement was, it, nonetheless, indicates Scorsese's desire to problematize race relations. More generally, the insertion of a new, black character in a narrative that had no Blacks suggests that the Italian/American director desired to include racial anger in his agenda. Better than that, Van Morton's blatantly political, almost propagandistic, trajectory shows that Scorsese did not fear the ridicule of taking clear stands in his films—to this day he is often accused of not being subtle enough.

The film in which Scorsese most explicitly touches on the theme of racial prejudice within the Italian/American community is *Mean Streets*. In the opening sequences, we see Charlie (Harvey Keitel) going first to church and then to Tony's bar. His voice-over directs the viewers' attention to the distinction between physical and spiritual pain, and as he enters the bar, we hear him saying that spiritual pain is harsher. At this point, the theme of racial difference is subtly and visually introduced by the fleeting sight, in the red-lit bar, of a black man comfortably sitting at the counter in the company of a white man. No sooner does the Rolling Stones's *Tell Me* replace Charlie's inner monologue than we see Diane's (Jeannie Bell) voluptuous body swaying in the crimson glow—she is a beautiful black woman who dances, seminude, her nipples barely covered, for an all-male audience. The synergism struck by an early gem of white rock music, Charlie's voice-over—so excruciatingly full of existential anguish— and the sexist depiction of the dancer send out reverberations of meaning that are open to different interpretations. What counts, for my thesis, is Scorsese's will to craft an interactive knot—that is, one in which the viewer chooses a path of "reading" and creates his or her own text—where race appears in connection to the film's central concerns.

It should be noted that Diane's body is fetishistically fragmented by extreme close-ups of its parts *before* she becomes the object of Charlie's appreciative stare. As the camera looks at her before she has a role in the narrative, this sequence becomes a wonderful example of the self-reflexibility that makes Scorsese's realism expressionistic: through Charlie's desire, Scorsese expresses his own. As a point of fact, *Mean Streets* abounds with those "free indirect subjective shots" theorized by Pasolini after a literary institution by Bakhtin, shots in which film directors use the gaze of a character in their films as an outlet for their own way of seeing. By means of this type of shot, a director's gaze may coincide with the character's, so the film acquires a strong expressionistic quality. In *Mean Streets*, Charlie's vision overlaps with Scorsese's, and it thus comes as no surprise that Charlie is, to the best of my knowledge, the only character in Italian/American cinema ever to problematize the racial bias that permeates his own (Charlie's *and* Scorsese's) culture. Let us see how.

As Charlie sits on a chair from which he patently enjoys Diane's seminaked body, his inner voice comments: "You know something. She is really good-looking. I gotta say that again: she is really good-looking. But she's black. And you can see that real plain, right? But there isn't much of a difference anyway, is there? Well, *is there*?" He then shakes the ice in his drink and gulps it down, the medium close-up of his face soon brutally interrupted by the two cartons of Marlboros thrown on the table by Michael.

Later in the film, as Diane switches wigs—from black to blond— in the backstage room, Charlie asks her out, making her believe that he wants to give her a job as a hostess in the place he dreams to open uptown. Intrigued by the chance of not having to dance anymore, Diane accepts. The film thus makes it clear that economic factors overdetermine their encounter. We then cut to a close-up of the lit panel on top of a cab, a blinking orange light on the words "on duty."

Inside the cab is Charlie, who does not have the courage to get out and meet Diane, saying to himself, "What are you, crazy?" He then tells the cab driver to drive slowly by her and then take him back to the neighborhood. Given the autobiographical dimension of Charlie's character, this sequence suggests Scorsese's awareness of not being immune from visceral, prerational racism himself. It is as if Scorsese wanted to exorcise the knowledge that he, too, takes part in racial prejudice simply because racism, just like sexual desire, is part of the cultural "duty" of Italian Americans. Of course, the impact of these sequences varies, depending on the racial and ethnic background of the viewer. Italian(/American) males certainly have the opportunity for an audiovisual interaction with their own myths and fears. It is because of such uncompromising will to stare at the petrifying Medusa at all costs—albeit in the safe narcissism of intellectual endeavors—that Scorsese earned my respect.

A racial subtext is present in *Taxi Driver* as well, for Travis (Robert De Niro) shows signs of hostility toward Blacks and does not hesitate to kill a black robber. Travis's hostility is not motivated by the narrative and can only be explained in terms of visceral dislike and prejudice—the kind of racism that seems to interest Scorsese. In fact, here, as in *Mean Streets*, the text somehow suggests that the director himself may be inextricably caught up in the deep-seated racism that we are "breastfed" in Western culture. One of Travis's customers, played by Scorsese himself, pays the fare just to sit in the cab and watch the windows of the apartment in which his wife is betraying him with a "nigger." In one of those moments in which transgression is so obvious and in such bad taste that it becomes sublime, Scorsese (as the husband threatened by "niggers") launches into a frantic monologue from the back of the cab:

> I'm gonna kill her. There's nothing else. What do you think of that? Huh? Don't answer. You don't have to answer everything. (Silence.) I'm gonna kill her. I'm gonna kill her with a .44 Magnum pistol. A .44 Magnum pistol. I'm gonna kill her with that gun.

Half-mocking and half-delirious, Scorsese's voice imitates the staccato delivery of the hysteric. And the silent Travis, in an interplay of eyes now glancing at the room where the fare's wife is making him compete with the black man's penis and then staring at the rearview mirror, has to sit through this excess of Italian/American male trouble:

> Did you ever see . . . did you ever see what a .44 Magnum pistol would do to a woman's face? It would fucking destroy it. It'd blow her right apart. That's what it would do to her face.

After the gun as gun has played its gruesome part and created its own sick image, the gun as penis cannot be far behind. Travis's fare takes a hysteric revenge on the member of the other race by ravaging the woman's genitals even more:

> Now, have you ever seen what it would do to a woman's pussy? That you should see, what a Magnum is going to do to a woman's pussy. That you should see.

The outrage has transgressed any limit. Scorsese, the client who wants the cab "on duty" just for him, tells Travis and the audience:

> You must think I'm pretty sick or something. You must think I'm pretty sick, right? I bet you think I'm sick. Do you think I'm sick? (Silence.) You don't have to answer. I'm paying for the ride. You don't have to answer.

The white men among the readers of this article know how much our sociocultural position is inescapably traversed by the fear of the black man's potency: we may extricate ourselves rationally, but the fear is, nonetheless, inscribed in that position; it is a cultural must. Once again, then, Scorsese confronts his viewer—and in particular the white male—with the quicksands of racism. It is easy to be liberal, to think that we are immune from it. Well, let us look at the place where fear and desire have their innermost origins, and we'll discover that, as *Taxi Driver* seems to say, racism is like sexuality: It does not always obey rational rules. The blinking orange light on the word *duty* epitomizes Scorsese's lacerating statements on racial problems: some gestures are a duty because a sociocultural passion has sedimented into second nature and has grown into the unconscious— and unconscious racism is perhaps more dangerous than its conscious counterpart. At the peak of his creative fury (which I locate in these years), Scorsese had the courage almost to excuse himself in advance for what he knows he has to do: to be racist in his portrayal of Blacks.

If *Mean Streets* represents the peak of Scorsese's deliberate representation of the racism of the Italian Americans, *Taxi Driver* is unique in its emphasizing white men's fears via the director's presence in the film. In some of his other films hatred and prejudice resurface ominously but almost never become autonomous subtexts as in these two films.

In *New York, New York* (1977), Scorsese's portrayal of a potentially touchy subject such as a white jazz musician in the 1940s is quite a-problematic. It is as if race had ceased to interest him, so that a certain mannerism vitiates the representation of the musical friendship between Jimmy Doyle (Robert De Niro) and Cecil Powell (Clarence Clemmons). The world of African/American music is, indeed, portrayed as marginal with respect to mainstream entertainment, but it is also romanticized and given a complacent Hollywood veneer. But then again, *New York, New York* belongs to the group of films over which Scorsese had less control and that he made to have the freedom to do what he wanted in other, more personally-felt ventures.

In *After Hours* (1985), Blacks are virtually absent if we exclude a brief appearance of two bouncers in the punk club and a black man in the posse that hunts Paul Hackett (Griffin Dunne). As *After Hours* is the story of man who is haunted by a bizarre chain of events, which turns an entire neighborhood against him, it is actually worth noting that Scorsese, in the mid-1980s and with racial relationships deteriorating in the Reagan's cultural climate, actually avoided including racial paranoia in his Kafkaesque fable.

Not surprisingly, the racial theme is more compelling in the films with ethnic situations. In *Raging Bull,* Scorsese implicitly takes up the theme of the rivalry between Italian Americans and Blacks in the boxing arenas. At least since 1935, the year in which Primo Carnera and Joe Louis squared off for the world heavyweight championship— and, ironically, the year in which Italy's fascist government invaded Abyssinia—Italian/American boxers (such as La Motta, Marciano, Graziano) have fought with Blacks, giving birth to a ruthless, if legal, battle that symbolized the black versus white antagonism. The symbolic arena in which these fights took place has of course been turned into a paternalistic, white epic with the *Rocky* series, in which Apollo Creed first fought and later befriended—in a Tom-like mode—the white champ. In *Raging Bull,* Scorsese does not make any explicit commentary on this situation. Visually, however, the images of La Motta's fights against "Sugar" Ray Robinson give a most effective account of the racial tension implicit in those matches.

Vincent Lauria (Tom Cruise) in *The Color of Money* (1984) is another racist Italian American in Scorsese's cinematography (although the film does not portray "the neighborhood"). When 'Fast' Eddie (Paul Newman) takes him to an all-black pool room, Vincent asks his girlfriend to leave because of the danger represented by a crowd of young black men. While not making an issue out of racial tensions *The Color of Money* reproposes the image of a conflict that may find different symbolic outlets: Every time Blacks and Whites confront one another, even under the aegis of fair play and Olympic spirit, the racial conflict at the root of our civilization raises its ugly head, whether or not we like it.

Finally, *GoodFellas,* Scorsese's most recent ethnic film, returns, albeit only tangentially, to the theme of the director's awareness of the racism in the Italian/American community. Significantly deviating from the literary original—Joe Pileggi's *Wise Guys*—Scorsese adds a few lines in which Tommy (Joe Pesci), at a dinner party in a restaurant, reprimands his girlfriend for being too soft on miscegenation. The general acquiescence with which Tommy's remarks are met reinforces the idea that racism is not the isolated opinion of a troubled mind—though Tommy's mind is indeed troubled—but, rather, the code of a territory. In addition to this minor but revealing reworking of the literary original, it should be noted that of all the murders ordered by Jimmy (Robert De Niro) after the Lufthansa heist, *Good-Fellas* depicts only one: Tommy's brutal shooting (played twice, the second time in slow motion!) of Stacks, the only black character in the film. Stacks, of course, is not murdered because he is black, but because he is one of the accomplices to the heist and thus could pose a threat to Jimmy. The fact remains, however, that Scorsese, intentionally or not, has chosen to put on the screen an aestheticized portrayal of violence by an Italian American against a black man. In effect, the two ways in which Blacks enter *GoodFellas* may be seen as convenient reminders of Scorsese's dual attitude with respect to race: denunciation of racism within the Italian/American community and, more important, (un)conscious awareness of his own inability to portray race relations in an unbiased manner. Like Charlie in *Mean Streets*, Scorsese has had the honesty to admit his "duty" to fear a confrontation with blacks in accordance with a preconstituted script. Second, Scorsese has often given the viewer the opportunity to react to and reflect on race relations simply by putting blacks and whites on the screen, even when an original literary work did not call for it. Scorsese's films reveal the director's will to give an unembellished portrayal of the nightmare haunting what was once the American dream. Although he has never made a film explicitly about race relationships, as has Spike Lee, Scorsese shares with the African/American director the desire to hurl his truth in the face of the audience with uncompromising passion—a blinking orange light on the word "realism."

## IV. CONCLUSIONS (STEPHANIE HULL)

De Palma, Coppola, Scorsese: these three directors' works, when viewed together in the context of their choice to confront race relations in the stories they tell, demonstrate the wide range of possibilities for the representation of Blacks in Italian/American cinema from

1970–90. While our approaches to their work resist synthesis (mainly because of Maurizio's more "personalized" voice), using both of our analyses, I have cautiously reached a general consensus in describing the directors in relation to one another.

De Palma's approach in his earlier films seems the least self conscious of the three. While he clearly intends to call attention to the ways in which Blacks and Whites interact, his characters at first lack the specificity that would make it possible to draw useful conclu sions about their representation. In *Sisters*, *Dressed to Kill* and *Wise Guys*, the black actors do not consistently portray human types, but where they do, their actions inspire us to question relations between people of different races. Even in *The Untouchables*, where Blacks are nearly invisible, their subtle presence reminds us of an important racial interaction in 1930s Chicago that simmers beneath the surface of the violent conflict in a city under siege by the mob. While the character manipulations in *Bonfire of the Vanities* are in many ways an unnecessary complication of Wolfe's plot, and the too-placid accep tance of oppression by Blacks in *Casualties of War* rings false, the intent in these two films to shed light on the unrest among Blacks, Whites, and Jews in New York City or Blacks, Whites, and Vietnam ese in Vietnam is patently clear and is laudable for this project's purposes.

I would place Coppola in the middle for his slightly more consisten and more open examination of the issues of racial interaction. As does Scorsese, Coppola takes the initiative to insert black characters even in literary adaptations—if such an insertion leads to an effective pro blematizing of race. His characters are more often than not developed in such a way that their interaction is multidimensional and thought provoking rather than merely stereotypical.

Yet neither of these two directors achieves the openness Maurizio justifiably attributes to Scorsese. Because Scorsese is willing to risk himself to reach a deeper understanding of others (and not only others *like him*), his depictions are a more controversial and more aggressive treatment of the social ills he perceives. He is set apart not by his product but by his process: identify a compelling topic (often a painful one) and make it the center of a thorough and multifaceted discussion after which no one leaves unscathed and no perspective is left unaf fected. While his director-colleagues have often hit on similar results theirs is an indirect approach that ultimately makes the films' mes sages more vulnerable while protecting the director. Scorsese make himself personally vulnerable and in exchange strengthens his charac ters and his examination of racial interaction.

I want to make it clear that these conclusions are the result of sort of "forced" dialogue between myself and our theme as a whole, and not the expression of any new beliefs. Looking at the three directors as objectively as possible (of course, this was easier while reading Maurizio's section than while reading my own), I tried to see a broader picture of the work all three had produced during this period. In doing so, I was most convinced by Maurizio's readings of Scorsese, and thus I concede that Scorsese makes the most conscious efforts of the three to problematize and develop our understanding of the relationships between Italian Americans and Blacks, both on-camera and off. While the conclusions have a certain validity and a definite necessity in the context of this project, I hesitate to let them have the last word. I remain more sceptical than Maurizio about the directors' motives and am still unwilling to espouse the sort of firm convictions his section expresses. I do, however, have a new appreciation of all three directors, in spite of their perspectives, because of their perspectives, or both at once.

## V. CODA: A MANTRA/POEM BY FRANCO BERARDI
### (WITH OUR TRANSLATION)

| | |
|---|---|
| Gli Italiani sono un popolo di merda. | The Italians are a shitty people. |
| I Francesi sono un popolo di merda. | The French are a shitty people. |
| Gli Svizzeri sono un popolo di merda. | The Swiss are a shitty people. |
| I Congolesi sono un popolo di merda. | The Congolese are a shitty people. |
| I Cinesi sono un popolo di merda. | The Chinese are a shitty people. |
| Gli Spagnoli sono un popolo di merda. | The Spanish are a shitty people. |
| Gli Inglesi sono un popolo di merda. | The English are a shitty people. |
| I Russi sono un popolo di merda. | The Russians are a shitty people. |
| I Giapponesi sono un popolo di merda. | The Japanese are a shitty people. |
| I Laotiani sono un popolo di merda. | The Laotians are a shitty people. |
| Gli Argentini sono un popolo di merda. | The Argentines are a shitty people. |
| I Peruviani sono un popolo di merda. | The Peruvians are a shitty people. |
| Gli Ungheresi sono un popolo di merda. | The Hungarians are a shitty people. |

| | |
|---|---|
| I Croati sono un popolo di merda. | The Croats are a shitty people. |
| I Bulgari sono un popolo di merda. | The Bulgarians are a shitty people. |
| Continuate voi perchè a me i popoli di merda mi danno sui nervi. | You go on, because shitty peoples get on my nerves. |
| Per fortuna ci sono anche degli esseri humani che non fanno parte di nessun popolo di merda. | Luckily there are also human beings who don't belong to any shitty people. |

## NOTES

We are aware that "African/American" would be more contemporary than "black." In our essay, however, we will use the latter, mainly to make our sentences less awkward. We have also capitalized "Black(s)" whenever it is a noun, and left it lower case when an adjective.

1. The former West versus East, capitalism versus communism, bipolarity has been replaced by the socio-economic gap dividing the North from the South. Although terribly vague because of its relativity (North of whose borders?) and because often the North vs. South polarity is reproposed within each country (Italy, Spain, India, etc.), this formulation seems to me rhetorically useful and discursively evocative: Most of the global wealth *is* concentrated in the hands of countries that are considered as "northern." According to many commentators, the Gulf war was the first manifestation of the South's resentment against the North.

2. Nykeisha Jenkins, a black student from Brooklyn in my Italian cinema class, had no knowledge of my observation and came to the same conclusions after watching several Italian films. Encouraged by me, she wrote an intriguing and convincing paper on the parallels between matriarchs in Visconti's *Bellissima* (1953) and Petrie's *A Raisin in the Sun* (1961).

3. Donald Bogle, *Toms, Coons, Mulattos, Mammies and Bucks* (New York: Ungar, 1989).

4. *Ibid.*, 81.

5. *Heart of Darkness*, Eleanor Coppola's documentary of the filming of *Apocalypse Now*, points out that forty years before this production, Orson Welles undertook and then abandoned the project of adapting Joseph Conrad's novel *Heart of Darkness* for his first major motion picture, following his dramatic reading of the text for a 1938 radio broadcast series. It is common knowledge that Conrad's novel reflects his own experiences while journeying upriver into "L'Etat indépendent du Congo" (the territory known as the Belgian Congo from 1908–1960, present day Zaire); this journey was the culmination of a childhood desire to travel into the unexplored expanses in the heart of Africa which were represented on maps of the time as "exciting spaces of *white* paper," "white and big" (Ross C. Murfin, ed., *Heart of Darkness: A Case Study in Contemporary Criticism*, New York: St. Martin's Press, 1989; my emphasis). While Conrad's novel is perceived as the expression of "a profound realization about human nature: whiteness and light may turn out to be blackness and darkness, and blackness and darkness may be relatively pure" (Murfin, 9; racial metaphors implied in text), Coppola's depiction alters the nature of this darkness by shifting the location of the "heart of darkness" to a country populated not by Blacks but by Asians and thus losing an integral aspect of Conrad's metaphors of European "exploration" and corruption of this African civilization; his elimination of the black characters before beginning to depict this central space of the film compounds his avoidance of the original text's major themes.

6. Among the reviewers of *The Cotton Club* were Steve Vineberg (*Cineaste*. XIX; 2:1985); Albert Johnson (*Film Quarterly*, summer 1985); Richard Corliss (*Time* 17 December 1984); and Bonnie Allen (*Essence*, December 1984).

7. As a character who is neither black nor white, she serves to remind us of the association of these two colors with negative and positive, respectively, and of the assumption that separating the two (putting things in black and white) implies clarity and resolution.

8. S. E. Hinton, *Rumble Fish* (New York: Dell Publishing, 1975); S. E. Hinton, *The Outsiders* (New York: Dell Publishing, 1967).

9. Tom Wolfe, *Bonfire of the Vanities* (New York: Farrar & Strauss, 1987). Subsequent references in text.

10. "*GoodFellas*," *Film Quarterly* 44, no. 3 (spring 1991): 43–50.

11. Although, for the purpose of this essay, I have viewed all of Scorsese's films, I will not mention here the films in which Blacks are either absent or when their presence seemed to me to have no interesting consequence for my argument, such as in *Cape Fear* (1991), where the only two black characters are the couple who have the judge's boat in custody.

# 10

## From Lapsed to Lost: Scorsese's Boy and Ferrara's Man

### REBECCA WEST

Abel Ferrara's *Bad Lieutenant* can profitably be read as a sequel to and completion of Martin Scorsese's *Who's That Knocking at My Door?*. There are many elements that link the two films: the setting in New York's "mean streets," the Italian American domestic background, the gritty realist style; none is as compelling, however, as the intense concentration on the male protagonists—J. R. in Scorsese and the unnamed "bad lieutenant" in Ferrara—both portrayed by actor Harvey Keitel. In the readings of these films that follow, my goals are, first, to analyze their representations of masculinities and male subjectivities, particularly in relation to Italian/American ethnicity, Catholicism, and the sphere that is gendered as feminine; next, to consider how and why Harvey Keitel is a particularly suitable, if complexly elaborated, embodiment of these representations; and, last, to posit some ways in which the roles Keitel embodies in these two films can be seen as challenges to the ostensible hegemony of the dominant fiction's normative heterosexual masculinity, a fiction that has historically conditioned both self-generated and externally imposed views of the quintessential "Italian" and "Italian/American" man.

Although I list these topics sequentially, I shall, in fact, move among them in a nonlinear manner, for they are inextricably bound up one with the other. In methodologically contextualizing my foray into the difficult terrain of gender, ethnicity, and cinematic representation, I privilege no one critical or theoretical take, although Kaja Silverman's work on "male subjectivity at the margins" and Paul Smith's study of Clint Eastwood as a "cultural production" were particularly helpful to me at the inception of this project. I shall reveal throughout this essay my debts to a diversity of approaches that have aided me in venturing to bring these films and this actor into a discursive space that seeks both to encompass and to transcend Italian/American issues. I hope to show that Scorsese's "boy" and Ferrara's "man" are readable as representations of masculinities in crisis and, further, that these films belie, with the force of their directors' internally generated critiques and deconstructions of the givens of their own inherited perspectives, what is too often seen as the unquestioned "macho-ism" of Italian/American male subjectivity. I also seek to bring to the fore the role of Harvey Keitel in this critique, an actor whose "passing" as an Italian American further complicates the issue of ethnicity, and whose recent personal and professional expressions of the importance of fatherhood are highly pertinent to constructions of masculinity.

As a parenthetical preface to my analyses, and to underline by contrast the representations of male subjectivities in Scorsese's and Ferrara's films, I want to make brief reference generally to the genre of action or adventure movies, and specifically to the recent Schwarzenegger blockbuster, *True Lies*. It is certainly a fact that the genre of action films has not functioned historically as a site of questioning of the phallic dominant fiction. We bring certain expectations to these "in-your-face" movies that we would be foolish to hope to see reversed or eroded. In the classic action or adventure flick, the hero is macho, violent, powerful, "all-man," while women are either motherly or highly sexualized accessories. *True Lies* draws on this tradition, but plays with today's awareness of how constructed these male and female representations are by having Harry, Schwarzenegger's character, be a "masked" double identity. To his wife and daughter, he is a rather boring computer salesman who is always late to family events, is absent-minded, and is, in summary, lacking in any charisma or, we adduce, sexual imaginativeness with his wife Helen (Jamie Lee Curtis). Helen is herself a "double" or "masked" character as well, for she appears to Harry to be a long-suffering, meek, and rather boring working housewife (she works as a paralegal but her major identity is as a wife and mother), when she, in fact, has become involved (nonsexually) with a man who claims to be a spy, and who is fulfilling her strong need for adventure and intrigue. Unbeknownst to her, her own husband Harry is a real spy who lives incredibly dangerous and sexualized adventures. This all provides a possibly revisionist depth to the film, as both male and female identities are questioned by the "doubling" effect, but the resolution of the film makes abundantly clear that women can have access to their desires only by recognizing and acquiescing to the dominant phallic fiction. Helen is thoroughly humiliated, endangered, and almost killed because of her attempt to

enter into Harry's world of adventure, and she and their daughter
Dana are saved only because Harry is restored to his "true" role as
classic adventure hero, supermacho representative of the traditional
dominant fiction. In the end, Helen gets what she wants; as she says,
"I married Rambo." And Harry gets what he wants as well; a sexy
wife whose excesses of desire and fantasy are all well incorporated
into his world (she becomes his partner in spying) and whose identity
is simply a version of his (her code name is Doris, his Boris).[1] There
is much more that could be said about this film in terms of its "tam-
ing" of women, its blatant racial stereotyping, and its rampant fixation
on the metaphoric phallus (big guns, huge pointy airplanes, Arnold
Schwarzenegger himself, whose body, unlike that of Jamie Lee Curtis, is never uncovered since he possesses the Phallus, not the penis),
but my point is that Hollywood, in this and so many other recent
films, sustains the dominant fiction even while introducing a little
touch of political correctness regarding women and a little bit of vulnerability in men. All is put back into "proper" place in *True Lies;*
Arnold is "all man" and Jamie Lee is "all woman," brute force wins,
and the phallic order is undisturbed. I would add that Schwarzenegger
is here, as in other films, not only the epitome of phallic maleness
but also thoroughly de-ethnicized, that is, mainstream, white "all-
American," albeit with the continuing irony of his Austrian accent.

In contrast to this Hollywood model, at the time Scorsese made
*Who's That Knocking* (midsixties, that is), he was a debutant director
well outside of the Hollywood mindset. Likewise, Abel Ferrara had
been and remained, up to the success of *Bad Lieutenant,* a maverick,
"cult" director with little or no presence in the Hollywood scene.
From their position on the margins of the industry, both were freer
to pursue projects and shape visions less controlled by issues of mar-
ketability or conformity. In addition, then-unknown actor Harvey
Keitel made his film debut in *Who's That Knocking* and, over the
next twenty years before the making of *Bad Lieutenant,* remained a
nonmainstream actor, often working with first-time directors and on
projects in Europe. Scorsese and Ferrara are heavily identified with
Italian Americana, by dint of their actual ethnic backgrounds and,
to varying extents, by the themes of their films. Keitel has a more
complicated relation to ethnicity, although his debut with Scorsese,
subsequent work (as a criminal or a lawman) with Italian/American
directors (Scorsese, Ferrara, Tarantino), and physical believability as
an Italian American have conspired to identify him strongly with that
ethnicity. Keitel himself responded to a question about the difficulty
of playing an Italian American in *Who's That Knocking* and in *Mean
Streets* that it was not so hard: "I grew up in Brooklyn and went to

school in Coney Island, so my friends were everything: Jewish, Catholic, Irish, a real melting pot. It didn't matter that I was raised Jewish and Marty was raised Catholic, our place was beyond local religion" (Thompson, 24). Scorsese, Ferrara, and Keitel are all three "marked," then, as maverick, "ethnic" presences at variance with Hollywood mainstream types. Furthermore, Italian/American film is typically associated with gangster movies, a genre that has historically been the site of probing representations of and investigations into "deviant" or nonnormative male subjectivities.[2] Scorsese, Coppola, and others have, of course, contributed to this characterization with films such as *Mean Streets, GoodFellas,* and *The Godfather* series. Keitel too is associated with gangster and cop movies because of the many times he has so effectively played either a bad guy or an officer of the law. Although many Italian Americans themselves decry the stereotyping of their culture that they see at work in such films (mafiosi, extended families with food-and children-obsessed mamas, lower-class milieus, etc.), it is worth pointing out, I believe, that these settings and these roles have often permitted very acute inquiries not only into Italian/American cultural and interpersonal realities but also into so-called mainstream assumptions about overtly ethnic masculinities and femininities.[3] Be that as it may (I cannot explore this important issue further in the context of this paper), I have sought to highlight here a number of attributes shared by Scorsese, Ferrara, and Keitel: maverick, marginal, "Italian American," deviant (i.e., the gangster thematic). Contrast this to the mainstream, nonethnic, and law-and-order thematics of many cultural representations of the dominant fiction of masculinity (the clean-cut "All-American" model), and certain challenges to that fiction are already to be expected in the films by Scorsese and Ferrara that I intend to discuss. The embodiment of these deviations from the "All-American" norm in Harvey Keitel is also important, given the actor's personal and professional identities, which I shall discuss later.[4]

Let me begin my analysis of ethnic male subjectivities in Scorsese's and Ferrara's films by highlighting the central role of the Catholic Church in both. Western society's dominant fiction of phallic masculinity is deeply tied up with religions, and in certain sectors specifically with Catholicism. Scorsese's *Who's That Knocking* portrays the spiritual struggle of a young man, J. R., who is in the grip of a Catholic belief system that proves in the end to be both ethically disabling and psychically devastating. That is, it affects both his social and interpersonal "ethos"—understood as a collection of habitual characteristics that make up a self and form a character—and his inner, psychic self. We see the results of J. R.'s conditioning most

clearly in his relationship with a non-Catholic girl, played by Zina
Bethune (who is simply called the "girl" in the film) whom he first
perceives as embodying the essentialized "virgin" of the Catholic (and
I should say not only Catholic) binarism "virgin-whore" by which
women have tended to be categorized in our Western culture. When
she tells him that she was raped by an earlier boyfriend, J. R. rejects
her as a "whore," and enters into a full-blown crisis of self-identity
as the negative limits of this binary belief system seep into his consciousness. If this element of the symbolic order that bolsters the
dominant fiction of normative masculinity does not hold, the entire
fiction is in danger of collapsing and, along with it, J. R.'s understanding of his identity as a male and a holder of the Law. Although the
title of the film is taken from the pop song that plays on the sound
track at a crucial moment (more on that later), I think that it alludes
also to the concept of challenge or the breaking of constructed categories that I am arguing. Something is "knocking" at the church's
door, at J. R.'s psychic door, and at the boundaries of the dominant
fiction's construction of heterosexual masculinity. And not inciden-
tally, that challenge is advanced by means of the issue of rape, which
destabilizes the "virgin-whore," or "Mary-Eve" categorization of
woman historically supported by Catholic doctrine.

In 1992, almost a quarter of a century after the 1969 release of the
final version of *Who's That Knocking* (which had several earlier versions and different titles), Ferrara's *Bad Lieutenant* is released. The
lead role is again played by Harvey Keitel, whose spiritual struggles
are again focused on, in a virtuoso performance at once riveting and
deeply disturbing. And the Catholic Church is once again brought
into play as both the source and the emblem of the bad lieutenant's
crisis of male identity. The "virgin-whore" thematic is made even
more explicit in the figure of a young and beautiful nun whose violent
rape intensifies what is already a radically advanced case of disturbed
male subjectivity. While Scorsese's "boy," the young and relatively
unformed J. R., has made few choices regarding what sort of man
he will become, the bad lieutenant is precisely what J. R. *might* have
become: a cop who is a drug addict, a desperate gambler, a corrupt
officer of the law: in short, a fractured subjectivity *in extremis*. I therefore read the title as another metatextual indicator, as is *Who's That
Knocking*, for a *lieu-tenant* is, etymologically, a holder of the place, a
"doorkeeper," a lineman, so to speak, and this lieutenant has himself
crossed all lines between good and bad, right and wrong, normal and
deviant, as these lines have been drawn and maintained in society's
symbolic and legal orders. Furthermore, a lieutenant is also a stand-
in for a superior power (as in "lieutenant governor"), as Keitel's

character should be a stand-in for the Law, a literal embodiment of it as a cop of the system, yet this particular character breaks the law again and again as he sinks ever deeper into a no-exit of addiction, gambling debt, and self-degradation. The rape of the nun once again destabilizes ostensibly fixed female identity, and ultimately brings the bad lieutenant face to face with the limitations of his own assumed male identity.

Let me now turn from these introductory remarks to a closer look at the films in question: first, Scorsese and some general background on him up to and including the time of the making of *Who's That Knocking*. Martin Scorsese was born in 1942 in New York City's Little Italy, which runs from Houston Street to Canal Street where Chinatown begins. (The hostile divide between these two areas is the basis of Abel Ferrara's film *China Girl*.) An only child, Scorsese grew up a sickly asthmatic boy whose greatest escape was going to the movies. He has said that he understood early on that the powerful people in his neighborhood were the gangsters and the priests, and he decided at the age of eight or nine to become a priest. He has also said that for him the Catholic mass and movies were similarly fascinating because of their vivid spectacle, their grandiosity, and colors. Scorsese did not follow his early desire to become a priest, of course; rather, he opted for film studies at New York University where he was a student from 1960 to 1965. He made a few short features before *Who's That Knocking*, but it was his first distributed film, what Maurizio Viano calls "his first film to enter the international 'postal' system" (in reference to Derrida's concept of the "postal" as "a model of communication that assumes systems of address based on identity" [quoted from Peter Brunette's and David Will's *Screen/play* in "Scor-sampling," 135]. In simple words, Scorsese first became "Scorsese" with this film. *Who's That Knocking at My Door* is an excellent object of inquiry for genetic criticism—the study of the ways in which texts are born and evolve—because it is what Viano calls "a de-structured text partially because of its troubled genesis" (139). It, in fact, had at least two intermediate versions from 1965 to 1969 with different titles; the first, from 1965, is called *Bring on the Dancing Girls* and the second, from 1967, *I Call First*. Scorsese describes what happened when it was shown at the Chicago Film Festival: "It got good reviews from Roger Ebert. And then there was a probability of distribution if I put a nude scene in, and I did that in Amsterdam, Holland" (quoted in Viano, 138). The film we now see is that "final" 1968 version, without, of course, the benefit of the visual palimpsest created by the earlier texts underlying it.

For those who have not seen the film, let me give a summary of its diegetic content, its "plot," so to speak.[5] J. R., a young Italian American, meets a blond girl in the New York City ferryboat waiting room and begins a romantic relationship with her. As we follow him through his daily life, made up primarily of aimless paling around with his Italian/American buddies, we come to understand that the relationship is in the past and that we are seeing flashbacks to it, constructed as J. R.'s thoughts and memories. The film alternates between the present—J. R. with his friends—and the past—J. R. with the girl (who is never named)—in a sort of circular construction in that the ending takes us up to where J. R., in fact, is at the beginning: Without the girl and back with his friends. In the flashbacks, we learn that J. R. will not have sex with the girl, despite her willingness and his desire for her, because as he explains to her, she is a good girl, not a "broad." When the girl tells him one day that an ex-boyfriend whom she trusted raped her, J. R. characterizes her as a "broad," and rejects her. He later attempts a reconciliation, but when he tells her that he "forgives" her and will marry her "anyway," she rejects him. He then goes to church, apparently seeking some relief from his confusion and distress; the final scene shows J. R. saying goodnight to his friend Joey, back on the neighborhood streets.

This narrative summary of a fairly simple story does not in any sense capture the intricate semiotics of the film, which Viano calls "semantically ambiguous and visually unsettling" (138). Considering some specific scenes may permit us to capture that disturbing ambiguity. The first is the opening and first few minutes of the film in which we first see a close-up of a statue of the Virgin and Christ child, then, a woman in a kitchen preparing food (a *calzone*) and serving it to children who are sitting around the table. This scene is accompanied by a grating, disquieting noise. Then, there is a cut to someone's back and hands, in which is held a stick, and we soon see that we are watching the beginning of a streetfight. The next cut takes us to the "Pleasure Club" (there is a close-up shot of the sign naming it as such) where J. R., who has already appeared in the streetfight scene, is hanging out with his friends, Joey, Sally Gaga, and others. At one point, a close shot of a pensive J. R. takes us into his thoughts, and his memory of his first meeting with the girl takes over the diegetic space.

Of the wealth of semantic information that these syntactically imbricated scenes give us, I underscore the following: First, the binary logic regarding gender distinctions inherent in the dominant symbolic order of Western society, and basic to Catholic doctrine, is evoked in several ways. The woman is clearly a mother who is cooking for her children and, although there is nothing explicitly disruptive or odd about this presentation of traditional female identity, there *is* something disturbing about the grinding sound track, which evokes a response that happy "domestic" music would not. The ritualistic aura of the scene, which is entirely without dialogue, further contributes to an estranging effect. The female domestic space is thus "marked" as requiring special attention, as the stereotypical Italian mama in the kitchen takes on an ambiguously ominous quality. On the other hand, the cut to a streetfight, in which only young men are participating, presents a traditional male identity that is tied to violence, in contrast to the presumably nurturing activities of the mother. Yet this scene is also estranging in that the fight seems curiously and obviously choreographed—more like a dance than a rumble—and it, indeed, is accompanied by upbeat pop music. Nonetheless, female and male are traditionally binarized, separated out one from the other, and characterized by sharply contrasting spaces, the mother within an enclosed domestic space, the boys out on the public streets.

When we move to the scene in the "Pleasure Club," we may note that "pleasure" evidently excludes women, as all of the people present are male. However, when we then are taken into J. R.'s thoughts (and he, seated alone and apart, has already been placed in such a way as to establish a physical distance from the other guys in the club), we understand that he is internally as well as spatially distant from this homosocial scene, taken up with memories of the girl. Pursuing spatial semantics, it is furthermore significant that the enclosed space associated with the mother and the public, open space associated with the boys in the opening sequences are often reversed in the ensuing scenes of J. R. and the girl together, as well as in those of J. R. and his pals. He and the girl walk on the roof or stroll on the street in some remembered encounters, while the guys hang out in the club, in cars, or in apartments the hermetic quality of which is emphasized by Scorsese in close-up shots of locking doors. While J. R.'s everyday Italian American world is prevalently male, then, it is portrayed as overwhelmingly enclosed—womblike, we might say— and is thus coded as more traditionally "feminine" than the wide-open public spaces historically marked as "masculine." As J. R. seeks some alternative to quotidian homosociality, he escapes the enclosed spaces shared with his pals in strolls on the street and on rooftops with the girl and in a trip to the country (a highly significant scene that I shall analyze later).

In spite of the dominant "maleness" of J. R.'s daily interactions, his father never appears, and it is the maternal realm—established as foundational in the opening shots—that haunts the film. This is an essential attribute of the film's "ambiguity." Many critics of the film have responded to the mother as a strongly negative presence. One obvious reading is that she is a "typical" Italian/American mama who spoils and stifles her son to the point that he becomes a "mama's boy," akin to the "roughneck sissy" type investigated by Sklar, one incapable of "manly" sexual relations with a woman because of his unhealthy attachment to his mother. Viano hints at this fundamentally Freudian interpretation when he writes of J. R.'s fear of impotence with the girl, of "not performing as a mythical stallion" (147). This reading is certainly possible, but it is complicated by the fact that the mother in the first scene is Catherine Scorsese, the director's mother, and Scorsese is thus implicating his own identity in the portrayal of J. R. The asthmatic, sensitive "mama's boy," Scorsese himself, may then be seen as expressing his own deep ambivalence toward women, whether mothers, "broads," or good girls, not simply in a fairly banal representation of the Oedipal complex, but rather in a mode of self-critique and analysis. Given J. R.'s hesitations to take on the crass behavior and attitudes regarding women that his pals unthinkingly demonstrate, and taking into account as well his struggle to break out of the limits of his geographically (Little Italy), religiously, and ethnically predetermined role as a "real man" in his relationship with the "other" (the blond, educated, clearly non-Italian/American girl), we might see his sexual anxieties as positive "weaknesses." That is to say that from our perspective today, when "weakness" and "feminization" regarding masculinities are coded and interpreted in more complex ways, we can (and I do) see J. R. not as a "mother-whipped" sexual coward, but as Scorsese's *alter ego* whose portrayal is infused with the director's self-awareness and perturbation as they are generated by his grasp of the complexities of gender identification and male sexuality.

Many scenes in *Who's That Knocking* show violence as an activity that is gendered male. By means of the early streetfight, the angry, physically aggressive behavior of Joey in the club, and the many ways in which the pals revel in real and imagined scenes of violence, we see that J. R.'s contemporaries have unthinkingly bought into this element of normative masculinity, just as they accept the objectification of women and its attendant misogyny. J. R. is, however, consistently distanced from this mode of interaction, tending to hold himself spatially (as well as mentally) apart from his surroundings. Keitel's young looks also contribute to our sense of his difference, for he is almost delicately handsome and rather diminutive. J. R. is, nonetheless, filled with ideas of masculinity generated and sustained primarily by tough, macho-Western or bad-guy movie heroes like John Wayne, and Lee Marvin. In his first conversation with the girl, who is reading a French movie magazine, he comments on an article in it on John Wayne, and later he takes her to see *Rio Bravo*. There is also a scene of a party, again an all-guy affair, in which one of the young men waves a (very small) gun around and threatens Sally Gaga, all to the vast amusement of the other guys; at the end of this scene there is a quick cut to stills of John Wayne, Dean Martin, and Angie Dickinson from *Rio Bravo*, which leads into a shot of J. R. and the girl leaving the theater where they have just seen that film. When the girl comments that she liked Angie Dickinson's character in the movie, J. R. scoffs at her, saying that Dickinson was nothing but a "broad," thus connecting the violence-Western-macho subtext with gendered binarism, which is carried one step farther, however, in that females are now also binarized as "good girls" whom one marries and "broads" whom one has sex with and discards. In the references to movies that dot *Who's That Knocking*, Scorsese subjects not only his own ethnic and religious attitudes toward masculine and feminine roles to autocritique, but he also implicates cinema itself in a *mise en abyme* that adds yet another level of depth to his questioning of dominant models of normative masculine heterosexuality.

The issues of traditional models of masculinity, binarized gender roles, and powerfully defining ethnic and religious attitudes are all put into place in the early scenes of the film, and are kept in play throughout. As I have argued, J. R. can be read as "lapsing" from these dominant fictions into a crisis of male subjectivity that threatens to shatter the generally unquestioned solidity of the phallic symbolic order at work in his formation as a man. I have already highlighted a few of the ways in which he is separated out (his placement in scenes, his physique, his recourse to his own inner thoughts and memories). I believe that J. R. is shown as being both in and out of the limits of normative maleness, a liminal character who is "betwixt and between," a true "adolescent" who has not yet taken on the fixed attributes of what his ambiance supports as mature masculinity. He hangs out with the guys, sharing their taste for violence and the crass use of women, yet he has also sought a relationship with the girl, who is clearly not from his neighborhood and not Italian American, but rather someone who represents "otherness" and perhaps even transcendence of his life as it is given. In his refusal to have sex with her, he indicates his belief in a binarized view of women as good or bad, but he also reveals a desire for love and a meaningful relationship. J. R. wants and seeks a life that is not dominated by the aimlessness, violence, casual sex, and misogyny of his homosocial group, and this need for something "higher" is quite literally portrayed in the important episode of the film in which J. R. and Joey go to visit a friend of J. R.'s who lives in the country. The friend takes them on an outing during which they hike up a mountain to see the beautiful view. Joey complains the whole way up and, once on the top, he sees no point in having made the effort, while J. R. silently absorbs the landscape spread out before him with what is obvious thoughtfulness. This mountain-climbing scene makes use of a very old *topos* of spiritual struggle—we need only think of Dante's purgatorial mount—and I have suggested in an earlier essay that this film, in fact, has much in common with Dante's allegory; J. R. looks for "salvation" in his Beatrice, while fighting against his attraction to "vanities" and "pargolette" (broads); he attempts a similarly premature ascent, and he is in his own "selva oscura" or dark wood of confusion and error at the end of the film.

Rape is the issue that precipitates J. R.'s crisis, bringing together as it does the film's preoccupation with binarized views of women, the negativity of macho violence, and confused male sexuality. The girl's rape is presented as a stunningly effective flashback that is cut into J. R.'s and the girl's conversation, during which she tells him about this traumatic event. J. R.'s reaction is to respond to her that he cannot understand what she is saying and that he is incapable of believing "that story." It is clear from his rejection of her, both at the time at which she tells him about the rape and later when he goes to her apartment to seek a reconciliation and instead ends up calling her a "whore," that J. R. identifies strongly with the boyfriend who raped her. He has, in fact, been fighting against his own powerful sexual urges toward her, and as the interpolated nude scene with multiple sex partners shows, has himself committed, in his objectification of women, a lesser but related violence against them.[6] There is, therefore, a level of guilt in J. R.'s reaction that he projects onto the girl, since projecting it onto the boyfriend would be tantamount to admitting his own guilt. He then attempts to forgive her for her "transgression," (a sort of self-forgiveness by transference), and when she resists this characterization of herself as responsible for the rape, J. R. cannot find an alternative to flight from her, which is equal to a flight from his own sense of guilt.

That Scorsese should have chosen rape as a catalyzing element in J. R.'s crisis is yet another indication of the depth of his self-critique and of his desire to deconstruct the fictions underlying normative heterosexual masculinity. In the context of Catholic, Italian/American tradition—the roots of which can be found in centuries-old Italian traditions—rape occupies an ambivalent space somewhere between the "naturally" sexual and the transgressively criminal. In simple words, women are more often than not seen as "asking for it" or at least as stimulating such intensities of desire in men by means of their "evil" corporeality that men cannot be held responsible for seeking to fulfill their needs. It was, after all, Eve who seduced Adam into eating the apple. J. R.'s response to the girl's rape is in keeping with this belief; rather than looking to bring the boyfriend to justice or to take revenge on him, J. R. transfers responsibility to the girl, now perceived as a "broad" and, finally, a "whore." He characterizes his attitude as that of "any *reasonable* guy" (italics mine). Yet it is also true that he is tormented by this response and wishes to activate "forgiveness" as the means by which the girl can be "revirginized," and he can escape his own bad conscience. The final scene of the film is precisely one of forgiveness sought, in the place where J. R.'s experience has taught him to seek it: the Church. As J. R. kisses the crucifix in the confessional, the sound track plays the title song, and the camera pans around the statues of holy figures, creating something like a proto-rock video. J. R.'s mouth bleeds as he kisses the crucifix, underlining his masochistic need for punishment. There are flash-backs to the scene with the mother in the kitchen, to the rape, to J. R. and the girl, and to J. R. with the "broads" in the nude scene, all of which highlight the centrality of the feminine sphere to J. R.'s "hysteria" in the face of a badly fractured normative concept of mas-culinity. We then see him back on the neighborhood street, saying goodnight to his friend Joey; and the film abruptly ends. The ending can be read in a variety of ways, but I think that my reading of the film overall supports a view that sees J. R. as left suspended in a state of identity crisis wherein his constructed male subjectivity has been put to a severe test and found wanting. J. R. has seen the negative limits of the dominant fiction of normative masculinity in which he is trapped, but he has not succeeded in moving beyond it. The ending suggests that breaks away or "lapses" from the normative have been and will continue to be sutured by the powerful social and psychical threads of tradition: the Church, homosocial bonding, familiar and protective ethnic and domestic spaces. A lapse is, after all, a tempo-rary thing. Yet lapses are generally recurring phenomena that reveal the strength of needs and desires that knock at our doors, be they bulwarks built of laws, traditions, or psychic modes of censorship. Society's (and more particularly, a Catholic Italian/American) ethos or dominant fiction of what a "real" man must be is questioned in this film by means of J. R.'s "lapse," but it is by no means dismantled, discarded, or replaced.

Abel Ferrara's *Bad Lieutenant* was released in 1992, and with it Ferrara achieved a level of visibility and success that his prior films had not brought to him. Harvey Keitel was also catapulted to star status and with the success of Jane Campion's *The Piano*, in 1993, to superstar heights. This "instant" success came to both director and actor after years of work, however. It has been asserted that Ferrara "has survived on the edge of the mainstream movie business, half-aided, half-held back by his cult reputation as a maverick" (in "The Gambler," an interview with Gavin Smith). Ferrara was born in New York City in 1952, of Italian/American origin. He has said that his grandfather came to the States from Naples, where he changed his "too-southern" last name "Esposito" to the northern "Ferrara." (Ferrara "signs" his film *China Girl* with both names; in the opening shots of Little Italy, we see a sign indicating "Ferrara's Bakery," and a pan to a building inscribed with the name "Esposito.") Ferrara's first film, *Driller Killer*, made in 1979, was an extremely low-budget picture in which Ferrara himself, under the name of Jimmy Laine, played the lead character, an alienated, unsuccessful painter who, like Scorsese's taxi driver, is driven to distraction by the violence and degradation of New York street life. He begins killing street bums with a hand drill, and ends up killing his lover's husband. The films ends as he waits in his lover's bed, presumably to kill her as well. This movie was never produced on video (that I know of) and was, in fact, the stimulus in England for a film censorship code, which until its showing had never existed there. His next film, *Ms 45*, made in 1980, is instead available on video, presumably because it is not as "raunchy" as his first. It is obviously also a low-budget movie, and while not in any sense a great achievement, it is, nonetheless, an effectively seriocomic, black-humorous portrayal of a young mute girl (played by Zoe Lund, who co-wrote the movie and who appears as the bad lieutenant's partner in drug addiction in the later movie, which she also co-wrote) who is raped twice in one day and just isn't going to take it anymore. She kills the second rapist, takes his forty-five, dismembers him and stores the parts in her refrigerator. She then proceeds to shoot down men, whether directly menacing to her or not. Although this film can be and has been read as a "feminist" statement, I see it more as a witty reversal of action-film clichés and an exercise in transgressing ostensibly fixed codes not in the strict service of a feminist view, but rather in defiance of traditional gender, genre, and audience expectations.[7] In 1984 Ferrara made a psycho-on-the-loose thriller, *Fear City*, followed by two episodes of television's *Miami Vice* and the pilot for *Crime Story;* in 1987 *China Girl* came out (a sort of Chinese/American, Italian/American *Romeo and Juliet*), then, in 1990, *King of New York* starring Christopher Walken, and in 1992 *Bad Lieutenant*. Since then, Ferrara has made his version of the classic *Invasion of the Bodysnatchers*, called simply *The Body-snatchers*, and *Snake Eyes*, which was distributed in the United States under the title *Dangerous Game*. This last film stars Keitel, Madonna, and James Russo and was a big hit at the 1993 Venice Film Festival, where Keitel won the best actor award, and both Ferrara and Keitel were enthusiastically interviewed and written about in Italian venues such as *Vogue Italia* and the newspaper *La Repubblica*. Ferrara's most recent film is entitled *The Addiction* and interweaves drug addiction and vampirism: a not-unexpected project given the centrality of the theme of addiction in *Bad Lieutenant*.

The plot of *Bad Lieutenant* is, as in *Who's That Knocking*, relatively simple. The bad lieutenant has bet big on the Dodgers-Mets championship game, and he ups the stakes throughout the film, convinced in his desperation that the losing Dodgers will win due to the skill of Darryl Strawberry. He spends his days snorting cocaine, making drug deals, talking with his bookie, and listening to and watching the games. One day he learns of the violent rape of a young nun, which occurred on a church altar. Although he responds cynically to the crime and to the reward of fifty thousand dollars offered for any information leading to the capture of the rapists (he says that women are raped all the time, and just because this one was wearing a "penguin suit," he's "supposed to get bent out of shape?"), he is visibly disturbed when he witnesses (half-hidden behind a semiopen door) the medical examination of the naked nun. He eventually goes to the crime scene, already dazed with drink and drugs, and shows real distress as he surveys the desecrated altar on which is scrawled an obscenity. He tries to lift up a toppled statue of the Virgin Mary but is too stoned and ends up sleeping in a pew until other cops and investigators arrive to take evidence at the scene. The lieutenant then listens in to the interrogation of the nun (again, from outside the room), who refuses to say anything about her assailants. He next stops two young girls in a car, ostensibly because of a broken taillight; when he learns that they have taken their father's car without their parent's permission, he blackmails them into participating at a distance in his masturbation (he has one of the girls show him her bared rear end and the other use her mouth to fake oral sex while he masturbates outside the car in which they are seated). His self-hatred is shown with unforgettable force in this almost unbearably drawn-out scene.

As it becomes more and more clear that the Dodgers are going to lose, the bad lieutenant's desperation grows, and he ends up back in the church where the nun is praying. She tells him that she has forgiven the rapists and that he should not seek revenge but rather pray to Jesus and also forgive the boys. He cries out in despair and has a vision of Christ's standing in the aisle in front of him; he first hurls obscenities at Jesus, asking where Christ was when he needed him, then pleads for forgiveness for the many "bad things" he has done. The Christ figure turns into an elderly black woman who is holding the chalice that was stolen during the rape; she leads him to the rapists' basement hideout, where the lieutenant watches the ball game and shares drugs with the two boys while holding them at gunpoint. He then drives them to the bus station and puts them on an out-of-town bus, giving them a box of money that he has gotten from a dealer in exchange for drugs the lieutenant stole from a crime scene, gets in his car, drives to a rendezvous with the gangsters with whom he has placed his big bets on the losing ball team, and as they pull up alongside his car and shoot him to death, the film ends.

Keitel's character is clearly on the edge from the very beginning of the movie, which begins in medias res. He drives his two small sons to school and immediately takes a snort of cocain after they have gotten out of the car. This opening scene conveys a great deal of information, as was the case in Scorsese's film. We learn that the lieutenant is a lower middle-class family man (the family home in the first shot is clearly working class), Catholic (there is a crucifix hanging in the car window), and an addict. We see his edginess and foul mood, which are maintained throughout, modulating at times into stupor or anguished fury. Ferrara has said, in response to a comment that we know nothing of the lieutenant's past, that "I don't think the past necessarily tells you why somebody is the way they are. . . . Who cares? That's the way he woke up that morning" (Gavin Smith, 21). But I think that the opening scene *does* tell us something about the past: The lieutenant has chosen to marry, to have children, to live in a standard house in a modest neighborhood, and to take drugs. This could very well have been the life chosen by Scorsese's J. R. and as the film progresses, we see that the lieutenant is indeed a Catholic and Italian American (there is a scene in which his wife, who is dark-haired and looks quite Italian American, and their four children are taking communion), a man who no doubt married a neighborhood sweetheart, became a cop, and took on the responsibilities of support-ing a family (including his mother-in-law, a very thin old woman with wild, long white hair who, like an ancient fury, looks silently at him with stony loathing in scenes at his home). He has, in fact, followed the standard model of responsible masculinity as defined by his cul-ture but has been unable to live out this model (and this is where we do not get information regarding why). Ferrara says that the pain he is in "comes from his heart. I think pain is in one way or another in everyone" (Gavin Smith, 21). Without indulging too much in the fallacy of extratextual inference, I would go at least as far as to say that the film lets us conclude that this man feels trapped in his life, is gambling to find a way out, and seeks release from himself, from his given identity and existence, in drugs and alcohol. For example, when his bookie refuses to up the lieutenant's already hefty bet, saying that the gangsters he's dealing with will blow up the lieutenant's family home if he doesn't pay his debt, Keitel says that is fine with him, since he has always hated the house he lives in. He is thoroughly alienated from his wife, who in one scene at home asks him to come have a cup of coffee with her, her mother and her sister, and he simply lurches silently off into another room. He seems either indifferent to or gruff with his children, although he goes into his children's bedroom one night and looks tenderly at them as they sleep, indicating that he is not as indifferent as he appears. The film begins, then, with a standard male subjectivity already in a full-blown crisis, already "deviant" and fractured.

In a book entitled *Hearts of Men: American Dreams and the Flight from Commitment*, Barbara Ehrenreich examines standard models of masculinity in our society from the fifties to the eighties (the book was published in 1984), and in a chapter called "Breadwinners and Losers: Sanctions against Male Deviance," she discusses the pressures that men typically felt in the recent past to conform to societal expectations to be thought "real" men. Among these expectations one of the strongest was marriage and family, with the concomitant expectation that the man would be the primary (if not sole) breadwinner. Men deviating from this choice were commonly labeled "losers," and seen as "not fully adults or not fully heterosexual" by a number of psychologists of the fifties who published "scientific" studies to argue their views. Novels such as *The Man in the Gray Flannel Suit* and *Marjorie Morningstar* blatantly advocated traditional models of male maturity and identity, and films of the forties and fifties similarly often emphasized the dangers of any deviance from the norm (even in something as simple as a man who liked to cook or who wanted to travel and have adventures in the world outside of domesticity. Think of what happens to James Stewart in *It's a Wonderful Life* when he rejects his given role: he is totally "erased"!). As the sixties, seventies, and eighties rolled by, things changed, of course, and men had more space for rebellion, more alternative models for mature lifestyles, yet even now there is little doubt that men who remain unattached are still viewed with suspicion and unease by large sectors of our society. For men like the bad lieutenant who were born and raised in the forties and fifties, the alternative models were neither very accessible nor sanctioned. Given the strong emphasis on family in Italian/American culture, it is even less likely that another lifestyle would have been an acceptable choice. Keitel's character is, therefore, caught in the dualism "breadwinner-loser," and the gambling motif of the film becomes even more resonant when we think of his loss of the bet in metaphoric as well as real terms. An addict, an alienated family man, a corrupt law officer, the lieutenant loses big when his psychic pain takes him down errant paths in a search for some way out of the misery that the dominant fiction's version of normative masculinity has brought him.

Although *Bad Lieutenant* is much less obviously dedicated to the portrayal of a specifically Italian/American male subjectivity than is *Who's That Knocking*, the role of the Catholic Church and of the raped nun strongly marks it as partaking in some of the same ethnically determined preoccupations as Scorsese's film. The bad lieutenant is thrown into a final crisis by the rape of the nun, just as J. R.'s breaking point is reached on the girl's revelation of having been raped. The two characters' reactions to the rape of virginal females signal both important similarities and significant differences, however. If J. R. returns to the bosom of the Church in his search for forgiveness, and ultimately gives himself over once more to the comfortable homo-social and macho world of his pals, the lieutenant's response is more explicitly complex. The juxtapositioning of the scene in which he spies on the medical examination of the nude nun (who is exceptionally and clearly sexually desirable) with the masturbation scene makes clear his "transgressive" desire for the nun, which is transferred onto the two young girls in what might be called a "no-touch" form of rape. Consciously or not, the lieutenant has identified strongly with the rapists, as J. R. identifies psychically with the boyfriend, but rather than heaping scorn on the nun, he seeks to revenge the wrong done to her by "getting" the perpetrators. When the lieutenant meets up with the nun at the altar of the church where she was raped, he tells her of his intent to put the rapists away for their crime, emphasizing that other lawmen would just let them go through the system (and presumably get off easy), whereas he alone will see to it that justice is done. We see that a masochistic urge to be punished himself is behind his vehemence, but the nun insists on the necessity for altruism and forgiveness, to the confused and desperate amazement of the lieutenant. Acting on this lesson in forgiveness, he lets the rapists go, not only relinquishing the reward money that would save him from the gambling debts that are threatening his existence, but also giving them the large sum of money that he had made on a drug deal. How might we read this final gesture?

Some critics see "extreme religious orthodoxy" and an attendant "redemption motif" in *Bad Lieutenant* (Slawner) and write that the lieutenant, "thus redeemed" by his final act, is "swiftly removed from the horrors of earthly life, shot dead by a bullet which could itself be interpreted as divinely driven" (Kermode, 40). This view, like the strictly Oedipal reading of *Who's That Knocking*, implicitly characterizes these films as conservative, if not reactionary, in their treatment of the male protagonists' crises. Mama and Mother Church determine all. I prefer to follow another possible interpretive direction, one that is provided by Harvey Keitel himself in comments on the film made during an interview conducted after its completion. To do so, I want to shift gears and to investigate briefly Keitel's profile. This is warranted, I believe, by the undeniable centrality of Keitel to both films under consideration, as well as his extended collaboration with Scorsese and Ferrara on other projects. He is obviously not just any actor as far as these directors are concerned, but rather an integral element in the realization of their visions. Although at this juncture I wish to concentrate on Keitel's work with Ferrara, it is worth remembering as well his extensive work with Scorsese on *Street Scenes 1970, Mean Streets, Alice Doesn't Live Here Anymore, The Last Temptation of Christ, Taxi Driver,* and others.

Ferrara has said in relation to Keitel's part in the making of *Bad Lieutenant* that "how we work is organic. You work around the way he works. He's in every shot, usually alone, so that becomes part of the style of the movie" (Smith interview). In watching Keitel's films, one has the strong sense that his work is often "organic" in this way,[8] that strong interaction with his director is often a large part of the results. He has many times worked with first-time or young directors (Scorsese, Ridley Scott on *The Duellists,* Quentin Tarantino on *Reservoir Dogs,* Danny Cannon on *The Young Americans*), and he has taken on projects far afield from Hollywood, including several in Europe, which Keitel straightforwardly explains as the result of not being able to "get work in Hollywood for the most part," adding that "it turned out a blessing, because I worked with some great people" (Thompson, 24). Keitel, whose work in *Bad Lieutenant* has been called "the bravest performance by an actor in memory" (Erickson), has given many "brave" performances over the course of his more than twenty-five years in the film business, from his debut in *Who's That Knocking* (in which he shed his clothes for the nude sex scene) to his portrayal of a kind of aborigine by elective affinity in *The Piano* (where he also shed his clothes). I emphasize his willingness to appear naked in films because the issue of "bravery" and daring that often comes up in discussions of him has much to do, I think, with male full-frontal

nudity. Much of Keitel's power on the screen derives from his willingness—especially now that he is no longer in youthful perfect shape—
to be seen head-on as an unglamorized male body rather than a glamorized phallic symbol. He is "real" in a way that many actors are not,
not simply because he offers his body to our gaze but also because he
absorbs that gaze without "macho" preening for the feminine spectator or self-conscious anxiety toward the male look.

    Keitel's own looks are capable of soliciting diverse responses, but
normatively glamorous they are not. I would argue that they are perceived as generically "ethnic," and that this "ethnicity" contributes
to our reception of him as a "real" body rather than a sex symbol or
a he-man. There have been few overtly "ethnic" romantic or action-
genre lead actors; perhaps the most spectacular (in every sense of the
word) exception was and remains Rudolf Valentino, whose reception
was strongly gender-specific (generally, women loved him and men
disdained [envied, feared] him).[9] Certainly, some ethnically coded
actors have had success as romantic leads—Al Pacino, John Travolta,
Robert De Niro, Sean Connery, Liam Neeson come to mind—but
the more "Southern" or "Latin" they are (like the first three), the
more they tend to be associated with dangerous sexuality, and the
more "English" or "Anglo-Saxon" (like the last two), the more
suavely or sweetly sexual. Typically, actors who were marked as generically "ethnic," such as the Jewish John Garfield (Julius Garfinkle)
and the Eastern European Charles Bronson (Charles Buchinsky) were
character actors cast, as was Bronson, as "a variety of types, from
Russian to Red Indian," presumably at least in part because they
were "sombre-looking [and] deep-featured" (Walker, 114). They were
also often cast as criminal, tough-guy, and loose-cannon law enforcer
types, as if their "ethnicity" naturally linked them to deviance. This
has been the case with Keitel, who is more often than not cast as a
"dangerous" man on one side or the other of the law, but always in
a tensely equivocal relation to it. He is also thought to be Italian
American by many viewers, in spite of his name, such was the believability he brought to his early roles in Scorsese films. (In *Clockers*, his
"Jewish-Italian" hybrid identity is highlighted in his character's
name: Rocco Klein. When asked what he is, Rocco responds that he
is one of the lost Black tribe of Israel!) He has become, in short, the
"real" ethnic male body *par excellence*, in contrast to the glamorized
and spectacularized "fake" all-American Hollywood phallus. That he
has gained the status of superstar in recent years has as much to do
with transformed perceptions of ethnicity and sexuality as with his
exceptional acting talent. Women spectators have certainly had much
to do with his success; he has been called "the thinking woman's

heartthrob" (a woman friend quoted this label to me, but could not remember the source). One of the salient aspects of Keitel's recent personal and professional profile has been his emphasis on fatherhood, a topic that brings us back to *Bad Lieutenant*. In several interviews conducted after the great success of *The Piano* and *Bad Lieutenant*, Keitel has emphasized his concern for his daughter's well-being as well as the centrality of fatherhood to Ferrara's film.[10] He has also taken on several roles in which fatherhood is the primary issue. Immediately after *The Piano*, in a children's film entitled *Monkey Trouble*, he plays a gypsy organ-grinder who has trained his pet monkey to be a thief. The character is also a divorced man and a highly irresponsible father who gets his comeuppance in the end. The film is a sort of morality tale with laughs, directed squarely at children; of it, Keitel said: "it's as important to my mind as *The Piano* or *Bad Lieutenant*" (Tosches, 161). Another recent film, *Imaginary Crimes*, stars Keitel as yet another conman and deeply flawed father who, as a widower, struggles to keep his daughters in the dark regarding his shady business deals, abandons them to flee prosecution for swindling funds, and eventually returns to take his punishment and be reunited with his daughters. Fatherhood is also important to Ferrara's *Dangerous Game*, in which Keitel plays a philandering film director who, upon confessing his adulterous affairs to his wife, is confronted by her in terms of what his amoral behavior means for their son's perspective on women and life.

According to Keitel, *Bad Lieutenant* is "about a man who is a father, and he's losing his soul and becomes aware of it and tries to do some good. What I feel is that we have to write our own Bible, and not just rely on the experience of our ancestors . . . unless we deal with our own inner conflicts, then we will leave that legacy to our children to cope with because we failed" (Thompson, 25). This reading goes counter to those quoted earlier that see the film as imbued with "extreme religious orthodoxy"; Keitel is denying the adequacy of tradition to resolve our existential conflicts, asserting instead that we must "write our own Bible," as in his view the bad lieutenant presumably did. Now, it could be that Keitel's emphasis on fatherhood has originated in his real-life preoccupations as a recently divorced man with the resultant concerns about his children's well-being. If we attempt to analyze this emphasis in less literal terms, however, Paul Smith's reading of Clint Eastwood's concern with fatherhood as it impinges on the film projects he assumes may provide a useful starting point. Smith links Eastwood's focus on fatherhood with the actor-director's anxieties regarding auteurship, authority, and status as a cultural "father figure" (see his chapter, "Auteur-Father," 243–62). It may well be that Keitel now feels similar anxieties, brought on by the great success of *Bad Lieutenant* and *The Piano*, films that elevated him to super-star status and thus to a position of great "authority" as an actor and a celebrity to whom people would look for guidance or whom they might wish to emulate. Having spent a good deal of his career playing violent, deviant, dangerous men, Keitel may now wish to counter this fairly essentialized "lawless" profile with that of male characters whose flawed natures are more complex, more geared to moral and spiritual issues. Whether consciously or not, Keitel is, in my view, using his accumulated cultural capital as an ethnically marked maverick to highlight the ethical quandaries embodied in such masculinities. In *Bad Lieutenant*, addiction is added to the mix in such a way that it too is activated as a significant and complex aspect of identity construction. Although I cannot deal with the issue of addiction here, it is clear that there is much room for work on the connection between subjectivities and dependencies, be they drugs, food, sex, or mothers. Regarding male subjectivities specifically, Robert Sklar has written, in the context of his analysis of the "roughneck sissy" type of man personified by James Cagney in so many of his roles, that "dependence is a concern for every human being, and . . . particularly so for men in the development of their masculine self-image" (17). That the bad lieutenant is "losing his soul" primarily by means of radically addictive behavior is not incidental to the question of responsible fatherhood, for both addiction and flight from the paternal role are symptoms of broader and deeper sociosymbolic disturbances and excesses that are simultaneously stimulated and condemned in these times of late capitalism and waning patriarchy.

Near the end of *Bad Lieutenant*, the two rapists are placed in the lieutenant's car in the exact same positions as were his sons in the opening scene. His release of them is, therefore, a father's gesture, a gesture of hope for a future generation in which forgiveness rather than revenge will reign; it is a legacy. But as is true of all legacies, the father must die in order that his sons can take possession of it. The lieutenant's decision to let the boys go free is self-sacrificial, therefore, but it is not in my estimation an act that reinscribes him back into either "religious orthodoxy" or conservative patriarchy. Rather, I read both films as powerful critiques of the inadequacies of normative masculinity's dominant fictions whereby men introject psychically and socially damaging views on sexual, familial, and professional roles to the point that capitulation or self-immolation is the only option left to "real men." These films, centering on social sites and issues apparently far from "women's issues," and made by Italian/American men who themselves come from a highly masculine culture, share, in my view, a great deal with certain theoretical and practical aims of feminism. Like many feminist theorizations of gender, these films seek to expose and to renegotiate components of the dominant fictions by which both men and women construct themselves as psychic, spiritual, ethnic, gendered, and social subjectivities. Neither Scorsese nor Ferrara offers positive alternatives to their protagonists' entrapment in harmful versions of masculinity. Rather, their art shows, in the eloquent embodiment of suffering in Keitel's youthful body and, years later, in his aging form, that "lapsed" boys still become "lost" men, and that all of us, whatever our gender positioning, need to go on knocking at doors.

## NOTES

1. In *Clint Eastwood: A Cultural Production*, Paul Smith writes regarding action film that "one of the most frequent functions of the women characters is to represent a resistance to the masculinist ethos, politics, and violence of the hero. In those narratives, however, the women's role is also to finally alter their relation to that ethos and give their consent to its heroics" (119). Even though Jamie Lee Curtis's character appears to go counter to this standard function in that she starts out as a woman who craves the masculinist ethos, in the end her complete inscription into that ethos puts her squarely back into the tradition as defined by Smith. For a much more complex portrayal of women's relation to the "man's world," see Curtis's performance in the film *Blue Steel*, in which she plays a cop whose needs and desires as a woman are not either subsumed or deformed.

2. In *City Boys: Cagney, Bogart, Garfield*, Robert Sklar presents a history of the emergence of the "urban tough guy" personified by the three actors he studies, a type that represents a new cultural icon most often embodied in the gangster or private eye. Sklar writes as well of the "roughneck sissy," whom Cagney played in several of his roles; this masculine type was " a figure strikingly different from the main masculine types in popular entertainment" of the twenties and thirties, in that he "neither escaped from women nor conquered them. His most important relation to women was not as lover but as son" (15). Sklar further comments: "This powerful strain of dependence [on the mother] underlies the character type James Cagney brought to his career in the movies. The extraordinary late-twentieth-century project of psychoanalytic and feminist theorists to reconceptualize gender can provide important insights toward understanding this fictional character structure" (16–17). I concur, and would add that ethnicity as well as gender could profitably be brought into the consideration, as I attempt to do particularly in the case of Scorsese.

3. See Canadé-Sautman's article for a reading of Italian/American self-representations in film that is highly critical. I tend instead to see cinema as the site where some of the most acute self-critiques of the givens of Italian/American culture have been elaborated, especially in the work of Scorsese, Cimino, and Ferrara.

4. Paul Smith interweaves the personal and professional identities of Clint Eastwood, and traces the ways in which they resonate with national myths, politics, and beliefs regarding masculinity from the fifties to today. Among other topics, Smith analyses the semiotics of Eastwood's body, seen as the site of both a ratification of normative masculinity and a breaking of that norm by means of hysterical and mas-

ochistic excesses. I believe that Keitel is particularly suited to similar study, and later on in this essay I adumbrate some of my views regarding him, to be developed in a longer work.

5. This summary, like all summaries, is already interpretive, in that others would no doubt tell the film's "story" in different ways. Description, although fundamental to analysis, is never neutral.

6. It is not clear if we are to read this scene as "real" or imagined, although it does create a dreamlike atmosphere not at all similar to the rest of the film. The problem is compounded by the fact that Scorsese put this scene in after the film had been completed, presumably to comply with the suggestion that the film would sell better if it contained a sex scene. "Real" or not, it represents J. R.'s desire for sexualized women, and underlines the intensity of his sexuality, which is suppressed with the girl.

7. In his thought-provoking piece on rape-revenge films, Peter Lehman mentions the good critical reception *Ms 45* enjoyed and adds in a note that it is "in fact an extremely interesting film, partly because of the way it positions the mute woman and, symbolically, women in general in relationship to male dominated language; she is not only raped and harassed by men but, also, oppressed by her exclusion from the powerful realm of speech" (116). I agree, but would emphasize that I see the film as much more self-consciously witty and transgressive than such a "politically correct" feminist imputation would suggest.

8. Ferrara has also commented that "with *Bad Lieutenant* we felt an immediate mutual understanding. If I were a woman, I would be crazy about him. He's the sexiest man I've ever met, he gives me shivers" (my translation of a quotation printed in *Vogue Italia*). I find this "deviant" avowal of sexual attraction to Keitel by a presumably straight Ferrara (he is married and has adopted two Indian children) a small but fascinating sign of nonphallic maleness; it is "normal" that women comment on other women's sexual desirability, but straight men seldom assess other men in this way—or at least not publicly!

9. See Part III of Miriam Hansen's *Babel and Babylon: Spectatorship in American Silent Film* for an outstanding analysis of Valentino's reception. See also Gaylyn Studlar in Cohan and Hark, eds.

10. Of his daughter Stella, Keitel said: "What do I need to do to open her mind so that she will be able, when the time comes, to suffer and change [suffering's] sound to poetry?" (in Tosches). He has also said: "I feel unless I can confront my own difficulty, my primal furies, I cannot pass that legacy on to my children. Somewhere in there, for me, is a knowing of that woman [sic!] we call God" (in Forde). Regarding his untraditional gendering of God, Keitel has studied the *Gnostic Gospels* by Elaine Pagels, which he said "changed his life." According to the 3 April 1995 *New Yorker* piece on Pagels, "when Vogue asked the actor Harvey Keitel for an interview before the release of *The Piano*, Keitel asked that the interviewer be Pagels" (Remnick, 62). She refused but did sit in on the interview.

## WORKS CITED

Aspesi, Natalia. "Questo mio cinema così depravato" and "Che bello lavorare con la star Madonna." *La Repubblica* (11 September 1993): 31.

Berger, Maurice, Brian Wallis, and Simon Watson, eds. *Constructing Masculinity.* London and New York: Routledge, 1995.

Bruno, Edoardo, ed. *Martin Scorsese.* Rome: Gremese Editore, 1992.

Casillo, Robert. "Moments in Italian-American Cinema: From *Little Caesar to Coppola and Scorsese*." In Tamburri et. al., eds. pp. 374–396.

Cohan, Steven and Ina Mae Hark, eds. *Screening the Male: Exploring Masculinities in Hollywood Cinema.* London and New York: Routledge, 1993.

Cremonini, Zoraide. "The Damned Movie." *Vogue Italia* 519 (November 1993): 38.

Dyer, Richard. *Stars.* London: British Film Institute, 1979.

Ehrenreich, Barbara. *Hearts of Men: American Dreams and the Flight From Commitment.* Garden City, N. Y.: Anchor Books, 1984.

Forde, Noah, interviewer. "Harvey Keitel." *Venice: Los Angeles' Arts and Entertainment Magazine* 4, no. 9 (January 1993): 28.

———. "The Knight of Night: Abel Ferrara." *Venice: Los Angeles' Arts and Entertainment Magazine,* 4, no. 9 (January 1993): 29–30.

Hansen, Miriam. *Babel and Babylon: Spectatorship in American Silent Film.* Cambridge: Harvard University Press, 1991.

Horrocks, Roger. *Male Myths and Icons: Masculinity in Popular Culture.* New York: St. Martin's Press, 1995.

Kirkham, Pat and Janet Thumim, eds. *You Tarzan: Masculinity, Movies and Men.* New York: St. Martin's Press, 1993.

———. *Me Jane: Masculinity, Movies and Women.* New York: St. Martin's Press, 1995.

Lehman, Peter. "'Don't Blame This on a Girl': Female Rape-Revenge Films." In Cohan and Hark, eds. pp. 103–17.

Remnick, David. "The Devil Problem." *The New Yorker* (3 April 1995): 54–65.

Ronell, Avital. *Crack Wars: Literature, Addiction, Mania.* Lincoln and London: University of Nebraska Press, 1992.

Sautman, Francesca Canadé. "Women of the Shadows: Italian American Women, Ethnicity, and Racism in American Cinema." *Differentia: Review of Italian Thought* 6–7 (spring-autumn 1994): 219–46.

Seidler, Victor J. *Riscoprire la mascolinità: sessualità ragione linguaggio.* Rome: Editori Riuniti, 1992.

Silverman, Kaja. *Male Subjectivity at the Margins.* New York and London: Routledge, 1992.

Sklar, Robert. *City Boys: Cagney, Bogart, Garfield.* Princeton: Princeton University Press, 1992.

Slawner, Heath Jay. Review of *Bad Lieutenant. 34th Street* (January 1993): 5.

Smith, Gavin. "The Gambler." *Sight and Sound* (February 1993): 21–23.

Smith, Paul. *Clint Eastwood: A Cultural Production.* Minneapolis and London: University of Minnesota Press, 1993.

Studlar, Gaylyn. "Valentino, 'Optic Intoxication,' and Dance Madness." In Cohan and Hark, eds. pp. 23–45.

Tamburri, Anthony Julian, Paolo A. Giordano, and Fred L. Gardaphé, eds. *From the Margin: Writings in Italian Americana.* West Lafayette, Ind.: Purdue University Press, 1991.

Thompson, David. "Harvey Keitel: Staying Power." *Sight and Sound* (January 1993): 22–25.

Tosches, Nick. "Heaven, Hell, Harvey Keitel." *Esquire* (September 1993): 118–23; 161.

Viano, Maurizio. "Scorsampling." *Differentia: Review of Italian Thought* 6–7 (spring-autumn 1994): 133–52.

Walker, John, ed. *Halliwell's Filmgoers and Video Viewer's Companion.* 10th edition. New York: HarperCollins, 1993.

West, Rebecca. "Scorsese's *Who's That Knocking At My Door?:* Night Thoughts on Italian Studies in the United States." *Romance Languages Annual* (1991): 331–38 (double-columned).

# Part 4
## Further Readings

# 11

## Emigrants, Expatriates, and Exiles: Italian Writing in the United States

### PAOLO A. GIORDANO

"Di tutte le lontananze, l'America è la più vera ed esemplare."
—Mario Soldati, *America Primo Amore*

"Exile is a slinking beast; it bides its time, without hurry, but it gets you in the end"
—Paolo Valesio, *Italian Poets in America*

Italians are a nation of emigrants. During the last two centuries, the train, the ocean liner, and the airplane have been the symbols of our fate. Whether it has been internal emigration to Northern Italy and to France, Switzerland, Germany, Belgium, and other European countries, or the mythical attraction of America, we always seem to be on the move. Whatever the reasons, millions of Italians are destined to die away from their native land. Truly, we are the children of Columbus.

Italians have accomplished some of their greatest achievements in all fields of endeavor outside Italy, or before unification, outside the native city-state, republic, or principality. Dante wrote the *Comedia* while in exile; Petrarch wrote while wandering from Provence to Milan to Venice and other places before finally coming to rest in Arquà; Columbus discovered the New World for the king and queen of Castilla and Aragon; Giordano Bruno, wandered Italy, Switzerland, France, Germany, and England before coming back to Italy, where he is tried by the Inquisition and, after a long trial, he is burned at the stake in Rome for his ideas; Enrico Fermi ushered in the nuclear age while living in self-imposed exile in the United States because he feared Fascist repercussions. The list could go on.

226     PAOLO A. GIORDANO

In the field of literature, which this chapter concerns itself with, beside Dante, Petrarch, and Bruno many other literary figures have, for various reason, suffered the same fate. A short list would include Ugo Foscolo, who spent time in England for political reasons; Giuseppe Ungaretti, who grew poetically in the cultural milieu of Paris in the 1920s; Filippo Tomaso Marinetti, who gave life and direction to futurism while living in Paris; Italo Calvino, who spent the last years of his life between Paris and Rome.

Throughout the twentieth century the myth of America has attracted Italian writers and intellectuals. Some came for short visits and wrote about their travels and perceptions, though limited they may have been; the literary critic Emilio Cecchi's *America amara*, the futurist Fortunato Depero's *Un Futurista a New York* (notes published posthumously), Mario Soldati's *America primo amore*, and Goffredo Parise's *Odore d'America* come to mind. Others stayed longer and their impact was more lasting; Giuseppe Prezzolini, Professor of Italian at Columbia University and director of its Casa Italiana, was a missionary of Italian culture and a highly respected intellectual who wrote, among other things, *I trapiantati* (Florence: Vallecchi, 1953), *America in pantofole* (Florence: Vallecchi, 1950), *America con gli stivali* (Florence: Vallecchi, 1954) and a provocative article "America and Italy: Myths and Realities" (*Italian Quarterly*, spring 1959).

Today, in the United States we are witnessing the emerging awareness of a new poetic voice—that of Italian literature written in America. Several writers, born and culturally trained in Italy, live in the United States and produce a substantial amount of poetry and prose, both in the Italian language and in the English language. The list is long: Pier Maria Pasinetti, Franco Ferrucci, Joseph Tusiani, Giovanni Cecchetti, Giose Rimanelli, Peter Carravetta, Luigi Fontanella, Paolo Valesio, Rita Dinale, Luigi Ballerini, Irene Marchegiani Jones and Alessandro Carrera are some of the names that come to mind. Through their writing a distinctive American voice in Italian literature, or maybe an Italian voice in American literature is starting to define itself.

On the phenomenon of the different aspects of Italian/American culture, as manifested through its literature, it's worth keeping in mind what Paolo Valesio wrote in is article "The Writer between Two Worlds: Italian Writing in the United States Today" (*Differentia* [spring–autumn, 1989]: 259–76):

It is worth keeping in mind a motto from the Medieval Scholastics: *Distingue frequenter*. The confusing of codes, registers, genres (be they literary or cultural) often lead to reciprocal misunderstandings. In the case of a community such as those "with a hyphen" (Italo-American, Spanish-American, Afro-American, etc.) the risk is even greater. The danger lies in a growth of pseudo problems (monstrously mushrooming) that slip into demagoguery. It becomes necessary, therefore, to distinguish between the following:

1. Not strictly literary autobiographical and memorial texts, whose collection and systematic analysis is, nonetheless, important for a dialectical understanding of the various components of literary history.
2. Novels or short stories written in English by members of the Italo-American community, containing predominance of themes that can be considered characteristic of such a community.
3. Works by those that I have called writers between two worlds: the Italian expatriates in the United States who write exclusively or largely in Italian.

*Italian Poets in America,* a special edition of *Gradiva: International Journal of Italian Literature,* edited by Luigi Fontanella and Paolo Valesio, and *Poesaggio,* edited by Paolo Valesio and Peter Carravetta, are representative of Valesio's third category, that of "writers between two worlds." Writers who are born in one country and receive their education in the country of birth, in this case Italy, but are culturally and intellectually active in another, the United States, thus operating in and from a reality that is "bilingual, bicultural [and] biconceptual" (Hicks, xxv). "Juxtaposed between multiple cultures" (Hicks, xxiii), these individuals create literature that explores, is influenced by, and is sensitive to the different cultural and linguistic referents that help mold it. They are "cultural border writers."

*Italian Poets in America* anthologizes thirteen poets: Luigi Ballerini, Peter Carravetta, Alessandro Carrera, Ned Condini, Alfredo De Palchi, Luigi Fontanella, Marisa Marcelli, Mario Moroni, Giose Rimanelli, Tonia C. Riviello, Emilio Speciale, Joseph Tusiani, and Paolo Valesio. The poems are divided into three sections: Poetry and the Tension of the Word; Poetry and the Narration of the Word; and Poetry and the Dream of the Word. This is followed by a questionnaire to the poets that elicits responses from the poets about their formation and influences, about living and writing poetry in America, and about their poetics.[1] All the poems in *Italian Poets in America,* originally written in Italian, are offered in both the original version and with an English translation, the exception is Joseph Tusiani's "Nocturnum neo-arboracense," which appears in Latin with Italian and English translations. In the foreword to the volume, Fontanella writes that this is a first attempt to offer the public a representative selection of Italian poets that live and work in America, and clearly

states that the literary production of these poets is not to be classified
under the rubric of "Italian-American Literature":

> it is difficult—I recognize it—not to classify as "Italian American, *tout
> court*, some for the poets here anthologized; that is, poets who have been
> living in America for the major part of their life, and who, by now, feel
> equally familiar with Italian and/or English, or even prefer, at this point
> of their literary life, to write almost exclusively in English, the language
> that they have better internalized. . . . But despite the time the poets of
> this anthology have spent in the United States and the inevitable American
> references in some of their works . . . that one should dismiss all attempts
> to hyphenate them. (*Italian Poets in America*, 3)

*Poesaggio* was born of a different matrix. *Poesaggio*, a word coined by
Peter Carravetta, from "poesia" and "saggio," is a program of poetry
readings established by Carravetta to bring the poetry of Italians living in the United States to the attention of the public. From 1984 to
1990, Carravetta organized a number of *poesaggi* at various conferences and universities. The book was conceived from this intensive
poetic activity. The volume is divided into five sections: an introduction by Carravetta, the poetry, critical and aestethic reflections by the
poets, an essay by Valesio, and bibliographical information on the
poets. The novelty of this book is in the structure of the poetry
section. The poems, all except one written in Italian, are not presented
by author, as is usually common in anthologies of this nature, but
according to a narrative and thematic plan. The sole poem written in
English is to remind us, the readers, that although these compositions
are in Italian these poets function in an everyday reality that is that
of an English speaking world. Carravetta and Valesio weave the poems
from the twelve authors anthologized (no author has two poems in
succession) creating a stimulating dialogue among the poets—a dialogue that binds them in a literary community, or to use Valesio's
words, "una tribù letteraria" (a literary tribe).

By bringing together authors that find themselves in a peculiarly
displaced position, all educated in Italy, all who write and probably
think in Italian, all living in North America from anywhere between
five and forty years, and who, by definition, are not American, not
Italian, and not Italian American,[2] *Italian Poets in America* and *Poesaggio* give voice to the Italian diaspora in the United States.[3]

For the remainder of this essay, I would like to turn my attention
to two writers, Jospeh Tusiani and Giovanni Cecchetti, also representative of Valesio's third category, that of "writers between two worlds,

and who represent two of the many paths that Italian writing in the United States has taken.

Tusiani, born seventy years ago in the town of San Marco in Lamis in the southern Italian region of Puglia, is the emigrant who came to the United States in 1947 at the age of twenty-three, with a university degree in hand, in search of his father, the father who emigrated when Tusiani's mother was pregnant with him, the father he had never seen. In the United States he became a recognized poet in the English language, receiving many awards for his writing: the Greenwood Prize from the Poetry Society of England (1956—the first time they bestowed this honor upon a poet from the United States), and the Spirit Gold Medal from the Poetry Society of America (1969). Tusiani is internationally known for his translations of Italian classics, among which are *The Complete Poems of Michelangelo*, Torquato Tasso's *Jerusalem Delivered*, *From Marino to Marinetti*, and the recently published *Dante's Lyric Poems*. He is the author of three collections of poems in English, *Rind and All*, *The Fifth Season*, and *Gente Mia and Other Poems*. Furthermore, his poems in English have appeared in prestigious journals as *The New Yorker*, *Yale Review*, *The Poetry Review*, and *Spirit* among others. Tusiani is also internationally known for his Latin verses. He is the author of four collections of Latin verses: *Melos Cordis*, *Rosa Rosarum*, *In Exilio Rerum*, and *Confinia lucis et umbrae*. He has also published his Latin verse *Latinitas* (Vatican), *Vita Latina* (France), *Vox Latina* (Germany), and *The Classical Outlook* (United States). Most recently, he has published his autobiography in three books, *La Parola Difficile*, *La Parola Nuova*, and *La Parola Antica;* two volumes of poetry, one in his native dialect of the *gargano* region of Italy, *Bronx America*, and one in Italian, *Il ritorno;* and a translation of the English poems of Giuseppe Antonio Borgese.

With the now relatively famous verses from "Song of the Bicentennial" (*Gente Mia*, 7), "Two languages, two lands, perhaps two souls . . . / Am I a man or two strange halves of one?" Tusiani perfectly verbalizes the plight of the emigrant/immigrant. In *Gente Mia and Other Poems*, and in the autobiographical trilogy *La parola difficile*, *La parola nuova*, and *La parola antica*, Tusiani, with eloquence and dignity, addresses the experience of immigration to the United States. In these works Tusiani's muse inspires him to examine the major themes that are associated with immigration: the spiritually and psychologically violent act of division from one's family and native land (which is the first experience of the new emigrant), the dreams of the emigrant/immigrant, the prejudice he or she encounters, the process of Americanization, the question of language, the alienation and the realization that the new world is not the "land of hospitality" he or she believed it was.

When the emigrant, after a long and wearisome crossing, arrived at Ellis Island he or she was immediately faced with the first major obstacle of his new American life—a strange language. Tusiani knows, as do most of those who were born in another country, that the emigration odyssey takes many forms. First and foremost, he or she must face and come to terms with the actual, physical separation from the country of birth, and from family and friends. This most evident element of the emigration/immigration process is initially the most traumatic. When the emigrant arrives to the new country, the voyage is not finished. He or she will have to undertake other "voyages" in his or her quest to assimilate into mainstream American culture. The most important of these "voyages" is the linguistic/cultural one. He or she must immediately begin the journey from one language, one of the many Italian dialects, to another, American English. Once this process has begun, the emigrant, whose status now is changing to that of immigrant, begins to lose his or her native language and the ideas and cultural values that language transmits. In other words, a cultural transformation begins to take place, and he or she begins to lose a part of himself or herself. The question of language, or, rather, loss of language, is of primary importance to our poet when discussing the experience of emigration. Tusiani introduces this argument in "Song of the Bicentennial" by as series of questions:

> Do I regret my origins by speaking
> this language I acquired? Do I renounce,
> by talking now in terms of only dreams,
> the *sogni* of my childhood? What has changed
> that I had thought unchangeable in me? (5)

Tusiani looks at the language question not only as a sociological problem but also as a spiritual dilemma. The answer to these questions is that something *has* changed and that every phrase, every word uttered in English separates him a little bit more from his roots:

> Now every thought I think, each word I say
> detaches me a little more from all
> I used to love—

For Tusiani, when "sogni" becomes dreams, "cielo" becomes sky, and "mamma" is translated to mother, much more transpires than the immigrant's process of Americanization and acculturation. Tusiani is aware of the fact that words communicate a plethora of memories, images, and emotions; the poet knows that "cielo" elicits mythicized visions of the old world and that "sky" will only remind the immigrant of the ghetto in the immense concrete jungle he now calls home, and that when "mamma" is translated to mother much of what was your life begins to disintegrate will eventually be lost as the immigrant moves toward assimilation into American life and culture.

> Mother, I even wonder if I am
> the child I was, the little child you knew,
> for you did not expect your little son
> to grow apart from all that was your world.
> Yet of a sudden he was taught to say
> "Mother" for mamma, and for cielo "sky"
> That very day, we lost each other. (5)

Loss of the Italian language is for our poet "a betrayal or denial of his original world—indeed his very origin, his very self" (Tusiani, 153–54).

In the autobiographical trilogy Tusiani again takes up the problem of language. He returns to the question of bilinguism in *La parola antica*, the third volume of the trilogy, and discusses it at length:

> Due lingue. La realtà dello sbarbicamento (uso questo termine per indicare lo sradicamento completo) comporta diversi problemi o traumi, prima di tutto quello di un nuovo linguaggio. Progredendo nell'acquisizione della lingua straniera, si corre il rischio, per ragioni di umana vanità, di ritenere inferiore quella materna? . . .
>
> Non si cade in questo pericolo se il fenomeno del bilinguismo lo si considera non come conquista ma come rinnegamento forzato delle proprie origini e di se stessi. Il bilinguismo, cioè, diventa sinonimo di disintegrata unità familiare, per cui una madre non è più in grado di comprendere il proprio figlio. Dal giorno in cui il figlio dice «Mother» per «mamma» e «sky» per «cielo», fra madre e figlio c'è già una separazione spirituale che lo studioso di linguistica non può catalogare. Se le parole sono suoni articolati che simboleggiano e comunicano un'idea, il termine «mamma», a differenza di «mother», il nuovo termine acquisito, simboleggia e comunica un intero mondo di sentimenti che nessuna espressione straniera può comprendere e rispettare. Abolirlo significa rigettare l'esistenza di una fanciullezza intimamente legata a tutti gli episodi, piccoli e grandi, e a tutte le emozioni, importanti e non importanti, connessi ed ispirati da quell'unica parola. Non assimilazione o americanizzazzione, dunque, ma ambivalenza, un'ambivalenza di pensiero e sentimento, di dubbio e di certezza, di sogno e realtà. (*La parola antica*, 143–44)[4]

The consequence of this transformation is that the immigrant, by expressing himself or herself in the acquired tongue, translates not only the language but his or her very soul, and in that process of translation he or she slowly and unrelentingly begins to change. He or she now has the language and the culture of two lands: "America e Italia; in quale ordine, però? Non dovremmo dire: Italia e America?" (*La parola antica*, 143).[5] Tusiani poses these questions because he believes that the immigrant cannot ever be totally assimilated into his or her adopted culture:

> fino a qual punto l'emigrato può assimilare la nuova lingua e la nouva civiltà, e in che maniera dimenticare e rinnegare se stesso in mezzo alle nuove e impellenti esigenze della sua vita? Anche se la risposta sia priva di validità scientifica, il poeta ci dice che non esiste, e non può esistere, un assorbimento totale, e che non potrà mai esserci un'accettazione totale, cioè *spirituale*, delle tradizioni della nuova terra. (*La parola antica*, 143: emphasis mine)[6]

Tusiani's continuous feeling of "uprootedness" lies primarily within this context of never having fully "spiritually" assimilated into American culture. He expressed it best in his "Song of the Bicentennial":

> Then who will solve this riddle of my day?
> Two languages, two lands, perhaps two souls . . .
> Am I a man or two strange halves of one?

It is precisely the unsolved riddle, and the feeling of being suspended between two worlds, of not belonging, and of navigating between two cultural systems that, I believe, pushes Tusiani to return to Italian, the language of his native land, for his autobiography.[7]

*La parola antica*, which concludes the trilogy, signals the end of immigration. The word has become ancient because Italian immigration has come to an end, and the cultural conflicts that marked the relationship between Michael Tusiani's American-born brother and his mother, between Michael's children and their grandmother, will dissapear within a generation. For the Italian American, finally on the threshold of assimilating into American society, Italy has little if no meaning at all. It has become just a place where his ancestors came from, a possible tourist attraction. For Tusiani, instead, "la parola antica" becomes stronger and spiritually pulls him back to the land and culture of his birth. His progressive, linear voyage in American society and culture is over and he longs for a *return*. The problem is that forty years of experienced American reality cannot be erased, they have had a profound effect on his life and on his work as a poet, translator, and scholar. In the last episode of the book, Tusiani, on his way back fom Italy, dreams that he finds himself alone with his mother in a long corridor bathed with a blinding white light, with many doors on the sides and one door on each end—one which said "Exit," the other, "Entrance." They begin walking toward the door marked "Exit." When they arrive, he notices that it now says "Entrance" and that the sign on the door at the opposite end of the corridor has changed accordingly to "Exit":

> Arrivai sotto quella scrittura e lessi «Entrata». Mi voltai e vidi, lì dov'era mia madre la parola «Uscita». . . . Rifeci il cammino, ma quando raggiunsi mia madre, in alto, al posto di «Uscita» lessi nuovamente «Entrata». . . . E per quaranta volte, affannato, ansioso, con la speranza e la disperazione che mi spingevano e guidavano, corsi da un'estremità all'altra di quell'enorme corridoio. (308)[8]

On the brink of being overtaken by panic, Tusiani notices that the corridor has doors along its sides. On each door is written the name of a person that has had a profound impact on his life: Francis Winwar, Cocò, Onorio Ruotolo, l'architetto Giusto, Giuseppe Antonio Borgese, Louise Townsend Nicholl, Arturo Giovannitti, Martin Luther King, Antonietta Lombardi, an immigrant neighbor, and Father Walsh, a Jesuit mentor. He knocks on all their doors but no one answers. Finally, bathed by the light he sees the shadow of his father who had died a few years earlier:

> «Papà! Papà!» gli dissi, andandogli incontro, «ci siamo perduti io e mamma; non possiamo trovare l'uscita.»
> «Sei proprio un bambino», mi rispose mio padre, sorridendo. «So io dov'è l'uscita: venite con me.» Cominciavamo a seguirlo. . . . (309)[9]

The dream ends abruptly when Tusiani is suddenly awakened by the flight attendant announcing the imminent landing at Kennedy Airport. No one can help him find the exit; it is an existential problem to which only he can supply an answer. The book, and the autobiography, ends with this short paragraph:

> Andando verso il Bronx, nella limousine della Poten (his brother's petroleum company), notai un altro particolare: i tergicristalli, strusciando da destra a sinistra, da sinistra a destra, sembravano dire Entrata-Uscita, Uscita-Entrata, ma non sapevo più che cosa significassero quelle due parole, né a chi fossero rivolte. (310)[10]

If the reader does a superficial reading of the last paragraph he or she would probably conclude that Tusiani does not find an answer to his dilemma, and may conclude that he is more confused than ever about his identity. But a closer reading tells us, I would contend, that Tusiani has, after forty years of American life, come to a resolution of his "problem." The resolution is his awareness of being suspended between two worlds, his acceptance of his biculturalism, for which, instead of seeing himself as not belonging to either one or the other world, he can accept himself as being the man of "two languages, two lands, . . . two [socio-cultural] souls," which he had previously questioned in his poetry:

> Then who will solve this riddle of my day?
> Two languages, two lands, perhaps two souls . . .
> Am I a man or two strange halves of one?

After forty years the riddle has been solved. The questions posed in "Song of the Bicentennial" have now become statements.

★ ★ ★

Giovanni Cecchetti, born in the town of Pescia in Tuscany, is the expatriate who came to this country right after the World War II and, while developing his poetic voice, went on to become one of the leading scholars of Italian letters in the United States. He developed programs of Italian studies at Tulane University, in New Orleans, Stanford University, and UCLA. Cecchetti has always written his verses and his prose in Italian; not because of a lack of skill and mastery of the English language, a quick cursus through his critical studies written in English would instantly dismiss such a notion, but because of a never wavering loyalty and devotion to the culture of Italy and a belief that the only true poetry is written in one's native language. In a short essay that appeared in the spring issue of *Forum Italicum* 26, no. 1, 1992, "Sullo scriver poesia," Cecchetti writes the following:

E la lingua? E' quella in cui si è nati; è la lingua d'un'infanzia trasfigurata, carica di quei sensi che allora sarebbero stati irragiungibili. Nessuno può scrivere poesia in un'altra lingua, sovrapposta e quindi fittizia, che non gli può diventare linguaggio, sebbene ci stia dentro quotidianamente. In questa può scrivere versi, magari dei buoni versi, ma non poesia—la quale non può nascere in chi si trova bloccato nella prigione dell'artificio. Noi che abbiamo avuto un'infanzia in Italia (quell'infanzia che in certo modo include anche l'adolescenza) possiamo scrivere poesia solo in italiano. L'inglese è la lingua della prosa.[11]

Among his many publications one finds critical studies of Leopardi, Verga and Pascoli; *La poesia del Pascoli* (Goliardica, 1954), *Leopardi e Verga* (Florence: La Nuova Italia, 1962), *Il Verga maggiore* (Florence: La Nuova Italia, 1975), *Giovanni Verga* (Boston: Twayne University, 1978); his translation into English of Giovanni Verga's *Mastro Don Gesualdo* (University of California Press, 1984) and Giacomo Leopardi's *Operette Morali / Essays and Dialogues* (University of California Press, 1983); four collections of poetry *Diario nomade* (Padova: Rebellato, 1967), *Impossibile scendere* (Milano: Scheiwiller, 1978), *Nel Cammino dei monti* (Florence: Vallecchi, 1981), *Favole Spente* (Venezia: Edizione del Leone [Collana "I Piombi"], 1988); and three volumes of prose, *Il villaggio degli inutili* (Venezia: Rebellato, 1981), *Spuntature e intermezzi* (Pisa: Giardini, 1983), and *La danza nel deserto* (Rebellato, 1985).

Cecchetti made his debut in print in 1967 with the poems of *Diario nomade*, while his second collection of poetry, *Impossibile scendere* appeared in 1978. These two works were intelligently and favorably discussed by two leading scholars of Italian letters residing on the North American continent; Fredi Chiapelli discussed *Diario Nomade* in volume nine of *Forum Italicum*, and in the pages of volume 13 of the same journal Danilo Aguzzi Barbaglia discussed *Impossibile scendere*. In these review essays, Chiapelli and Aguzzi Barbaglia identified exile, memory, the inexorable passage of time, modern man's existential and spiritual battle among alienated and alienating landscapes and occurrences as the salient thematic elements in Cecchetti's work.[12]

In considering his last work of prose, *Danza nel deserto*, we see that the thematic elements that Chiapelli and Aguzzi-Barbaglia identified in Cecchetti's first two volumes of poetry, and that Rebecca West put in perspective in her review of *Nel cammino dei monti*, Cecchetti's third collection of poems, are still present and reinforced by his use of the California desert as stage and frame for the twelve short stories that comprise this volume of 127 pages.[13] Cecchetti has lived on the Pacific coast and on the margins of the California desert for the last thirty years. The stories of *Danza nel deserto*, while echoing Dino Buzzati's *Il deserto dei tartari*, strongly reflect Cecchetti's experiences of living and working in the American landscape for such a long time. The desert for Cecchetti is a metaphor for the solitude that envelops humanity in contemporary society and the squalor that that solitude represents. In the desert, nature breaks the boundaries that we consider "normal," that is livable; it seems that the desert "does not comprehend man because man does not comprehend the desert." With the desert as stage and frame, these stories acquire a highly surrealistic quality. They portray a world of fantasy were reality is in constant flux and transfiguration. The stories, as the author himself stated in an interview with Michael Lettieri,[14] are nothing more than "immagini del mondo in cui viviamo, quasi forme simboliche, ossia forme quasi allegoriche" (123).[15]

The men and women who populate *Danza nel deserto* are indivduals who live in solitude, and the more they try to break the wall of solitude, the stronger and more imprenetrable that wall becomes. *Danza nel deserto* is a book about *communication* or, better yet, the *lack of communication* in contemporary society:

> E' il mondo in cui vivo ancora: un mondo di gente che ride e che piange di là dalle vetrate, che muove serissima le labbra, senza che non ci sia mai un interlocutore. So che tutti cercano parole, dimentichi del nido del grillo canterino, e poi si contentano della risata solitaria o del sussurro di colomba.[16]

In the story "Il telefono," the traveler/narrator of *Danza nel deserto* visits an old school chum who lives in a small one room house away from civilization. Inside the small house the traveler sees statues of men and women that are really telephones:

> "Non capisco niente," dissi. M'avvicinai a un uomo con gli occhi tesi.
> "Non codesto. E' un ventriloquo. Ha il telefono in pancia; ripete solo quel che dicono i vicini." . . .
> "Prova a parlare con qualcuno," disse; "forse risponde . . . Questo."
> M'avvicinai e dissi nel ricevitore: "Come sta?" Mi giunse una risposta monosillabica, un suono agglutinato, come in cinese.
> Provai le altre statue; le risposte non cambiarono. A volte i suoni scivolavan via; a volte si gonfiavano in modo da sembrar grida disarticolate da giungla. M'arresi.
> "Senti," disse il vecchio compagno di scuola. "Credevo che con un estraneo diventassero normali. Invece . . . Da principio cominciarono a farmi degli scherzi. Se dicevo qualcosa in un ricevitore, rispondevan con lunghi discorsi in coreano, in persiano, in armeno . . . o almeno così credevo, perché spesso non riuscivo nemmeno a riconoscer la lingua. . . . Pensai che si fossero abituati a questi scherzi perché li avevo collegati alle linee internazionali. Allora li misi sulla rete nazionale. Peggio che peggio: colpi di tosse, abbai, grida, addirittura canzoncine a boccha chiusa. *Insomma voci, non parole.* . . . C'è da disperarsi. (30–31)[17]

The protagonists of *Danza nel deserto* attempt communication but are constantly frustrated in their attempts, either by their own doing or by events that are outside of their sphere of control. They live as in a dream world. Their need to communicate is so intense that they invent ways of communication. They need to invent ways of communication because they are incapable of communication, as is the case, the author tells us, of contemporary wo/man in general. Why is communication so difficult? Cecchetti offers an answer in the above mentioned interview with Micheal Lettieri:

Il mondo che sognano, quello in cui poi finiscono per vivere, a volte è molto insolito, come è sempre il caso dei sogni; e quindi non è percepibile dagli altri. E' percepibile solo da loro stessi, perché gli altri hanno un loro mondo di sogni che è totalmente diverso. Questo spiega perché la comunicazione è così difficile, anzi direi impossibile. E lo è naturalmente non solo per queste persone, ma per tutti gli altri che io non considero. (125)[18]

The theme of the "impossibility of communication" is one that ties a number of Cecchetti's works together. In *Il villaggio degli inutili*, a collection of stories that were written when the author was a young man, eighteen-or nineteen-years-old, but only recently published, the initial story, "La sporta del viandante," clearly explores the themes of the impossibility of communication among men/women and the continuous flux of reality:

Ogni tanto aprivo la sporta e ne tiravo fuori una casa o dei brandelli, e mi mettevo a studiarmeli in mano. Non mi ci volle molto ad accorgermi che nella sporta avevo creduto di metter l'infinito, ed invece non avevo depositato altro che una gran quantità di limiti. Continuai lo stesso a raccogliere e conservare. . . . Però troppe eran le cose che avevo e che dovevo portarmi dietro. Un giorno cominciai a tirar fuori quel che ci avevo messo, ma tutto era incredibilmente cambiato. Ciò che era originariamente bianco s'era fatto rosso, e viceversa. Le cose azzurre eran diventategrigie. Ma che c'era dentro quella sporta per causare simili trasformazioni? Non lo mai saputo." (17–18)[19]

The American desert returns as a protagonist in *Nel cammino dei monti*. In the poem titled "Las Vegas" Cecchetti deposits the reader in that most surrealistic of experiences: Las Vegas the city of metal, neon, and glass that rises, like the Phoenix out of the Nevada desert; the city where America plays. When faced with this surrealistic sight the poet's agony over the faith of society overwhelms him. Las Vegas is a metaphor for contemporary society, a society that has no foundation, a society built on sand:

Se si stacca una scaglia ecco che crolla
a briciole la rete, e non c'è più nemmeno
un'ampolla opaca al chiodo
della parete . . . (43)[20]

Thus the desert is a metaphor for our life and society, and of an emptiness that is within all of us and that we are not able to fill, because modern man, in his quest for happiness and knowledge, has fallen into the abyss of despair and all he can see, according to Cecchetti, is the infertile, arid desert.

★ ★ ★

## CONCLUSION (SORT OF)

Joseph Tusiani and Giovanni Cecchetti, whose work I have only briefly examined in this essay, have taken different roads in addressing their status as *other* on the American landscape. Tusiani addressed the plight of the immigrant with some of the most poignant verses written by an Italian living in the United States, and, in his later years, he has returned to writing in Italian and in the dialect of the Gargano region of Italy where he was born. This return to his native language may be interpreted as an attempt at a resolution of his status as a man divided between two lands and two cultures. The problem is that forty years of experienced American reality cannot be erased because they have had a profound effect on his life and on his work as poet, translator, and scholar. The resolution to Tusiani's dilemma comes in his awareness of being suspended between two worlds, and of the acceptance of his biculturalism allowing him to accept himself as being a man of "two languages, two lands, . . . two [socio]cultural souls."

For Cecchetti, his American cultural odyssey took a different path. Throughout the years he has remained faithful to his Italian culture. Throughout his artistic life he has steadfastly written in Italian, both prose and poetry. Cecchetti's intimate ties with Italian culture, his native culture, and with the American West, his adopted culture and landscape, make him a most original multifaceted poetic voice in Italian literature. His cultural border crossings produce a literature that captures "both the concrete and the ephemeral nature of the seen world and of lived experience, and concentrates on the struggle of human consciousness to move beyond space and time into an acceptance of the limits of both that might lead to the repatriation of the exiled soul" (West, 98).

## NOTES

1. The following are excerpts from the interviews on the influence American life has had on their writing:

Peter Carravetta—Some of the aspects of living in the United States which could not but pluck the chords of the poet's lyre: the uprootedness, the mobility, the endless spaces, its being the quintessence of modernity, the diversity and tensions between natural forces and the padded mechanization of everything, the deep restless solitude of its peoples (124).

Alessandro Carrera—. . . , in America, I felt a vertigo, at the new physical and linguistic space offered to me, that has generated a more relaxed approach to writing (125).

Ned E. Condini—The untiring energy and brutal honesty of its citizens; their indifference to the world of poetry (128).

Alfredo de Palchi— . . . the ambivalence of life in America discouraged and yet angered me enough to write (129).

Giose Rimanelli—More than with the place (US), which however is extraordinary from any side you look at it. I am in love with the language of the place. In England it gets on my nerves, in the United States it warms my heart (134).

Mario Moroni: The plurality of spaces, languages, and ethnic presences is an aspect of American Society which has stimulated my writing, . . . In the United States I have acquired a different manner of perceiving things, under the influence of a modern American aesthetics which tends to name physical and mental objects more directly (*Italian Poets in America*, 133).

2. See Valesio's "I fuochi della tribù," in *Poesaggio* (255–90).

"Il modo migliore di definire questo gruppo di poeti è, in prima istanza, la via negativa: quello che questi poeti non sono e non possono essere né come italiani, né come americani, né come italiani-americani (257).

Distinguiamo dunque in questo territorio, quattro gruppi: (1) poeti americani; (2) poeti italani; (3) poeti italiani americani; (4) poeti tra i due mondi (259).

. . . chi scrive poesia in una data lingua mentre è immerso nel flusso e realtà quotidiana di una lingua diversa (260).

[The best way to define this group of poets, at least in a first instance, is in the negative: that which these poets are not and cannot be—not as Italians, not as Americans, not as Italian Americans.

We then distinguish four groups: (1) American poets; (2) Italian poets; (3) Italian American poets; (4) poets between two worlds.

He who writes in a language while he is immersed in the flux and reality of a different language].

3. In a recent conversation, Peter Carravetta said the following about the place of Italian writers in the United States: "Displaced as poets in society at large, the *Poesaggio* twelve are displaced also in terms of their identity and role within a community called Italian culture, criticism and cultural discourse as takes place in most cities in Italy today. Suddenly, despite the ready-at-hand freedom and possibilities of telephone, fax machines, airplanes and high speed trains and cars, these poets acknowledge and demonstrate that being away from the country of origin (whether as *patria* or *madrelingua*) greatly enhances their potential for exclusion and non-recognition in an already competitive, amorphous and distrustful community. Developing this further, it became evident to me that with their individual voice what was passed over in silence and ignored is also a potential collective formation to join the ranks of many others now on the scene both in North America and in Europe, a new and problematic discourse (such as letting more women poets tell their side of being an exile or expatriate), or a poetics (see for example Valesio's concluding essay, which revolves around the metaphor of the tribe, but a scattered and heterogenous one at that) as a *caso storico:* and the debate on an italophone literature, or an Italian literary diaspora *for our times,* has only just begun." (This conversation was published in a series of short interviews that appeared in a special issue of the *Canadian Journal of Italian Studies,* 1996: 218).

4. Two languages, the reality of eradication (I use this term to indicate total uprootedness) brings on different problems or traumas. First of all that of a new language. Then while learning that foreign language, one runs the risk, for reasons of human vanity, to think of your native language as inferior.

One does not fall into this trap if the phenomenon of biligualism is considered not as a conquest but as the forced reneging of one's origins and of one's self. Bilingualism becomes synonymous with the disintegration of family unity, for which a mother is not able to understand her own son. From the day when the sone says "Mother" instead of "mamma" and "sky" for "cielo," between a mother and a son there already is a spiritual separation that the scholar of linguistics cannot catalog. If words are articulated sounds that symbolize and communicate an idea, the term "mamma," different from "mother," the newly acquired term, symbolizes and communicates an entire world of sentiments that no foreign expression can comprehend and respect. To abolish it means to renege the existence of a childhood intimately tied to all the episodes, small and large, and to all the emotions, important and not important, connected and inspired by that singular word. Not assimilation or Americanization then, but ambivalence of thought and sentiment, of doubt and certainty, of dream and reality.

Also see "Song of the Bicentennial" in *Gente Mia and Other Poems*.

5. "America and Italy; in what order though? Should we not say, Italy and America?"

6. "to what point can the emigrant assimilate the new language and the new society, and how does he forget and renege himself in the middle of all the new and pressing exigencies of his life? Even if the answer lacks scientific validity, the poet tells us that complete assimilation is not possible, that it cannot be possible, and that there can never be complete acceptance, in the spiritual sense, of the traditions of the new land."

7. Although my statement is technically correct, Italian is the language of Italy and Tusiani was born in Italy, Tusiani's native language, the language that is full of cultural significance and remembrances, is, in effect, not standard Italian but the dialect that is spoken in San Marco in Lamis. We know that during Tusiani's youth, living in a small town meant growing up speaking the local dialect as your first language, Italian was a language that was acquired in school.

8. "I arrived under that sign and I read "Entrance." I turned and saw, there where my mother stood, the word "Exit." . . . I retraced my steps, but when I rejoined my mother, high on the wall, in place of "Exit," I again read "Entrance." . . . And forty times, anxiously, pushed by hope and despair, I ran from one end to the other of that enormous corridor."

9. "Father! Father!" I called, while moving toward him, "Mother and I have lost our way, we cannot find the exit."

"You really are a child," my father answered with a smile, "I know where the exit is, come with me." We were beginning to follow him.

10. "Driving towards the Bronx, in the limousine of the Poten Company, I noticed another detail; the windshield wipers, moving from right to left and from left to right, seemed to be saying Entrance-Exit, but I had lost the meaning of those words, and for whom they were meant."

11. "What about language? It is the one we were born into, the transfigured language of our childhood, charged with meanings and rhythms that at that time would have been beyond reach. An individual can never write poetry in another language which is superimposed and thus fictitious. This new language can never become his personal language even if he is immersed in it daily. In this case, one can

write verse, even good verse, but not poetry; for poetry cannot issue from the prison of linguistic artificiality. . . . Those of us who have lived our childhood in Italy (that childhood which in some way also includes adolescence), we can write poetry only in Italian. For us, English is the language of prose."

12. See Rebecca West's review of Cecchetti's *Cammino dei monti* (Florence: Vallecchi, 1980) in *Forum Italicum* 15, No. 1 (1981): 102.

13. The short stories of *Danza nel deserto* are: "Danza nel deserto," "Il telefono," "Il molo," "Il viale dei pirati," "La baia secca," "Le lettere," "Gl'ingessati," "Il castello," "Gl'ingabbiati," "Il cassone," "La macchina dell'aria," and "L'ascensore."

14. Michael Lettieri. "*Danza nel deserto:* intervista a Giovanni Cecchetti," *Ipotesi 80* (giugno, 1989): 123-30.

15. "images of the world in which we live, forms that are almost symbolic, that is forms that are almost allegorical."

16. "It is the world in which I live in: a world of people that laugh and cry from the other side of glass walls, that moves its lips with severity, without there ever being an interlocutor. I know that everyone seeks words, forgetting the nest of the talking cricket, and then finds contentment in a solitary laugh or the cooing of a dove."

17. "I don't understand anything," I said as I approached a man with tense eyes. "Not that one. He is a ventriloquist. He has a telephone in his belly and repeats only that which his neighbors say." . . .

"Try speaking with someone," he said," maybe they will answer. . . . This one."

I moved closer and spoke into the receiver: "How are you?" I heard a monosyllabic response, a garbled sound, as if in Chinese.

I tried the other statues; the answers were all the same. At times the sounds slithered away; at times they were so bloated they resembled inarticulate jungle screams. I gave up.

"Listen," my old classmate said. "I thought that with a stranger they would act in a normal way. Instead. . . . They began playing tricks on me from the beginning. If I said something into one of the receivers, they would answer with long discourses in Korean, in Persian, in Armenian . . . or at least that's what I thought, because on numerous occasions I could not identify the language. . . . I thought that they played these tricks because I had connected them to an International cable. So I connected them to the national cable. Worse than before: coughs, barks, yells, even little ditties sung through closed lips. In short, voices not words. . . . One can go crazy."

18. "The world they dream, the one which they end up living in, is at times quite unusual, as always is the case with dreams; hence it is not perceptible by others. It is noticeable only to them, because others have their own world of dreams that is totally different. This explains why communication is so difficult, more than that I would say it is impossible. Not only does this apply to these persons, but for all those others that I am not even considering."

19. "Every once in a while I opened the bag and extracted from it a house or some rags, and studied them in my hands. I thought that I had put infinity in that bag, but it didn't take me long to realize that I had only deposited a great quantity of limitations. Nonetheless I continued to gather and conserve. . . . But there were too many things that I had to carry with me. One day I began taking out all that I had put in. Incredibly everything had changed. That which had been white came out red. Blue things had turned to gray. What was inside that bag to cause such transformations? I never found out."

20.

"If a chip falls the whole net collapses
into crumbs, and there isn't even
an opaque phial hanging from a nail
in the wall"

## WORKS CITED

*Canadian Journal of Italian Studies.* Special Issue on Italian American Writing. 19.55 (1996). Guest Editors Paolo A. Giordano and Anthony Julian Tamburri.

Carravetta, Peter. "Poessay VI: Voices from the Italian Diaspora." Concept, Direction, Introduction. *Romance Language Notes* II (1991): 13–15.

Carravetta, Peter & Paolo Valesio, eds. *Poesaggio.* Quinto di Treviso: Pagus editore, 1993.

Cecchetti, Giovanni. *Diario nomade.* Padova: Rebellato, 1967.

———. *Impossibile scendere.* Milano: Scheiwiller, 1978.

———. *Nel Cammino dei Monti.* Florence: Vallecchi, 1981.

———. *Il villaggio degli inutili.* Venice: Rebellato, 1981

———. *Danza nel deserto.* Venice: Rebellato, 1985.

Fontanella, Luigi and Paolo Valesio, eds. *Italian Poets in America*, a special edition of *Gradiva: International Journal of Italian Literature* 5, No. 1 Stony Brook, N.Y., 1993.

Hicks, D. Emily. *Border Writing the Multidimensional Text.* University Minnesota Press, 1989.

Lettieri, Michael. "*Danza nel deserto:* intervista a Giovanni Cecchetti." *Ipotesi 80* (giugno 1989): 123–30.

Tusiani, Joseph. *Gente Mia and Other Poems.* Stone Park, Ill: Italian Cultural Center, 1978.

———. *La parola antica autobiografia di un italo-americano.* Bari: Schena Editore, 1992.

———. *La parola nuova autobiografia di un italo-americano.* Bari: Schena Editore, 1991.

———. *La parola difficile autobiografia di un italo-americano.* Bari: Schena Editore, 1988.

Valesio, Paolo. "Writer Between Two Worlds: Italian Writing in the United States Today." *Differentia* 3–4 (spring-autumn 1989): 259–76.

West, Rebecca. Review of Cecchetti's *Cammino dei monti* (Florence: Vallecchi, 1980) in *Forum Italicum* 15, no. 1 (1981):102.

# 12

# Rethinking Italian/American Studies: From the Hyphen to the Slash and Beyond

## ANTHONY JULIAN TAMBURRI

> Most [people] do not think things in the way they encounter them, nor do they recognize what they experience, but believe their own opinions.
>
> —Heraclitus

> If every picture I made was about Italian Americans, they'd say, "That's all he can do." I'm trying to stretch.
>
> —Martin Scorsese, in *Premiere*

## A PREMISE OF SORTS

The fortune of Italian/American literature is somewhat reflective of the United States mind-set vis-à-vis ethnic studies. Namely, until recently, ever since the arrival of the immigrants of the 1880s, the major wave of western-European emigration, the United States has considered ethnic/racial difference in terms of the melting-pot attitude. The past two decades, however, have constituted a period of transition, if not a change, in this attitude. Be it the end of modernism, as some have claimed, be it the onslaught of the postmodern, as others may affirm, in academic and intellectual circles today, one no longer thinks in terms of the melting pot. Instead, as is well known by most, one now talks in terms of the individual ethnic/racial culture and its relationship—and not necessarily in negative terms only—with the long-standing, mainstream cultural paradigm. It is, therefore, with the backdrop of this new attitude of rejecting the melting pot and supplanting it with the notion of Americana as a "kaleidoscopic, sociocultural mosaic,"[1] that we should consider an attempt to (re)define Italian/American literature and recategorize the notion of

243

the *hyphenate writer.* By using the phrase "kaleidoscopic socio/cultural mosaic," I mean to underscore how the sociocultural dynamics of the United States reveal a constant flux of changes originating in the very existence of the various differentiated ethnic/racial groups that constitute the overall population of the United States. As an addendum, furthermore, I suggest that we must still come to understand that the population of the United States is indeed similar to that of a mosaic in that this country consists of various bits and pieces (i.e., the various peoples, ethnic and racial, of the United States) each one unique unto itself. The kaleidoscopic nature of this aggregate of different and unique peoples is surely descriptive of this constant flux of changes that manifests itself as the various peoples change positions, physical and ideological, which ultimately change the ideological colors of the United States mind-set.

Borrowing from Aijaz Ahmad's notions immediate to post-colonial literature, of *ethnic*—or for that matter any *other*—literature we may indeed state that, first of all, such a notion cannot be "constructed as an internally coherent object of theoretical knowledge"; that such a categorization "cannot be resolved . . . without an altogether positivist reductionism."[2] Secondly, *other* "literary traditions [e.g., third world, ethnic, etc.] remain, beyond a few texts here and there, [often] unknown to the *American* literary theorist" (5). While it may be true that Ahmad's use of the adjective *American* refers to the geopolitical notion of the United States of America, I would contend that the situation of ethnic literatures within the United States is analogous to what Ahmad so adroitly describes in his article on, for lack of a better term, "third-world literature." Thus, I would suggest that we reconsider Ahmad's *American* within the confines of the geopolitical borders of the United States and thereby reread it as synonymous to *dominant culture.* Third, "[l]iterary texts are produced in highly differentiated, usually over-determined contexts of *competing ideological and cultural clusters, so that any particular text of any complexity shall always have to be placed within the cluster that gives it its energy and form, before it is totalised into a universal category*" (23; my emphasis). Thus, it is also within this ideological framework of cluster specificity that I shall consider further the notion of Italian/American literature as a validifiable category of United States literature and (re)think the significance of the Italian/American writer within the recategorization of the notion of the hyphenate writer.

Finally, I should specify, at the outset, that which I have in mind for Italian/American writer throughout this essay. Because of language plurality—standard Italian, Italian dialect, and United States English[3]—I believe that there are different types of writers that may fall under the general category of Italian/American writer. They range from the immigrant writer of Italian language to the United States-born writer of Italian descent who writes in English; and in between, of course, one may surely find the many variations of these two extremes.[4] Here, in the pages that follow, therefore, I shall use the phrase Italian/American writer in reference to that person who—be he or she born in the United States or in Italy—is significantly involved in creative literary activity in the English language.[5]

## [RE]DEFINITIONS AND CATEGORIES

In the past, Italian/American art forms—more precisely, literature and film—have been defined as those constructed mainly by second-generation writers about the experiences of the first and second generations.[6] Robert Casillo defined Italian/American cinema as "works by Italian-American directors who treat Italian-American subjects."[7] In like fashion, Frank Lentricchia had previously defined Italian/American literature as "a report and meditation on first-generation experience, usually from the perspective of a second-generation representative."[8] Indeed, both constitute a valid attempt at constructing neat and clean definitions for works of two art forms—and in a certain sense we can extend this meaning to other art media—that deal explicitly with an Italian/American ethnic quality and subject matter.[9] Such definitions, however, essentially halt the progress and limit the impact of those writers who come from later generations, and thus may result in a monolithic notion of what was/is and was/is not Italian/American literature. Following a similar mode of thinking, Dana Gioia has more recently proposed yet another limiting definition in his brief essay, "What Is Italian-American Poetry?"[10] There, Gioia describes "Italian-American poetry . . . only as a transitional category" for which the "concept of Italian-American poet is therefore most useful to describe first- and second-generation writers raised in the immigrant subculture" (3).

One question that arises is What do we do about those works of art—written and visual—that do not *explicitly* treat Italian/American subject matter and yet seem to exude a certain ethnic Italian/American quality, even if we cannot readily define it? That is, can we speak to the Italian/American qualities of a Frank Capra film? According to Casillo's definition, we would initially have to say no. However, it is Casillo himself who tells us that Capra, indeed, "found his ethnicity troublesome throughout his long career" (374) and obviously dropped it. My question, then, is Can we not see this *absence*, especially in light of documented secondary matter, as an Italian/American signifier *in potentia?*[11] I say yes. And in this regard, I suggest an alternative perspective on reading and categorizing any Italian/American art form.[12] That is, I believe we should take our cue from Scorsese himself and, therefore, "stretch" our own reading strategy of Italian/ American art forms, whether they be—due to content and form— *explicitly* Italian American or not, to accommodate other possible, successful reading strategies. Indeed, recent (re)writings of Italian/ American literary history and criticism have transcended a limited concept of Italian/American literature. New publications (literary and critical) have created a need for new definitions and new critical readings, not only of contemporary work, but of the works of the past. In addition, these new publications have originated, for the most part, from within an intellectual community of Italian Americans.[13] Therefore, I propose that we consider Italian/American literature to be a series of written enterprises that establish a repertoire of signs, at times, *sui generis,* and therefore create verbal variations (visual, in the case of film, painting, sculpture, drama, etc.) that represent different versions—dependent, of course, on one's generation, gender, and socioeconomic condition—of what can be perceived as the Italian/ American signified.[14] That is, the Italian/American experience may indeed be manifested in any art form in a number of ways and at varying degrees, for which one may readily speak of the variegated representations of the Italian/American ethos in literature, for example, in the same fashion in which Daniel Aaron spoke of the "hyphenate writer."[15]

Within the general discourse of American literature, Daniel Aaron seems to be one of the first to have dealt with the notion of hyphenation.[16] For him, the hyphen initially represented older North Americans' hesitation to accept the new/comer; it was their way, in Aaron's words, to "hold him at 'hyphen's length,' so to speak, from the established community" (213). It further "signifies a tentative but unmistakable withdrawal" on the user's part, so that "mere geographical proximity" denies the newly arrived "full and unqualified national membership despite . . . legal qualifications and . . . official disclaimers to the contrary" (213).

Speaking in terms of a passage from "'hyphenation' to 'dehyphenation'" (214), Aaron sets up three stages through which a non-Anglo-/ American writer might pass.[17] The first-stage writer is the "pioneer spokesman for the . . . unspoken-for" ethnic, racial, or cultural group—that is, the marginalized, who writes about his or her co-others with the goal of dislodging and debunking negative stereotypes ensconced in the dominant culture's mind-set. In so doing, this writer

may actually create characters possessing some of the very same stereotypes, with the specific goals, however, of (1) winning over the
sympathies of the suspicious members of the dominant group, and (2)
humanizing the stereotyped figure and thus "dissipating prejudice."
Successful or not, this writer engages in placating his or her reader
by employing recognizable features the dominant culture associates
with specific ethnic, racial, or cultural groups.[18]

Less willing to please, the second-stage writer abandons the use of
preconceived ideas in an attempt to demystify negative stereotypes.
Whereas the first-stage writer might have adopted some preconceived
notions popular with the dominant culture, this writer presents characters who have already sunk "roots into the native soil." By no
means, therefore, as conciliatory as the first-stage writer, this person
readily indicates the disparity and, in some cases, may even engage
in militant criticism of the perceived restrictions and oppression set
forth by the dominant group. In so doing, according to Aaron, this
writer runs the risk of a "double criticism": from the dominant culture offended by the "unflattering or even 'un-American' image of
American life," as also from other members of his or her own marginalized group, who might feel misrepresented, having preferred a more
"genteel and uncantankerous spokesman."

The third-stage writer, in turn, travels from the margin to the
mainstream "viewing it no less critically, perhaps, but more knowingly." Having appropriated the dominant group's culture and the
tools necessary to succeed in that culture—the greater skill of manipulating, for instance, a language acceptable to the dominant group—
and more strongly than his or her predecessors, this writer feels entitled to the intellectual and cultural heritage of the dominant group.
As such, he or she can also, from a personal viewpoint, "speak out
uninhibitedly as an American."[19] As Aaron reminds us, this writer
does not renounce or abandon the cultural heritage of his or her
marginalized group. Instead, he or she transcends "a mere parochial
allegiance" in order to transport "into the province of the [general]
imagination," personal experiences which for the first-stage ("local
colorist") and second-stage ("militant protester") writer "comprised
the very stuff of their literary material" (215).[20]

An excellent analog to Aaron's three stages of the "hyphenate
writer" can be found in Fred L. Gardaphé's three-fold Vichian division of the history of Italian/American literature. Gardaphé proposes
a culturally "specific methodology" for the greater disambiguation of
Italian/American contributions to the United States literary scene. In
his essay, he reminds us of Vico's "three ages and their corresponding
cultural products: the Age of Gods in which primitive society records

expression in 'poetry' [*vero narratio,*] the Age of Heros, in which society records expression in myth, and the Age of Man, in which through self-reflection, expression is recorded in philosophic prose." These three ages, Gardaphé goes on to tell us, have their parallels in modern and "contemporary [socio-]cultural constructions of realism, modernism, and postmodernism" (24). And ultimately, the evolution of the various literatures of United States ethnic and racial groups can be charted as they "move from the poetic, through the mythic and into the philosophic" (25).[21]

For the first-stage writer, then, a type of self-deprecating barterer with the dominant culture, the *vero narratio* constitutes the base of what he or she writes. He or she no more writes about what he or she *thinks* than what he or she *experiences,* his or her surroundings. His or her art, in a sense, then, records more her or his experiential feelings than her or his analytical thoughts. This writer is not concerned with an adherence to or the creation of some form of objective, rhetorical literary paradigm. He or she is an expressive writer, not a paradigmatic one—his or her ethnic experiences of the more visceral kind serve more as the foundation of his or her literary signification.

The second-stage writer, the "militant protester" who is by no means conciliatory as was the first-stage writer, belongs to the generation that re/discovers or reinvents his or her ethnicity. While he or she may present characters who have already "sunk roots in the native soil," he or she readily underscores the characters' uniqueness vis-à-vis the expectations of the dominant culture. As Gardaphé reminds us, before this writer can "merge with the present," s/he must recreate—and here I would add, in a *sui generis* manner—his past: He or she must engage in a "materialization and an articulation of the past" (27).

The use of ethnicity at this second stage shifts from the expressive to the descriptive. As a rhetorico-ideological tool, ethnicity becomes much more functional and quasi descriptive. It is no longer the predominantly expressive element it is in the premodernist, poetic writer (i.e., the bartering, first-stage expressive writer). Whereas in the premodernist, poetic writer ethnicity, as theme, is the conduit, hence expressive, through which he or she communicates his or her immediate, sensorial feelings, for the modernist, mythic writer, ethnicity becomes more the tool with which he or she communicates his or her ideology. In this second case, the ethnic signs constitute the individual pieces to the ethnic paradigm this second-stage writer so consciously and willingly seeks to construct.

While this modernist, mythic second-stage writer may engage in militant criticism of the perceived restrictions and oppression set forth by the dominant group, *expressive* residue of the evolution from the premodernist to the modernist stage, the third-stage writer (i.e., Gardaphé's postmodernist, philosophic writer) may seem at first glance to rid himself or herself of his or her ethnicity.[22] This writer, as Aaron reminds us, will often view the dominant culture "less critically" than the previous writers but indeed "more knowingly." This should not come as any surprise, however, since, as Gardaphé later tells us, this writer finds himself or herself in a decisively self-reflexive stage for which he or she can decide to transcend the experiential expressivity of the first two stages by either engaging in a parodic tour de force through his or her art or by relegating any vestige of his or her ethnicity to the background of his or her artistic inventions.[23] In both cases, the writer has come to terms with his or her personal (read, ethnic) history, without totally and explicitly renouncing or abandoning cultural heritage. This writer, that is, transcends "mere parochial allegiance" and therefore passes completely out of the *expressive* and *descriptive* stages into a third and final (?) reflexive stage in which everything becomes fair game. All this is due to the "postmodern prerogative" of all artists, be they the parodic, the localizers, or others simply in search of rules for what will have been done.

What then can we finally make of these writers who seem to evolve into different animals from one generation to the next? Indeed, both Aaron and Gardaphé look at these writers from the perspective of time, their analyses are generationally based—and rightfully so. However, we would not err to look at these three stages from another perspective, a cognitive Peircean perspective of firstness, secondness, and thirdness as rehearsed in his *Principles of Philosophy*.[24] All three stages, for Peirce, represent different modes of being dependent on different levels of consciousness. They progress, that is, from a state of nonrationality ("feeling")[25] to practicality ("experience")[26] and on to pure rationality ("thought")[27]—or, "potentiality," "actuality," and "futuribility."

If firstness is the isolated, *sui generis* mode of possibly being Peirce tells us it is, we may see an analog in the first-stage writer's *vero narratio*. For it is here, Gardaphé tells us, that primitive society records expression in poetry, in unmitigated realism, by which I mean that which the writer experiences only.[28] In this sense, the writer's sensorial experiences, his or her "feelings," as Peirce calls them, constitute the "very stuff of [his or her] literary material." Namely, those recordings of what he or she simply experiences, without the benefit of any "analysis, comparison or any [other] process whatsoever . . . by which one stretch of consciousness is distinguished from another."

As the second-stage writer shifts from the expressive—"that kind

of consciousness which involves no analysis," Peirce would tell us—
to the descriptive, he or she now engages in some form of analysis
and comparison, two processes fundamental to Peirce's secondness.
This writer, that is, becomes aware of the dominant culture—"how
a second object is"—and does not repeat the conciliatory acts of the
first-stage writer—he or she undergoes a "forcible modification of . . .
thinking [which is] the influence of the world of fact or *experience*."

The third-stage writer transcends the first two stages of experiential
expressivity either through parody or diminution of significance of
his or her expressivity because he or she has seen "both sides of the
shield" and can, therefore, "contemplate them from the outside only."
For that "element of cognition [thirdness, according to Peirce] which
is neither feeling [firstness] nor the polar sense [secondness], is the
consciousness of a process, and this in the form of the sense of learning, of acquiring, mental growth is eminently characteristic of cognition" (1.381). Peirce goes on to tell us that this third mode of being
is timely, not immediate; it is the consciousness of a process, the
"consciousness of synthesis" (1.381), which is precisely what this
third-stage, postmodern writer does. He or she can transcend the
intellectual experiences of the first two stages because of all that has
preceded him or her both temporally (Aaron, Gardaphé) and cognitively (Peirce).[29]

What we now witness after at least three generations of writers is
a progression from a stage of basic realism to that of incredulous
postmodernism, with passage through a secondary stage of mythic
modernism in which this monolithic, modernist writer believes to
have found all the solutions to what he or she has perceived as the
previous generation's *problems*. In light of what was stated above, we
may now speak in terms of a twofold evolution—both a temporal and
intellectual process—that bears three distinct writers to whom we
may now attach more precise labels. The *expressive* writer embodies
the poetic realist who writes more from "feelings." Through the process of analysis, on the other hand, the second is a *comparative* writer
who sets up a distinct polarity between his or her cultural heritage
and the dominant culture in that he or she attempts to construct a *sui
generis* ethnic paradigm. The third writer, instead, through "mental
growth," as Peirce states, can embrace a consciousness of process
(i.e., self-reflexivity) and consequently engage in a process of synthesis
and "bind . . . life together" (1.381)—this I would consider to be the
*synthetic* writer. The following graph charts my use of the above-
mentioned terminology in what I have proposed as three possible
categories of the Italian/American writer—or, for that matter, any
ethnic/racial writer:

| Aaron | | Gardaphé | | Peirce | | |
|---|---|---|---|---|---|---|
| first-stage<br>"local<br>colorist" | ↔ | poetic<br>"premodernist" | ↔ | "firstness" | → | expressive |
| \| | | \| | | \| | | \| |
| second-stage<br>"militant<br>protester" | ↔ | mythic<br>"modernist" | ↔ | "secondness" | → | comparative |
| \| | | \| | | \| | | \| |
| third-stage<br>"American" | ↔ | philosophic<br>"postmodernist" | ↔ | "thirdness" | → | synthetic |

Having proposed such a reclassification, I believe it is important to reiterate some of what was stated before and underscore its significance to the above-mentioned categories. First and foremost, it is important to emphasize that the three general, different categories, while generationally based for Aaron and Gardaphé and cognitively based for Peirce, should not, by any means, represent a hierarchy—they are, simply, different. For in a manner similar to Peirce's three stages, these three general categories also represent *different* modes of being dependent on *different* levels of consciousness. The key word here, of course, is different. These categories are different precisely because, just as literary texts in general, as Ahmad reminded us, "are produced in highly differentiated, usually overdetermined contexts of competing ideological and cultural clusters," so too do each of the three categories constitute specific cognitive and ideological clusters that ultimately provide the energy and form to the texts of those writers of the three different stages.

Second, these stages do not necessarily possess any form of monolithic valence. What I am suggesting is that writers should not be considered with respect to one stage only. It is possible, I would contend, that a writer's opus may, in fact, reflect more than one, if not all three, of these stages.[30] In this respect, we should remind ourselves that pertinent to any discourse on ethnic art forms is the notion that ethnicity is not a fixed essence passed down from one generation to the next. Rather, "ethnicity is something reinvented and reinterpreted in each generation by each individual,"[31] which, in the end, is a way of "finding a voice or style that does not violate one's

*several components of identity*" (my emphasis), these components constituting the specificities of each individual. Thus, ethnicity—and
more specifically in this case, *italianità*[32]—is redefined and reinterpreted on the basis of each individual's time and place, and is therefore always new and different with respect to his or her own historical
specificities vis-à-vis the dominant culture.

This said, then, we should also keep in mind that we may now
think in terms of a twofold evolutionary process—both temporal and
cognitive—that may or may not be mutually inclusive. The temporal
may not parallel the cognitive and vice versa. Hence, we may have,
sociologically speaking, a second- or third-generation writer—according to Aaron's distinction, he or she would have to be a "second-"
or "third-stage" writer—who finds a voice or style in his or her recent
rediscovery and reinvention of his or her ethnicity. This writer,
though a member of the second or third generation, may actually
produce what we may now expect from the *expressive* or *comparative*
writer—namely, the first- or second-generation writer. Conversely, we
may actually find a member of the immigrant generation—undoubtedly, a "first-stage" writer from a temporal point of view—whose
work exudes everything but that which we would expect from the
work of a first- or even a second-generation writer (that is, Aaron's
"first-" or "second-stage" writer). This immigrant writer may indeed
fall more easily into the category of the *synthetic* writer rather than
that of the *comparative* or *expressive* writer. For my first hypothesis,
then, I have in mind a writer like Tony Ardizzone, a third-generation
Italian American whose work fits much better the category of the
*expressive* and *comparative* writer. My second hypothesis is borne out
by the example of Giose Rimanelli, an Italian born, raised, and educated in Italy, who has spent the past four decades in the United
States. His first work in English, *Benedetta in Guysterland,* is anything
but the typical novel one would expect from a writer of his migratory
background. Much less problematic, instead, is the second-stage category, the *comparative* writer, that I exemplify with a reading of Helen
Barolini's first novel, *Umbertina.*

## WRITERS AND CATEGORIES

### TONY ARDIZZONE

Tony Ardizzone's *The Evening News*[33] is a collection of short stories
that won the Flannery O'Connor Award for Short Fiction in 1986.[34]
This collection of eleven stories offers its reader a portrait, for the

most part, of the North Side of Chicago where Ardizzone spent his childhood. He presents his reader with both working- and middle-class citizens of all ages, men and women, mostly of Italian descent. Except for a few stories about college, Ardizzone's characters are the so-called hyphenated Americans who occupy a world seemingly different from what one might expect; they are very much ensconced in a world of memory and recollection that keeps them ineluctably tied to their past either in search of some form of understanding their present situation or, in certain cases, in an attempt to escape from their present situation.

In articulating a sense of empathy for his characters, Ardizzone is also, to paraphrase Daniel Aaron, a sort of pioneer spokesperson—similar to Aaron's "first-stage" writer—for the unspoken-for marginalized Italian/American citizen of, in his case, Chicago's North Side.[35] Undoubtedly, he offers portraits of his co-ethnics with the goal of dislodging and debunking negative stereotypes ensconced in the dominant culture's mind-set. In so doing, he also creates characters possessing at times some of the very same stereotypes that some sensitive types—for example, thin-skinned Italian Americans—would rather see debunked.[36] In this manner, he surely succeeds in humanizing the stereotyped figure. At the same time, he does not necessarily engage directly in militant criticism of any preconceptions, restrictions, and oppression of ethnic set forth by the dominant group. As a result, demystification of negative stereotypes is, at best, left for the reader to infer,[37] for which the general reader's strategy for and interpretation of "dissipating prejudice" is called to the fore, and the semiotic responsibility of any sort of finalized act of signification is shifted from that of being entirely the author's to a more complicit act between author and reader. What I thus propose here is a reading of some of Ardizzone's stories as an example of his *expressivity*, as it pertains to what I have outlined earlier in my reconsideration and redefinition of the Italian/American writer.

In Ardizzone's opening tale, "My Mother's Stories," the narrator clearly speaks in his own, personal voice, offering us a moving tribute to his ill mother of German descent married to his Italian/American father. The story opens with a brief description of how his mother was born frail and sickly. In fact, we read that "they were going to throw her away when she was a baby. The doctors said she was too tiny, too frail, that she wouldn't live" (1). What becomes significant here at the outset is that this is also the opening of the entire collection, for which the frailty of the narrator's ethnic mother is also, I would contend, a signal of the frailty of the immigrant and his or her progeny. Such frailty of one's existenial condition, I would suggest here, will reappear at the end of the collection in the figure of "Nonna."[38]

All this is couched in a much more intimate rapport between the narrator and his reader, when he soon passes to direct discourse with his reader, in a Calvinian sense, as he adopts the "You" in "You can well imagine the rest."[39] Such a shift of immediately placing the relationship between narrator and reader on a much more personal level, now transforms the reader, semiotically, into a type of listener and, emotionally, into a type of confidant. Thus, from the viewpoint of both representation and content, a shift in modality also occurs. Such a shift in levels between narrator and reader—or for that matter, any transformation in one's narrative technique—is part and parcel of the author/narrator's sense of self-awareness that informs much of this story, signaled here at the beginning:

> "my mother and her stories. For now the sounds and pictures are *my* sounds and pictures. Her memory, my memory." (1)

Such self-awareness first of all also puts the narrator on the same level as his mother, and, in a certain sense, his storytelling replicates that of his mother, that which he now recounts. Thus, we become witness to a type of circularity between who tells and what is being told. The narrator thus engages in an act of identification with what and about whom he recounts. This identification becomes more significant here precisely because the person in the narrator's story is indeed a story-teller. Thus, the act of narration is underscored both by the fact that the narrator alludes to his narrating as well as to his mother, the storyteller as protagonist, and her previous storytelling to him and his family. Such a layered, narrative situation might be mapped out by a curious set of graphs. First, in modifying slightly Seymour Chatman's 1978 schemata,[40] we may chart the overall narrative communication act in the following manner:

|  |  | Narrative Text |  |  |
|---|---|---|---|---|
| Real | Implied |  | Implied | Real |
|  | -> (Narrator) -> | MOTHER'S STORIES | -> (Narratee) -> |  |
| Author | Author |  | Reader | Reader |

What we see is that Ardizzone sets up a multilayered narrative text that has embedded in his narrative communication act a second one—his mother's stories—that includes him as character. Second, in charting further the relationship between our narrator (N) and his narrated protagonist, his mother (M), we see the circularity of identification between who narrates (N) and what/whom (M) is being narrated:

$$N \rightarrow M = M/N \ (mother< = >narrator)< = \ N$$

The narrator (N), we see, discusses ($\rightarrow$) his mother who soon becomes ($< = >$) for us also the mother/narrator (M/N) with whom our narrator eventually identifies ($< =$), as we saw above: "For now the sounds and pictures are *my* sounds and pictures. Her memory, my memory."

A secondary level of identification becomes equally sigificant here, this time in relationship to the theme of ethnicity. Whereas above, on the one level, the narrator becomes a storyteller like his mother, the protagonist of his story, here, on another level, the narrator also becomes a (metaphoric) first-generation hyphenate that is also his mother. The storyteller's story thus replicates the life of his character. We therefore see the polysemy of the above-cited act of identification insofar as the storyteller—that is, Narrator—as both raconteur and ethnic, becomes his character the storyteller—that is, his mother. In so doing, he signals to us that, like his mother, he is a first-generation storyteller. Thus, it is in this framework that I would suggest we read Ardizzone's *The Evening News*. Namely, in spite of his actual ethnic status of second or third generation, Tony Ardizzone's stories may often appear as examples of that type of narrative a first-generation writer might readily construct.

This story has everything in it necessary for examination. Along with the author's self-consciousness, we see that ethnicity is not limited to Italian Americans only; the character's mother is, in fact, German. Second, the difference in immigrant groups is underscored with colors; the Germans are light, the Italians are dark, "dark Sicilians" as is her girlfriend and sister of her future husband who, in turn, is "finely muscled, dark, deeply tanned" (2). Thus, we have the usual light versus dark binary opposition among ethnic groups. Indeed, lest we forget, Italians were considered people of color by some sociologists in the early years of the twentieth century.[41] The initial description of the character, in fact, is presented from the young woman's perspective, the narrator's frightened young mother:

> Perhaps our Mary, being young, is somewhat frightened. The boy behind the dark fence is older than she, is in high school, is *finely muscled, dark, deeply tanned. Around his neck hang golden things glistening on a thin chain. He wears a sleeveless shirt—his undershirt.* Mary doesn't know whether to stay with her young friend or to continue walking. She stays, but she looks away from the boy's dark eyes and gazes instead at *the worn belt* around his *thin waist.* (2; emphasis added)

We see above that the father, as a young man, is an Adonis-like individual, a handsome replica of a Greek stature, who, nevertheless, readily recalls an image representative of the stereotype of the working-class Italian and Italian American both of long ago as well as that of today. Tony, the multi-referential irony of which should not be lost on us, wears a sleeveless shirt, the classic *guinea t-shirt*, as it was often called years ago, and sports, again according to what we might consider a classic Italian/American semiotic, a golden chain laden with what can only be easily recognizable amulets—indeed, so recognizable that it is not necessary to specificy and enumerate them. The Italian/American sign system is further employed in the phyical description of the narrator's young father. Both his physical attributes of corpular muscularity and his olive complexion, dark and deeply tanned, are presented as integral parts of one another; for he is "finely muscled, dark, [and] deeply tanned," as we read. In addition, his working-class status is signaled at the end of this brief description together with his physical attributes, as Mary, too shy from her proper raising, does not look him in the eyes, but instead "gazes . . . at the worn belt around his thin waist." This portrait of the narrator's young father thus figures as a most reminiscent interpretant (i.e., signifier) of the Italian and/or Italian American of a certain social class of the early and mid-twentieth century. The good looking athletic type— that is, muscular—often ended up in professional sports— professional or semiprofessional—if not, on those rare occasions, in the movies.[42]

As one might suspect, the father in this story is also a positively framed character. Different from some father figures in the writings of some other Italian Americans,[43] Tony is a good husband and father, a sensitive man. Toward the end of this story, in fact, his sensitivity comes to the fore. In discussing his wife's terminal illness with his son, the narrator, we are witness to this serious demeanor; he was, as we are told, "not a man given to unnecessary talk" (12). Tony's ability to communicate his feelings of imminent loss and seeming desperation belie any notion of the stereotypical macho, emotionally hard-nosed—that is, paralyzed—Italian or Italian/American male. For the father now confides in his son, seeking obvious comfort and reassurance, as is evident from he following conversation:

> I don't know what I'd do without her, he says. I say nothing, for I can think of nothing to say. We've been together for over thirty years, he says. He pauses. For nearly thirty-four years. Thirty-four years this October. And, you know, you wouldn't think it, but I love her so much more now. He hesitates, and I look at him. He shakes his head and smiles. You know

what I mean? he says. I say yes and we walk for a while in silence, and I think of what it must be like to live with someone for thirty-four years, but I cannot imagine it, and then I hear my father begin to talk about that afternoon's ball game—he describes at length and in comic detail a misjudged fly ball lost in apathy or ineptitude or simply in the sun—and for the rest of our walk home we discuss what's right and wrong with our favorite baseball team, our thorn-in-the-side Chicago Cubs. (12)

As we look further, we find other dynamics at work in the above-cited passage. While it is true that the son cannot identify with his father's thirty-four years with his mother, an identification process between father and narrating son, analogous to what we saw between mother and son, is also at work. We see, first of all, that the dialogue recounted in an indirect format does not immediately distinguish between the "I" of the father and the "I" of the son: "*I* don't know what *I*'d do without her, he says. *I* say nothing, for *I* can think of nothing to say." But if this initial amalgamation of the two "I"s seems to be belied by the narrator's admitted inability to empathize and comprehend his father's feelings—"*I* cannot imagine it?"—such inability is further countered by the transformation of the two singular, first-person pronouns ("I") into the first-person, plural adjectives ("our") and pronouns ("we"). Such transformation, I would further add, takes place on two occasions. Immediately after the first two ambiguous "I"s we have a "we": "*I* don't know what *I*'d do without her, he says. *I* say nothing, for *I* can think of nothing to say. *We*'ve been. . . ." The second occurrence can be found in the final, complete sentence of the paragraph, as the son responds to his father's question, "You know what I mean?" he says:

> *I* say yes and *we* walk for a while in silence, and *I* think of what it must be like to live with someone for thirty-four years, but *I* cannot imagine it, and then *I* hear my father begin to talk about that afternoon's ball game—he describes at length and in comic detail a misjudged fly ball lost in apathy or ineptitude or simply in the sun—and for the rest of *our* walk home *we* discuss what's right and wrong with *our* favorite baseball team, *our* thorn-in-the-side Chicago Cubs. (12; emphasis added)

What starts out as an inability to undertsand his father's sentiments vis-à-vis his wife transforms itself into a total amalgamation of the two men as they now discuss something they both know intimately: "*our* thorn-in-the-side Chicago Cubs."[44]

As apparent from a number of stories in *The Evening News*, Ardizzone's characters, as Gino the young altar boy (of the collection's second story, "The Eyes of Children") tells us, occupy a "big dark world," one that in effect is metonymous of the world of the ethnics that inhabit Ardizzone's world.[45] The estrangement that they experience is an easy metaphor for the more general ethnic estrangement that the immigrant and, in some cases, the first generations especially feel. Like Ardizzone's characters, the members of these generations are often caught between two worlds. They are neither the *Americans* they traveled to be nor are they any longer members of the world from which they emigrated.

Part of what marks this and other stories of the collection as what I have constructed as "expressive" is the so-called time warp in which many of Ardizzone's characters seem to be fixed. Some of the male characters, for instance, are most sentimental, often thinking back to their old girlfriends or mothers. Needy to know what has touched them, they are reluctant to let go of these old emotional bonds in order to move on, and so they remain in a most modernist framework, undesiring of the somewhat detached postmodern.

Ardizzone's style and narration vary with each story. Simple on the surface, Ardizzone at the same time challenges his reader to delve deep below the surface in order to grapple with the sense of some sort of existential unease, if not a seeming dispair and hopelessness, often present in his stories. Equally significant, then, is Ardizzone's self-awareness of story-teller and crafty builder of tales. As he tends to lie outside his stories as omniscient narrator, he also inserts himself in stories masked as one of the characters, usually—as expected—the storyteller. In fact, as the narrator of "My Mother's Stories" tells us, writers engage in what I would label narrative *irresponsibility*, to echo the long-forgotten Wayne Booth in our theoretical/critical world of a sometimes narrow-mindedness poststructuralism:[46]

> I stand here, not used to speaking about things that are so close to me. I am used to veiling things in my stories, to making things wear masks, to telling my stories through masks. (12)

The "here" of where our narrator stands is, first or all, an ambiguous one. This paragraph, which appears at the end of Ardizzone's opening story, is set apart form the main text by spaces inserted before and after the preceding and subsequent paragraphs. Thus, we must, as involved readers, look for whatever possible bits of evidence lying beneath the surface—that is, "veil[ed in] masks," as Ardizzone's narrator would tell us—that might lead us down one or the other interpretive path. For we should not forget what Ardizzone's narrator tells us at the end of his first story: "but [my mother] never said what it was that she saw from the front windows. A good storyteller, she leaves what she has all too clearly seen to our imaginations" (13). We may surely borrow our initial narrator's words and, in considering Ardizzone's storytelling, state that, like his narrator's mother, Ardizzone the "good storyteller, . . . leaves what [he] has all too clearly [crafted] to our imaginations."

Indeed, as his characters seem to inhabit a certain period or possess characteristics of a period long gone, in his own way Ardizzone inhabits, in a thematic sense, an ethnic warp. To cite one of his reviewers, he "can't seem to cut himself free [from working-class, ethnic, city life]. And that's good, because his book not only entertains, it fills a void."[47] He does not engage in the militant criticism we would expect of a *comparative* writer; nor does he go beyond the ethnic in an attempt to *synthesize* his stories and characteriers with irony and ethnic dispassion. He succeeds, like those who (re)turn to their ethnicity and (re)invent it through their craft, while filling in the above-mentioned void. It is, in fact, this filling of such a void—an ethnic void, I would add at this point—that, in one sense, makes Ardizzone the "expressive" writer that I suggest he is. The characters he presents are still very much tied to individuals with the vicissitudes of those whom Aaron outlined in his essay. Ardizzone, that is, writes from the heart of the North Side of Chicago, a socioeconomic melieu where ethnicity is still very much alive and well, and class issues are up front and personal.

## HELEN BAROLINI

Helen Barolini's first novel, *Umbertina* (1979), deals directly with the Italian immigrant's assimilation process in the United States. She presents the lives of three women of the Longobardi family: Umbertina, the immigrant; Marguerite, Umbertina's granddaughter, and Tina, Marguerite's daughter. Each, in fact, represents a different stage of the Italian and Italian/American assimilation process to American culture. *Umbertina* is a fictionalized account of the social changes and the conflicts within the Italian/American family as it grew and developed from one generation to the next—those generations Joseph Lopreato describes and analyzes in his study *Italian Americans* (1970): "peasant," "first-," "second-," and "third-generation."[48] His "peasant" family comes to life in the figure of Umbertina, a shepherd-girl from a small mountain village in Calabria, who tended goats in the burned-out hills near her birthplace until she married. After her marriage to Serafino—a marriage of convenience rather than one of love—they acquired a parcel of secularized land and gave it their best at farming. However, their attempts at making a better life for themselves were futile because of the barrenness of the land and the exorbitant taxes. It was, then, soon decided that they would go to the United States, where Serafino had spent a good part of his youth. Their subsequent move to the United States and the hardships of the trip and of their initial years in New York City are representative of those experienced by most southern Italians who made the journey during the great wave of immigration at the turn of the century. Their later years of life also correspond to the general pattern of behavior among their *paesani* in the new country: the father was considered the head of the family; the "boys" enjoyed more freedom than the "girls."

Barolini does not deal directly with the second-generation family. Instead, the members of this type of family are presented intermittently, as part of the life stories of the three women who make up the book. Yet, even here, some classic stereotypes are presented.[49] What stands out most significantly of this generation is the "apathetic individual," who tends to see things from an economic perspective and avoids the conflict of cultural duality by de-emphasizing and "de-emotionalizing" natural origin (Lopreato, 42), if not at times rejecting it and proclaiming him/herself American rather than Italian.

Marguerite is prototypical of Lopreato's "second-generation" (i.e., third-generation) family, which he considers to be the first "to make the big cultural break between the old society and the new" (Lopreato, 74). He goes on to describe three different types of individuals who make up this group: the "rebel," the "apathetic individual," and the "in-grouper." Of the three, Marguerite best represents the "rebel," whose "impatience [and] intensity of [her] negative attitude toward the ways of the old folks" (Lopreato, 76) were dominant characteristics of hers at an early age. Like Aaron's second-stage writer, Marguerite also engages in a type of critical militancy in her socially rebellious acts. She rebelled against middle-class malaise: the religiosity of the traditional family and her mother's middle-class civility. In fact, we read

> At school, where all the daughters of the top Irish families went, including the mayor's daughter, she got to be known as Mad Marguerite—because she read books that no one else had hear of (Voltaire, Spengler, T. S. Eliot, Ivy Compton-Burnett) and because she defied convent ways. She wore her uniform too tight, she studied too hard, her answers were delivered in a deprecating way, and for religion class she had written a notorious answer on a test that the Virgin birth could be explained by *coitus ante portam*—"intercourse outside the door," i.e., without penetration. (152)

Indeed, we see that her defiance was not at all limited in scope: She rebelled against everything her parents' generation, as also some peo-

ple of her own, considered proper and sacred. Her contempt for imposed roles is represented by her mode of dress and behavior at
school. More significantly, we find a great deal of contempt for the
specific role of the female, as her uniform was too tight—most *unladylike*—and her answers were offered in a deprecating manner. In addition, she studied too hard: This also was unladylike, since education
was usually reserved for the male, and once having finished, he believed he would enjoy economic success. Marguerite's contempt for
an imposed female role is manifested as well in her attitude toward
religion. In reference to the most holy of Catholic beliefs, she describes it with what may be considered by some, a most desecrating
and *vulgar* description.[50]

In her rebellion, Marguerite disagreed with the Old World idea
that children *owed* their parents respect. She saw, to her dismay, the
parent-child relationship of the Italian family set in economic terms:
Children *owed, paid back, bore dividends* for having done good deeds.
Thus for her, the family motto could have been "Money Talks," as
it was also the motto for their concept of social mobility and individual
development. But Marguerite believed there was more to life than
material well-being; and she turned to literature and other arts as a
means of achieving some sort of personal fulfillment. Thus, her rebellion was aimed at the traditional form of education, more specifically,
the overall ideological viewpoint of the parochial school, which is
"person-oriented [since it] teaches children rules of behavior appropriate to the adult peer group society, and it stresses discipline."
The public school, on the other hand, is "object-oriented and teaches
[children] aspirations and skill for work, play, family life and community participation."[51]

With regard to her Italianness as both a child and an adult, Marguerite found herself in a "confusion of roles." And it was precisely this
confusion that seemed to spark her rebellious acts. Her desire to break
away from first- and second-generation (i.e., ethnic) bonds and her
belief in freedom and spontaneity are evidenced by both her "quickie
marriage" to Lennert Norenson "the Nordic" (as her cousin labeled
him) and her later trip to England, where she strikes up an affair
with a self-exiled literary type. Her subsequent marriage to Alberto,
a wise and philosophical older Italian writer, and her later trips to
Italy reveal, on the other hand, the extent to which she accepts her
ethnicity. Yet her marriage is, at best, an ambivalent one for both
personal and cultural reasons; and she is reluctant to stay in Italy for
long. Thus she seems to exhibit signs of confusion indicative of the
third-generation Italian. Namely, while this individual seems to be

more self-confident and secure about his or her life's trajectory, there still remains some cultural residue from the previous generation.[52]

This antagonism between Americanness and Italianness is a major theme both in Marguerite's story and the novel itself. In the prologue of the novel, in fact, which takes place in her analyst's office, he interprets her dream as an expression of her "feeling of alienation . . . anxiety as to whether she is American, Italian, or Italo-American" (17). And she, soon after, recalling a picture of her father, describes him in a manner similar to that in which her analyst described her.

> I remember a picture of him in our album, at eighteen on his motorcycle when he had already organized the business but was still just a kid full of God knows what kind of dreams of an exciting future. I thought of him separating himself from the Italians of the North Side to make himself into a real American. He turned reactionary to do it, but he started courageously. He was caught in a terrible trap; he couldn't be either Italian like his father and mother or American like his models without feeling guilty toward one or the other side. And even now he doesn't know how to be American while accepting his Italianness because it's still painful to him. So there's conflict and bitterness. (19)

The conflict and bitterness she sees in her father is equally as strong in her: For she too was *caught in a trap*. Marguerite was an intellectually curious child of a culturally unsophisticated family, who was often chided for having her "nose in a book," something deemed ever "so impractical."[53] Throughout her life, she was constantly trying to live according to "everyone else's idea of what [her] life should be" (19). This included her parents, her husband, Alberto, and even her Italian lover. In the first case, she lay victim to her parents' shame of their Italianness that they tried not to pass on to her. In the second and third cases especially, while her Italianness was partially satisfied, she was, nevertheless, dependent on them more specifically because of her gender. Consequently, she felt personally unfulfilled, that she was not her own person but rather a part of everyone else.

Tina's story may seem slightly different from the usual fourth-generation experience because she is the child of an Italian/American mother and Italian father. Yet, her father's situation notwithstanding, she does still reflect those characteristics that, according to Lopreato, the fourth-generation individual may possess.

She is introduced to us as a young American feminist of the 1960s generation, completely unidentifiable as Italian. Yet, she too struggles with the Italian/American dilemma. Like her mother, she experiences a love/hate relationship with Italy and with America. When in Italy, she is enamored of the "natural, human life": but she also realizes that as an individual, or better yet, as a woman, "it won't get [her] anyplace and that [she has] got to go back [to the United States] and plug into the system" (298).[54]

Tina's experience, however, differs greatly from that of her mother and from her great-grandmother's as well. Indeed, two major reasons come to the fore with regard to this distinction. Tina is, first of all, a member of a generation that initiated a cultural and sexual revolution, and thereby challenged an entire set of norms that trapped women, especially, of previous generations. Secondly, she is a fourth-generation Italian who was, like most members of this group, according to Lopreato, "deliberately educated in the ways of the middle-class, [according to which] education is highly valued" (86). Education is highly valued precisely because it becomes an end in itself, "used to maximize individual development of the person" (Gans, 247).[55]

Tina, in fact, wants to be a "scholar who teaches for a living"; she does not want to end up both emotionally and financially dependent on marriage. Indeed, she adamantly refuses to repeat the experiences of both her mother and great-grandmother;[56] and she decides to define herself as an autonomous individual before becoming permanently involved with a man. Thus, she places her degree over her love for Jason, even at the risk of losing him, because she firmly believes that there would not exist between them a relationship "in which individuals seeking to maximize their own development as persons come together on the basis of common interests" (Gans, 247). It is therefore through education that she achieves not only material well-being but also self-expression, self-fulfillment, and empathy for the behavior of others. It is precisely this last characteristic that eventually helps her understand and ultimately resolve her ethnic (if not also gender) dilemma.[57]

As witness to the Italian ethnic dilemma, Barolini indeed succeeds in creating experiences similar to those reported by sociologists such as Gambino, Gans,[58] and Lopreato. Likewise, she succeeds in portraying those experiences and difficulties of the Italian/American female, which have been recorded by Winsey, Yans-Mclaughlin, and those who have contributed to the volume *The Italian Immigrant Woman in North America*.[59] Yet, *Umbertina* is more than just a fictionalized account of those experiences. For while it is enhanced by this documentary quality, it also enjoys an unsparing true-to-life characterization of the protagonists, and thus proves to be extremely intriguing and, at times, provocative.

Of the three stages we saw earlier, Barolini surely represents the second-stage writer, that "militant protester," especially illustrated by her character Marguerite, who, by no means conciliatory, belongs to the generation that re/discovers and reinvents his or her ethnicity. Barolini, that is, presents characters who have already "sunk roots in the native soil" and readily underscores the characters' uniqueness vis-à-vis the expectations of the dominant culture. Indeed, as Gardaphé reminds us, before a writer like Barolini can "merge with the present," she must recreate—and here I add, in a *sui generis* manner—her past: She engages in a "materialization and an articulation of the past" as we saw above. Umbertina, for example, is not the stereotypical, dominated female Italian *momma* that the dominant culture might readily expect. Instead, and in a certain sense in spite of her inner strength, she is one of the strongest characters of the novel. She is the catalyst and, I would add, business acumen behind the Longobardi family's success.

Therefore, as the use of ethnicity at this second stage shifts from the expressive to the descriptive, as a rhetoric-ideological tool, it becomes much more functional. No longer the predominantly expressive element it is in the premodernist writer, for the modernist, mythic writer, ethnicity becomes more the tool with which she communicates her ideology. In Barolini's ethnic/gender case, the ethnic signs constitute the individual pieces of the ethnic paradigm she so consciously and willingly seeks to construct in an overall cultural paradigm that is still predominately male.

Finally, the figure of the woman in Italian/American literature has been portrayed, for the most part, in a traditional female role by a male author. And even in those few exceptions written by women, the female has still occupied a fixed role—that of the central position in the family.[60] The novelty of *Umbertina* lies precisely in Barolini's treatment of women as individuals, who, at one point or another in their lives, become aware of their true plight—the duality of gender and ethnic oppression—and, especially with regard to Marguerite and Tina, attempt to free themselves from the prison house of patriarchy.

## GIOSE RIMANELLI

*Benedetta in Guysterland. A Liquid Novel* is Giose Rimanelli's first book-length prose fiction in English. Written well over twenty years ago—conceived, processed, and finally drafted into manuscript form during the 1961–72 decade—it was published only recently by Guernica Editions (1993). While it may not be ironic that this work is published twenty years later—for he tells us that he wrote it for love, not money—it does seem a bit ironic that it be published by a Canadian house for two diametrically opposed reasons: (1) Rimanelli spent most of his adult life outside Italy in the United States; (2) perhaps a sweeter irony, Rimanelli was born in Italy of a Canadian mother and a United States grandfather. He thus returns not to one or the other of the two North American English-speaking countries—that is, the United States or Canada—but indeed to the two non-Italian countries that contributed in different ways to his general, adult cultural specificity. *Benedetta in Guysterland. A Liquid Novel*, in this sense, represents the amalgamation of two socio-cultural experiences—the Italian and the North American—which, in turn, constitute Rimanelli's status as true bicultural (as well as bi-continental) writer.

One premise already discussed earlier that crosses generations with regard to the image of Italy and Italian America in Italian/American art is the general notion of cultural specificity. Namely, that literature and film, as is the case with any other artistic form, are conceived and produced in highly differentiated contexts of culturally specific ideological clusters, and that any particular work will have to be viewed against the backdrop of that specific cluster in which it was produced, as well as the viewer's intertextual cultural reservoir. Another premise, analogous to the general notion of cultural specificity and more specific to the Italian/American experience, that links many Italian/American art forms is the notion of ethnogenesis—namely, again as we saw earlier, that ethnicity is not a fixed element, some unchanging form that is passed from one generation to the next. Rather, ethnicity is something that is continuously regenerated, through the following generation's discovery of it, hence, reinvented according to this new generation's ideological specificities.[61]

Also pertinent to an understanding of the Italian American's relationship to Italy and Italian America is the notion of the hyphenated individual. With regard to literature, people have already spoken of the "hyphenate" writer—in our case I remind the reader of Aaron and Gardaphé. Sociologists have likewise spoken of the hyphenated ethnic—here, too, I remind the reader of Lopreato and Campisi. In both cases, the characteristics of each group overlap and the progression from one generation to the next follows a similar trajectory.[62]

Of the different stages of the hyphenate writer, Giose Rimanelli represents the third-stage writer who travels from the margin to the mainstream "viewing it (i.e., mainstream = dominant culture) no less critically, perhaps, but more knowingly" than the previous first- and second-stage writer. Having appropriated the dominant group's culture and the tools necessary to succeed in that culture—the greater skill of manipulating, for instance, a language acceptable to the dominant group—and more strongly than his predecessors, this third-stage writer feels entitled to the intellectual and cultural heritage of the dominant group. As such, he or she can also, from a personal viewpoint, "speak out uninhibitedly as an American."[63] This writer, moreover, as Aaron reminds us, does not renounce or abandon the cultural heritage of his or her marginalized group. Instead, he or she transcends "a mere parochial allegiance" to transport "into the province of the [general] imagination," personal experiences that for the first-stage ("local colorist") and second-stage ("militant protester") writer "comprised the very stuff of their literary material" (215). This, in fact, is precisely the case with Giose Rimanelli's *Benedetta in Guysterland*. His novel is chock full of all that is Italian and/or Italian/American, so much that it could not exist without the "stuff" of ethnic experiences with which Rimanelli informs his text.

To be sure, Rimanelli's Italian/American cultural specificity is an important component of *Benedetta in Guysterland*. In what follows, I shall deal with the questions of text and textual boundaries as they relate to the structural division of *Benedetta in Guysterland. A Liquid Novel* and how, in the general scheme of things, the novel's structural division is also representative of different voices that replicate the overall polyphony of society. If we consider, in a general sense, a text to be a series of signs transmitted through a verbal or visual medium with the intent of comunicating a message of any sort, regardless of how easy or difficult it may be to decode such a message, then the notion of text is not so much a significant matter; *Guysterland* surely satisfies this general definition.[64] "What is more significant here, I would contend, is the notion of textual boundaries. Looking at the book's table of contents, we find the following:

As is evident from the graph, we find a preface by Fred Gardaphé and four other sections; three written by Giose Rimanelli, the fourth a collaborative effort. What we may normally consider the narrative text—that is, a succession of events which constitute the "story"—is the second section, "Benedetta in Guysterland," the longest of them all. But there is also a "For-a-word" and a "Post-word" written by Rimanelli, or, as he refers to himself, "the Author," that special construct that is and may be Rimanelli, in this instance; and what concludes this succession of internal texts—or better, "microtexts," to borrow from Maria Corti[65]—is an "Appendix" consisting of a series of responses to "Benedetta in Guysterland" (31–204) by Rimanelli's friends and colleagues of the early 1970s, capped by two minisections—responses and thank-yous—written by Rimanelli himself.

Gardaphé's preface is precisely that, an outsider's view of the book intended to lay some foundation for any reader's encounter with the narrative text. Some poststructuralist critics, however, might want to see this, too, as part of the overall text. Indeed, from a hermeneutico-semiotic point of view, the idea is not too farfetched; after all, any information the reader may gather from Gardaphé's preface will influence her or his reading of Rimanelli's novel. Yet even if, for argument's sake, we decide to eliminate Gardaphé's preface and the multi-authored "Appendix," we find ourselves, nevertheless, with three other microtexts, not just "Benedetta in Guysterland," for which the question of textual boundaries persists. Namely, we still have a similar textual lineup of a "For-a-word," "Benedetta in Guysterland," and "Post-word"; and the reader, whoever he or she may be, will most likely consider, at least at his or her first encounter with the book, the central microtext "Benedetta in Guysterland" to be the *novel*.

What further complicates the matter is that the narrating voices of each of these three microtexts is a different one. The narrator of the "For-a-word" may readily be identified with the actual penholder—or, as we might say today, wordprocessor user—whom we know as Giose Rimanelli, "emigré," as he readily defines himself here ("when the Author was still an emigré in U.S.A." [29]), to the United States in 1961. Here, in a somewhat personal way,[66] Rimanelli offers a few interpretive keys to his reader. We find out that "Benedetta in Guysterland" is, in a very Gozzanoan and Palazzeschian way, "made up by the careful use of famous and infamous quotations, scraps of personal *co co rico co co rico* lyrics, confessions of country girls with kitsch and poetry pap, advertisements" (28), and so on, as he continues to tell us.[67] We also come to know that the "Author" is a lover of words and sees himself here as a

> free collector of paper joy and paper anguish instead of a producer of them—in order to attempt a new experiment on verbs and syntax, speech, writing, and paranoia. I stretched my hands out and found what we usually produce: dreams, love, murder, golden charades, lampoons. (28–29)

Two things stand out in the above-cited quotation. First, we see that the Author's intent is to experiment as free collector—again, Gozzanoan/Palazzeschian reverberations come to the fore—not as producer, for which the production of the "paper joy and paper anguish," what we may consider a metaphor for meaning/signification, becomes an act of coproduction. Second, such coproduction is implicit, I would suggest, in his shift from a singular first-person pronoun to the plural form: "*I* stretched my hands out and found what *we* usually produce: dreams, love, murder, golden charades, lampoons." This desire for coproduction—the connection between author and reader—is underscored by the physical act of stretching, the Author's literal reaching out to his reader. We see, in fact, that as the *I* of "I stretch" transforms into the *we* of "we usually produce," coproduction takes place; and what follows—those "dreams, love, murder, golden charades, lampoons"—may easily constitute thematics of an author's work as well as those of a reader's list of desired motifs.

Benedetta's story is not an easy one to recount; or, for that matter, to follow and understand.[68] Born Clarence Ashfield, she gets her name Benedetta from the mobsters she meets once she enters the underworld. They meet her as Benie, a nickname bestowed upon her by mob lawyer Willie "Holiday Inn" Sinclair, from the Italian adverb *bene*. However, they believe the nickname is a shortened form of Benedetta, whence therefore she gets her name, thus becoming the blessed among "guysters," Rimanelli's idiosyncratic sign for gangster. Leaving her home town of New Wye, in Nabokov County, in Appalachia, Benedetta becomes intricately involved in the underworld of organized crime, falling in love with and, eventually, yearning for the exiled Joe Adonis, Santo "Zip the Thunder" Tristano's nemesis. Through a series of episodes, events, and adventures (some more realistic, others more fantastical), Benedetta does not actually tell her story as we might expect from traditional first-person narrative; rather, in her dialogue with her beloved exiled mobster, Joe Adonis, Benedetta's story unfolds.

The novel begins in the present, so it seems, with Benedetta, in the first person, directly addressing Joe Adonis: "I love you, Joe Adonis" (33). But we soon find out that she is not actually *talking* to him; instead, she is *writing* to him, as we find out in chapter 2: "I am now pounding on the typewriter" (40). Benedetta's letter writing is an obvious act of any author's self-reflexivity, and indeed of Rimanelli's as well, we can readily state. But it is not just Benedetta's act of writing that reflects Rimanelli's writing; to be sure, it is also how and what she writes that reflects the Rimanelli we encountered in the "For-a-word." There, we saw Rimanelli's desire for experimentation, his wish to write a novel free of tradition, without a narrative, lacking any sense of logical plot or storyline. Benedetta, in her letters to Joe Adonis, reflects similar hermeneutico-semiotic actions and creative desires early on in the first two chapters. In chapter 1 we see that she misses "sharing non-senses" (34) with Joe Adonis. In chapter 2, where we find out that she is actually writing to Joe, Rimanelli's "free collector" status is mirrored in Benedetta's description of her own writing:

> These thoughts live in my mind as they appear on the paper, muddled and, as I know only too well, unorganized. I feel that if I organize them, they will seem like an essay to me and I would not be writing for myself if I spent time arranging ideas into neat little compartments. Do you understand me, Joe? While I am writing, I am far away; and when I come back, I have already left. I am now pounding on the typewriter, talking to myself and at the same time listening to Zip and the band downstairs. (40)

"Muddled" and "unorganized," adjectives that describe Benedetta's thoughts above, figure as logical metaphors for that which does not adhere to tradition, since tradition is, as implied immediately above, organized and essayistic, ideas and emotions arranged "into neat little compartments" according to, we might add, neat little rules. Binary oppositions of this sort, the sensical versus the nonsensical and the organized versus the unorganized, constantly reappear in Benedetta's story both on a formalistic and contextual level. More significantly, the three central texts—"For-a-word," "Benedetta in Guysterland," and "Post-word"—rely on a very strong dose of irony, be it directed inward—self-parody as writer, thinker, Italian American—or outward—parody directed toward various cultural phenomena such as the mafia, sexual liberation, and both popular and high cultures of various societies and countries of the Western World. This is indeed Rimanelli's legacy *qua* Italian/American writer. He has not only *mastered the master's tool*—that is, language—but he has succeeded, in transcending the first two stages of parochial allegiance, in contemplating his world of Italian Americana "from the outside only," as Peirce tells us.

Ultimately, the act of semiosis involved in Rimanelli's *Benedetta in Guysterland* is a restructured and redefined act of sign interpretation dependent on a sign repertoire no longer consonant with that of the literary canon—that is, the dominant culture. What occurs concomitantly, then, is Bakhtin's previously noted concept of the decentralization of the "verbal-ideological world."[69] More specifically, along the lines of sign-functions, one sees that the two functives of expression and content are no longer in mutual correlation. The content, at this point in time with regard to a non-canonical (read, ethnic) literature, is different from that of the canon. The sign-function realized in this new process of semiosis is now in disaccord with the dominant culture's expectation of the coding correlation.[70] Another important consideration here, as was apparent earlier, is the interpreter's fore-understanding "drawn from [his/her] own anterior relation to the subject" (Gadamer, 262). This notion of fore-understanding is surely a basis for both the sender's and the addressee's use and interpretation of signs. That is to say, the sign (or sign-function) is not ideologically neutral. Rather, its use and interpretation are dependent on *both* the sender's and addressee's prejudgments.[71] In a general sense, then, language—i.e., its sign system—cannot be but ideologically invested. As an ideological medium, as it can become restrictive and oppressive when its sign system is arbitrarily invested with meanings by those who are empowered to do so—that is, the dominant culture—so can it become empowering for the purpose of privileging one coding correlation over another (in this case the canon), by rejecting the canonical sign system and, ultimately, denying validity to this sign system vis-à-vis the interpretive act of a noncanonical text.[72] Then, certain ideological constructs are de-privileged and subsequently awarded an unfixed status; they no longer take on a patina of *natural facts*. Rather, they figure as the *arbitrary categories* they truly are. All this results in a pluralistic notion of literary invention and interpretation which, by its very nature, cannot exclude the individual—author and reader—who has [re]created and developed a different repertoire of signs.

The resultant noncanonical text that arises from such an unorthodox creative act, that is Rimanelli's, may initially problematize and frustrate a reader's interpretive act. But more than an attempt to frustrate or block his reader's semiotic *iter*, I would contend that such problematics in textual boundaries and framing, discussed above, constitute Rimanelli's desire to involve intimately his reader in the coproduction of textual signification. That is, the purpose of Rimanelli's sign-system is not to elicit, simply, pleasant and unpleasant memories and imagery in his reader's mind. Rather, he attempts to render his reader complicit in an emotional and sensorial state as expressed through his prose that would then lead his reader to engage in an act of signification. Indeed, then, it is provocation, not description, that defines Rimanelli's prose. And his reader, in his or her complicity in this polysensorial state, becomes a coparticipant in Rimanelli's sign production and signification. Hence, his *liquid* novel, precisely because it acquires its signifying shape from, metaphorically speaking, the form of its reader's hands—like any liquid that takes the shape of the container in which it is situated.

## SOME "CULTURAL" CONSIDERATIONS FOR BEYOND

In rejecting the melting-pot attitude (a metaphor for assimilation) and supplanting it with the notion of Americana as a kaleidoscopic, sociocultural mosaic (a metaphor for multiculturalism), the role of Italian/American intellectuals inevitably undergoes changes that, if not already, will eventually reshape their roles, even if ever so slightly, from that of a raccontuer of what took place—a role that may lean more toward nostalgia than analysis—to that of cultural examiner and, eventually, cultural broker.

It is precisely with regard to this possible new role, something that has already manifested itself in a number of Italian/American intellectuals, that new and more recent methodologies and reading strategies, as I have presented here, can prove helpful in broadening our various perceptions of Italian/American art forms in general. Also helpful in this type of epistemological reconfiguration are the general notions and tools of what we know as cultural studies and multiculturalism. In general, we may consider cultural studies as that mode of analysis that takes as its focal point of argument, as Stuart Hall tells us, "the changing ways of life of societies and groups and the networks of meanings that individuals and groups use to make sense of and to communicate with one another."[73] What is of primary significance is Hall's insistence on plurality—that is, societies and groups—and interconnectedness—that is, to communicate with one another. Hall's plurality and interconnectedness form an obvious and necessary couplet that resulted from the changing attitude toward the notion of melting pot—that is, the rejection of assimilation—that was ultimately supplanted by any one of the many metaphors and similes which readily connote difference and individuality of all groups that constitute the United States population.

But cultural studies must also be "critical" insofar as it must be more than the "mere description of cultural emergents that aims to give voice to the 'experience' of those who have been denied a space to talk," as Mas'ud Zavarzadeh and Donald Morton describe what they distinguish as "dominant" or "experiential cultural studies," which "offers a 'description' of the exotic 'other' and thus provides the bourgeois reader with the pleasure of contact with difference."[74] Instead, for them, critical cultural studies "is not a description but an explanation, not a testimonial but an intervention: it does not simply 'witness' cultural events, but takes a 'position' regarding them" (8).[75] As both Hall and Zavarzadeh and Morton underscore, change is the operative word. For Zavarzadeh and Morton, especially, critical cultural studies should constitute "an articulation of the cultural real that will change the conditions that have blocked those voices from talking" (8).

If we accept the premise that cultural studies represents, among other things as stated above, "the weakening of the traditional bound-

aries among the disciplines and of the growth of forms of interdisciplinary research that doesn't easily fit . . . within the confines of
exisiting divisions of knowledge" (Hall, 11), then we may surely open
ourselves up to different modes of analysis that go beyond those "traditional boundaries" of literary study so often concerned with the
formalistic and the thematic. Mere rhetoric and signification should
not suffice; other critical perspectives should become part of our interpretive arsenal. This is especially true since many contemporary Ital-
ian/American writers today avail themselves of certain generative tools
that were not necessarily popular a decade or two ago; generative
tools that have their origin in a number of different sources—in different national cultures, if not the *epistemological collision* of different
national cultures;[76] in critical thinkers becoming creative writers; in
the influence of other media on the written word; in the incorporation
of popular cultural forms with those considered more high-brow; or
in the *high-browization* and glorification of the popular arts—for example, film, romance narratives, and music videos.

As we stated in the introduction to this volume, great strides have
been made in the past fifteen years by critical thinkers such as Helen
Barolini, Robert Viscusi, Mary Jo Bona, and Fred L. Gardaphé, as
well as Edvige Giunta and Pasquale Verdicchio along with others
more recently, in framing an Italian/American critical discourse in
more contemporary terms. My own reading presented herein has obviously profited from the works of those mentioned above, all of
whom are directly involved in Italian/American studies. What should
also be evident at this time is that I have depended to a similar degree
on some general studies such as Aaron and Peirce, to name a few, to
bring forth yet another reading strategy that would help us expand
further still the interpretive arena of aesthetic discourse in general vis-
à-vis Italian Americana. Therefore, while I have presented Ardizzone,
Barolini, and Rimanelli as prime examples, respectively, of my three
categories of *expressive, comparative,* and *synthetic* writers, I offer for
further speculation other names that might readily fit into these different categories.[77] While we may surely place someone like Pietro Di
Donato, Jerre Mangione, and Mari Tomasi as *expressive* writers, we
might add to this list Rita Ciresi as a generational analog to Ardizzone's case. Likewise, John Fante and Mario Puzo make fine partners
with Helen Barolini as *comparatively* militant writers. Third, I contend, writers such as Don DeLillo, Carol Maso, Gilbert Sorrentino,
and Anthony Valerio pair nicely with Rimanelli and others we might
place among the *synthetic* writers.

Our new aesthetic reconfigurations, however, should not be limited
to the literary. As I have implied earlier in this essay, we should

bring our new modes of interpretation to other art forms such as, for example, cinema and painting. In bringing such provocative notions to these and other art forms, in what other way might we read a Scorsese film from the point of view of ethnicity? Indeed, we saw earlier how Robert Casillo, in his 1991 essay on Italian/American cinema in general, brought forth the case of Frank Capra and the question of ethnicity, or absence thereof.[78] We might see in those cases of explicit ethnicity that some filmmakers are actually more positive than initially perceived, I contend, in their overall portrayals of ethnic cultural, and that the alleged romanticization of the gangster image is, in reality, a critiqué. Further still, in passing on to the figurative arts, how may we reconcile the content and sign-functions of the paintings and drawings of Ralph Fasanella, Robert Buono, or Bob Cimbalo vis-à-vis their own specific, ethnic culture as well as the United States at large?

These and other questions not only broaden our horizons with respect to our specific ethnic experience; in addition, they ultimately— and indeed should—bring us into contact with many of the other groups that constitute our greater kaleidoscopic, sociocultural mosaic so that Italian Americans—as a whole, especially, as well as from the point of view of both an artistic aesthetics and general ideology— begin to speak in terms of us *and* them, not us *against* them. Ethnicity is a sociopolitical construct, and as such it differentiates only insofar as it points out the major characteristics of one group as compared to those of another. These differences, moreover, may also have corollaries and analogues in certain characteristics of other ethnic groups. Let us not forget that zoology is different from sociology, and that one's cellular make-up—that is, his or her race—does not necessarily override one's long-term social and cultural experiences—that is, her or his ethnicity.[79] Italian/American cultural interlocutors must therefore eschew the discourse of binary oppositions—the us *against* them—and adopt, instead, one that also takes into consideration the similarities—albeit of varying degrees and intensities—of experience that Italian Americans and all the other ethnic/racial/sexual groups— minority *and* majority—have and continue to encounter. We must learn, that is, not to speak in terms of racism or prejudice in the singular, "but of *racisms* [as also prejudices] in the plural."[80]

Such a strategy responds to a necessity of inclusiveness of all groups. For until all groups—the so-called dominant class *and* minorities—are included in a cultural discourse, we risk: (1) maintaining the obvious aesthetic hierarchy of a major literature and numerous minor literatures; (2) remaining stuck within a thematically grounded discourse of nostalgia, for which leitmotifs such as *pizza* and *nonna* continue to possess high aesthetic currency; (3) losing "Italian/American" authors to what some have called either "residual multiculturalism" or "the reductiveness of multiculturalism," both being synonymous with [total?] assimilation; and (4) conserving the divisiveness that seems to exist today, precisely because an aesthetic hierarchy is maintained, both within and outside of the Italian/American community of creative writers and critical thinkers. With "its focus on the politics of the production of subjectivities rather than on textual operations, [cultural studies] understands 'politics' as access to the material base of [power, knowledge, and resources]" (208). Cultural studies also "insists on the necessity to address [these] central, urgent, and disturbing questions of a society and a culture [in] the most rigorous intellectual way . . . available" (Hall, 11). It thus "constitutes one of the points of tension and change at the frontiers of intellectual . . . life, pushing for new questions, new models, and new ways of study, testing the fine lines between intellectual rigor and social relevance" (Hall, 11). For only when all these concerns are addressed and all United States identifiable groups and their differences are foregrounded on equal terms, through a general exploratory lens of cultural studies, can then the notion of multiculturalism function effectively as a useful expression of difference,[81] leading ultimately to a more level field of play for critical discourse and intellectual exchange.[82]

## NOTES

This essay represents, in a significantly reduced version, some major parts of a much larger study: *A Semiotic of Ethnicity: In (Re)cognition of the Italian/American Writer* (SUNY Press, forthcoming).

For more on the use of the slash in place of the hyphen, see my *To Hyphenate or Not To Hyphenate? The Italian/American Writer: An* Other *American* (Montréal: Guernica, 1991). With regard to the Italian/American writer, see especially 20–27, 33–42.

1. See my *To Hyphenate or Not To Hyphenate?* 48.

2. See Aijaz Ahmad's response: "Jameson's Rhetoric of Otherness and the 'National Allegory'," *Social Text* 17 (1987): 4.

3. Because of nuances, subtleties, and semantic and grammatical differences between the various English languages spoken throughout the world, I believe it is necessary to recognize these different languages. And since American, as adjective, can refer to any one of the many geographical and cultural zones of the Americas, for the sake of convenience and economy, I shall refer to United States English in the following pages as, simply, English.

4. While there does not yet exist an exhaustive study on the various categories of the Italian/American writer, Flaminio Di Biagi has offered us a valiant first step in that direction. See his "A Reconsideration: Italian American Writers: Notes for a Wider Consideration," *MELUS* 14, nos. 3–4 (1987): 141–51.

Also, with regard to the Italian writer in the United States, I would remind the reader of Paolo Valesio's substantive essay, "The Writer between Two Worlds: The Italian Writer in the United States," *Differentia* 3–4 (spring / autumn 1989): 259–76. Gustavo Pérez Firmat, in an analogous manner, takes the matter one step further and offers an equally cogent exegesis of the bilingual writer—in his case the Cuban American—who, in adopting both languages (at times separately, at other times together in the same text), occupies what he considers the "space between" (21); see his "Spic Chic: Spanglish as Equipment for Living," *The Caribbean Review* 15, no. 3 (winter 1987): 20ff.

5. In stating such, I do not intend to ignore the bilingual Italian/American writer: he or she who operates in both linguistic melieus. Hence, the presence of Joseph Tusiani in this essay and possible topics of discussion in any further versions of this type of study may indeed include the works in English by someone like Giose Rimanelli, Peter Carravetta, and/or Lucia Capria Hammond.

6. In this poststructuralist, postmodern society in which we live, my essay casts by the wayside any notion of universality or absoluteness with regard to the (re)definition of any literary category vis-à-vis national origin, ethnicity, race, or gender. One can, and should, readily equate the above-mentioned notion to some general notions associated with the postmodern. Any rejection of validity of the notion of "hierarchy," or better, universality or absoluteness, is characteristic of those who are, to paraphrase Lyotard, "incredul[ous] toward [grand or] metanarratives" (Jean-François Lyotard, *The Postmodern Condition: A Report on Knowledge*, trans. Geoff Bennington and Brian Massumi with a foreword by Fredric Jameson [Minneapolis: University of Minnesota Press, 1984], xiv).

7. See his "Moments in Italian-American Cinema: From *Little Caesar* to Coppola and Scorsese," *From the Margin: Writings in Italian Americana*, ed. Anthony Julian Tamburri, Paolo A. Giordano, and Fred L. Gardaphé (West Lafayette: Purdue University Press, 1991), 374.

8. He then continues to say that "in such writing Italian-American experiences and values are delineated in dramatic interaction with the mainstream culture." See his review of *Delano in America & Other Early Poems*, by John J. Soldo, *Italian Americana* 1, no. 1 (1974): 124–25.

9. One problem with definitions of this sort is that they exclude any discourse on the analogous notion of, for example, the "hyphenate" filmmaker. I refer to Daniel Aaron's "The Hyphenate Writer and American Letters," *Smith Alumnae Quarterly* (July 1964): 213–17; later revised in *Rivista di Studi Anglo-Americani* 3, nos. 4–5 (1984–85): 11–28.

10. Dana Gioia, "What Is Italian-American Poetry?" in *Poetry Pilot* (December 1991): 3–10.

11. At this point I would wonder if Casillo's definition of Italian/American cinema with regard to his opening remarks on Capra may not possibly create a type of *have your cake and eat it too?*

12. What is important to keep in mind is that one can perceive different degrees of ethnicity in literature, film, or any other art form, as Aaron already did with his "hyphenate writer."

13. For more on the origins of recent Italian/American, critical self-inventory I refer the reader to our introduction to this volume.

14. For a recent rehearsal of a "postmodern," critical analysis specifically focused on Italian/American literature can be found in Fred L. Gardaphé's excellent essay, "Visibility or Invisibility: The Postmodern Prerogative in the Italian/American Narrative," *Almanacco*, 2, no. 1 (1992): 24–33.

15. See his "The Hyphenate Writer and American Letters." Here, I quote from the original version.

16. Aaron is not alone in discerning this multi-stage phenomenon in the ethnic writer. Ten years after Aaron's original version, as stated in our introduction, Rose Basile Green spoke to an analogous phenomenon within the history of Italian/American narrative; then, she discussed her four stages of "the need for assimilation," "revulsion," "counterrevulsion," and "rooting" (see her *The Italian-American Novel: A Document of the Interaction of Two Cultures*, especially chapters 4–7).

As I have already rehearsed elsewhere (*To Hyphenate or Not To Hyphenate? The Italian/American Writer: An* Other *American*), I would contend that there are cases where a grammar rule/usage may connote an inherent prejudice, no matter how slight. Besides the hyphen, another example that comes to mind is the usage of the male pronoun for the impersonal, whereas all of its alternatives—e.g., *s/he, she/he,* or *he/she*—are shunned.

17. In order to avoid repetitive textual citations, I should point out that Aaron's description of these three stages are found on page 214.

I would also point out that Daniel Aaron's three stages of the hyphenate writer have their analogs in the different generations that Joseph Lopreato (*Italian Americans* [New York: Random House, 1979]) and Paul Campisi ("Ethnic Family Patterns: The Italian Family in the United States" [*The American Journal of Sociology* 53.6 (May 1948)]) each describe and analyze: i.e., "peasant," "first-," "second-," and "third-generation." With regard to this fourth generation—Lopreato's and Campisi's "third generation"—I would state here, briefly, that I see the writer of this generation subsequent to Aaron's "third-stage writer," who eventually returns to his/her ethnicity through the process of re(dis)covery.

18. Aaron considers this first-stage writer abjectly conciliatory toward the dominant group. He states: "It was as if he were saying to his suspicious and opinionated audience: 'Look, we have customs and manners that may seem bizarre and uncouth, but we are respectable people nevertheless and our presence adds flavor and variety to American life. Let me convince you that our oddities—no matter how quaint and amusing you find them—do not disqualify us from membership in the national family'" (214).

19. There are undoubtedly other considerations regarding Aaron's three categories. He goes on to discuss them further, providing examples from the Jewish and Black contingents of American writers.

20. One caveat with regard to this neat, linear classification of writers should not go unnoticed. There undoubtedly exists a clear distinction between the first-stage writer and the third-stage writer. The distinction, however, between the first- and second-stage writer, and especially that between the second- and third-stage writer, may at times seem blurred. In his rewrite, in fact, Aaron himself has recognized this blurring of boundaries, as these "stages cannot be clearly demarcated" (13). This becomes apparent when one discusses works such as Mario Puzo's *The Godfather* or Helen Barolini's *Umbertina*. More significant is the fact that these various stages of hyphenation may actually manifest themselves along the trajectory of one author's literary career. I believe, for instance, that a writer like Helen Barolini manifests, to date, such a phenomenon. Her second novel, *Love in the Middle Ages,* revolves around a love story involving a middle-aged couple, whereas ethnicity and cultural origin serve chiefly as a backdrop. Considering what Aaron states in his rewrite, and what seems to be of common opinion—that the respective experiences of Jews and Italians in the United States were similar in some says (23–24 especially)—it should appear

as no strange coincidence, then, that the ethnic backgrounds of the two main characters of Barolini's second novel are, for the woman, Italian, and, for the man, Jewish.

21. In making such an analogy, it is important to remember, as Aaron had already underscored, that personal experiences "comprised the very stuff of . . . literary material" for both the first-stage ("local colorist") and second-stage ("militant protester") writers; whereas the third-stage writer, on the other hand, travels from the margin to the mainstream without either renouncing or abandoning his/her cultural heritage. For Gardaphé, Vico's three ages (read, Aaron's three stages) constitute the pre-modernist (the "poetic" = "realism"), the modernist (the "mythic" = "modernism"), and the postmodernist (the "philosophic" = "postmodernism").

22. For a cogent example of ethnic signs relegated to the margin—what at first glance may seem to be an absence—see Gardaphé's discussion of DeLillo (30–31), where he also rehearses his notions of the "visible" and "invisible" Italian/American writers.

23. Again, I refer to Gardaphé's analyses of Rimanelli and DeLillo (28–31), the first the parodist (the "visible"), the second the *assimilated* (the "invisible").

24. *Principles of Philosophy* in *Collected Papers*, ed. Charles Hartshorne and Paul Weiss, Vol. 1 (Cambridge, Mass: Harvard University Press, 1960). Peirce offers numerous versions of his definitions of these three modes of being and examples throughout his writings, especially in this volume.

25. "By a feeling, I mean an instance of that kind of consciousness which involves no analysis, comparison or any process whatsoever, nor consists in whole or in part of any act by which one stretch of consciousness is distinguished from another" (1.306).

26. Secondness, as "the mode of being of one thing which consists in how a second object is" (1.24), provokes a "forcible modification of our ways of thinking [which is] the influence of the world of fact or *experience*" (1.321; emphasis textual).

27. "The third category of elements of phenomena consists of what we call laws when we contemplate them from the outside only, but which when we see both sides of the shield we call thoughts" (1.420).

28. I make this distinction in order not to contradict myself vis-à-vis Peirce's use of the term "real" when he discusses secondness. There, he states: "[T]he real is that which insists upon forcing its way to recognition as *something* other than the mind's creation" (1.325).

29. As an aside, I would merely point out that Gadamer's notion of one's anterior relationship to the subject may also come into play. I shall reserve this, however, for another time and place.

30. Indeed, I would also contend that, in a similar vein, any number of these stages may even be inferred in a single work of a writer.

31. Michael M. J. Fischer, "Ethnicity and the Post-Modern Arts of Memory," in *Writing Culture. The Poetics and Politics of Ethnography*, ed. James Clifford and George E. Marcus (Berkeley: University of California Press, 1986), 195.

32. For more on *italianità*, see Tamburri, Giordano, Gardaphé, "Introduction," *From the Margin: Writings in Italian Americana*.

33. Tony Ardizzone, *The Evening News* (Athens, GA: University of Georgia Press, 1986). Three of the four Italian/American stories that I examine in my *A Semiotic of Ethnicity* curiously reappear in Ardizzone's latest collection of short fiction, *Taking It Home. Stories from the Neighborhood* (Urbana: University of Illinois Press, 1996).

34. The Flannery O'Connor Award is sponsored by the University of Georgia Press, that has, over the years, unearthed some fine Italian/American writers. Along with Ardizzone, other winners include Salvatore La Puma (1987) and Rita Ciresi (1991).

35. See Aaron's "The Hyphenate Writer and American Letters."

36. As thin-skinned Italian Americans, I have in mind those persons who see absolutely no thematic value to the works of those like Mario Puzo, Nick Pileggi, Frances Ford Coppola, Nancy Savoca, or Martin Scorsese, for example, because such works, in their opinion, glorify a negative stereotype. This is, to be sure, a curiously superficial reaction by the likes of those who then turn around and call for the biographical rendition, written or visual, of the life of someone like Amedeo Giannini (something which, in fact, is now available from the University of California Press). Not only this, but they call for the preservation of the Italo Balbo monument donated by Mussolini, or extol the "virtues," as they say, of Mussolini's corporate state, or, *last but surely not least,* invite Italy's leading neo-Fascist, Gianfranco Fini, not to mention Mussolini's own ideologically sympathetic granddaughter, to their annual showcase events.

37. Again, I remind the reader that the distinction I point out between these categories is by no means to be perceived as an indication of any sort of hierarchical valence.

38. "Nonna" is one of the three other stories I deal with of Ardizzone's collection in my *Semiotics of Ethnicity: In (Re)cognition of the Italian/American Writer.*

39. Indeed, other writers have engged in direct conversation with their readers. However, given the success and popularity of Italo Calvino's penultimate novel, *If on a winter's night a traveler* (HBJ 1981 [1979]), this technique has become increasing identified with him.

40. See Seymour Chatman, *Story and Discourse* (Ithaca: Cornell University Press, 1978), 151.

41. For an example of those who, directly or indirectly, classified Italian Americans in this manner see Bernard Rosen, "Race, Ethnicity and the Achievement Syndrome," *American Sociological Review* 24 (October 1959): 47–60; William Whyte's study also proves unflatteringly race-conscious (see his *Street Corner Society* [Chicago: University of Chicago Press, 1960, 2nd edition]). Such notions notwithstanding, I would point out that while this may seem to be a negative commentary of sociologists early on, today the notion of Italians and Italian Americans as people of color is a more recently positive consideration. See Lucia Chiavola Birnbaum's "The History of Sicilians," *Italians and Italian Americans and the Media,* ed. Mary Jo Bona and Anthony Julian Tamburri (Staten Island: AIHA, 1996) 206–15, and Rose Romano's essay "Coming Out Olive," in *Social Pluralism and Literary History,* ed. Francesco Loziggio (Toronto: Guernica, 1996).

42. One need only think back to some of the classic names associted with Italian Americans and Hollywood.

43. One of the less sensitive figures of the Italian and/or Italian/American father figure is found in Rachel Guido deVries's *Tender Warriors* (Firebrand, 1986). Other figures can be found in the fiction of Helen Barolini's *Umbertina* (Seaview, 1979), in Mario Puzo's *The Godfather* (Putnam, 1969), or in the poetry of Gianna Patriarca's *Italian Women and Other Tragedies* (Guernica, 1994).

44. At this point, it is also important to note that one of Ardizzone's early novels is thematically couched in the metaphor of baseball: *In the Heart of the Order* (Holt, 1986).

45. Be it because it is his first book, be it the subject matter, whatever the case, *The Evening News* has yet to have a full-fledged essay dedicated to it. One of the better reviews, both in length and insight, is by Mark Shaffer, who points out the similarity between Gino's specific world and the rest of Ardizzone's characters. See

his "Streets of Chicago Yield Faith and Fire," *The Washington Times Magazine* (24 November 1986).

46. I am aware of the irony involved in my paraphrasing of Booth (*The Rhetoric of Fiction* [Chicago: University of Chicgo Press, 1960]). But it is true that we, in our poststructuralist theoretical mind-frame, must not forget where the foundations of some of our new ideas lie. Our debt is too big to ignore.

47. Jim Spencer, "N. Sider's Tales of Urban Life," *Chicago Tribune* (13 January 1987), sect. 5: 3. Another reviewer suggests that Ardizzone become "a free agent from his past" (Mary Elizabeth Courtney, "Making Games of Allegories," *Columbus Dispatch* [19 October 1986]). It is his attachment to his past that indeed has made Ardizzone the Italian/American writer he is. Humor, as Courtney would have it, is not necessarily a requirement, it is a choice of style, technique, and rhetoric.

48. Both Joseph Lopreato (*Italian Americans*) and Paul Campisi ("Ethnic Family Patterns: The Italian Family in the United States") use similar tags in distinguishing the various Italian/American generations: "peasant," "first-," and so on. The common practice among sociologists, however, it to use a slightly different set of tags. Thus, Lopreato's and Campisi's "peasant" family corresponds to the more widely used "first-generation" family; and their "first-," "second-," and "third-generation" families correspond to the more popular "second-," "third-," and "fourth-generation" families. In this essay I have opted for the more commonly used set of tags, which are also those Barolini occasionally adopts throughout her novel.

49. We can find those Italian Americans with the seemingly insignificant desire to Americanize their names—Giacomo and Benedetto soon want to be called Jake and Ben. We also encounter the more enterprising "status climber" who makes attempts at all sorts of endeavors that the previous generation cannot understand: such is the case with Paolo—soon to become Paul—who, "filled with ambitions for himself that had nothing to do with the kind of hard work and drudgery the rest of the family engaged in" and believing himself "too smart to waste his time around two-bit family stores" (123–24), suddenly finds himself without a home since he refuses to do his part in the family business.

50. Along with Marguerite's defiant efforts to break away from the Old World ways, we also see in the above-cited passage the second generation's attempt at shedding its Italianness: her parents sent her to a school "where all the daughters of the top Irish families went, including the mayor's daughter." Implied here is the belief that economic success leads to individual amelioration. Indeed, it was at this school, according to her mother, where Marguerite could meet "worthwhile girls" whom she could invite over because her family had "a nice home now" (153).

51. Herbert J. Gans, *The Urban Villagers*, 129.

52. In his study of the Italian/American family in the United States, Campisi found that there was, indeed, more security fostered in the third-generation individual than in the second generation. However, he also found what he calls "conflict lags"; and because of these lags, this third-generation family many times reflects a "confused American situation" (Campisi, 446). In Marguerite's case, her initial breaking away demonstrates her desire to live a life different from her parents'. Yet, she also feels a strong tie to Italy; and it is precisely her oscillation between America and Italy, between American culture and Italian culture, that perpetuates her identity confusion.

53. We have already seen this notion expressed by her father in his conversation with Tina.

54. At other points during her story, we can find Tina comparing the two different countries, and herself as well in each place. For example: "Her sense of illimitable

possibilities awaiting her could not stop at the softness and languor of Rome, beneath which, she knew, there were deadly poisons of unrest and discontent. Rome is too old, she thought; nothing matters anymore. In New York everything does. In New York she felt competitiveness throbbing in the air and became frenetic because of so much going on, because of the sense of space to fill. In Rome she was squelched by the sense of time: Everything had already been thought of and done—it was time to rest and savor" (300). To her future husband, Jason, she later described herself in the following matter: "I'm two different people, Jason. The Italian part, when I get back to Rome, likes civilized comforts: eating well, having Giovanna go out and do the shopping and prepare the *caffè-latte* for me each morning while I sleep. Here I like to get all dressed up and go shopping and have Mauro cut my hair. I dress in blankets and clogs when I'm in the States and sometimes don't comb my hair for days. I drive my grandmother in Gloversville crazy when I go see her because she says I'm a hippy. But in Rome I'm purely a sybarite" (323).

55. Also significant here is her father's educational background. While it is true that he too was very much part of the Old World, he held a university degree, and Tina initially identified intellectually with his side of her heritage.

56. Umbertina became a sort of past idol for Tina; and only after she makes a trip back to Umbertina's native village in Italy does she begin to understand truly the hardships that all her relatives who came before her, the women especially, had encountered.

57. After Tina's conversation with her grandfather, when he objected to her choice of Italian as a field of study, she demonstrates a good deal of understanding with regard to his ethnic dilemma. She thought: "What was wrong with the immigrant's children that left them so distrustful of their *italianità*? It was, she knew, the burden of the second generation, who had been forced too swiftly to tear the Old World from themselves and put on the new. They were the sons and daughters ashamed of their illiterate, dialect-speaking forebears—the goatherds and peasants and fishermen who came over to work and survive and give these very children, the estranged ones, America. Tina was torn between compassion and indignation: She understood him, why couldn't he understand her?" (398).

58. Richard Gambino, *Blood of My Blood* (New York: Double Day and Co, 1974); Herbert J. Gans, *The Urban Villagers* (New York: The Free Press, 1962).

59. Valentine Rossilli Winsey, "The Italian American Woman Who Arrived in the United States before World War I," *Studies in Italian American Social History*, ed. Francesco Cordasco (New Jersey: Rowman & Littlefield, 1975); Virginia Yans-McLaughlin, *Family and Community. Italian Immigrants in Buffalo, 1880–1930* (Ithaca: Cornell, 1977); and Betty Boyd Caroli, Robert F. Harney and Lydio F. Tomasi, eds. *The Italian Immigrant Woman in North America* (Toronto: The Multicultural History Society of Ontario, 1978).

60. See, Rose Basile Green, "The Italian Immigrant Woman in American Literature," in *The Italian Immigrant Woman in North America*, 342.

61. As we saw earlier, Michael M. J. Fischer ("Ethnicity and the Post-Modern Arts of Memory," 195; my emphasis) indeed tells us, I remind the reader, that "ethnicity is something reinvented and reinterpreted in each generation by each individual," which, in the end, is a way of "finding a voice or style that does not violate one's *several components of identity*," these components constituting the specificities of each individual. Thus, ethnicity—and more specifically in this case, one's *Italianness*—is redefined and reinterpreted on the basis of each individual's time and place, and is therefore always new and different with respect to his/her own historical specificities vis-à-vis the dominant culture.

62. The hyphen, as Aaron told us, initially represented older North Americans' hesitation to accept the new/comer; it was their way to "hold him at 'hyphen's length,' so to speak, from the established community" (213). It further "signifies a tentative but unmistakable withdrawal" on the user's part, so that "mere geographical proximity" denies the newly arrived "full and unqualified national membership despite . . . legal qualifications and . . . official disclaimers to the contrary" (213).

63. There are undoubtedly other considerations regarding Aaron's three categories. He goes on to discuss them further, providing examples from the Jewish and Black contingents of American writers.

64. I shall use *Guysterland* as an abbreviated form of *Benedetta in Guysterland. A Liquid Novel.*

65. I refer to Maria Corti's essay, "Testi or microtesti? I racconti di Marcovaldo di Italo Calvino" (*Strumenti critici* 27 [June 1975]: 182–93), where she defines the macrotext as follows: "Una raccolta di racconti può essere un semplice insieme di testi or *configurarsi essa stessa come un macrotesto;* nel secondo caso ogni racconto è una ministruttura che si articola entro una macrostruttura, donde il carattere funzionale e 'informativo' della raccolta; nel primo caso la definizione di una raccolta come insieme di testi è soltanto tautologica" (182; emphasis added. My translation: A collection of stories can be a simple gathering of texts or it can take the form of a macrotext; in the second case every story is a ministructure that defines itself within the macrotext, whence the collection's functional and "informative" character; in the first case the definition of a collection as a gathering of texts is merely repetitive).

66. In a sense, this microtext, as therefore the entire book, throws the reader *in medias res.* The opening words—"Just after finishing *this*, I went out in the open . . ." (27; emphasis added)—make reference to a previous act/thing, that being the act of writing and/or the actual finished product. This beginning, however, I would contend, also adds a personal touch in that it simulates an exchange between author and reader, as if the author were handing the book over to the reader.

67. With regard to possible Italian intertexts in Guido Gustavo Gozzano's and Aldo Palazzeschi's poetry, I would point out that Gozzano's borrowings from other European poets are well known and have been studied and examined by a number of Italian critics. Similarly, Palazzeschi also spoke in terms of other poets' work, though differently. In describing his "strofe bisbetiche," he states: "Sapete cosa sono? / Sono robe avanzate, / non sono grullerie, / sono la . . . spazzatura / delle altre poesie" ("E lasciatemi divertire"; my translation: Do you know what they are? / They're leftover things, / they're not silly acts, / they're the . . . garbage / of other poerty ["And Let Me Have My Fun"]). In his Appendix 15, Luigi Ballerini makes a parenthetical allusion to both Gozzano and Palazzeschi.

68. From the New Americanist perspective, Fred L. Gardaphé, more than he does in his preface to Rimanelli's book, deals with *Benedetta in Guysterland* in his penetrating, book-length study, *Italian Signs, American Streets: Cultural Representation in Italian/American Narrative Literature* (Raleigh, N.C.: Duke University Press, 1966). Gardaphé offers an excellent analysis of Rimanelli's sociocultural parody that lies at the base of *Benedetta in Guysterland.*

69. See Mikhail M. Bakhtin, *The Dialogic Imagination*, ed. Michael Holquist, trans. Caryl Emerson and Michael Holquist (Austin: University of Texas Press, 1981), 258ff.

70. For more on sign-functions, see Umberto Eco, *A Theory of Semiotics* (Bloomington: Indiana University Press, 1976), 48–62.

71. For more on prejudgments see Hans-Georg Gadamer, *Truth and Method* (New York: The Crossroad Publishing Company, 1988), 234–75.

72. Again, I remind the reader of V. N. Volosinov's notion of ideology and semiotics: "Every sign is subject to the criteria of ideological evaluation. . . . The domain of ideology coincides with the domain of signs. . . . Wherever a sign is present ideology is present also. *Everything ideological possesses semiotic value*" (Volosinov, *Marxism and the Philosophy of Language* trans. Ladislav Matejka and I. R. Titunik [Cambridge, Mass: Harvard University Press, 1986], 10; emphasis textual).

73. See his essay, "Race, Culture, and Communications: Looking Backward and Forward at Cultural Studies," *Rethinking Marxism* 5, no. 1 (1992): 10–18.

74. See their co-authored study, *Theory, (Post)Modernity Opposition. An "Other" Introduction to Literary and Cultural Theory* (Washington, D.C.: Maisonneuve Press, 1991), 8. For Zavarzadeh and Morton, the proponents of the dominant cultural studies include the likes of John Fiske and Constance Penley.

75. I would point out here that Stuart Hall tends to be much more reticent about real (radical?) change; almost as if to suggest something to the sort that, *if it happens fine, if not, oh well*. Hall, in fact, seems to limit his vision of change to the academy: "It is the sort of necessary irritant in the shell of academic life that one hopes will . . . produce new pearls of wisdom" (11).

76. I have in mind the case of the bicultural and bilingual writer. As stated earlier, with specific regard to the Italian/American experience, see Paolo Valesio's working paradigm in his essay, "The Writer between Two Worlds: The Italian Writer in the United States," *Differentia* 3/4 (Spring/Autumn 1989): 259–76; and my review essay, "From *Simulazione di reato* to *Round Trip*: The Poetry of Luigi Fontanella," *Voices in Italian Americana* 3, no. 2 (1992): 125–34, which is an abbreviated version of my later essay "Italian/American Writer or Italian Poet Abroad?: Luigi Fontanella's Poetic Voyage," *Canadian Journal of Italian Studies* 18 (1995): 76–92. In the analogous case of the Cuban American, I remind the reader of Gustavo Pérez Firmat's cogent exegesis of the bilingual writer who, in adopting both languages (at times separately, at other times together in the same text), occupies what he considers the "space between" (21); see his "Spic Chic: Spanglish as Equipment for Living."

77. At this point, I would remind my reader of what I already stated in footnote 21, 31, and what I underscored at the end of part two of this essay, regarding these three stages: that a writer may actually experience two, if not three, of these stages throughout his or her career.

78. With regard to a seemingly absent ethnicity, I refer the reader to my Barthian reading of Joseph Greco's short film, *Lena's Spaghetti*, in my "What Is [Not] Italian/American about *Lena's Spaghetti?*" *Voices in Italian Americana* 6, no. 1 (1995): 169–82.

79. For more on this idea in general, see Ernest Renan, "What Is a Nation?" in *Nation and Narration*, ed. Homi K. Bhabha (London: Routledge, 1990), 8–22.

For an example of what we should eschew as Italian/American critical thought is Ferdinando Alfonsi's notion of biology *qua* ethnicity (*Dictionary of Italian-American Poets* [New York: Peter Lang, 1989]), that blood "is a force of such inevitableness that it conquers time and space and even individual will" (9). For a response see my review in *Voices in Italian Americana* 1, no. 2 (1990), 135–37 and Fred L. Gardaphé's review of Alfonsi's bilingual study, *Poesia Italo-americana: saggi e testi/Italian American Poetry: Essays and Texts* in *Italica* 70, no. 2 (1993), 219–21.

For an interesting read on ethnicity as chiefly representative of cultural characteristics, not biological characteristics, see Tommy L. Lott, "DuBois on the Invention of Race," *The Philosophical Forum*, 1–3 (fall–spring 1992–93): 166–87.

80. See Hall (11) for more on his notion.

81. For an excellent example of this notion put into effect, see Sneja Gunew,

"Denaturalizing Cultural Nationalisms: Multicultural Readings of 'Australia'" in *Nation and Narration,* ed. Homi K. Bhabha (London: Routledge, 1990), 99–112.

82. Like most things, ideas are to be shared and discussed. I did so first, *ante-litteram,* with Paolo A. Giordano, Fred L. Gardaphé, and John Kirby; I thank them for their helpful suggestions for and comments on earlier versions of this essay.

# Notes on Contributors

MARIO DOMENICHELLI is Professor of English at the University of Pisa. He has written numerous essays and books on topics such as Ezra Pound and English Romanticism. His books include *Wyatt, il liuto infranto: formalismo, convenzione e poesia alla corte Tudor* (Longo, 1975); *Narciso al buio: analisi digressiva e contraddittoria di Cuor di tenebra di Joseph Conrad* (Longo, 1978); *Il mito di Issione: Lowry, Joyce e l'ironia modernista* (ETS, 1982); and *Il limite dell'ombra: le figure della soglia nel teatro inglese fra Cinque e Seicento* (F. Angeli, 1994).

FRED L. GARDAPHÉ, Professor of English at Columbia College Chicago, is coeditor of *From the Margin: Writings in Italian Americana* (Purdue University Press, 1991) and the semiannual *Voices in Italian Americana*. His books include *The Italian-American Writer: An Essay and Annotated Checklist* (Forkroads, 1995); *Italian Signs, American Streets: The Evolution of Italian American Narrative* (Duke University Press, 1996); *Dagoes Read: Tradition and the Italian/American Writer* (Guernica, 1996); *Moustache Pete Is Dead! Evviva Baffo Pietro!* (Bordighera, 1997).

PAOLO A. GIORDANO, former director of the Loyola University Rome Center Campus (1989–92), is Professor of Italian at Loyola University Chicago. He is the editor of *Joseph Tusiani: Poet Translator Humanist* (Bordighera, 1994); coeditor of *From the Margin: Writings in Italian Americana* (Purdue University Press, 1991) and the semiannual *Voices in Italian Americana,* and also founding coeditor of the serial *Italiana.* He has written widely on Italian and Italian/American literature, and he is associate editor of *Italica.*

EDVIGE GIUNTA is Assistant Professor of English at Jersey City State College. She has written on Italian/American literature and cinema and Joyce. She is the author of the afterword for the reprint of Tina De Rosa's novel *Paper Fish* (Feminist Press, 1996). She has also guest-edited the special volume of *Voices in Italian Americana* (7.2 [1996]) dedicated to Italian/American women.

RENATE HOLUB teaches social theory and European Studies at the University of California at Berkeley. Among her numerous publications on feminism, philosophy, and Italian culture, she is the author of *Antonio Gramsci: Beyond Marxism and Postmodernism* (Routledge, 1992).

STEPHANIE J. HULL, Ph.D., is Assistant Dean of First-Year Students and Adjunct Assistant Professor of French and Italian and Women's Studies at Dartmouth College. She has published on the representation of eighteenth-century France in the cinema and on fashion. Her research interests also include music video and pop music.

ERNESTO LIVORNI, poet and literary critic, teaches Italian literature at Yale University. He is the editor of *L'Anello che non tiene* and coeditor of *Yale Italian Poetry*. Forthcoming are a book of poetry, *L'America dei Padri*, and a book of literary criticism, *Avanguardia e tradizione: Ezra Pound e Giuseppe Ungaretti*.

A native of Idaho, DIANE RAPTOSH has two collections of poetry: *Just West of Now* (Guernica, 1992) and *Labor Songs* (Guernica, 1998). Her poems have appeared in journals and anthologies across the United States and Canada. She is Professor of English at Albertson College of Idaho.

ANTHONY JULIAN TAMBURRI, Professor of Italian and Comparative Literature at Purdue University, is coeditor of *From the Margin: Writings in Italian Americana* (Purdue University Press, 1991) and the semiannual *Voices in Italian Americana*. His books include *Of "Saltimbanchi" and "Incendiari": Aldo Palazzeschi and Avant-Gardism in Italy* (Fairleigh Dickinson University Press, 1990); *To Hyphenate or Not to Hyphenate* (Guernica, 1991); *Per una lettura retrospettiva: prose giovanili di Aldo Palazzeschi* (Gradiva, 1994); and *A Semiotic of Ethnicity: In (Re)cognition of the Italian/American Writer* (SUNY University Press, 1998).

MAURIZIO VIANO is Associate Professor of Italian at Wellesley College. He has written widely on modern Italian culture, cinema, women's literature, and political criticism. He is the author of *A Certain Realism: A Study of Pasolini's Cinema* (California University Press, 1993).

ROBERT VISCUSI is Professor of English at Brooklyn College of the City of New York, where he has directed the Wolfe Institute for the Humanities since 1982. He is the author of numerous essays on Italian/American culture and literature and the novel *Astoria* (Guernica, 1995) for which he won the American Book of the Year Award from the Before Columbus Foundation. He is the President of the Italian American Writers Association.

JUSTIN VITIELLO is Professor of Italian at Temple University. He has published numerous scholarly articles on and translations of medieval, Renaissance, and modern Italian, Sicilian, and Spanish poetry. Among his publications are the volume of poetry *Subway Home* and the critical book *Poetics and Literature of the Sicilian Diaspora: Studies in Oral History and Story-Telling*.

REBECCA WEST, Professor of Italian in the Department of Romance Languages and Literatures, Professor in Core Faculty of Program in Cinema and Media Studies, University of Chicago, is recipient of numerous awards, including the Howard Marraro Prize (best work on an Italian subject) by MLA in 1982 for her book, *Eugenio Montale: Poet on the Edge* (Harvard University Press, 1982), and a Guggenheim Fellow in 1984–85. Among her fifty-plus essays, she is coeditor (with Dino Cervigni) and author of Introduction to the *Annali d'Italianistica* volume "Women's Voices in Italian Literature and Culture." She is currently coediting (with Z. Baranski) a volume for Cambridge University Press on postunification Italian literature and culture.

# Index

287